BRIDE'S.

Lifetime Guide
to Good Food
& Entertaining

BRIDE'S

Lifetime Guide to Good Food & Entertaining

BONANZA BOOKS

New York

Designed by Maxine Davidowitz

Drawings by Lauren Jarrett

Photo credits: David Frazier — Floral Fantasy Luncheon;
André Gillardin — Bountiful Breakfast; Bill Helms — Con-
temporary Combinations, Country-Style Elegance, In
Celebration of Spring; Horst — The Ultimate Luxury,
Autumnal Tailgate Fête; Bradley Olman — Candlelight
Supper for Two, Afternoon Tea and Tarts, Dining Alfresco
by Candlelight; J. Barry O'Rourke — Leisurely Garden
Lunch, A Creative Reception, Midsummer Repast
European Style, Pasta Party, Sun and Fun Picnic, Sunset
Tête-à-Tête; Joe Standart — Come-and-Get-It Buffet, A
Feast for Friends.

Table settings designed by Donna Ferrari

This 1985 edition is published by Bonanza Books,
distributed by Crown Publishers, Inc., by arrangement
with Congdon & Weed.

Printed and Bound in the United States of America

Library of Congress Cataloging in Publication Data

Main entry under title:

Bride's lifetime guide to good food & entertaining.

   Compiled by Donna Ferrari.
   Includes index.
   1. Cookery. 2. Entertaining. I. Ferrari, Donna.
II. Bride's magazine. III. Title: Lifetime guide to good
food & entertaining.
TX715.B84148   1985   642'.4   85-14932

ISBN: 0-517-491761
h g f e d c b a

Contents

· CONTENTS ·

Color photographs follow page 210.

Foreword

In this year of BRIDE'S Fiftieth Anniversary, it seemed the perfect, if not golden, opportunity to put together a complete, *basic* book of cooking and entertaining that would become a lifetime treasure and indispensable guide. Since 1934, BRIDE'S has advised its readers about entertaining, counseling brides and grooms alike on menus, stocking kitchens, pantries, and bars, setting tables, and in general getting over a billion households off to a good start . . . gastronomically speaking.

And now, here it is. A complete manual of cooking and entertaining knowledge, gathered from our fifty years of expertise and experience.

Obviously, this is a book about food—an essential element in our everyday life, a necessity for health and well-being, a vital part of our cultural heritage. But this is also a book about . . . LOVE! For throughout time and around the world, beautiful food, aromatic and delicious, artistically arranged, presented with ceremony, has always been one of love's greatest gifts.

The great gourmet and food writer M.F.K. Fisher once conceived a satiric dinner that was the antidote to sensual pleasures. Composed of a succession of rich dishes and liberally laced with alcohol, it attacked rather than soothed the senses. But consider the alternative repast: light and fresh and colorful—lingering more in the mind than the stomach—and you have the food of love and laughter, the ultimate gastronomic satisfaction.

To whom do these gifts of love belong? To the ultimate loved one, of course. Lovers find endless enjoyment in tempting each other with fragrant offerings from the kitchen: breakfast in bed, a picnic luncheon, candlelit dinners created out of cherished recipes . . . and a desire to please. These are expressions of a deeper craving, a hunger for intimacy, for time alone to talk and dream and plan for the future.

Beautiful meals are also special presents for family and friends. For implicit in the invitation to share home and hearth is the promise of friendship, of affection that enfolds each guest as he or she enjoys your own very personal ceremony. There are endless pleasures to savor. The table is an arena for exchange, a meeting place of ideas, a warm and bountiful center of home life that reassures all who approach it. Preserve the tradition of these dining hours, and they will see you through a lifetime of more difficult moments. For food is nourishment . . . for the soul as well as the senses.

Barbara Tober
Editor-in-Chief
BRIDE'S Magazine

ix

Introduction

This book is designed to start the two of you on your way to cooking-skill virtuosity and entertaining aplomb. Contained within these covers is a timeless collection of recipes, cooking charts, creative ideas, rules of etiquette, and countless hosting suggestions to which you can return time and time again. From step one of your maiden-voyage dinner party all the way through years of holiday feasts, creative theme parties, and romantic dinners for two, you will find this book to be your lifetime guide to good cooking and entertaining.

Part I includes the fundamentals that are essential to the preparation of every good meal—from information on how to select the right cookware and the freshest ingredients for the best results, to explanations of cooking techniques and convenient reference charts. This part of the book, including illustrations, can be as helpful as personal cooking lessons in your own kitchen.

Part II is a compendium of valuable information on selecting and utilizing most foods from the different food groups. In addition, this section is filled with a wealth of classic, all-time-favorite recipes, which can be the focal point or complement to any of the meals you plan each day.

Part III offers suggested menus for all occasions—from casual weekend brunches and beautiful buffets to meals that richly enhance the most celebratory and festive of events. The emphasis in these menus is on food that is beautiful, sumptuous, and nutritious—a winning combination that will delight any appetite. As the host and hostess using these recommended menus and wines, you can be assured of presenting meals that will be creative, and will offer a harmonious balance of color, texture, aroma, and flavor—all important elements in a truly memorable meal. In recognition of today's busy schedules for two-career couples, many of these recipes are quick to prepare, or are outlined with time-saving instructions for preparation in advance of your entertaining plans. At first, a few recipes may seem a bit complicated, but the skills required will become second nature as you develop your cooking expertise.

Part IV is devoted to party giving. It includes entertaining etiquette, stylishly creative suggestions for table settings and the presentation of food, and a myriad of useful hints and answers to frequent hosting questions.

In total, all of these sections will provide the two of you with the inspiration and know-how to plan and execute well-organized, successful parties of your own. Familiarize yourselves with the contents of this book. If you put into practice what you learn, you will quickly discover how simple and enjoyable cooking and entertaining can be. Cook together and you will find that it is twice as easy, and so much more fun! But don't stop there—share the wealth. Once the two of you have developed confidence in the kitchen, invite your families and friends to join you in the convivial exchange of good conversation, good food, and good cheer. Imagine how proud you two will feel when you are able to extend heartfelt hospitality to your guests in the home you created together as a reflection of your love. Yours will be a home imbued with the irresistible qualities that make visitors feel welcome and at ease—the center of your joint universe, brimming with the unique touches and attention to detail that reveal your distinctive style and signature as a couple.

On behalf of BRIDE'S Magazine, and myself, I would like to thank the people with whom I worked to create this book. First and foremost, I would like to thank Daniel Mattrocce, whose culinary expertise and imagination, combined with extraordinary good taste, have helped to ensure that the recipes in this book are both foolproof and delicious. I also want to thank the following: Lea Guyer Gordon, editor at Congdon & Weed, for her warmth, incisive judgment, unflagging guidance, and indefatigable contributions to every part of this book; Margaret Swendseid, who worked diligently to research and write parts of the text; Lauren Jarrett, for her artistic prowess with pen and ink in expertly rendering illustrations to accentuate the book's practical and informative objective; Greta Lauria, whose skill and competent hand at the typewriter transformed practice-stained pages of recipe notes and reams of partially handwritten material into an orderly manuscript; Maxine Davidowitz, for her creativity in carefully planning the graphic design of this book so that it would be visually useful and beautiful.

When you cross the threshold into married life, you embark together on a new course—one charted by mutual hopes, aspirations, and dreams. Each and every day, for a lifetime, you two will have the chance to reward yourselves with the pleasure of all your personal and professional accomplishments, and the fulfillment derived from sharing what you have achieved with the one you love. Let this book help you enjoy the full potential of your home as you celebrate the joy of each new day.

Donna Ferrari
Tabletop, Food & Wine Editor
BRIDE'S Magazine

PART I

Preparation

To all the pleasures and contentments of your new life together you will want to add the enjoyment of good food. Consider the rich array of piquant sauces, fragrant herbs and spices, luscious ripe fruits, exotic vegetables, and delicacies from far-off places. By including these treasures in your cooking repertoire, you can conjure up travel experiences without ever leaving the kitchen. Happily, food's fundamental purpose does not preclude its ability to amuse and comfort the senses and to feed the soul as well as the body. Like any new discovery, your taste buds are a fascinating area to explore. As the two of you travel this journey to good taste, utilize all of your senses to fully appreciate and acquaint yourselves with the myriad of food varieties and flavors within your reach.

Even as you start to cook a meal, the shapes and colors of beautiful fruits and vegetables should be no less an inspiration than the flavors you know they contain. Famous French artists like Cézanne and the Dutch still-life painters endlessly challenged themselves to reproduce on canvas the exact blush of a peach or the elusive dimensions of an egg. A wise cook has an advantage over even the greatest artists in being able to capture the jewels fresh from nature to produce a culinary masterpiece.

Learn to enjoy the many sounds and smells of food. How disappointing it is, for example, when biting into an apple does not produce that refreshing crunch, when bread does not live up to its crusty promise, when the salad is limp. Tempting aromas not only prepare the mouth for the meal to come, they also possess a curious ability to summon memories of tastes past. Can you even count the number of times a familiar scent reminded you of a comforting childhood experience? All of these faculties— sight, sound, taste, smell, and touch—realized in unison are inseparable parts of the total eating experience.

These same elements must be addressed when planning a menu. Always appeal to the senses with a variety of colors and textures as well as compatible flavors to ensure a truly satisfying meal.

With all the pressures of contemporary living, try to think of cooking as a welcome and relaxing diversion, not a chore. Shop together. Cook together. Dine and take more time for dinner conversation together. Even cleaning up can be less effort and fun when shared by two.

It has been said that if you can read, you can cook. Essentially, cooking is based on logical step-by-step procedures. Begin by taking the time to read the recipe thoroughly. Buy the freshest ingredients you can find; truly great food can be achieved only when you start with the best. When it is time to cook, prepare your kitchen by clearing counterspace, organizing equipment and utensils, and setting out the ingredients. Play some favorite music and pour an aperitif. As you prepare your feast, savor every moment, and discover how easy it is when you divide the tasks. He cuts the vegetables for the salad and side dishes, you prepare the sauce; he sets the table, you add the finishing touches to dessert. Alternate these activities each time, so you will both learn how to prepare and present food.

As the two of you begin your adventures in cooking, it is also important to remember that all of your first endeavors may not turn out to be masterpieces. You may scorch the sauce, dry out the roast, or even forget a basic ingredient, such as sugar in the cake. Fear not. Every cooking couple has several kitchen mishaps. When one of yours happens, just laugh, learn from it, and go out for pizza. In fact, you can even do better than that. You can let someone else cook *for* you. Gourmet takeout shops have become increasingly popular because they offer a variety of items—from a course to a whole meal—that are fresh, flavorful, and ready to serve. When you and your husband are not in the mood to cook, or when time is short, takeout fare can be the perfect solution for an entire meal. For entertaining, try combining certain prepared dishes with your own carefully rehearsed specialties to create a menu that will not only delight your guests but will also allow you time and energy to enjoy their company.

As the two of you gain experience and become more knowledgeable cooks, you will eagerly experiment with your own ideas. As you gain confidence and skill, do not hesitate to improvise with new ingredients, spices, sauces, and combinations. Many a great recipe evolved from the imagination of curious cooks who tested and retested with differing (and often startling) results—until perfection.

Once you feel comfortable with your pots and pans, spices and herbs, and are confident with a few good recipes, you will have countless opportunities to share your expertise. There will be Sunday dinner with your families, a get-acquainted brunch for new neighbors, and your own romantic suppers in front of the fireplace on special occasions. The possibilities and the pleasures are endless. And, of course, the ultimate reward of good cooking speaks for itself.

SHOPPING

•••

With a delicious meal as the ultimate reward, one would think that food shopping should always be a delightful, pleasurable adventure. But this is not always the case. Crowded stores, low-quality merchandise, and undisciplined selection can yield you less than you want—at higher prices than you bargained for.

You will find your market basket filled primarily with everyday essentials. But from time to time, why not treat yourselves to a few unfamiliar items that can satisfy both your curiosity and your desire to experiment? You will find that there are always beautiful, fresh, and nutritious foods to inspire your culinary creations, whether at a roadside farmer's market or your local supermarket. As your knowledge of different foods expands, along with ways to use them, you will add excitement and versatility to your cooking repertoire. The key, of course, is to organize your food marketing to save time and money, both of which can certainly be well spent in other ways.

Here are some tips and advice on buying food and on shopping strategies.

Shopping Lists

First and foremost, put together a shopping list and take it along to remind you of the items you need. A handy way to keep a current, running list of these necessities is to write them down on a roll of adding-machine paper which you can hang on the kitchen wall with a piece of string; simply tear off the list on your way to the store.

Store Specials and Comparison Shopping

Stores generally advertise their weekly specials in local newspapers. You should always check these sales, because they can represent terrific savings for you on items you really need or want. But remember, the store's primary objective is to attract customers by promoting these selected items, and thereby its image as the store that saves you the most money. Actually, no store can undersell its competitors on every item in stock, so expect to find that most items will fluctuate and vary in price from store to store.

Be wise when you comparison-shop among stores, otherwise you will find yourself spending too much time, effort, and possibly gasoline pursuing slight variations in price that ultimately result in minimal savings. Generally, the best way to shop is by frequenting one or two convenient stores that serve the majority of your needs. In this way you can familiarize yourself with each store's pricing patterns and learn to spot its traditional bargains. For instance, one store may offer better savings in the produce department, whereas another store may be the better choice when buying meat.

Coupons

Coupons are a controversial subject. On the one hand, they offer the consumer an immediate savings on the market price of the item. On the other hand, the cost of producing and distributing the coupon to the consumer, and then reimbursing the retailer for the face value of the coupon plus a handling fee, must eventually be built into the cost of the item. A good rule of thumb is to use coupons only for items you will really use. No matter how you look at it, coupons do not represent a savings if you let them influence you into buying an item you can easily do without.

Clipped coupons inevitably have a way of either getting misplaced or being left behind at home when you arrive at the store. Solve these problems by keeping a little coupon notebook that you always take to the store. You might find one at a stationery store, or make it yourself. Just staple together pages in a notebook to make individual pockets, and label each pocket with an identifying category, such as "Dairy," "Canned Goods," "Cleaning Supplies," etc. File coupons accordingly.

Timing

The peak traffic times for food shopping are weekends and just before dinner. If at all possible, try to avoid shopping at these hours, to save yourself the time lost maneuvering through crowded aisles or waiting on long checkout lines. Shop when the store will have the freshest and most choice selection. As you work your way through the store, save your refrigerated and frozen purchases for last so they will stay cold till you get them home.

The standard and classic piece of advice is never to shop when you are hungry, or you might buy far more than you need.

Package Information

If you read a label carefully it will tell you what you are paying for and what you will receive in content, calories, and nutritional value. By law, the ingredients must be listed in descending order, the most substantial ingredient first. Nutrients, vitamins, and minerals listed are those deemed essential to good health, along with the percentage a specific serving of that product fulfills in your daily need for these nutrients.

Freshness dates are a quality-control measure to indicate to the consumer the last date recommended for enjoyment of the product at its peak quality. When you buy a product it is dated to allow you ample time to use it at home before its quality significantly declines.

What follow are a number of checklists for stocking your cupboards, refrigerator, and freezer.

STOCKING THE PANTRY

Tea—loose leaf, bags, and herbal
Coffee—regular, instant, and decaffeinated
Granulated sugar
Confectioners' sugar
Brown sugar
All-purpose flour
Instant flour
Baking soda
Baking powder
Evaporated milk
Canned chicken broth
Canned beef broth
Cornstarch
Vegetable shortening
Vegetable oil
Olive oil
Vinegar—wine and white
Pasta and noodles—assorted sizes and shapes
Assorted canned beans—garbanzo, lentil, kidney, etc.
Grains—rice, cornmeal, barley, bulgur, hot and cold cereals
Bouillon cubes—chicken and beef
Consommé
Unflavored gelatin
Crackers
Bread crumbs
Raisins
Honey
Jams, jellies, and marmalades
Tomatoes—canned, sauce, and paste
Peanut butter
Cookies and wafers
Cocoa powder
Olives

Tuna fish
Vegetable and fruit juices
Nuts
Canned soups
Vanilla and almond extracts
Dried beans
Salt
Pepper
Allspice
Basil
Bay leaves
Cinnamon
Cloves
Curry powder
Dill
Dry mustard
Garlic powder
Nutmeg
Onion flakes
Oregano
Parsley flakes
Paprika
Rosemary
Tarragon
Thyme

REFRIGERATOR/ FREEZER

Milk
Butter and/or margarine
Eggs
Cheese
Yeast
Onions
Garlic
Lemons
Pickles
Relishes
Catsup
Mustard
Mayonnaise
Heavy cream
Breads
Frozen vegetables
Frozen pie shells

SPECIALTY FOOD ITEMS

Worcestershire sauce
Tabasco sauce
Steak sauce
Hot sauce
Chili peppers
Jalapeño chilies
Sesame seeds
Sesame oil
Soy sauce
Dried mushrooms
Peanut oil
Oyster sauce
Rice wine vinegar
Taco shells
Prepared horseradish
Chutney

KITCHEN SUPPLIES

Paper towels
Paper napkins
Aluminum foil
Waxed paper
Plastic wrap
Toothpicks
Garbage bags
Copper cleaner
Silver polish
Glass cleaner
All-purpose kitchen cleanser
Scouring pads—steel wool and nylon
Sponges
Ammonia
Hand soap
Dishwashing detergent—hand and dishwasher
Dish towels
Potholders
Bleach
Rubber gloves
Scouring powder
Stain remover

KITCHEN EQUIPMENT AND UTENSILS

Have you ever entered a kitchen and felt instantly at home? Perhaps the rustic curtains or the lush array of plants helped create the warm and cozy atmosphere. Or, letting your eyes wander, perhaps it was the display of worn and well-loved cookware that filled the room, like portraits of friends proudly mounted on the walls: an earthenware crock hugging weathered wooden spoons; copper-bottomed pots with rich amber tones; or festive Italian tiles for cooling dishes. Favorites of yours make a personal statement about the two of you and your love of cooking. These are the familiar objects you handle most frequently throughout the course of your life. Treat them with care and they will serve you well.

Many of the cookware items in our homes have stayed the same throughout the centuries: spoons and forks, bowls, pots and pans. In early history, our ancestors heated rocks by a fire to warm foods, then later hollowed the rocks out to heat water and other liquids. Animal skins sewn together were the first containers for transporting water. Knives were formed by splitting rocks to create a cutting edge. All sizes and shapes of bowls were fashioned by mixing clay with water and baking it.

Unlike the chefs of yesteryear, however, you have the advantage of using electrical appliances that make the job of cooking easier and more efficient. Whether you favor the latest in chopping and grinding gadgets, classic cookware, or a combination of both, in time you will discover your own culinary style, and which equipment and utensils best serve your needs.

When shopping for kitchen equipment, research brands carefully by reading manufacturers' labels and consumer literature. There are many resource manuals available—some with brand comparisons—that will greatly aid your investigation of cookware. Do not hesitate to seek the advice of friends or family members on tried-and-true products.

The most important factors to consider when selecting equipment are durability, practicality, and quality of materials. While sturdy, reliable brands tend to be a bit more costly than inferior products they are economical in the long run, because you will not have to replace them as often. A quality utensil will also facilitate the cooking process—which can make the difference between a scorched sauce and one that is velvety-smooth and delectable. What follows is a brief discussion of some of the most common materials used in kitchen equipment, as well as a checklist of essential cookware and utensils. Always read the manufacturers' labels carefully on the maintenance and cleaning of these tools, as it will increase their longevity.

Pots and Pans

The most frequently used kitchen items, pots and pans are available in a wide range of materials, from clay to copper. Look for pots and pans with tight-fitting lids and heat-resistant plastic handles, or handles that stay cool to the touch. Heavier metals are desirable, because they conduct heat more evenly, thus cooking foods thoroughly and uniformly.

CAST IRON AND ENAMELED CAST IRON

As a base material for cookware, cast iron is a heavy metal that holds heat well and allows for even browning of foods. Cast iron needs to be "seasoned" before initial use and intermittently as time goes by, because it is porous and prone to rust. To season, simply coat the pan with oil and heat in a 250-degree oven for 30 to 60 minutes. Let the pan cool to room temperature. Following seasoning, the pan can simply be wiped clean with paper towels after each use. If you must wash the pan, use sudsy water, dry thoroughly, and reseason. Do not use this pan for cooking foods that contain acid or wine, as cast iron discolors these food preparations.

Enameled cast iron offers the advantage of being easy to clean, with no seasoning necessary. The coating protects highly acid foods that discolor with cast iron. Because this material can crack or chip, handle the pot with care. Do not use abrasive cleaners and scrubbers, such as steel wool. Use mild copper cleaner, bleach, or baking soda to remove discolorations on the outside or inside of enameled utensils.

STAINLESS STEEL

Stainless steel pots and pans are easy to clean and they resist rust and corrosion. However, stainless steel is a poor conductor of heat, so select utensils with bottoms of aluminum or heavy copper cladding.

ALUMINUM

Thicker-gauge aluminum conducts heat well, but thin aluminum does not. This material tends to be inexpensive and lightweight, and is rust-resistant. Acid foods can pit aluminum cookware, and alkaline foods can stain it. Use a brush or a nylon scourer to remove burned-on food. To clean stains, boil a weak solution of vinegar and water in the pan.

NONSTICK SURFACES

No fuss and little or no oil needed are the main advantages of nonstick pots and pans. Anyone who is dieting or who hates to scrub will appreciate this equipment.

While high-quality nonstick surfaces are durable, be careful not to scratch them with metal utensils or scouring pads. Low-quality surfaces may eventually wear away with use. Season these pans according to manufacturers' directions.

GLASS

Pyroceramic is stronger than heat-resistant glass and is designed to withstand direct heat or flame and extreme temperature variations. Transparent heat-resistant glass offers the advantage of allowing you to see the food as it cooks, but cannot withstand extreme temperature changes. It is best to preheat glass by filling it with hot tap water before putting it in the oven. Glass and pyroceramic cookware are easy to clean with hot sudsy water and a nylon brush or nonabrasive liquid cleaner. Always read and adhere to manufacturers' instructions for use and care of these products.

COPPER

Tin-lined copper pots and pans may be the most expensive, but they are also the cookware most highly regarded by gourmet chefs the world over. This is because copper conducts heat uniformly throughout the bottom and sides of a utensil. Because copper by itself reacts toxically with the acids in many foods, it must be lined with a nonreactive metal. Tin is excellent, but the tin will periodically wear out and require retinning, which is a costly process. Many copper pots and pans are now available with durable stainless steel linings, and there are even some sold with silver linings. Some copper utensils come shellacked to prevent tarnishing. This is fine if you only keep the piece on display, but for cooking, the copper must first be immersed in boiling water and the shellac scrubbed off. During regular use, copper should be cleaned with hot water and a soapy nylon brush, then polished dry with a soft cloth. To remove tarnish, shine copper with a metal cleaner or a combination of salt and lemon or vinegar.

Knives

A good knife is indispensable in the kitchen and can do the job of many other space-consuming gadgets. Knives are made from various metals. One metal is high-carbon stainless steel, which resists rust and staining and can easily be kept sharp; another is carbon steel, which sharpens well but can stain and rust even with careful cleaning and drying between use. Knives are also made of stainless steel, which does not rust or stain and is very durable, but because it is so hard, it is difficult to resharpen at home.

Knife handles are also made of a number of materials: wood, plastic, or plastic-impregnated wood. The important features to look for in a quality knife are:

1. Tang. The tang is the end of the blade that extends into or is sandwiched between the two parts of the handle. It is important that the tang be the full length and width of the handle, to provide strength and balance to the knife.
2. Rivets. Rivets are used to attach a two-part handle to the tang. They should be of a rust-resistant material, to prevent loosening of the handle. Where the rivets are placed indicates how far the tang extends in the handle. Some plastic handles are molded around the tang and do not require rivets.
3. Heel or guard. The heel or guard is at the base of the blade, before it meets the handle. This feature is found on large knives to guard the hand from slipping to the blade.
4. Balance. A good knife should be balanced to feel comfortable in the hand and have sufficient weight to facilitate chopping.

KEEPING KNIVES SHARP

Sharpening steels are made from high-carbon steel, harder then the metal used for knife blades. The steel is used to realign the existing edge to keep a blade sharp. Regular steeling each time you use a knife will reduce the need to put a new edge on a worn blade. The proper technique for steeling is as follows:

1. Hold the handle of the sharpening steel and point the steel away from you.
2. Start at the top of the steel, directly under the handle, and place the knife blade at a 20-degree angle against the steel. Using medium pressure, stroke the knife blade from heel to tip across the steel. Ten strokes are generally sufficient to maintain a sharp edge.
3. To sharpen the other side of the blade, hold it at a 20-degree angle against the steel. This time start with the heel at the sharpening steel's tip and stroke blade along the steel toward you.

Sharpening hones and oilstones are either coarse ceramic or man-made compositions of silicon carbide that are used to put a new edge on a dull, excessively worn blade. These tools remove tiny bits of steel from the blade. If a knife has been carefully maintained with the steeling process it should be necessary to sharpen it with a hone or oilstone only a few times a year.

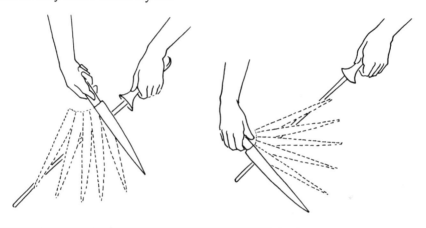

The following are particularly useful knives:

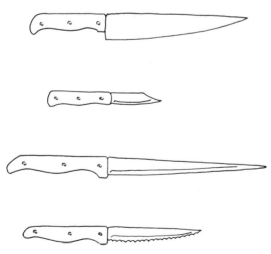

CHEF'S KNIFE: This is a heavy, large-bladed knife. Keeping tip on cutting board, use it with a rocking motion to chop, slice, mince, and dice. PARING KNIFE: With its small, easily maneuvered blade, this knife should feel like an extension of your hand. Make sure the tip stays sharp so that you can use it to dig out stubborn potato eyes, hull strawberries, core apples, and peel thin-skinned fruits and vegetables. SLICING KNIFE: The long, rigid blade of this knife will shave smooth slices from vegetables and meat. UTILITY/STEAK KNIFE: This knife is best with a serrated edge. Terrific for slicing tomatoes, trimming fatty meat, and removing the rind and pith of citrus fruits.

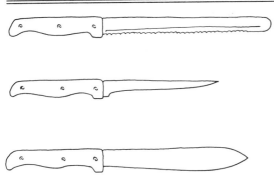

BREAD KNIFE: This knife is essential for slicing all breads—crusty French or Italian, date-nut, etc.—without a mess of crumbs or a ragged loaf. BONING KNIFE: This knife should be razor-sharp and very pointed to reach between chicken ribs and small fish bones. Invaluable for salvaging meat from boned roasts, filleting fish, and boning poultry. BUTCHER KNIFE: You will need this knife for heavy-duty tasks like disjointing a large turkey. Also good for dealing with big, firm fruits and vegetables like pineapples, melons, and cabbages.

Cutting and Pastry Boards

Hard woods, such as maple, are preferred as cutting boards over soft woods, because they are less porous and more moisture-resistant. To season the wood, rub it well with oil and heat it in a 200-degree oven for about 1 hour. To clean the board, scrub with a nylon scrubber and a damp cloth or rub it down with coarse salt for a thorough cleaning. Dry immediately. Keep a separate board for cutting garlic and onions, which are easily absorbed by wood and can impart their flavor to foods when you least want it—when cutting fruit, for instance.

Molded plastic boards are a good second choice to a hardwood cutting board, and are easy to keep clean. Get one with some weight or grip so that it does not skid on the counter when you use it.

Marble is the ideal choice for working pastry. This nonporous stone remains cool, which is a help when working with the fats in pastry dough. Do not use marble for acidic foods, which would corrode it.

The following list of equipment and utensils is a basic prescription for culinary preparation. The more adept you become at cooking, the more equipment you will want to acquire.

COOKING AND BAKING

POTS AND PANS
Baking/cookie sheet
Bar cookie pan
2 bread loaf pans, 4 × 9 × 3 inches
2 cake pans, 9 inches in diameter
2 casseroles or Dutch ovens, 8 and 12 inches in diameter, with lids
Double boiler
2 frying pans or skillets, 8 and 10 inches in diameter, with lids
3 baking dishes, 8 inches square, 7 × 10 × 2 inches and 8 × 12 × 2 inches, with lids
2 pie pans, 9 and 10 inches in diameter
Roasting pan with a rack, 13 × 9½ × 2 inches
Saucepans, 1-, 2-, and 3-quart, with lids
Steamer for vegetables—metal or bamboo
Muffin pan
Springform pan
Bundt pan
Jelly roll pan
1½-quart soufflé dish

2 or more ramekins
Stockpot

**MIXING AND MEASURING
  EQUIPMENT**
Mixing bowls, 6, 7, 8, 10 and 12 inches
  in diameter
1 set dry measuring cups
1 set measuring spoons
2 rubber spatulas
Wooden spoons, different sizes
Thermometers—meat, candy, oven, and
  deep-fry

PREPARATION UTENSILS

Apple corer
Vegetable peeler
Rolling pin and cover
Cake rack
Cookie cutters
Can opener
Flour sifter
Colander
Sieve
Tea strainer
Grater
Cheese cutter or cheese plane
Cutlery set: chopping, carving, slicing
  knives, 2 paring knives, serrated-edge
  bread knife, and sharpener
Cutting board—wooden or plastic
Funnel
Marble pastry board
Pastry brush
Pastry scraper
Pastry tube and basic tips
Pepper mill
Wire whisk, 10-inch
Slotted spoon

Two-pronged fork
Pancake turner
Trussing needles
Bulb baster
Soup ladle
Skewers
Jar opener

ELECTRICAL APPLIANCES

Toaster
Electric hand beater
Blender
Food processor
Hot plate
Slow cooker (crock pot)
Coffee maker

MISCELLANEOUS

Rotary eggbeater
Cooking tongs
Garlic press
Potato masher
Coffeepot
Teakettle (for boiling water)
Salad bowl with fork and spoon
Salad spinner/dryer
String
Kitchen shears
Juicer
Zester
Butter curler
Cheesecloth
Cookie jar
Storage containers
Timer
Metal tongs
Wooden toaster tongs

Use and Description of Certain Kitchen Tools

The following is a list of some of the more common kitchen equipment and utensils and their uses.

EQUIPMENT	USE
Baking dishes	Relatively shallow and straight-sided, baking dishes are ideal for cooking solids with liquids evenly and gently; where moisture evaporates and food must "set." Eggs, fish, braised vegetables, and lasagna are best suited to this dish. Best materials are glass, porcelain, and earthenware.
Bulb basters	Designed for basting, also ideal for skimming fat from soups and gravies. Select one that has a sturdy bulb that will not collapse or stick together.
Casseroles (Dutch ovens), round and oval	For baking foods slowly and gently in the oven. A deep, heavy dish that should have a tight-fitting lid to keep moisture in, the round casserole is most often used for combinations of foods, such as meat with vegetables. Oval casseroles are designed to conform to certain cuts or shapes of meat and poultry—a whole chicken, for instance, or a boned leg of lamb. Enameled cast iron is a fine choice for this utensil. It should be usable both on top of the stove and in the oven.
Double boiler	For gently heating and warming foods that should not be cooked over direct heat, as in making sauces and melting chocolate. The double boiler is made of two pots, one of which nests in the other. Water is heated in the bottom pot.
Loaf and pie pans	Many bakers claim that black steel pans are the best for producing a crisp crust and evenly baked bread. But a heavy-gauge aluminum pan or a glass loaf pan can also produce a fine bread, with the latter letting you see the dough as it turns golden. Special clay pottery bakers also yield excellent results.
Roasting pans	Feature anything from high to low sides; you will have to judge for yourself the design that best suits you. The pan is designed for roasting meat and poultry. The thickness of the metal is more important than what kind of metal, as it must be able to support a weighty roast and not flex or warp from the heat.
Saucepans	The most utilitarian piece of equipment in the kitchen, the saucepan is simply a sauté pan with higher sides. This multipurpose pan is good for cooking vegetables, soups, sauces, and other foods. Stainless steel, aluminum-based material, and lined copper are generally preferred.

Frying and sauté pans	Frying and sauté pans are a more developed form of the primitive griddle, a flat cooking surface. The low raised sides allow you to cook solids in fat or liquid.
	The principal difference between sautéing and frying is that generally less fat is used in sautéing and sautéed foods are cooked more quickly. A frying pan has sloping walls to facilitate the use of a lifter to turn food onto its other side. A sauté pan has straight walls to facilitate rapid tossing to stir or shake ingredients such as meat, poultry, or vegetables. A good frying or sauté pan can be made of lined copper, copper- or aluminum-clad stainless steel, or enameled cast iron.
Soufflé dish	To create soufflés, those light and airy imports from France, it is necessary to use the proper dish. It should have straight walls to direct the expansion of the egg whites upward to form a high fluffy crown. The shape of the dish is round to provide even heating. It can be made of glass, porcelain, or stoneware. The latter two ceramic materials should be left unglazed on the bottom so that heat can quickly penetrate from underneath. The bulging rim at the top enables an extra paper or foil collar to be fastened to the top if a higher soufflé is desired.
Scraper or spatula	A useful tool, the scraper or rubber spatula scrapes frostings, purées, batters, and doughs from dishes or bowls. Select one with a sturdy but flexible rubber blade. They are also handy for folding and blending mixtures. Be careful not to use them in contact with hot pans—they melt.
Wooden and metal spoons	Hard woods such as beech, ash, and sycamore are preferable for wooden spoons, as softer woods can be porous and absorb flavors and smells easily. Wash these spoons quickly in soapy water and thoroughly air-dry before putting them away. Do not soak them in water and do not put them in the dishwasher, which makes them soften and crack. Wooden spoons do not get hot when used for stirring or for tasting. Spoons with deep bowls are good for soups and stews. Angled spoons have little points to reach into the corners of straight-sided pans. A flat spoon with a hole in it facilitates stirring thick foods like oatmeal or beating air into a batter. Stainless steel spoons are easy to clean. They often have wooden or plastic handles to protect your hands from the heat; be careful not to burn or melt these handles.
	Slotted spoons have holes to allow you to easily lift such solids as bones, poached eggs, chunks of meat, and vegetables out of a sauce or broth.
	The all-purpose ladle is good for preparing and serving foods, skimming liquids, and scooping a large portion from the pot to the serving dish.

Steamers	The steaming method, which originated in the Orient, cooks foods in a way that preserves their nutrients, textures, and flavors. Electric steamers are available, but a stainless steel basket steamer is a fine and inexpensive choice, because it transfers heat well and requires little cleaning. Simply put the steamer basket in a saucepan partly filled with water and fitted with a tight lid. Put food in the basket, over the water. After the food is cooked, open the pot carefully a safe distance from exposed skin, as steam can scald you.
Stockpots	The high sides of the homey, lovable stockpot help conserve liquid. Many cooks keep this pot on the stove to turn scraps of meat, fish, or vegetables into always useful stocks, which can be kept frozen. A stockpot is essential for preparing soups and stews, simmering meats, and boiling pasta. It can also be used for preparing chili and boiling or steaming lobsters. When shopping for a pot, make sure the bottom is thicker than the sides, and of good quality, to avoid scorching.
Turners	Think of the turner as an extension of your hand. This utensil is so named because you literally turn or flip foods over with it—pancakes or hamburgers, for instance. Make sure it has a comfortably long wooden handle, to keep your hand away from heat or frying fat. Select a turner that is wide enough to let you turn larger items over in one piece.
Whisks	There are many different types of whisks, which vary in weight, length, and degree of flexibility. Each is designed for a specific function. For whipping egg whites, which are light and will greatly increase in volume, use a light, round-ended balloon whisk; the large size also makes the work go faster. For heavy pastries and thick sauces use a stiffer whisk made of heavier wire. Use a rounded shape when working in a round mixing bowl, and a longer, tapered whisk to reach the corners of a saucepan.
Wok	The wok, another import from the Orient, is set directly over heat, cradled in a metal collar that keeps it from tipping. Those made of iron are best, because of their ability to heat foods quickly. The rounded bottom and curved walls allow for rapid tossing and stir-frying of foods. With extra attachments the wok can also be used for deep frying and steaming. Smoking is also possible in the wok, using the traditional flavors of burning tea leaves or a rice-and-brown-sugar mixture.

COOKING AND FOOD PREPARATION TERMS

••

al dente:	All pastas should be cooked *al dente*—firm and slightly chewy "to the tooth."
aspic:	A cold, usually molded dish that contains gelatin.
au gratin:	Creamed food covered with bread crumbs, butter, and/or grated cheese and baked or broiled until the top is browned.
au jus:	Any meat served in its natural juice.
bake:	To cook in an oven.
bard:	To wrap meat with fat (such as bacon or salt pork) before roasting, to keep from drying.
baste:	To ladle or brush drippings, melted fat, or sauce over meat while it cooks. Basting keeps food moist.
beat:	To blend by mixing with rapid over-and-over or rotary motion.
beurre blanc:	White butter sauce, served over some fish and vegetables.
beurre noir:	Brown butter sauce made from clarified butter.
blanch:	To immerse briefly in boiling water, then in cold to stop the cooking.
blend:	To mix together two or more ingredients until thoroughly combined. Also, to purée in an electric blender.
boil:	To cook in water or other liquid at a temperature at which the liquid comes to bubble rapidly and continues to do so.
bone:	To remove meat from the carcass of an animal or from a large bone, such as a leg of lamb.
braise:	To brown quickly in fat and then cook in a small amount of liquid, either on top of the stove or in the oven.
bread:	To coat with fine bread crumbs or cracker crumbs.
broil:	To cook in the broiler part of a stove, directly under the heat source.
brown:	To cook in hot fat until brown. Usually done in a frying pan on top of the stove.
brush:	To dab melted fat or a liquid on food with a pastry or cooking brush.
caramelize:	To melt sugar until it turns golden brown. Commonly done as a delicate and delicious glaze for pastries and custard.
charlotte:	A molded gelatine dessert with ladyfingers and whipped cream.
chill until set:	To refrigerate a gelatin mixture until firm.
chop:	To cut up food with a knife or cleaver so that it is in equal small pieces.
clarify:	To make a cloudy liquid clear. To clarify butter, melt, let stand a few minutes, and skim off foam and solids. Clarify stock by adding an egg white and eggshell and beating over heat. Then strain the stock; the food particles will cling to the egg.
coat:	To cover a food thoroughly, generally with a liquid or crumbs.
court bouillon:	A highly seasoned fish stock or broth.

cube:	To cut into small dice.
cut in:	To work butter or shortening into flour when making pastry.
deep dish:	Dish baked as a pie without the bottom piecrust.
deep fry, *deep-fat fry*:	To cook in a deep skillet with fat and a frying basket, as in preparing of Southern-fried chicken or french-fried potatoes.
deglaze:	To pour liquid into a degreased roasting or sauté pan, and scrape the browned bits into the liquid as it simmers.
deviled:	A sharply seasoned food cooked with a crumb topping and served with a piquant sauce.
dissolve:	To melt or liquefy a solid food.
dot:	To cover with small bits of butter.
dredge:	To coat food with flour or sugar.
dust:	To sprinkle lightly with flour or sugar.
fines herbes:	Minced mixed herbs used for seasoning in a dish, such as an omelet or soufflé.
flake:	To break into small pieces with a fork.
flambé:	To pour liquor over food and light it.
fold:	To combine two ingredients by gently turning one over into the other, using a folding motion with a rubber spatula or large spoon.
french fry:	Same as deep fry.
fricassée:	A type of stew. Chicken or meat is simmered, and then the liquid is thickened and served over it.
fry:	To cook on the top of the stove in butter or fat.
glaze:	To coat food with a glossy covering using aspic; a thin sugar syrup; or cheese or a sauce run under a broiler.
grate:	To rub on a grater, shredding food into tiny particles.
grill:	Same as broil, but usually over coals.
julienne:	To cut into fine strips, as with vegetables.
knead:	To mix and roll with the hands, as in pastry and bread making.
lard:	To insert thin strips of bacon or salt pork in a piece of meat.
macédoine:	A mixture, usually of vegetables or fruits.
marinate:	To soak food in a liquid (the marinade) that adds tang and flavor, and often makes the food more tender.
mask:	To cover or coat thoroughly, usually with aspic or a sauce.
meunière:	To sauté lightly floured food quickly in butter, a traditional method of preparing sole and other fish fillets.
mince:	To chop into tiny bits.
panbroil:	To cook in a heavy pan over direct heat on top of the stove with little or no fat added. The pan may be sprinkled with salt or rubbed lightly with butter or oil.
parboil:	To partially cook food in a boiling liquid, usually in preparation for further cooking.
pare:	To remove the skin or rind.
parfait:	A frozen custard or ice cream layered with fruits or whipped cream.
pâté:	A purée of meat, vegetable, or seafood, served as an hors d'oeuvre or a first course.

pinch:	An old-fashioned expression meaning to use as much as you can hold between thumb and forefinger.
poach:	To cook in a simmering liquid.
pot roast:	Meat cooked by braising in a covered Dutch oven.
purée:	To make into a paste or thick liquid by using a food processor, blender, food mill, or sieve.
reconstitute:	To restore a concentrated food to its original state by adding a liquid, such as water to frozen orange juice.
reduce:	To evaporate some of the water out of a stock or sauce by boiling rapidly.
refresh:	To plunge hot food into very cold water to stop the cooking process.
render:	To melt a piece of solid fat by cooking it slowly in a frying pan.
roast:	To cook in an oven, in a pan without a lid.
roux:	A blend of butter and flour used for sauces and gravies.
sauté:	To cook on top of the stove in a small amount of butter or fat.
savory:	English term meaning something that is not sweet (thus, a cheese soufflé as opposed to a chocolate soufflé).
scald:	To heat a liquid to just short of boiling, so that bubbles gather only around the edge of the saucepan.
scallop:	To bake food in layers, covered with sauce and/or crumbs, in an oven-proof dish.
score:	To make shallow cuts or gashes with a knife in meat, as with ham.
sear:	To brown quickly over high heat.
shred:	To cut into thin slivers.
shuck:	To remove shellfish from their shells or husks from ears of corn.
sift:	To shake through a fine sieve, as with flour or sugar.
simmer:	To cook gently at just under a boil. The liquid should barely move.
skim:	To remove the fat or scum from the surface of a liquid with a spoon. Also, to remove cream from milk.
sliver:	To slice into long, thin lengthwise pieces. Almonds are often slivered.
sorbet:	French for sherbet; frequently less sweet than sherbet, when used to cleanse the palate between courses.
soufflé:	A savory or sweet dish made with beaten egg whites folded into other ingredients. It puffs up when baked.
steam:	To cook food in the vapor from boiling water, as in a steamer with a rack.
stew:	To cook slowly in a liquid for a long time until tender.
stir:	To mix ingredients with a spoon by using a wide, circular motion.
torte:	Cake made with little or no flour; ground nuts take the place of the flour.
turban:	A mousse baked in a ring of fish fillets.
whip:	To beat an ingredient rapidly so that it becomes puffy, with an electric beater, a whisk, or an eggbeater.
zest:	Outer rind or peel, without any white membrane, of fruit, usually lemon or orange; it adds tang and flavor to food and drinks.

HERBS AND SPICES, EXTRACTS AND FLAVORINGS

Good cooks through the years have used seasonings to enhance the delicate natural flavors of foods. Among the seasonings most popular with cooks are herbs. Herbs are essentially fresh or dried plants. They may be chopped or minced in small pieces, but they are usually not ground. The life of a dried herb's flavor is short; it lasts only four or five months. That is why it is wiser, when available, to buy fresh herbs, as their flavor is purer, although you will need to use a larger quantity of a fresh herb. Dried herbs should always be stored in a dark place.

By contrast, spices, the other most popular group of seasonings, are chiefly derived from seeds or bark and always sold in ground form. Their shelf life is about the same as that of dried herbs, and they, too, should be stored in a dark place.

Both herbs and spices should be used in small amounts so that the foods being seasoned are not overpowered or overwhelmed.

Extracts differ from herbs and spices. They are prepared from natural foods and preserved in an alcohol base. They include vanilla, almond, lemon, rum, spearmint, peppermint, wintergreen, and anise. Flavorings can be either from natural foods or synthesized. They are generally not as strong as extracts. Flavorings include black walnut, butterscotch, maple, banana, caramel, cherry, strawberry, and other subtle taste delights. Extracts and flavorings add interest to cakes, cookies, pies, fillings, frostings, whipped cream, candies, and meringues. Cordials and liqueurs are also used as flavorings.

The lore of spice and herb cookery is worldwide, and interest in it is growing all the time. Most cooks enjoy building up a spice and herb shelf to suit their family's preferences. The chart below shows the more familiar herbs and spices.

HERB OR SPICE	FLAVOR	USE
Allspice	Resembles a blend of cloves, cinnamon, and nutmeg.	In pot roasts, pickles, mincement, and baked goods.
Anise	Sweetish, licorice-like flavor.	In baked goods, shellfish dishes, and fruit and vegetable salads.
Basil	Subtle, spicy, distinctive flavor.	Superb in all tomato sauces, with pasta, and in Italian dishes. Also used on sliced raw tomatoes and in tomato juice.

Bay leaf	Aromatic laurel tree leaf.	Whole in meat and fish dishes, soups, seafood, and pasta sauces.
Caraway seeds	Dark brown seeds that add a sharp tang.	In rye bread, cottage cheese, potato and cabbage dishes.
Cayenne pepper	Hot ground red pepper.	In seafood and egg dishes.
Chervil	Slightly licorice-tasting, looks slightly like parsley.	Chiefly in egg and vegetable dishes.
Chili powder	Very hot dark red pepper blend.	Notably used in Spanish and Mexican cuisine, particularly in chili con carne and other rice, bean, and meat dishes.
Chives	Mild onion flavor.	Minced in cheeses, eggs, salads, soups, and vegetables. Also as a decorative garnish.
Cinnamon	Spicy bark of a tree.	In baked goods, drinks, desserts, pickles, fruit dishes, and some winter-squash recipes.
Cloves	Spicy, sharp, pungent.	Whole are pressed into ham, onions, oranges; ground is used like cinnamon.
Curry powder	Golden yellow in color, a blend of a number of aromatic spices.	Egg, chicken, lamb, fish dishes; most notably in Indian curry sauces.
Dill	Sweet pickle taste.	Chicken and fish dishes, salad dressings, and, of course, in pickling.
Fennel	Licorice-like in flavor.	In salads or raw vegetable dishes; cooked with fish.
Garlic	Strong, onion-like odor and taste.	With meats, frequently In Italian and French cuisine, sauces, fish, poultry, salads and salad dressings, soups.

Ginger	Pungent, intense, peppery flavor.	In Chinese food, baked goods, meats, preserves, ginger beer.
Juniper berries	Spicy, piny berries.	In lamb, game, sauerbraten, sauerkraut, and spicy sauces.
Mace	Delicate and nutmeg-like.	In baked goods, preserves, fish stews, and soups.
Marjoram	Spicy odor but delicate flavor.	In egg dishes, stuffings, fish, salads, sauces, soups, stews, and with vegetables.
Mint	Fresh, clean, distinctive taste.	In drinks, desserts, jellies, salads, lamb dishes, and with certain vegetables.
Mustard	Sharply spiced flavor.	In salad dressings, dips, meat glazes, sauces, and with cold meats and fish dishes.
Nutmeg	Mellow spicy taste.	In vegetable and egg dishes, sauces, soups, drinks, and baked goods.
Oregano	Aromatic taste.	In many Italian dishes, notably pasta sauces, pizzas, and some egg and cheese dishes.
Paprika	Spicy red pepper—can be sweet or sharp and biting.	To give color and taste, and sometimes as decorative garnish. Notably used in Hungarian and Spanish dishes.
Parsley	Mildly bitter taste.	In meat, fish, poultry dishes, soups, salads, stews, and as a decorative garnish.
Pepper, black	Zesty, when freshly ground.	As much used as salt.
Pepper, white	Similar to ground black pepper.	Used where visual effect of black pepper is undesirable.
Poppy seeds	Tiny round seeds with distinctive grainy texture.	Sprinkled on rolls, pastry, noodles, and in some pork dishes.

Rosemary	Distinctive aromatic taste.	In lamb and egg dishes, in stews, soups, and sauces.
Saffron	Slightly bitter taste; its color is reddish yellow.	In fish, rice, and egg dishes and in Spanish, French, and Italian cuisine.
Sage	Spicy grayish green leaf.	In pork, fish, game, veal, poultry dishes, also in stuffings, soups, and sauces.
Savory	Piquant dark green leaf.	In egg and poultry dishes, salads, and stuffings.
Sesame seeds	Distinctive nut-like taste.	Sprinkled on cookies, rolls, cakes, soups, and casseroles. Also toasted as a garnish.
Shallots	Subtly onion-like but milder than garlic.	In egg dishes, casseroles, sauces, and dressings and many French dishes.
Tarragon	Slightly anise-like taste.	In chicken, meat, fish dishes, as well as salads, sauces, dressings, soups, marinades, and as a garnish.
Thyme	Pungent flavor.	In soups, seafood, meat, and poultry dishes, in stuffings, chowders, stews, salads, and salad dressings.
Turmeric	Rich, sweet, slightly spicy, orange red in color.	In curry blends and pickling. Can be substituted for saffron; although flavor is different, it adds color like saffron.
Vanilla bean	Subtle, sweet, delicate flavor.	Buried in sugar to give flavor.
Watercress	Tangy and biting.	Popular garnish, also used in salads, soups, sandwiches, and with cold fish and meats.
Woodruff	Sweet-smelling.	In May wine, fruit drinks, and fruit cups.

FREEZING

Whether you own a freezer or have a freezing compartment in a refrigerator, there are many basic tips and thoughts on the subject for new couples and new households.

There are many reasons for owning a freezer, but not all of them are valid. A freezer can increase the variety of foods that are readily available. Recipes can be doubled and tripled so whole preparations can be frozen, or parts of recipes are prepared in advance and frozen. This is a great convenience and time-saver. There is, however, a hidden cost, not only in the freezer itself, but also in the consumption of electricity and in packaging materials for the foods.

While for some the freezing compartment of the refrigerator has sufficient space, for others, who may have access to farm-fresh vegetables or fruits, for those who have a source of supply for a large quantity of meat, chicken, or fish, or for people who do a great amount of entertaining, a freezer is more of a necessity than a luxury. (The freezer part of the refrigerator cannot maintain zero degrees, the ideal temperature for freezing, so food cannot be stored for long periods of time without deteriorating.) If you do decide to buy a freezer, the convenience of a self-defrosting model is worth the extra cost.

If you are reasonably neat, it is easier to see all the foods at a glance with an upright rather than a chest type of freezer. For the maximum operating economy, a freezer should be kept three-quarters full.

Here are some tips to remember in freezing foods:
- The foods that are most successfully frozen are bread, pastry, and unfrosted cakes.
- Stews, soups, and sauces, except egg-based sauces, also freeze well. Meats and poultry also do well in the freezer.
- Fruit purées, and fruits and vegetables after a preliminary blanching, also freeze successfully, as do mousses and cold soufflés.
- All hard cheeses and some soft ones, such as Brie, can be frozen.
- Butter and margarine can be frozen.
- Milk can be frozen; containers take about 6 hours at room temperature to defrost.
- Do not freeze whole eggs, cream, sour cream, or yogurt.
- Potatoes do not freeze unless they are cooked and become part of another dish, and they are best if they are mashed.
- Crisp vegetables lose their crispness in the freezer, and batter-fried foods become soggy.
- Apples are best frozen in the form of pies.
- Do not freeze raw tomatoes and celery; they get too mushy.
- Do not freeze mayonnaise.
- Do not season food you plan to freeze, as the flavor gets lost in the process.
- Pat dry all meats and poultry before wrapping for the freezer.
- Baker's yeast freezes well.

PREPARING FOOD FOR THE FREEZER

Wrap all food, including ice cream, in special freezer wrap, preferably transparent wrap. Seal, label, and date the package. It should not be possible for air to enter or for moisture to leave the package. If you do not wrap food airtight, it will get freezer burn and dry out and lose flavor.

Chill food before freezing. Do not overload the freezer with huge quantities of unfrozen food, because it takes too long for the food to freeze. Ice crystals form within the packages, causing the food to lose flavor, color, and texture. Add foods to be frozen a little at a time, making sure that each batch is solidly frozen before adding more.

BLANCHING VEGETABLES

For the small household that occasionally may want to put fresh vegetables in the freezer, the most efficient way is by blanching. Blanching requires a good deal of water. For every pint of vegetables to be blanched you will need 1 quart of water, a large kettle with a cover, and a wire basket or a piece of cheesecloth fashioned and tied into a bag. To begin the blanching process, bring the water to a boil, put the vegetable (shelled, sliced, or otherwise prepared) in the wire basket or cloth bag, and submerge the vegetable in the boiling water. Keep the heat high, the kettle covered, and the water boiling. Start counting the time *immediately*—a timer is the best device for this job. Each vegetable requires a different blanching time. Do not overblanch. If you live at a high altitude, add half a minute to the time for 2,000 to 4,000 feet, add 1 minute for 4,000 to 6,000 feet, and add 2½ minutes to the time given over 6,000 feet.

As soon as the vegetable is blanched, plunge the basket or cloth bag into ice water (add ice cubes to keep it cold). This rapid chilling helps retain the nutrients and makes for better quality. To test for sufficient chilling, bite a few pieces. If the vegetables feels cold to your tongue, drain *immediately* in a colander, wrap, and put in the freezer.

Here are the recommended blanching times for a number of vegetables the small or new household might undertake:

Asparagus	3 minutes	Green peppers	
Beans	3 minutes	(halves)	3 minutes
Broccoli	4 minutes	Okra	3 to 4 minutes
Brussels		Snow peas	2½ to 3 minutes
sprouts	4 minutes	Turnips	
Carrots	3½ minutes	(½-inch cubes)	2½ minutes
Cauliflower	4 minutes	Zucchini	
Green peas	1½ to 2 minutes	(¼-inch slices)	3 minutes
		(1½-inch slices)	6 minutes

To freeze fresh herbs, wrap a few sprigs or leaves of the herb in foil or seal in sandwich-size plastic bags and put in a glass jar or plastic container, label, and freeze. Some of the herb's color is lost in the freezing process, unfortunately.

DEFROSTING FOOD

Ideally, foods should be defrosted slowly in the coldest part of the refrigerator. This will prevent any serious deterioration in texture and flavor. If this is not practical, stand meats on a rack on the kitchen counter. Brush meats with oil. The oil will prevent, or partially prevent, loss of juices.

Some foods can be taken directly from the freezer and cooked in their frozen state. If the food is raw, increase the total cooking time by half as long again. Thus, if you expect a raw steak to cook in 16 minutes, cook a frozen steak for $16 + 8 = 24$ minutes. Frozen foods can be taken directly from the freezer and cooked in an electric slow cooker (the slow-cooking utensil made of stoneware).

Freezing Foods

PRODUCT	MAXIMUM STORAGE TIME AT 0°F.
FISH	
Fatty	6–8 months
Lean	10–12 months
FROZEN VEGETABLES (commercially prepared)	
Asparagus	8–12 months
Green beans	8–12 months
Corn	8–10 months
Spinach	14–16 months
ICE CREAM	2 months
POULTRY (raw)	
Chicken	12 months
Duck	6 months
Turkey	12 months
MEATS (raw)	
Beef	6–12 months
ground beef	3–4 months
Lamb	6–9 months
ground lamb	3–4 months
Pork	3–6 months
ground pork	1–3 months
bacon	1 month
smoked ham	2 months
Veal	6–9 months
ground veal	3–4 months
Wild game	9 months

FOOD SAFETY

Many foods must be handled with special care to avoid infective or toxic gastroenteritis.

Dairy products, mayonnaise, meats, poultry, and seafood are one group of foods that are susceptible to the bacteria salmonella. Poultry is particularly notorious as a source of this bacteria. Always wash poultry with cold water before cooking it—particularly the body cavity. To avoid salmonella, the best rule of thumb is to keep all cooked poultry, meats, and seafood hot and to keep all cold foods, such as dairy products and mayonnaise, cold. Also, keep all cooked poultry, meats, and seafood to be eaten cold in the refrigerator until serving time.

Salmonella bacteria can also be spread via counters and table tops, cutting boards, and knives used in the preparation of these foods. *Always* scrub surfaces, cutting boards, knives, and hands before and after handling any dairy products, mayonnaise, meats, poultry, or seafood. Occasionally give boards, tops, and knives a good cleaning using 1 or 2 tablespoons of chlorine bleach in a gallon of water.

Other foods that should be checked are canned and bottled products. They are susceptible to *Clostridium botulinum*, the bacteria whose toxin causes botulism. This poison affects the nervous system and can result in death. If the bacteria is not killed in the canning or bottling process, it can thrive in this anaerobic environment. Anyone eating the contaminated canned goods will ingest the toxin. Swollen cans and lids indicate possibly infected food and should be immediately discarded.

The following are further food-safety suggestions:

MILK AND CHEESE

• For best flavor, milk, cream, and cottage cheese should be used within 3 to 5 days. Soft cheese such as Camembert and Brie can be stored for up to 2 weeks. Hard cheese can keep up to several months, when protected from drying out. Plastic wrap is best for wrapping cheese, because it sticks to the sides of the cheese. Be sure to wrap tightly to keep out air. To be on the safe side, discard any cheese that develops mold.
• Processed cheeses should be refrigerated.
• Store dry milk in airtight containers, away from heat. Unless kept in a tightly closed container, dry milk becomes stale and lumpy. Treat reconstituted dry milk as if it were fresh—refrigerate it.
• Store canned, evaporated milk at room temperature until opened, then refrigerate as you would fresh milk.

EGGS

• Keep eggs dry, cool, and covered in the refrigerator. Do not buy eggs that are cracked in their cartons. If they crack at home, use them in foods that are cooked for a long time in the oven or on top of the range, such as custards or soufflés.

- After opening a package of dried eggs, store them in a tightly closed container in the refrigerator. Freeze them if you intend to keep them longer; they will retain their flavor for about a year.

POULTRY

- Store fresh poultry in the refrigerator at or below 40 degrees Fahrenheit, for no more than 2 days.
- Do not thaw frozen raw poultry at room temperature. It should thaw in the refrigerator.
- Never let cooked poultry stand at room temperature for very long.
- Poultry should always be cooked until well done.
- Never stuff chicken or turkey the night before cooking. Bacteria love to grow in the warm dressing inside the bird. Pack stuffing lightly to prevent spoilage and to let heat penetrate quickly.
- Never refreeze stuffed poultry.

MEAT

- Luncheon meat, such as salami and bologna, should be used within a week, and kept tightly sealed.
- Be sure to completely thaw large cuts of frozen meat, otherwise the outside may be cooked while the inside is barely warm.
- Always use a meat thermometer to measure the internal temperature of meats that need to be thoroughly cooked.
- Pork should *never* be cooked or served rare because of the extreme danger of trichinosis parasites. The rule of thumb with pork: Cook until there is no pink color in the meat or juices. Always follow your oven temperature guide when cooking pork. This includes uncooked fresh hams.

SEAFOOD

- When purchasing fresh fish, it should not smell fishy but clean and mild. Frozen fish should be solid and have very little odor.
- All shellfish should be alive when purchased.
- Wrap fresh fish in heavy waxed paper or put on a plate and cover with aluminum foil or plastic wrap. Store in the coldest part of the refrigerator. Handle it gently so that it is not bruised, which can accelerate deterioration.
- If you do not use fresh fish within two days, freeze it at zero degrees Fahrenheit or below. Thaw frozen fish in the refrigerator. Never thaw it at room temperature or in warm water.
- Canned fish should be used within a year.

FRUITS AND VEGETABLES

- In general, inspect produce carefully for bruises, soft or mushy spots, mold, rotten odors, and dirt and insects. Fruit and produce should have intact skins and a healthy overall appearance.
- Do not store bruised fruit or vegetables near firm ones, as they can hasten decay.

• After frozen vegetables have been cooked, do not let them stand for a long time. Do not refreeze vegetables that have been thawed.

• After a few months, most dried fruit will start to deteriorate and can attract insects.

• The maximum advisable storage time for canned fruit and vegetables is a year. Canned goods survive best in cool storage; freezing them can adversely affect their taste and appearance.

GENERAL TIPS

• Never leave cooked foods out at room temperature for very long, because they can cause food poisoning. Refrigerate foods as soon as the table is cleared.

• When you shop for food, make sure that packages are in good shape and whole. Avoid dented or sticky cans; ripped or battered frozen food packages; and fish, meat, or poultry with torn plastic wrapping.

• Read all labels on food packages carefully for storage and preparation.

• For efficient refrigerator storage, air must circulate around foods; do not overcrowd it. Regularly wash out your refrigerator with baking soda to give it a clean, fresh smell and to keep the interior shelves and boxes clean.

PART II

Recipes

F

ashions and styles of eating are constantly changing, and we are increasingly being influenced by social, political, and economic factors over which we have little control. Anthropologists claim that our origins lay in foraging vegetarianism, and we became meat eaters only over an incalculable period of time. Though we read historical accounts of vast orgies of food, the sheer quantity is impossible for us to contemplate in our present lifestyle.

Today, the emphasis is on fresh food and all the enjoyment and good health it embodies. The recipes that follow are intended to help you explore some of the new (and traditional) techniques of preparing and cooking as well as to help you enjoy many of the new foods now available to us. If you start off with good food, and good basic equipment, you cannot go wrong.

M EAT AND POULTRY

Buying

You will probably be buying most of your meat and poultry prepackaged at the supermarket. Most packaged fresh and processed meats are dated. It is important to understand what each date means.

"Sell by" or "pull" date indicates the last day the product can be sold in the supermarket. This date allows for limited safe home storage after the date.

"Use by" date, often found on processed meats, suggests the date after which the food will no longer be at peak freshness.

"Pack date" indicates the date the product was packed or processed by the manufacturer.

"Expiration date" is the last day the product should be used.

If you are unsure of any date on your meat or poultry purchases, be sure to ask your meat retailer for an explanation.

Meats bought through a community cooperative plan cost less than those in a supermarket, where overhead has to be included in the price.

Meat from a butcher shop almost always costs more than meat from a supermarket. It is important to remember, however, that comparing the cost of meat is like comparing apples and pears. Supermarket meat is not necessarily the same quality as butcher-shop meat. You may arrive home with two pounds of ground chuck from one place that will be full of fat and shrink when it is cooked; two pounds of ground chuck from another place will yield a greater amount of cooked meat. While the two packages appear to be identical, one may cost more because the meat in it is of better quality.

For most consumers, trying to stretch the food dollar has become a way of life. One of the best ways to get the most for your meat dollar, according to the National Livestock and Meat Board, is to compare cost per serving rather than cost per pound. Meat with minimum bone and fat may cost more per pound but less money per serving because it yields more servings per pound. To calculate cost per serving, simply divide the cost per pound by the number of servings per pound you expect to get.

When buying beef or pork, look for fine lines of fat running through the meat. This fat, or marbling, keeps the meat juicy. Beef should have a red to dark red color. Pork should be pink and firm, with a substantial coating of white fat. Veal is usually a pink color, although the choicest milk-fed calves produce veal that is white. Very special prime-meat butcher shops carry such veal, and it is expensive. Lamb has a firm coating of white fat. The darker the color of the meat, the older the animal is.

Poultry should be plump and firm, with a slightly yellow skin and some yellow fat under the skin.

Variety meats should also be plump, firm, and fresh-smelling. Select calf's or beef liver that is light brown in color, as it is more tender than dark brown liver.

To buy meat intelligently, here are some guidelines:
1. Look for the inspection label on the meat.
2. Larger cuts are often sold as "specials." If you have the storage room, buy them and have the butcher cut the meat in two. A leg of lamb can serve as a roast as well as being cut into steaks or cubes for stew. Many stores offer combinations—so much chopped meat with a roast or steaks, however you want the meat cut.
3. Boneless meat, although more expensive to buy, may prove less expensive per serving because there is no waste.
4. If you are buying from a butcher, watch the scales with him.
5. When buying poultry, look for a bird with a well-filled-out breast for the most white meat.
6. You know better what you are buying if the prepackaged meat is in a transparent tray so you can inspect both sides.

Storage in the Home

Keep meat and poultry in the coldest part of the refrigerator. Try to cook the meat or poultry as soon as possible, within 3 to 4 days.

If you want to keep meat or poultry longer you must wrap it in moisture-vapor-proof wrapping, excluding as much air as possible, and seal the package. Store it in the freezer compartment of the refrigerator or in the freezer. Meats stored in the refrigerator freezer do not keep as long as those frozen in a freezer. Ground meat should be shaped into patties before freezing, as large lumps of ground meat do not freeze properly and will spoil in the center, causing off-flavors. Do not freeze bologna, frankfurters, bacon, or sausage for very long, since the salt in them interferes with proper freezing. When freezing chops, individual steaks, etc., put two thicknesses of freezer wrap between them so they can be pulled apart easily when frozen.

Wrap meat in meal-size portions. Prepare meat in the style in which you plan to cook it—trim and cube, slice, or grind it before freezing. Freeze meat quickly in a single layer against the freezer coils, then store it in another part of the freezer. Allow 12 hours for complete freezing.

Label packages with type of meat, weight, and date. Use the oldest packages first, since they can be stored for only a limited time. See Index for chart on freezing foods.

Thaw large pieces of frozen meat in the refrigerator, wrapped, and then cook as usual. Thin cuts can be cooked in the frozen state if you allow a little extra cooking time.

Methods of Cooking

ROASTING

Preheat oven to the right temperature. Put the roast or thoroughly washed bird on a rack in a shallow pan. Sprinkle on all sides with pepper and desired spices and herbs.

Put meat on a rack, fat side up. Insert a meat thermometer in the thickest part of the meat, being careful not to touch a bone, and roast for the time specified in the following charts. Roast poultry breast side down in a V-shaped rack. Turn for the last 30 minutes so breast skin can brown. The meat thermometer should be inserted between the thigh and the body, not touching a bone.

Meat can be roasted in two ways—it can be roasted at one temperature throughout the whole cooking time, or it can be seared first at a high temperature and then roasted at a lower temperature until done. The first method provides a juicy roast with less pan drippings and less spatter in the oven. A meat chart can give the approximate length of time a piece of meat takes to roast, but only a meat thermometer will tell you just when the meat is ready. Personal preferences as to the doneness of meat must be considered, and the cooking time requires adjustment for each individual family. When it is done, remove meat from the oven and let stand at room temperature for 20 minutes, to give it time to set and make carving easier.

MICROWAVE COOKING

Microwave cooking is another way to roast and bake food. One of the chief benefits of microwave cooking is that busy couples can cook food in much less time than by conventional roasting and baking methods. Another bonus is that you can arrange and cook the food on individual plates that can be brought directly to the table. Yet another advantage is that you can prepare a meal in advance and reheat it in minutes.

To use any microwave oven, follow the manufacturer's instructions *carefully*.

BROILING

Use only tender meat. Do not broil veal, since it is a lean meat that toughens when broiled. Do not broil pork, since it must be very well cooked and will dry out first.

Preheat the broiler. Grease the rack on which the meat or poultry will be placed. Line the broiler pan with foil, to avoid messy cleanup. Do not season the meat until after cooking. Cut the fatty edge of the meat at 1-inch intervals to keep it from curling during cooking. The distance from the source of heat should be about 3 inches. Use tongs to turn meat; a fork would pierce it and let juices escape. To check whether the meat is done, make a small cut near a bone and look for redness. Continue cooking until redness disappears, if you want well-done meat.

PANBROILING

Put tender cuts of meat, such as minute steaks and fillets, in a hot heavy skillet. To keep meat from sticking, rub the pan with a little fat or sprinkle it with salt. Panbroil the same length of time required for broiling. Turn and panbroil the other side.

PANFRYING/SAUTÉING

Use only slices of tender meat, such as veal scallopini. Heat a small amount of fat in a skillet. If you like, coat the meat with flour or crumbs. Add meat to hot fat and cook over medium heat. Continue cooking with skillet uncovered, turning meat to brown both sides. If meat or poultry is thick you can cover until meat is tender. To recrisp meat, uncover the pan for the last 10 to 15 minutes.

BRAISING

Use less tender cuts of meat and poultry. Meat can be larded to increase tenderness. Cut holes in the piece of meat and push in thin strips of bacon or salt pork (or use a larding needle). Meat can also be barded, or covered with strips of bacon or salt pork. To braise meat or poultry, first brown it on all sides in very hot fat. Add a small amount of liquid, cover tightly, and cook over low heat, replenishing the liquid from time to time. If you want to add vegetables, put them in about 30 minutes before meat is done.

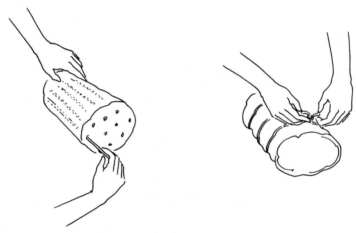

STEWING AND FRICASSÉEING

Cube meat or poultry or cut into smaller pieces. Brown on all sides in hot fat and cover with liquid. Add seasonings. Cover the pan and cook over low heat until meat is tender. Vegetables can be added. You can thicken the pan juices with flour or cornstarch.

POACHING OR SIMMERING IN WATER

This method is used for older chickens, very tough cuts of meat, cured or corned meat, tongue, and oxtail. To the meat or poultry add water just to cover. Frequently an herb bouquet—made of sprigs of parsley, thyme, and a bay leaf tied together in a small cheesecloth pouch—is added. Cover the pan and simmer over low heat until tender; do not let the water boil, as this toughens meat. The cooking water and herb bouquet are usually discarded. Meat or poultry can be marinated to add flavor. The acid in the marinade also slightly tenderizes the meat. When adding wine to meat during cooking, use just enough to season, not enough to overpower the meat.

Roasting Chart

All these times are approximate; meat should be at room temperature before placing in the oven. When using a meat thermometer, remove the meat from the oven when the thermometer registers 5 to 10 degrees below *that indicated on the chart, as the meat will continue to cook internally and will reach the desired temperature while standing. The following meats should be roasted at 350 degrees.*

MEAT	INTERNAL TEMPERATURE (°F.)	COOKING TIME IN HOURS
Beef, standing rib,	130 (rare)	1
4 pounds	140 (medium)	1¼
	150 (well done)	1½ to 1¾
Sirloin tip, eye	130 (rare)	1
round, 3 pounds	140 (medium)	1¼
	150 (well done)	1½
Lamb		
Leg, 6 to 7 pounds	165 (well done)	1½ to 1¾
Leg, half, 3 to	165 (well done)	1 to 1¼
4 pounds		
Veal		
Loin, 5 pounds	170	1¾ to 2
Shoulder, 6 pounds	170	2½
Stuffed chicken		
2½ pounds	180	1¼
Roaster 4½	180	2
pounds		
Capon, 6 pounds	180	2¼
Duck, 5 pounds	180	2
Goose, 10 pounds	180	3
Stuffed turkey*		
6 to 8 pounds	175	2 to 2½
8 to 12 pounds	175	2½ to 3
12 to 16 pounds	175	3 to 3¼
16 to 20 pounds	175	3¾ to 4½
20 to 24 pounds	175	4½ to 5½
24 pounds and over	300	14 minutes per pound
Frozen boneless		
turkey roll,		
thawed		
3 to 5 pounds		2½ to 3
5 to 7 pounds		3 to 3¾
7 to 9 pounds		3¾ to 4½

*Figures provided by the California Turkey Advisory Board.

The following meats should be roasted at 350 degrees.

MEAT	INTERNAL TEMPERATURE (°F.)	COOKING TIME IN HOURS
Pork, fresh		
Leg (fresh ham), 6 pounds	185 (well done)	3 to 3½
Loin, 5 pounds	185 (well done)	1½
Shoulder butt or cushion shoulder, 5 pounds	185 (well done)	2¾
Pork, smoked		
Ham, not precooked, 12 pounds	160 (well done)	3½
Ham, fully cooked, 12 pounds	130	2¾

Broiling

MEAT	WEIGHT	THICKNESS	MINUTES PER SIDE
Steak	⅓ to ½ pound	1 inch	3 (rare) 5 (medium) 6 (well done)
		2 inches	7 (rare) 9 (medium) 10 (well done)
Hamburger patties	⅓ to ½ pound	1 inch	4 (medium)
Lamb chops	½ to ¾ pound	1 inch	5 (medium)
Chicken halves	½ to ¾ pound		13

Braising

MEAT	THICKNESS OR WEIGHT	COOKING TIME IN HOURS
Beef		
Pot roast	3 to 5 pounds	3½ to 4
Swiss steak	1 to 1½ inches	2 to 2½
Short ribs		2 to 2½
Stew beef	1½-inch cubes	2½ to 3
Oxtail		3 to 3½

MEAT	THICKNESS OR WEIGHT	COOKING TIME IN HOURS
Lamb		
Shoulder chops	¾ inch	40 minutes
Shanks	1 pound	1½ to 2
Stew meat	1½-inch cubes	1½ to 2
Veal		
Stew meat	1-inch cubes	1½ to 2
Pork		
Rib and loin chops	¾ to 1 inch	50 to 60 minutes
Shoulder steaks	¾ inch	45 minutes
Spareribs		1½ to 2½
Tenderloin	½ inch	30 minutes

Cooking in Liquid

	WEIGHT	COOKING TIME IN HOURS
Corned beef	3 pounds	3 to 3¾
Beef tongue	3 to 4 pounds	3 to 3½
Pork hocks	¾ to 1 pound each	2½ to 3
Stewing chicken	3 to 4 pounds	2½ to 3
Oxtails	2 pounds	4

Carving

Carving is a skill that can be developed and polished only with practice—and a good sharp knife. It helps to know a little bit about the animal's anatomy—where the bones are located and how the grain of the meat runs. Most meats are cut against or across the grain to ensure juicy, nonstringy slices. There is a correct way to carve every type of roast and fowl—the way the meat is set on the platter, the way the knife is used, and the angle at which the meat is sliced. Carve on a wooden board whenever possible so the knife will not scratch a good china piece. As you cut slices, transfer them to a small, warm platter next to the cutting board. If the carving knife does not have a keen edge, sharpen it on steel or stone. (See Index on keeping knives sharp.) When carving, use a long, light stroke, pushing and pulling the knife with a saw-like movement. Keep the fork behind the knife on the side next to you for better anchorage and protection. A good carving fork will have a thumbpiece or shield to protect you further.

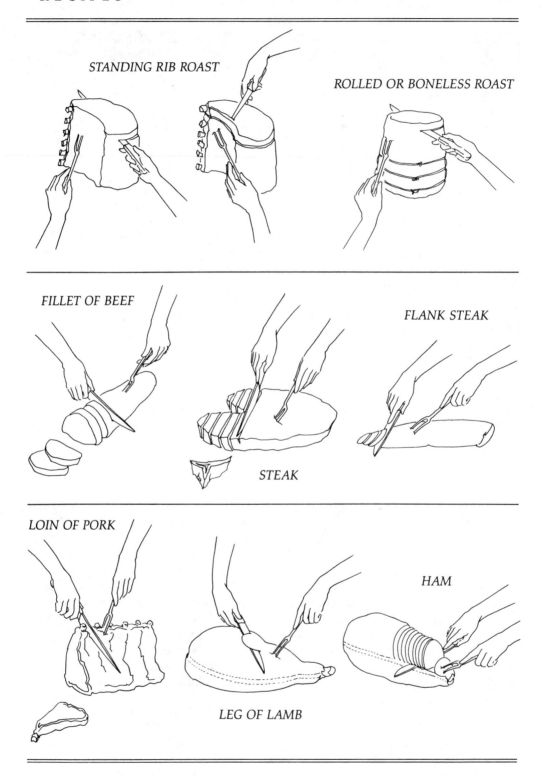

STANDING RIB ROAST

ROLLED OR BONELESS ROAST

FILLET OF BEEF

FLANK STEAK

STEAK

LOIN OF PORK

HAM

LEG OF LAMB

STANDING RIB ROAST. Put the meat on the platter, ribs to the side, the larger end at the bottom for a firm base. Carve crosswise toward the bone, cutting the slices to desired thickness. Carefully cut along the bone to free the slices. Reverse each slice over the knife and put on the warm platter to save the meat juices.

ROLLED OR BONELESS ROAST. Carve across in the same way, as you would a standing rib roast, cutting the slices as thick as you want them. Sever the strings and remove any excess fat with the point of the knife.

FILLET OF BEEF. Hold the fillet in place on a board with the back of the fork, not with the tines, because of the tenderness of the meat. Starting with the widest end, use the slicing knife to cut straight down and through in one motion. Cut thick slices, from ¾ inch to 1 inch.

STEAK. Cut out and remove the bone with the point of the steak or boning knife, holding one end with a fork. Slice crosswise at an angle to retain the juices.

FLANK STEAK. Holding the steak firmly with a fork, and holding the slicing knife at an angle, start at the small end and cut very thin diagonal slices. If the meat is not cut across the grain it will be stringy.

LEG OF LAMB. Put the roast, leg bone side down, on the platter with the exposed tip of the leg to your left. Using the carving knife, start a third of the way down the leg, slicing across to take off a small shallow piece from the top. Continue across the top, making thin slices. Lamb is cut with the grain of the meat.

HAM. Cut a piece from the bottom to make the base flat. Turn over and put the ham on a board, preferably one with spikes for better anchorage. Cut a small wedge down to the bone near the shank end (where the bone is exposed) and remove. Continue slicing down, working toward the butt end. Free a series of slices from the bone at one time by making one parallel cut. For cold ham, angle the slices more and make them thinner.

LOIN OF PORK. Stand the roast with the ribs on top, where the backbone has been removed. Holding firmly with the fork, cut down between the ribs for individual servings. For thinner slices, cut down near the rib several times and free the slices from the bone with one cut.

TURKEY. Put the turkey on a platter, breast up, drumsticks toward the carver. Cut down between the thigh and the body; push the leg away from the body with the fork to separate it at the joint with the tip of the knife. Put the piece on a warm platter and separate the thigh from the leg. Holding the drumstick by the bone, slice downward

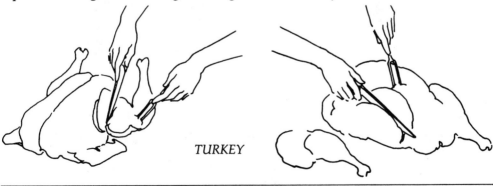

TURKEY

for servings of dark meat. To remove the wing, slant the knife very low at the base of the same side and remove the wing at the joint. Make a horizontal cut at the base of the breast on the side so the breast slices will fall away easily. Starting at the front side, carve thin slices at a downward angle until you reach the widest part of the breast. Alternate carving from the side front and the side back to give even slices. After carving one side, spoon out the stuffing from the body cavity.

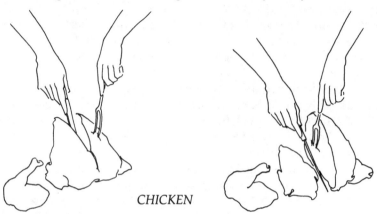

CHICKEN

CHICKEN. A large roasted chicken can be carved in much the same way as a turkey. A smaller chicken is quartered. Sever the leg and thigh section at the joint and remove to a platter. Starting at the top of the breastbone, cut down, as close to the bone as possible, press the meat aside, and continue cutting until the wing is separated. The wing and breast will be all in one piece.

OTHER GENERAL MEAT HINTS
• Do not salt meat until it is three fourths cooked, or well browned, to make sure it does not lose its juices. Salt causes a "bleeding" of the rich, flavorful juices.
• Many B vitamins, in addition to flavor, are lost when the drippings or juices from cooked meat are thrown out. Juices are also lost as meat thaws or is sliced. Save these precious juices for a meat stock or sauce.
• When broiling or stewing a tough cut of meat, add a couple of teaspoons of vinegar to the liquid to make the meat more tender. Another tenderizer: Cut a kiwi fruit and rub it over the raw meat.

Beef

It is very difficult to choose from all of the attractive beef packages, except by price, unless you know something about the cuts of meat and how they should be cooked.

Beef is the meat most often graded; beef shipped across state lines must be inspected by the federal government. Lamb and veal are sometimes graded, but pork is not. Many states and cities have their own inspection laws, but not all do. You can tell if the meat has been graded and inspected by the round purple stamp marked "U.S. Inspected" that is affixed to the meat, certifying that it is safe, untainted, and free from disease. The grades and what they stand for are:

USDA Prime. The best and most expensive quality of meat—tender, juicy, and well textured, with good marbling (fat distribution) through the lean meat. The fat encasing the outside is thick and creamy white. Most of the prime-quality meat goes to the best restaurants and hotels, but you may be able to find some in the better butcher shops.

USDA Choice. The next best grade, with less fat but still very tender and juicy. Good butcher shops and supermarkets carry this grade.

USDA Good. A good quality of meat with less fat; relatively tender, with little or no marbling. It has a mild flavor but lacks the juiciness of the top two grades.

USDA Standard. Meat from young low-quality animals, which is less tender, less flavorful, and has very little fat.

USDA Commercial. Meat from older animals. It has flavor but is tough and coarse.

Every cut of beef provides the same food value in terms of protein, vitamins, and minerals, but just as some parts of the human body are more muscular than others, some cuts of meat are naturally more tender. The methods of cooking must be matched to the characteristics of the meat to obtain the best results.

The most tender and expensive cuts of beef (sirloin, T-bone, porterhouse, and prime rib roast) are better cooked by the dry-heat methods: broiling, roasting, panbroiling, and barbecuing. Heat seals the surface, keeping the juices and nutrients from escaping. The less tender cuts, those with connective tissue and fiber (chuck, brisket, and short ribs), need to be cooked longer in moisture—stock, wine, or water—to become tender. Try braising, stewing, pot roasting, and poaching. Chopped meat

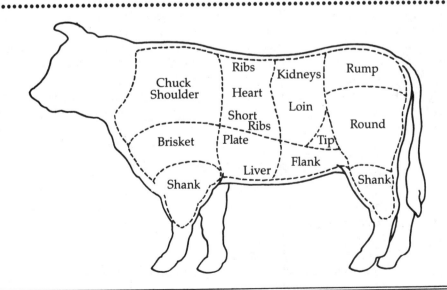

41

can come from the scraps of any number of cuts—sirloin, round, chuck, or a hodgepodge that is unidentified by cut. Chopped sirloin and ground round have less fat than chuck.

When buying beef, count on ⅓ to ½ pound of boneless beef per person, or ½ pound beef with a small bone, such as sirloin steak. For each person allow ¾ pound of beef with a prominent bone, such as standing rib or short ribs.

In storing beef, keep in mind that a 3- to 4-pound piece of beef for roasting will keep in the refrigerator for up to 4 days. Keep it loosely wrapped in the original paper so it can "breathe," or rewrap it if it comes packed in plastic wrap. The beef must be able to breathe or it will deteriorate rapidly. Steak and stewing meat will keep for 3 days, but ground beef and liver should be eaten as soon as possible, and certainly within 2 days. See Index for chart on freezing food.

◆

STEAK WITH PEPPERCORNS
Serves 4

This is a special dish for birthdays, anniversaries, or when you want to give guests the royal treatment.

1 tablespoon peppercorns	2 tablespoons finely minced
4 10-ounce shell steaks	shallots
3 tablespoons vegetable oil	½ cup dry white wine or
4 tablespoons butter	vermouth
	½ cup heavy cream

Crush peppercorns, but not too finely, with the bottom of a heavy frying pan or a meat pounder and sprinkle equally on both sides of each steak. Use your hands to work peppercorns into the meat. Heat oil in a large heavy frying pan. When it begins to sizzle, put steaks in pan and cook for about 3 minutes on one side; turn steaks and cook about 2 to 3 minutes (or longer if you want meat better done) and remove to a warm platter. Pour off oil and add 2 tablespoons butter with the shallots and cook until they are just soft. Add wine and cook, stirring with a wooden spoon, until wine is almost totally reduced. Pour in the cream and cook over higher heat for about 1 minute. Add the remaining 2 tablespoons butter and serve steaks, spooning a little sauce over each.

◆

ALL-AMERICAN BEEF STEW
Serves 4

This is even tastier the second day.

2 pounds boneless beef chuck,	2 teaspoons salt
cut in 1-inch cubes	¼ teaspoon pepper
¼ cup all-purpose flour	¼ cup peanut oil

1 cup beef stock or canned
   broth
1 can (8 ounces) tomato
   sauce
1 garlic clove, chopped
6 large potatoes, peeled and
   diced

1 cup sliced celery
6 large carrots, peeled and
   sliced
6 white onions, peeled
½ pound fresh mushrooms,
   sliced and sautéed

Choose a well-marbled cut of chuck for this stew. Trim off excess fat and remove gristle and any long fibers or tendons. Roll meat in flour mixed with salt and pepper. Heat oil in a large frying pan and brown meat cubes on all sides. Cook in batches until all meat is browned. Add stock, tomato sauce, and garlic to the frying pan and mix with drippings in pan. Transfer meat and liquid to a heat-proof casserole that can be used on top of stove, or to a casserole that can be used only in the oven. Cover casserole tightly and either simmer over low heat on top of stove or bake in a preheated 325-degree oven until meat is tender, about 2 hours. Add vegetables, except mushrooms, cover, and simmer until vegetables are tender. Add mushrooms and simmer another 10 minutes. Gravy can be thickened with a mixture of flour and water, if desired.

◆

SWISS STEAK
Serves 4

2 pounds round steak, about
   1 inch thick
1 garlic clove, mashed
Pepper
½ cup all-purpose flour
¼ cup vegetable oil

1 large onion, sliced
½ cup sliced celery
1 can (1 pound) tomatoes,
   undrained
6 carrots, quartered
   lengthwise

Rub steak with garlic and sprinkle with pepper. Pour ¼ cup of the flour onto the steak and pound it into the steak with a meat pounder or the edge of a heavy plate. Turn and prepare other side in the same way. Heat oil in a large frying pan and brown meat on both sides. Add remaining ingredients. Cover tightly and simmer over low heat for 1½ hours, or until meat is fork-tender. Cut into serving-size pieces and serve with gravy from pan and with noodles, rice, or mashed potatoes.

◆

BEEF STROGANOFF
Serves 6

3 pounds lean round steak
¼ cup (½ stick) butter or
   margarine

2 large onions, chopped
1 garlic clove, finely chopped

1 pound mushrooms, cut into quarters	1 cup beef stock or canned broth or consommé
2 tablespoons all-purpose flour	1 tablespoon Worcestershire sauce
1 tablespoon tomato paste (optional)	1 cup (½ pint) sour cream
	Salt and pepper
	Garnish: Minced parsley

Slice (or have butcher do this) beef into ⅛-inch lengthwise strips. Heat butter in a large frying pan and cook onions and garlic, stirring constantly, until golden. Add mushrooms and sauté until golden. Remove onions, garlic, and mushrooms to a small bowl. Add meat to pan and cook over higher flame until brown. Sprinkle flour over meat. Return onions, garlic, and mushrooms to the frying pan. Stir in tomato paste, stock, and Worcestershire sauce. Continue to stir until meat is tender and gravy is thickened. Just before serving, stir in sour cream. Reheat but do not boil. Season to taste with salt and pepper. Serve at once with rice or noodles and garnish with parsley.

◆

MEAT LOAF
Serves 4

There are countless recipes for meat loaf. It can be served hot or cold, reheated or used in sandwiches. This recipe is moist rather than dry. The vermouth gives it zing.

2 pounds lean ground chuck or 1 pound chuck and ½ pound each ground veal and pork	¼ cup finely diced celery
	Salt and ground pepper to taste
½ cup bread crumbs	¼ cup vermouth or dry white wine
1 large onion, minced	Paprika
¼ cup minced fresh parsley	

In a large mixing bowl, mix together all ingredients except paprika until well combined. Put mixture in an ungreased meat loaf or bread pan, dust with paprika, and bake in a preheated 350-degree oven for 1¼ hours. From time to time, pour off any pan juices that accumulate. Remove meat loaf and let stand for about 20 minutes before slicing.

◆

STEAK AND KIDNEY PIE
Serves 6

1 pound veal kidneys	2 pounds round steak
2 tablespoons vinegar	1 cup all-purpose flour

1 teaspoon salt
¼ teaspoon pepper
¼ cup vegetable oil
2 onions, peeled and chopped
1½ cups beef bouillon

½ cup beer
Pie dough (see Index) or 1
  package piecrust mix
  prepared according to
  directions

Kidneys should be light brown with white fat. Cut each half crosswise and cut out center fat and tubes. Soak kidneys in water with vinegar added for about 1 hour. Drain and rinse. Cut kidneys into ¼-inch slices. Cut round steak into 1-inch cubes. Mix flour with salt and pepper. Roll round steak in flour. Shake pieces to remove excess flour. Heat oil in a large frying pan and brown kidney slices, beef cubes, and onions. Pour mixture into a greased 1½-quart casserole. Add bouillon and beer. Cover and bake in a preheated 350-degree oven for 1½ to 2 hours, or until beef is tender. Remove from oven and measure top of casserole. Roll out pie dough on a lightly floured board to a round that will fit casserole plus 2 inches extra in diameter. Put dough on top of casserole and let hang over edge. Prick top with a fork to allow steam to escape. Raise heat to 400 degrees and bake pie for 15 minutes, or until crust is brown.

SAUERBRATEN
Serves 8

This wonderful cold-weather dish can be prepared ahead of time, refrigerated, and reheated.

4 to 5 pounds beef rump or
  pot roast
2 cups cider vinegar
1 cup water
1 cup beef stock or canned
  broth
1 cup sliced onions
1 lemon, sliced

12 whole cloves
3 bay leaves
8 peppercorns
1½ tablespoons salt
2 tablespoons sugar
3 tablespoons vegetable oil
8 crumbled gingersnaps
½ cup all-purpose flour

Use well-marbled beef with a good fat covering. Put meat in a deep glass bowl. Add remaining ingredients except oil, gingersnaps, and flour. Cover and refrigerate for 2 days, turning meat in marinade several times.

Heat oil in a Dutch oven and brown beef on all sides. Strain marinade and pour 1 cup over meat. Cover tightly and cook for 3 hours. Add more marinade from time to time to keep up original level of liquid. When meat is tender, remove from pan with a slotted spoon. Crumble gingersnaps and mix with flour in a saucepan. Gradually stir in 2 cups of the leftover marinade. Cook over low heat until mixture bubbles. Stir in hot pan drippings and cook until thickened. Slice meat and serve with gravy.

Veal

The most tender veal is from milk-fed calves that are three months or younger. After that the calves are fed on grain and allowed to graze. As their diet changes, the meat become pinker and pinker, until it is no longer veal, but baby beef. Because it is vastly more economical for farmers to fatten the cattle into mature animals, veal is one of the more expensive types of meat.

When you go to buy veal, look for white or very light pink meat with a firm texture. Avoid gray, watery-looking veal.

For two people buy ½ to ¾ pound boneless veal. Allow two rib chops per serving.

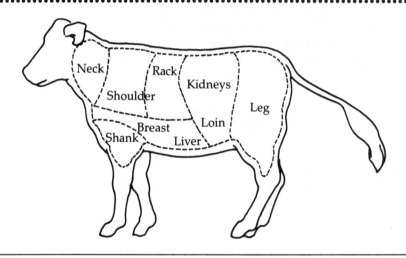

◆

VEAL SCALLOPINI WITH LEMON

Serves 2

Veal scallopini is a small, thin slice of pounded meat. It is rich; many people find two scallopini satisfying, although others can handle three. There are many ways to cook scallopini; with lemon is one of the most popular and basic.

4 to 6 veal scallopini,	Salt and pepper to taste
depending on appetites	Juice of 1 lemon
1 tablespoon butter	Garnish: 1 tablespoon minced
1 tablespoon peanut oil	fresh parsley

Dry scallopini with paper towels. Heat butter and oil in a heavy skillet (you may have to add a little more, depending on number of scallopini) until the mixture stops foaming. Add scallopini in one layer; do not crowd. Sauté quickly for about a minute on each side. Season with salt and pepper. Remove from skillet to a warm platter. Add lemon juice to pan, stirring with a wooden spoon to incorporate all the juices. Spoon pan juices over each serving and sprinkle with parsley.

• VARIATIONS •

Veal Scallopini with Vermouth. Substitute vermouth or dry white wine for lemon juice.

Veal Scallopini Marsala. Substitute Marsala for lemon juice.

Veal Scallopini with Herbs. Substitute vermouth or dry white wine for lemon juice and add 1 tablespoon each fresh minced tarragon, chives, and parsley.

◆

STUFFED SHOULDER OF VEAL
Serves 8 to 10

This is a dinner fit for a king or queen.

1 shoulder of veal, boned (3 to 4 pounds)	1 tablespoon fresh rosemary or 1 teaspoon dried
1 cup fresh bread crumbs	3 tablespoons melted butter
⅓ cup chopped fresh parsley	Salt and pepper to taste
⅓ cup minced onion	1 cup chicken or veal stock
½ cup sliced mushrooms	

Have the butcher bone the shoulder of veal. To make the stuffing, put the bread crumbs and all other ingredients except the stock in a large mixing bowl. Blend stuffing so all ingredients are well combined. Spread the stuffing over the fleshy side of the meat and roll the roast loosely. Tie with string and put in a roasting pan in a preheated 375-degree oven. Roast for 1½ hours, basting from time to time. When done, take roast out and pour off the pan juices, leaving about 2 tablespoons of fat. Add the stock to the roasting pan, and with a wooden spoon scrape sides of roaster to incorporate the browned bits. Cook at high heat on the stove until thickened. Slice roast in thin portions and pass the gravy separately.

◆

VEAL LOAF EN CROÛTE
Serves 8 to 10

2 pounds veal	2 teaspoons salt
1 pound chicken livers	¼ teaspoon white pepper
1 small onion, peeled	7 eggs
2 tablespoons chopped fresh parsley	¾ cup light cream
	2 packages piecrust mix

Choose pale pink veal cut from leg or loin. Trim tough fibers from veal. Finely chop veal with livers and onion in a food processor. Stir in parsley, salt, pepper, 4 well-beaten eggs, and cream. Beat until well blended. Pour piecrust mix into a bowl. Beat 2 eggs with ¼ cup water and add. Mix with a fork until particles clump together. Press large clumps together and knead on a lightly floured board until smooth. Roll out two thirds of the dough into an oblong 17 × 13 inches. Line a loaf pan with foil; let the foil hang over edges of pan. Grease the foil. Line the bottom and sides of the pan with the dough, which should hang over the edge of pan about 1 inch. Spoon veal mixture into pan. Fold dough over meat. Brush dough with the remaining egg, beaten with 1 tablespoon water. Roll out remaining dough into an oblong large enough to cover top of pan. Cover top with dough and trim edges. Press edges together. Brush top with beaten egg. Cut shapes out of any leftover trimmed dough and decorate top. Brush with egg again. Bake in a preheated 325-degree oven for 1½ hours, or until nicely browned. Let cool on a rack. Chill. Use foil overhang to pull loaf out of pan. Cut into thin slices and serve.

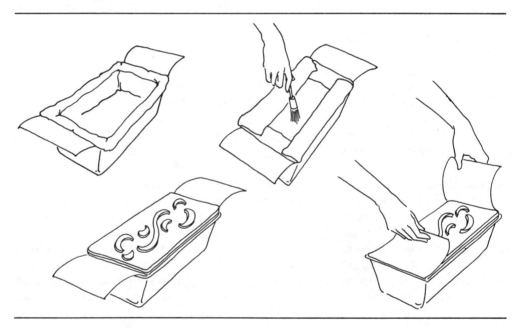

◆

VEAL RAGOUT
Serves 6

A veal stew is much more delicate than a beef stew, and it makes a nice change of menu during the cold months.

3 pounds veal shoulder, cut
into cubes

3 tablespoons vegetable oil
3 tablespoons butter

Salt and pepper to taste
1 large onion, thinly sliced
1 garlic clove, minced
1 can (16 ounces) tomatoes

2 cups green pepper strips
¾ cup dry vermouth or dry
   white wine
½ cup chopped fresh parsley

Dry veal cubes in paper towels. In a heavy, flame-proof casserole heat oil and butter until it sizzles. Add veal cubes, browning them in batches until all are done. Season meat, add onion, garlic, tomatoes, green pepper, wine, and parsley, and simmer, covered, for 1½ to 2 hours, or until veal is tender. When meat is done, turn heat higher and reduce sauce, uncovered, for about 5 minutes. Taste again for seasoning. Remove meat with a slotted spoon to a warm platter. Over high heat cook sauce for another 5 minutes to reduce further. Pour sauce over veal and serve with rice or noodles.

Lamb

The younger the lamb, the more tender the meat. Baby lamb, the most expensive, is less than four months old. The lamb that is regularly for sale in the supermarket is about a year old. The older the animal, the more pronounced the flavor becomes. The texture of meat from an older animal is coarser than that of a young lamb, and the fat tends to give it a somewhat gamy taste. Mutton, or older lamb, makes good-tasting chops but is more frequently used for soups and stews than for roasts.

For two people buy 1 pound boneless stew-meat lamb. Do not buy less than a 3-pound roast, or it will become dry before it is fully cooked. When roasting meat, it is better to buy more than you need for one meal and use the leftovers another day.

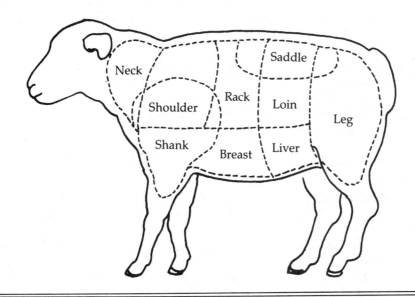

◆

BROILED BONED BUTTERFLY LAMB
Serves 6

Ask the butcher to butterfly a leg of lamb. You will get a wide, flat piece of meat that will cook under the broiler or over charcoal in 40 minutes. A 6-pound leg of lamb will serve 6 people when the bone has been removed (save the bone and use it for soup). The lamb is put in a zesty marinade to soak for several hours before it is broiled.

1 onion, finely chopped	*2 sprigs parsley*
2 garlic cloves, finely	*½ cup oil*
chopped	*1 cup vinegar*
1 teaspoon salt	*2 tablespoons soy sauce*
1 teaspoon peppercorns	*1 6-pound leg of lamb, bone*
1 teaspoon dried rosemary	*removed before weighing*

Combine all the ingredients in a large baking dish and marinate the lamb for 6 hours or longer in the refrigerator. Turn the lamb at least once.

Preheat the broiler. Take the lamb from the marinade and put it 4 inches from the heat. Cook for 20 minutes on each side, brushing with the marinade every 10 minutes.

◆

LAMB KEBABS
Serves 2

Some of the easiest dishes are the most spectacularly good. Part of the effect with this entrée is achieved by serving the food on a skewer. It looks beautiful and is far more attractive than if all the ingredients were put separately on the plates.

¾ pound leg of lamb	*1 teaspoon dried rosemary*
¼ teaspoon salt	*1 onion, cut into 8 wedges*
Freshly ground black pepper	*6 cherry tomatoes*
1 garlic clove, finely chopped	*1 green pepper, cut into*
¼ cup wine vinegar	*1½-inch pieces*
¾ cup oil	*8 mushrooms*
2 teaspoons soy sauce	

Cut the lamb into 1½-inch cubes. Trim carefully to remove all fat. Combine salt, pepper, garlic, vinegar, oil, soy sauce, and rosemary for marinade. Marinate the lamb for 2 hours, or longer if possible in the refrigerator. Preheat the broiler and put the rack on the lowest shelf. Alternate lamb, onion, tomatoes, green pepper, and mushrooms on two skewers. Brush all the ingredients with the marinade. Broil for 10 minutes, basting with the marinade once. Turn, baste again, and continue broiling for 5 minutes. Serve on a bed of rice.

◆
MIXED GRILL
. . . .
Serves 2

Sometimes called "English grill," this is an impressive lunch or dinner main course that takes only minutes to put together.

2 1-inch loin lamb chops
1 tomato
Salt and pepper to taste
4 medium-size sausages

6 mushrooms, sliced
Garnish: Minced fresh
parsley

Trim excess fat from chops. Preheat broiler to high. Cut tomato in half and season with salt and pepper. Put chops and tomato under broiler flame. Put sausage in a small frying pan and quickly sauté while chops and tomato are broiling. Do not let tomato get too brown. Cut into chops after 8 minutes to see if done to your taste. Remove sausage from frying pan and quickly sauté mushrooms in the sausage drippings. Arrange 1 chop, 2 sausages, ½ tomato, and mushrooms on each plate. Sprinkle with parsley for added color.

◆
LAMB STEW
. . . .
Serves 6

This is a delicate dish; many cooks forget that lamb makes a delicious stew. This recipe is based on a French one, as the French generally use turnip in this ragout.

4½ pounds of lean lamb
shoulder or breast of lamb,
cut into bite-size pieces
All-purpose flour
8 tablespoons vegetable oil
5 to 6 cups beef stock or
canned broth
Salt and pepper to taste
4 tablespoons butter
1 medium-size turnip, peeled
and cut into bite-size
pieces

12 small white onions, peeled
2 teaspoons sugar
2 garlic cloves, peeled
6 carrots, peeled and quar-
tered lengthwise
2 leeks, white ends only, cut
into 1-inch slices
12 small new potatoes or 8
medium-size older potatoes

Dry meat in paper towels and flour lightly. Put oil in a large frying pan, bring to a sizzle, and brown meat in batches in a single layer. Take time to brown each piece evenly and thoroughly. When browned, cover lamb with stock, scrape sides of pan to incorporate the browned bits, and season with salt and pepper. Cover the frying pan and simmer lamb gently for 45 minutes. Meanwhile heat butter in another frying pan and sauté the turnip and onions for 10 minutes, making sure they cook evenly. Sprinkle with sugar to glaze slightly. Transfer lamb to a large casserole and add the turnip and onions, garlic, carrots, and leeks. Add the potatoes—new potatoes whole and unpeeled, older potatoes peeled and quartered. Add enough stock to almost cover the ingredients. Cover casserole and bake in a preheated 350-degree oven for 1 hour, or until vegetables are fork-tender.

Pork and Ham

As with all meat, the younger it is, the more moist and flavorful it will be. Always buy firm, fresh-looking pork or ham. If it has been frozen and thawed in the supermarket, it will look gray and limp.

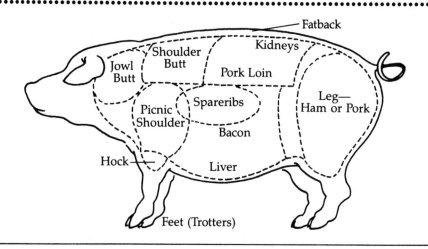

ROAST PORK LOIN WITH MUSTARD

Serves 6

It is impossible to prepare a small pork roast, because the outside becomes dry before the inside is fully cooked. A 2-pound roast is the minimum size that will cook satisfactorily, but a 3-pound roast will taste even better, and there are many ways of using the leftovers.

1 3-pound boneless pork loin
4 teaspoons prepared Dijon mustard

1 teaspoon dried rosemary
1 teaspoon crushed green peppercorns

Score the pork fat in a diamond pattern and put the loin on a rack in a shallow roasting pan. Combine the mustard, rosemary, and pepper and spread over the surface fat. Roast the pork in a preheated 350-degree oven for 1½ hours, or until a meat thermometer reaches 175 degrees. Let the pork rest for 20 minutes before carving.

◆

PORK CHOPS WITH TOMATO
Serves 2

This is a rich main dish and usually one chop per person is sufficient, but for hardy appetites plan on two chops per person.

2 loin pork chops, 1 inch thick
2 tablespoons vegetable oil
¼ cup vermouth
1 can (8 ounces) stewed tomatoes
1 medium onion, finely chopped
2 carrots, scraped and quartered lengthwise

2 stalks celery, cut into 1-inch pieces
2 tablespoons minced fresh parsley
1 tablespoon fresh rosemary or 1 teaspoon dried
Salt and pepper to taste

Remove excess fat from chops and pat dry with paper towels. Heat oil until sizzling in a frying pan and add pork chops. Brown chops on each side. It will take about 15 minutes to thoroughly do this. Add vermouth and with a wooden spoon scrape sides of pan to get all the browned bits. Add tomatoes, onion, carrots, celery, herbs, and salt and pepper. Cover pan and gently simmer for 1¼ to 1½ hours. Meat should be tender and show no sign of pink. Serve with rice and spoon sauce over chops and rice.

◆

ROASTED MARINATED SPARERIBS
Serves 4

This is a great informal meal to share with close friends on a weekend evening. The ribs go well with rice.

5 pounds lean spareribs
3 garlic cloves, minced
1 can (8 ounces) tomato sauce

1 cup beef consommé
1 cup orange juice

1 cup red wine	*½ cup honey*
½ cup vegetable oil	*1 teaspoon hot dry English mustard*

Dry ribs with paper towels and put in a large roasting pan. Combine garlic, tomato sauce, consommé, orange juice, wine, and oil in a small bowl to make the marinade and pour over ribs. Let ribs stand in this mixture in refrigerator for at least 24 hours. Turn ribs frequently to keep them coated with the marinade.

When ready to roast, lift ribs out of the marinade and put on a rack in a roasting pan. Roast, uncovered, in a preheated 350-degree oven for ¾ hour. From time to time baste with the marinade, and also pour off any fat that accumulates in the bottom of the roasting pan. Mix honey and mustard, increase oven heat to 400 degrees, and brush ribs with the honey mixture. Let ribs cook another 10 minutes, until they have a nice glaze or shine. Meanwhile, put marinade in a saucepan and heat until bubbly. Serve as a sauce with the ribs.

◆

APRICOT-GLAZED HAM
Serves 8 to 10

This makes a stunning focal point for a buffet table, a festive main dish for any dinner party or celebration.

1 precooked smoked ham (about 10 to 12 pounds)	*½ cup firmly packed dark brown sugar*
⅓ cup dried apricots	*½ teaspoon dry mustard*
Orange juice	*⅛ teaspoon ground cloves*

Choose a well-rounded, chunky-looking ham (with a short shank) that feels firm and has a fresh smoky odor. Put ham on a rack in a shallow baking pan, fat side up. Insert a meat thermometer into the center of the ham, not touching bone. Roast in a preheated 350-degree oven for 2½ to 3 hours, or until internal temperature registers 130 degrees. After 2 hours remove ham from oven, score fat into diamonds, and cut rind on shank into points with a pair of scissors. While ham is roasting, cook apricots in enough water to cover until tender. Purée apricots and blend in enough orange juice so mixture is the consistency of honey. Stir in remaining ingredients. Thirty minutes before ham is done, spoon glaze over ham and replace in oven. Continue baking, spooning additional glaze over ham for over 10 minutes.

• VARIATION •
The apricot glaze can be spooned over ham steaks or slices. Slash edges of 2 ham slices, 1½ inches thick. Put slices in a well-greased shallow pan. Bake in a preheated 350-degree oven for 30 minutes. Spoon glaze over steaks and bake another 10 minutes.

Poultry

You can tell the age and quality of a chicken just by looking at its skin and appearance. If it is plump with a well-filled-out breast and the skin fits the body as if it were custom-made, take it home. The breastbone will be red with bright blood. Beware the limp and jaundiced appearance of a skinny bird with flakes of ice beneath its back. It may have been frozen and defrosted more than once before being offered for sale. A frying chicken can be fried, braised, stewed, or roasted, but a roasting chicken (which is an older bird), turkey, or duck should be roasted. See roasting chart, pages 35 to 37.

For two people buy a 2½-pound chicken. There will be some left over.

Wrap chicken, turkey, or duck in waxed paper and cook it within 3 days.

When buying turkey, select one that is pink-skinned with a slight purplish tinge. Ducks, geese, game hens, and other wild birds should have pale, clear, clean skin.

How to Stuff and Truss Poultry

Allow ¾ cup stuffing for each pound of poultry. Stuff the bird just before it is to be roasted. Always wash the bird inside and out under cold running water. (See "Food Safety.") Sprinkle inside and out with salt and pepper. Do not pack stuffing tightly into bird, as stuffing swells during cooking, but spoon it in lightly. Skewer or sew neck opening. Twist wings back over the neck opening. Skewer or sew body opening. Then truss bird. Put cord through twisted wing into the crease between the breast and leg. Cross the string under and then over the legs and tie together as close as possible.

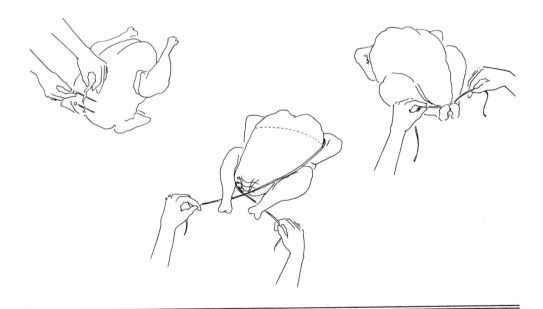

How to Cut Up a Chicken

Use a boning knife. To halve a bird, cut along the breastbone, cutting through the wishbone and the breast meat. Pull out the breastbone with your fingers. Open out the bird and put it on the cutting board, skin side up. Cut along the backbone to separate bird into halves. To quarter, cut these halves along the upper edge of the leg, or fold the half and cut along the fold.

To cut up a chicken or to remove breast meat: Remove the wings and legs first. Cut legs into drumsticks and thighs at the joint. To further cut the shell, place bird breast side up. Insert knife into bird's cavity and cut along both sides of the backbone. Remove backbone. Put breast skin side down and flatten. Remove breastbone with your fingers. Cut breast in half. Then cut each half in half again.

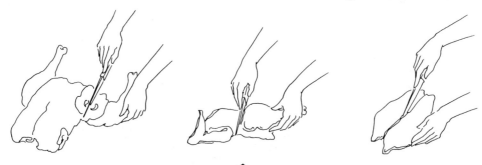

◆

ROAST CHICKEN WITH STUFFING

Serves 4

To make your own bread crumbs for stuffing, use stale bread and finely crumble by hand or in a food processor. To hasten drying fresh bread, put slices on a cookie sheet in a 200-degree oven until moisture evaporates.

3 tablespoons butter　　*1 stalk celery, chopped*
1 onion, finely chopped　　*1 chicken liver, cut in half*

1¼ cups freshly made bread
    crumbs
4 tablespoons finely chopped
    fresh parsley
2 teaspoons dried sage

½ teaspoon dried marjoram
½ teaspoon salt
Freshly ground black pepper
1 egg, lightly beaten
1 3-pound chicken

Heat 2 tablespoons of butter in a frying pan and fry the onion and celery over low heat for 10 minutes. Add the chicken liver and cook for 5 minutes. Remove from the heat and chop the chicken liver into small pieces. Return it to the pan and fold in all the remaining ingredients except chicken. Stuff and truss chicken and put in a baking dish. Dot the surface with the remaining butter and bake uncovered in a preheated 350-degree oven for 1¼ hours. Serve with Giblet Gravy (recipe follows), or see Index for plain pan gravy.

◆

GIBLET GRAVY
Makes 1 Cup

This recipe can be made with turkey or chicken innards. Do not use the liver, the flavor of which would be overpowering.

Chicken giblets and neck
½ onion, finely chopped
1 carrot, finely chopped
1 stalk celery, finely chopped
2 parsley sprigs
1 bay leaf
½ teaspoon dried marjoram

10 peppercorns
1¼ cups chicken stock or
    canned broth
1 tablespoon butter
1 tablespoon flour
2 teaspoons lemon juice

Put the giblets, neck, onion, carrot, celery, parsley, bay leaf, marjoram, pepper-corns, and stock in a saucepan. Simmer, uncovered, over low heat for 1 hour. Strain. Heat the butter in a saucepan and stir in the flour. Add the strained broth. Stir with a wire whisk until smooth. Stir in the lemon juice. Chop giblets and add to gravy.

◆

COQ AU VIN
Serves 6 to 8

2 broiler-fryers (about 2 to
    2½ pounds each)
¼ cup (½ stick) butter or
    margarine
¼ cup olive oil
1 carrot, chopped

1 onion, chopped
2 teaspoons salt
¼ teaspoon white pepper
Bouquet garni of bay leaf,
    celery stalk, parsley sprig,
    and 2 garlic cloves

2 cups white Burgundy
About 2 cups chicken stock or
   canned broth
2 tablespoons butter
2 tablespoons flour

12 small white onions, boiled
   and drained
1 cup sliced fresh mushrooms,
   sautéed

Leave chickens whole but thoroughly wash and pat dry. Tie legs together and turn back wings. Heat butter and oil in a frying pan and brown chickens on all sides. Put chickens in a large Dutch oven or casserole. Brown carrot and onion in same frying pan and add them with the pan drippings to the casserole. Add salt and pepper. Tie bouquet garni together in a small piece of cheesecloth and put in casserole. Add wine. Cover casserole tightly and cook over medium heat, turning chickens occasionally. Add stock, if necessary, so liquid covers chicken. When chickens are tender, in about 45 minutes, remove from pot to a serving platter and keep warm in the oven. Mix butter with flour and drop paste into hot pan drippings. Remove bouquet garni. Cook over low heat, stirring constantly, until mixture bubbles and starts to thicken. Add onions and mushrooms. Simmer for 10 minutes, stirring constantly. Serve sauce, onions, and mushrooms with chicken. Rice or fresh noodles go well with this.

◆

BROILED CHICKEN WITH LEMON BUTTER AND ROSEMARY
Serves 2

Broiled chicken is among the simplest and most satisfying of easy entrées. You can also cook it over charcoal. There will be some chicken left over for the next day.

1 2½-pound frying chicken,
   cut up and thoroughly
   washed
Freshly ground black pepper
3 tablespoons butter, melted
1 tablespoon oil
1 tablespoon fresh rosemary
   or 1 teaspoon dried

2 tablespoons finely chopped
   fresh parsley
2 tablespoons lemon juice
Coarse salt

Preheat broiler. Oil broiler rack with a little vegetable oil. Season the chicken with pepper and put on broiler rack. Combine the butter, oil, rosemary, parsley, and lemon juice in a small saucepan. Brush the chicken with the mixture. Broil the chicken parts, except breasts, for 12 minutes on each side, the breasts for 10 minutes on each side, basting frequently. (Broil chicken at least 4 inches from the heat, or the outside will be charred before the inside is cooked.) Season with coarse salt.

◆
CHICKEN LIVERS IN MADEIRA SAUCE
Serves 2

This is a fast, inexpensive, and flavorful main course. If you add only half the quantity of chicken broth, the recipe can be used as a filling for omelets or crêpes. The chicken livers cook quickly and are not improved by overcooking.

½ pound chicken livers
2 tablespoons butter
6 scallions, finely chopped
1 teaspoon prepared Dijon
  mustard
1 teaspoon tomato paste
1½ tablespoons all-purpose
  flour

¾ cup beef stock or canned
  broth
2 tablespoons Madeira
¼ cup heavy cream
Garnish: 2 tablespoons finely
  chopped fresh parsley

Cut each chicken liver in half. Wash and remove any membranes with a small sharp-pointed knife. Heat the butter in a frying pan. Add the scallions and sauté for 4 minutes. Add the chicken livers and cook over high heat for 5 minutes. Stir in the mustard, tomato paste, and flour. Add the stock and stir to form a sauce. Stir in the Madeira and cream. Continue cooking for 2 or 3 minutes, until hot. Garnish with parsley. Serve with rice.

◆
ROAST DUCK
WITH PLUM STUFFING
Serves 4

The butter and honey keep the duck moist and give the roasted skin a deep brown, almost black color.

1 large (12-ounce) can pitted
  plums
½ cup chopped walnuts

1 4½-pound duck
2 tablespoons butter
2 tablespoons honey

Combine plums and walnuts for the stuffing. Wash out cavity and fill and truss the duck. Put duck on a roasting rack and prick the skin with a fork. Combine the butter and honey and spread over the bird. Roast in a preheated 400-degree oven for 20 minutes. Reduce oven to 325 degrees and roast for 2 hours. Remove from oven and let sit 20 minutes before carving.

The duck skin is pricked so that the fat can run freely. There will be at least 1½ cups of fat, so make sure the duck is on a rack in a deep roasting pan or baking dish.

◆

DUCKLING À L'ORANGE
Serves 4

1 duckling, about 4½ to 5
   pounds
Salt and pepper
2 oranges, cut into quarters
¼ cup honey

¼ cup all-purpose flour
1 cup fresh orange juice
Rind of one orange, cut into
   thin strips
¼ cup currant jelly

Wash outside of duck thoroughly. Remove neck and giblets, and wash cavity under cold running water. Sprinkle inside and out with salt and pepper. Put orange quarters in body cavity. Put duckling on a rack in a shallow roasting pan. Prick entire body with a fork. Roast duckling in a preheated 325-degree oven for 2½ to 3 hours (internal temperature of 190 degrees). Cover neck and giblets with water and cook until tender. Drain and reserve 1 cup of the broth. Remove duckling from oven when roasted. Raise oven temperature to 375 degrees. Pour off drippings and reserve ¼ cup. Brush duckling with honey. Roast an additional 15 minutes. Mix reserved drippings with the flour. Gradually stir in orange juice, rind, broth, and currant jelly. Chop giblets and add to sauce. Cook over low heat, stirring constantly, until smooth and thickened. Remove and discard orange quarters, carve duckling, and spoon sauce over.

◆

ROASTED AND STUFFED ROCK CORNISH GAME HENS
Serves 2

1 cup cooked rice
¼ cup sliced fresh mush-
   rooms, sautéed
Salt and pepper to taste
Dash of nutmeg
2 tablespoons freshly grated
   Parmesan cheese

1 tablespoon chopped fresh
   parsley
2 Rock Cornish game hens
1 lemon quarter
¼ cup melted butter

Mix rice, mushrooms, seasonings, cheese, and parsley in a small bowl. Wash the hens inside and out and pat dry with paper towels. Rub the inside of both cavities with the lemon quarter. Stuff the cavities with the rice-mushroom mixture. Truss the hens and arrange on their sides on the rack of a roasting pan. With a pastry brush, dab melted butter over the skins of both hens. Roast in a preheated 400-degree oven for 15 minutes. Turn the birds over to the other side and baste with more melted butter and accumulated pan juices. Roast for another 15 minutes. Now turn birds on their backs, breast up, baste, and roast for another 15 minutes, or until tender. To test for doneness, puncture the joint between body and thigh with a sharp-pointed pairing knife; juices should run clear.

SEAFOOD

Fish and shellfish should be fresh when purchased. Here are a few tips as guidelines to freshness: To tell if a whole fish is fresh, check eyes (they should be well-rounded and clear), gills (bright red), and scales (they should adhere tightly to the skin). All fish should have flesh that feels firm and elastic and smells like a sweet sea breeze. Do *not* buy fish that has even a hint of an ammonia odor.

When buying fish for the freezer, be sure the fish is fresh and has not been previously frozen and thawed. Wrapped fish that is not to be frozen should be stored in the coldest part of the refrigerator and used immediately. If purchasing already frozen fish, be sure the package is hard to the touch. Put it in the freezer.

Assuming most household heads are not going to catch and clean their own fish, it is still important to know what some of the fish-store preparation terms mean.

Drawn: When the innards are removed and the fish is scaled, it is referred to as drawn.

Dressed: When the tail, head, and fins are removed, in addition to the innards and the fish scales, it is called dressed.

Pan-dressed: When all of the dressing preparation is completed and the fish is then split, with its backbone removed, it is referred to as pan-dressed.

Steaks: When the dish is dressed and the meat cut into crosswise slices, the slices are called steaks.

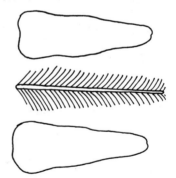

Fillets: When the fish is dressed and the meat is cut away from the bones, the boneless pieces of fish are called fillets.

Sticks: When fillets of fish are cut into long, thin slices, they are called sticks.

When purchasing steaks, fillets, or sticks, allow 3 servings per pound; when using dressed fish, allow 2 servings per pound; and when using whole fish, allow 1 serving per pound.

When poaching a whole fish, as soon as the liquid returns to a simmer, count on 10 minutes of cooking time for every inch of thickness of the fish. For example, if the fish is 2 inches thick, it should poach 20 minutes in the simmering liquid.

Incidentally, any good seafood cookbook will tell you how to gut, clean, scale, and cut up freshly caught fish. It is a messy operation, but not at all difficult once you get the hang of it. Besides, it gives the cook immense personal satisfaction, and is an excellent relaxing exercise for frustrated surgeons!

When buying shellfish, it is extremely important to know the source of the fish, because shellfish taken from polluted waters can cause hepatitis and many serious gastric disorders. If your seafood shop is worth its salt, it will know where its shellfish were harvested.

Another warning: Shellfish should be alive when bought. Carefully examine the shells of any clams, mussels, scallops, or oysters you are about to cook to make sure the shells are *tightly closed*. Any live clam or mussel will part its shell slightly when cooked. A dead clam or mussel will not open its shell when cooked and should be discarded. Members of the shellfish family include clams, oysters, scallops, mussels, crabs, lobsters, and crayfish. Crabs, lobsters, and crayfish should be also alive and kicking right up until the time of cooking.

Fish and shellfish provide an excellent source of protein, vitamins A and D, and minerals. The keys to successful fish cookery are gentle, quick cooking, subtle seasonings, and light, delicate sauces.

Seafood can be baked, broiled, deep fried, panfried, sautéed, and steamed. Line the baking or broiling pan with foil to eliminate pan scrubbing and fish after-odors. Fatty fish can be broiled easily, but leaner fish requires basting with butter or oil.

Shellfish are sold alive in the shell (clams, crabs, lobsters, mussels, oysters, snails), canned, cooked in the shell (some crabs and lobsters), cooked (lobster, crab), frozen raw and cooked (scallops, oysters, shrimp, king crab), shucked (oysters, clams, scallops), and smoked (oysters and mussels).

Almost all fish dishes must be made at the last moment, because the timing is so critical; the fish tends to become overcooked if it is reheated.

OTHER GENERAL FISH HINTS

• To test fish for doneness, push a fork gently into the thicker part of the body; if it flakes, it is cooked. Another test: Once the clear part of the flesh becomes opaque, the fish is done.

• When cooking fresh fish, leave the head and tail on. It locks the juices into the flesh, which adds to the flavor. The head and tail can be removed before serving, although it will lose juices even then.

• When cooking thin fish fillets, the second side will not require as much cooking time as the first side.

• To ease the transfer of a large, whole cooked fish to a serving platter, line the pan with a large, well-greased piece of foil before putting the fish in the oven. Holding the foil, use it to gently slide the fish onto the platter in one piece.

• When poaching or steaming, first wrap the whole fish in cheesecloth. After the fish is cooked, you can lift it out of the poaching liquid by the cloth handles.

◆

BAKED BLUEFISH
Serves 2

A quickly prepared and extraordinarily good-tasting dish. It can be made in the same way with other fish, such as snapper, striped bass, weakfish, cod, and haddock.

¾ pound bluefish
4 scallions, finely chopped
2-ounce jar chopped pimientos, drained, or several strips fresh green pepper

2 tablespoons finely chopped fresh parsley
2 tablespoons butter
1 tablespoon lemon juice

Put the bluefish on a piece of aluminum foil large enough to enclose it completely. Cover the fish with the remaining ingredients. Fold the edges of the foil together to form a neat package, making sure none of the juices can escape. Put the package on a baking sheet and bake in a preheated 350-degree oven for 15 minutes.

◆

STEAMED RED SNAPPER WITH DILL SAUCE
Serves 4 to 6

1 red snapper (about 4 to 5 pounds), dressed, with head left on
Salt and white pepper
4 tablespoons chopped fresh dill
1 lemon, sliced
1 onion, sliced
2 carrots, diced

6 peppercorns
2 bay leaves
1 cup sliced celery
2 cups water
2 cups dry white wine
3 tablespoons butter
3 tablespoons all-purpose flour
1 cup heavy cream

Wipe fish inside and out with a damp cloth. Sprinkle inside and out with salt and pepper. Wrap fish in a long piece of cheesecloth so that cheesecloth extends 12 inches beyond the head and the tail. Put 2 tablespoons dill, lemon, onion, carrots, peppercorns, bay leaves, celery, water, and wine, in a roasting pan or fish steamer large enough to hold fish flat. Put fish in pan, letting cheesecloth ends hang outside pan. Cover tightly and put cheesecloth ends on lid to keep them from burning. Bring water to a boil, lower heat, and simmer for 30 to 35 minutes. Uncover, lift out fish using cheesecloth ends, and place on a heat-proof platter. Cover with foil and set over hot water to keep warm, or put in a low oven.

To make sauce, strain broth in skillet. Measure out 1 cup. Heat broth to the boiling point in a saucepan. Cream together butter and flour and form into small balls. Drop balls into hot broth. Cook over low heat, stirring constantly, until broth bubbles and thickens. Beat in cream and remaining dill. Season to taste with salt and pepper. Reheat slightly. Remove cheesecloth carefully from fish and pour sauce over fish. Serve at once. To cut fish for serving, remove head with a sharp knife. Then cut into crosswise slices.

◆

STUFFED WHOLE BAKED SEA BASS
Serves 4 to 6

1 dressed striped bass, about
   4 to 5 pounds
Salt and pepper
1 small onion, chopped
¼ cup chopped celery
½ cup (1 stick) butter
2 cups soft bread crumbs

1 package (6 ounces) frozen
   king crab meat, defrosted
   and drained, or ½ pound
   fresh crab meat
2 tablespoons chopped
   scallions
1 cup chicken stock or canned broth
1 onion, cut into thin slices

Wipe bass inside and out. Sprinkle inside and out with salt and pepper. Sauté chopped onion and celery in ¼ cup of the butter in a skillet until golden brown. Add bread crumbs, crab meat, and scallions. Use mixture to stuff bass. Sew or skewer opening together. Put fish in foil-lined shallow baking pan. Add stock. Melt remaining butter and brush over fish. Top with onion slices. Bake, uncovered, in a preheated 350-degree oven for 40 to 45 minutes, or until fish is easily pierced with a fork. Cut into crosswise slices to serve.

◆

FLOUNDER POACHED IN CIDER
Serves 4

1 teaspoon butter
4 scallions, finely chopped
2 pounds flounder fillets
½ teaspoon salt
Freshly ground black pepper
1 cup apple cider
2 tablespoons apple brandy

1 tablespoon lemon juice
2 tablespoons butter
1½ tablespoons all-purpose
   flour
⅓ cup heavy cream
4 tablespoons freshly grated
   Parmesan cheese

Butter a broiler-proof baking dish with 1 teaspoon butter and sprinkle with scallions. Cut each flounder fillet in half lengthwise. Roll it up like a jelly roll to make a more attractive presentation. Arrange flounder fillets in the dish. Season fish with salt and pepper. Add cider, brandy, and lemon juice. Cover dish with aluminum foil, put in a preheated 350-degree oven, and poach fish for 12 minutes. Strain off the liquid carefully. Keep the fish warm. Melt the 2 tablespoons butter. Stir in the flour and add the strained liquid and cream. Pour the sauce over the fish. Sprinkle with cheese and brown under the broiler for 3 minutes.

◆

SALMON EN PAPILLOTE
Serves 4

The fish can be prepared and wrapped ahead of time, refrigerated, and baked at the last minute.

4 salmon steaks, about 1 inch
   thick
Softened butter
1 large onion, sliced
1 bay leaf

⅓ cup melted butter or
   margarine
Juice of 1 lemon
Garnish: Lemon wedges

Wipe steaks with a damp cloth. Open out a brown paper bag or use a piece of parchment or brown paper, cutting a piece 16 × 20 inches. Grease paper thoroughly with softened butter, using a pastry brush, and put paper in a shallow roasting pan. Put steaks on paper and top with onion, bay leaf, melted butter, and lemon juice. Wrap paper tightly around steaks. folding in ends, and tie with string. Bake in preheated 425-degree oven for 15 to 20 minutes. Unwrap, discard bay leaf, and serve immediately, garnished with lemon wedges.

◆

STEAMED MUSSELS OR CLAMS

Allow 12 per serving. Mussels or clams should be cooked as soon as possible after purchase. Scrub shells with a vegetable brush in cold water. Pull or snip the black hairy threads, called the beard, from the mussels. Wash mussels or clams in several changes of cold water. Discard any that float. Heat ½ inch of water in a large kettle. Add mussels or clams, cover, and steam over high heat until shells open—3 minutes for mussels, 6 minutes for clams. Remove mussel or clam from shell. Dunk mussels in melted butter. Dunk clams in cups of hot broth to wash off any sand and then dip in melted butter.

• VARIATIONS •

Mussels or Clams Marinière. In a large heavy kettle put 1 finely chopped onion, ½ cup chopped fresh parsley, ½ teaspoon dried thyme, ground pepper to taste, and 1½ cups white wine. Heat until simmering. Add mussels, cover kettle, and steam for about 3 minutes or until shells open. To serve, ladle seafood and broth into deep soup bowls.

Mussels or Clams Marinière with Tomatoes. Add 1 medium can of tomatoes to the kettle.

Mussels or Clams Marinière with Cream. After mussels or clams are cooked and removed from kettle, stir ⅔ cup heavy cream into the hot liquid and bring to a boil. Pour over shellfish in the soup dishes.

◆
BOILED LOBSTER

Boiling is the most common way to cook lobster. Most lobsters are pegged or banded to keep their claws from opening. If they are not, grasp the lobster's back firmly at the point where the solid body joins the jointed tail section.

Select 4 lobsters, each weighing 1¼ to 1½ pounds. In a large kettle bring to a boil enough water to cover the lobsters. As soon as water is boiling rapidly, drop in the lobsters, one by one. Cover pot with a lid and boil for 10 to 12 minutes after water returns to a boil. Lobsters turn red when cooked, and the meat on the underside of the tail will feel tender to a fork. Remove lobsters with tongs. Slit down the center of the bottom with a large knife. Turn over, shell side up, and let water drain out. Serve warm with melted butter, flavored with a dash of lemon and Tabasco sauce. You can serve cold with mayonnaise. Leftover lobster can be used in salad or made into a curry dish.

◆
STEAMED LOBSTER
Serves 4

Steamed lobsters tend to be less watery than boiled ones.

3 quarts water	2 teaspoons dried
12 peppercorns	2 bay leaves
2 tablespoons fresh thyme or	4 1¼- to 1½-pound lobsters

Bring water with peppercorns, thyme, and bay leaves to a boil in a large kettle with a lid. When water is rapidly boiling, drop in the lobsters, one by one, cover kettle, and steam for 12 to 15 minutes after water returns to a boil. Remove with tongs. Split lengthwise with a sharp knife and drain. Serve with melted butter and lemon or with mayonnaise.

◆
BROILED LOBSTER
Serves 2

If you feel squeamish about running a sharp knife down the center of a live lobster, do not undertake this method of cooking. (Some seafood shops will do the task for you, but you should *immediately* bring the lobster home and broil it.)

Insert a sharp knife between the body and tail shell of the lobster to sever its spinal cord. Then turn the lobster on its back and with a sharp knife make a deep cut through the entire length of both the body and tail. Spread the lobster open and remove the intestine and stomach sac. Put in a preheated broiler and dot with butter, or pour melted butter all over the cavity. Broil 15 to 20 minutes, or until flesh is lightly browned. Serve warm with more melted butter and lemon.

◆
STEAMED CRAB
Serves 4

In various parts of the country where crabs are abundant, a crab feast can be a joyful way to entertain. Count on about 6 crabs per person and use any left over in a salad, cocktail, or creamed dish.

3 cups flat beer or water
3 cups vinegar
1 cup commercial seafood
   seasoning or 1 cup mixed

fresh dill, parsley, and
   celery leaves
2 to 3 dozen live hard-shell
   crabs

Bring all ingredients except crabs to a boil in a large kettle with a rack or a steamer. With long tongs transfer crabs to the rapidly boiling liquid. (Some may be a bit feisty and lively.) Put lid on pot and hold it for a minute or two in case any crabs try to escape. Steam crabs for 20 to 25 minutes, or until they are bright red. Remove from heat and let cool for 5 minutes. Picks and crackers are necessary to pick out the meat. The average crab will yield 2 or 3 ounces of solid crab meat. Dunk the meat in mayonnaise, vinegar, or melted butter with Tabasco sauce.

◆
SOFT-SHELL CRABS
Serves 2

4 tablespoons butter
4 soft-shell crabs
Juice of 1 lemon

Garnish: Minced fresh
   parsley

Put butter in a large skillet and heat until foaming. Add crabs and sauté for a minute or two on each side according to size. Squeeze lemon over the cooked crab. Serve immediately and pour pan juices over the crabs. Garnish with parsley.

◆
MARYLAND CRAB
CASSEROLE
Serves 6

1½ pounds crab meat
1 green pepper, seeded and
   chopped
1 can (4 ounces) pimientos,
   drained and chopped

2 teaspoons dry mustard
2 eggs, well beaten
⅔ cup mayonnaise
Salt
Paprika

1 medium head broccoli,	1½ cups bread cubes
cooked and in small spears,	¼ cup melted butter
or 2 packages (10 ounces	
each) frozen broccoli spears	

Remove cartilage from crab meat. Mix crab with green pepper, pimientos, mustard, eggs, and mayonnaise. Add salt and paprika to taste. If using frozen broccoli, wash under running water to thaw enough to loosen spears. Put broccoli in the bottom of a casserole and spoon crab mixture evenly over top. Cover with bread cubes mixed with melted butter. Bake in a preheated 350-degree oven for 30 to 35 minutes, or until top is golden brown.

◆

BOILED OR POACHED SHRIMP
Makes 4 Shrimp Cocktails

The classic way to boil or poach shrimps is in a court bouillon. Shrimps prepared this way are used in shrimp cocktails, salads, and various shrimp casseroles and dishes.

1 pound fresh medium-size	1 small onion, minced
shrimps (about 20	¼ cup minced fresh parsley
shrimps)	or celery leaves
2 bay leaves	Flat beer or water
12 peppercorns	

Peel off the shell of each shrimp, but if you want to serve shrimps as an appetizer to be eaten with the fingers, leave the tails on, as it makes them easier to eat and decorative. With a small, sharp-pointed knife (or the pointed end of a beer can opener), remove the black intestine that runs down the back of the shrimps. Rinse shrimps and put in a medium-size kettle with the bay leaves, peppercorns, onion, and parsley. In a separate saucepan bring to a boil enough beer to cover the shrimps and pour it over them. Cook shrimps no longer than 3 to 5 minutes. Shrimps turn pink when cooked. Do not overcook, or they will be tough. Drain and let cool if using in cocktail or salad.

• VARIATIONS •
Boiled Shrimp in the Shell. Many people enjoy shrimps boiled in the shell and make it a "shrimp feast" for informal occasions. To prepare, count on ½ pound raw shrimps per person and follow preceding cooking instructions, leaving the shells on. Cook shrimps for about 3 minutes, or until shells turn a translucent pink. Drain and serve immediately with melted butter mixed with Tabasco sauce; tomato-and-horseradish seafood sauce; or mayonnaise mixed with lemon juice and Dijon mustard. Each person shells his or her own shrimps; a large bowl for empty shells is a must.
Broiled Shrimp. Prepare and cook shrimps as for Boiled Shrimp, counting on ½

pound raw shrimps per person. When shrimps are cooked and drained, put them in a large buttered broiler-proof baking dish (or about 10 individual baking dishes). Dot shrimps with a mixture of minced garlic, chopped chives, minced tarragon, minced parsley, pepper, fine bread crumbs, and softened butter. Pour a little white wine or vermouth over shrimps and put under the broiler for a few minutes, until golden brown and bubbly.

SCAMPI
. . . .
Serves 4

Scampi are jumbo shrimps. This is a quick and popular way to serve them.

2 pounds jumbo shrimps
1 garlic clove, minced
¼ cup (½ stick) butter
¼ cup olive oil

¼ cup white wine
Juice of 1 lemon
Pepper

Wash shrimps and drain well. Shell and devein. Cook garlic in butter and oil in a large skillet until golden brown. Add wine, lemon juice, and shrimps. Stir over high heat until shrimps turn pink and flesh is white, about 2 to 4 minutes. Sprinkle with pepper. Serve at once with some of the pan drippings.

SHRIMP JAMBALAYA
. . . .
Serves 8

¼ cup olive oil
2 garlic cloves, chopped
1 large onion, chopped
1 small green pepper,
* chopped*
2 cans (1 pound each)
* tomatoes*
1 quart chicken stock
2 cups long-grain rice
2 teaspoons salt

⅛ teaspoon cayenne pepper
1 pound shelled and cleaned
* raw shrimps*
1 cup diced smoked ham
1 cup sliced pitted ripe olives
1 package (10 ounces) frozen
* okra, cut into slices or ½*
* pound of fresh okra, cooked*

Heat oil in a skillet. Add garlic, onion, and green pepper and cook, stirring, until onion is golden brown. Add tomatoes, stock, rice, salt, and cayenne pepper. Stir to blend. Cover tightly. Cook over low heat until rice is almost tender, about 20 minutes, stirring occasionally to keep rice from sticking. Add shrimps, ham, olives, and okra. Stir to blend. Cover tightly. Cook over low heat until shrimps are pink and liquid has been absorbed. Serve immediately.

◆
SHRIMP CURRY
Serves 4

4 tablespoons vegetable oil
2 garlic cloves, minced
2 medium onions, chopped
1 large (2-pound) can whole
   tomatoes
½ cup tomato purée
1 to 2 tablespoons curry
   powder, according to taste

Salt
½ cup dry white wine or
   vermouth
2 pounds raw shrimps,
   shelled and cleaned
Condiments: sliced bananas,
   chopped salted peanuts,
   chutney, coconut, etc.

Heat oil in a large frying pan and sauté garlic and onions. Cook until soft but not brown. Add tomatoes and cook gently, covered, over very low heat for about ¾ hour. Add the tomato purée and simmer for another 15 minutes. Add the curry powder and salt to taste. Heat a few minutes and put sauce through a strainer. Return sauce to the frying pan and add wine. Let liquid come to a boil and add the shrimps. Simmer about 5 minutes, until shrimps turn pink. Serve at once with rice and offer a selection of condiments for the curry.

◆
SAUTÉED SCALLOPS
Serves 2

Tiny bay scallops are a great delicacy, and those who love them adore them almost any way; sautéing, however, preserves their delicate flavor. Larger scallops, called sea scallops, are cut into smaller pieces and are also best sautéed.

¾ pint freshly shucked scallops (or 1 pint for very
   large appetites)
Instant flour
2 tablespoons peanut oil

4 tablespoons butter
Salt and pepper to taste
Chopped fresh parsley, lemon
   wedges

Wash scallops and dry with paper towels or dish towel. When thoroughly dry, roll scallops in a dish of flour, just enough so scallops are evenly and lightly floured. Put aside. Heat oil and butter to a sizzle in a large frying pan. Quickly, with a slotted spoon, put scallops in the frying pan and sauté, turning scallops so that they brown on all sides. The browning process should take a few minutes. Do not overcook, as scallops become tough and watery. Sea scallops will take somewhat longer than bay scallops. Immediately put sautéed batches on paper towels to drain. Season to taste and garnish with parsley and lemon.

· VARIATIONS ·

Sautéed Scallops with Wine. Add ½ cup white wine or vermouth to frying pan after removing scallops. Deglaze with a wooden spoon and pour over the scallops.

Broiled Scallops. Wash and dry scallops on paper towels or dish towel. Put in a broiler-proof baking dish and pour ½ cup of white wine or vermouth over the scallops. Dot with butter and dust with paprika. Run under the broiler for 5 minutes, giving them one turn with a slotted spoon. Serve immediately, garnished with minced fresh parsley and lemon wedges.

◆

OYSTERS ON THE HALF SHELL
Serves 2

Oysters are more stubborn than scallops, harder to open, and for that reason almost everyone except a seasoned bayman or experienced chef usually leaves the job to the fish store. A good seafood store will open them and put them on a bed of ice. If you want to learn to open your own oysters, ask your friendly seafood-shop owner for a demonstration. You will need a special oyster knife for the operation.

Oysters should be rushed home and put in the refrigerator immediately, although they can be held on ice for an hour or two without losing flavor. If the seafood store wraps the oysters on ice in a plastic bag, remove the bag where you put oysters in the refrigerator. Count on 4 to 6 oysters per serving, depending on appetites. Serve with seafood sauce, lemon wedges, Tabasco sauce and Worcestershire sauce, and oyster crackers.

See Index for other oyster recipes.

◆

OYSTER STEW
Serves 4

Most men have a weakness for a steaming hot bowl of oyster stew. This makes a nice weekend lunch or supper dish.

1½ pints freshly shucked oysters with their liquid	*Salt, pepper, and cayenne pepper to taste*
1 cup light cream	*Paprika*
2 cups milk	*Butter*

Drain liquid from oysters and put in a large heavy-bottomed saucepan. Add cream and milk and heat almost to a boil. Add seasonings and oysters and cook only a few minutes, until edges of oysters begin to curl and float. Do *not* let the cream and milk boil. Ladle into soup bowls, dust with paprika, and dot each bowl with a generous piece of butter.

VEGETABLES AND FRUITS

....

Vegetables

A vegetable is at its peak of perfection when it has fully ripened in the sun. Ideally it should be eaten as soon as possible after being harvested. If you find asparagus in January, grown in a faraway place, it will not only be higher-priced than a local vegetable in season, but it will neither taste as good nor have as high a nutritional value.

It is a sad fact that unless you grow your own vegetables or buy them locally in season, commercially canned and frozen vegetables have a greater food value than many "fresh" but underripe imported vegetables at the supermarket. Frozen and canned vegetables are cooked briefly before being processed, so they need only be reheated, not actually cooked. Canned vegetables should be reheated only in their own liquid for the most nutritional value. Vitamins and minerals are destroyed by prolonged heat, so frozen and canned vegetables should be added to stews only in the last few minutes of cooking time. Frozen vegetables should be reheated in as little water as possible.

BLANCHING AND PARBOILING

This is a method used for softening vegetables slightly before adding to other quick-cooking dishes. For example, carrots are partially cooked before being glazed in butter; onions and green peppers are blanched for a few minutes before being threaded on skewers for shish kebab. Plunge the vegetables into a large pot of boiling salted water. Cook uncovered over high heat for 30 to 40 seconds and drain in a colander. Green beans and tougher vegetables will take a few seconds longer. Rinse immediately with cold water to stop the cooking. The vegetables will be crisp and bright in color. When you are ready to finish the cooking, return them to a pan of boiling water, or toss them quickly in hot butter.

STEAMING

Steaming is one of the most nutritious ways to cook vegetables. Use a steamer or pour an inch of water into a saucepan. Put the vegetables in a vegetable steamer, or on a perforated plate or metal strainer, and suspend over the water. Cover and steam until just tender.

PUREEING AND MASHING

Vegetables seem to have an exciting and different taste when they are puréed or mashed. Maybe it is because they look so decorative. The easiest way to purée is to put the cooked vegetable, such as peas, broccoli, cauliflower, spinach, or carrots, in a blender or food processor. Add a tablespoon or two of butter and just enough cream or chicken stock so the blades can turn easily. Taste, add more seasoning if necessary, and return the vegetable to a buttered saucepan. Reheat until it is very hot. The easiest way to mash a cooked vegetable is to first use a hand potato masher; then use an electric hand-held beater to whip them light. Add heated milk and butter in small quantities to get the desired consistency.

BRAISING

Carrots, celery, leeks, white onions, and Belgian endives are particularly good braised or cooked in a liquid in the oven. Parboil the vegetable for 5 minutes to soften it slightly. Put in a buttered baking dish and add about ¼ inch of heavy cream, chicken or beef stock, a small onion, finely chopped, a pinch of salt, and a tablespoon of herbs. Cover the pan with aluminum foil and cook in a preheated 300-degree oven for 30 to 40 minutes, until completely tender. Remove the vegetable from the braising liquid with a slotted spoon and serve.

BAKING

Potatoes, acorn squash, and other varieties of winter squash are delicious baked in the oven until tender. Potatoes should be rubbed with oil and pricked with a fork in one or two places after the skin is washed and scrubbed. Pricking allows the steam that builds up inside a baking potato to escape. If you fail to do this, you will have an oven full of exploded potato pulp! Potatoes require 1 hour in a 400-degree oven. Test with a fork to see if they are tender and done.

FRYING AND DEEP FRYING

Mushrooms, eggplants, onions, and zucchini are some of the most frequently used vegetables for frying. They can be fried in oil, butter, or a combination of oil and butter. They can be cooked as they are or coated with egg and bread crumbs. Vegetables other than potatoes are usually dipped in batter and deep fried for 3 to 6 minutes.

STIR-FRYING

More and more cooks are stir-frying vegetables to keep them crisp and nutritious. Among the most popular vegetables are snow peas, carrots, broccoli, mushrooms, asparagus, cucumbers, spinach, peppers, and sliced onions. There is no magic to stir-frying; all that is necessary is split-second timing and having all the vegetables prepared when you start. To cook most vegetables takes 1 to 2 tablespoons oil. The oil is heated to a sizzle, and the vegetables are added and quickly turned several times. The whole cooking process should take roughly 30 seconds to 1 minute. A 14-inch wok is a practical size for any household. A wok with two handles is much easier to hold and lift. Iron woks are the best; forget the nonstick and aluminum linings.

New woks, like crêpe and omelet pans, must be seasoned before being used. Clean it first: Fill the wok with hot water and add 2 tablespoons baking soda. Simmer on top of the stove for 15 to 20 minutes. The film can then be scrubbed off; if not, repeat the procedure. Now you are ready to season the wok. Heat it and wipe the inside with paper towel dipped in oil (peanut oil is best). The paper towel will look rusty. Let the wok cool and rinse it with lukewarm water. Repeat wiping with oil until rusty color is gone. When cooking with a wok, make sure the wok is thoroughly hot before adding the cooking oil; then let the oil become hot before adding the vegetables or other ingredients. Always scrub a wok gently; never use steel wool or a harsh powder. If necessary, soak to remove food remains. Make sure it is completely dry before storing.

Guide to Buying and Cooking Vegetables

VEGETABLE	QUANTITY NEEDED FOR 2 PEOPLE	AVAILABLE SEASON
Artichokes	2	October–May.
Asparagus	12 stalks	February–June.
Beans, green or yellow wax beans	½ pound	Available almost year round in markets. Peak season is spring and summer.
Beans, lima	1 pound	July–September.
Beets	6 medium	Available almost year round. May–October is peak season.
Broccoli	½ small head	Available year round. Peak season is fall.

BUYING TIPS

Choose fresh green color, closed firm buds with little or no brown discoloration.

Choose long, straight stalks of uniform size with tightly closed buds and almost entirely green stem.

Choose firm beans that snap and break rather than bend.

Choose uniformly filled pods. Flat pods contain baby limas and are hard to shell.

Choose firm beets with fresh green tops.

Choose dark green, closed buds with firm crisp stems.

PREPARATION AND COOKING

• Cut off stem so artichoke can sit on a plate. Soak in cold salted water to remove dirt or grit. Cook in large pot of simmering water with 1 tablespoon lemon juice. Cover and simmer for 40 minutes, or until a leaf can easily be pulled off. Drain and serve with hot butter, or serve cold with vinaigrette sauce or mayonnaise dressing. Can also be steamed.

• Soak in cold water to remove any sand. Discard tough white end and remove large leaf scales on stems with a vegetable peeler. Steam in 2 inches of water for 10 minutes, until just tender. Also can be stir-fried.

• Cut off ends. String or cut in half lengthwise or cut whole into any desired length. Yellow and green beans mixed together make a pretty vegetable offering. Simmer for 5 minutes in salted water, until just tender. Drain and season. The French method, which keeps beans beautifully green, is to parboil, rinse in cold water, and sauté in a skillet with butter until just tender. Also can be stir-fried in a wok.

• Shell limas and simmer in salted water for 5 minutes, or until just tender. Drain, season, and serve.

• Cut off leaves an inch from beet. (Leaves are a delicacy; cook and eat like spinach.) Wash beets but do not peel. Cook in boiling salted water, simmering covered for about 20 minutes, or until tender. Drain. Peel when cool enough to handle. Slice or serve whole with butter and salt and pepper.

• Soak in salted cold water to remove any debris. Discard lower third of stems. Cut stems lengthwise. You can further quarter stem to speed cooking. Steam or simmer in boiling water 3 to 5 minutes, or until just tender. Drain and season. Can also be stir-fried. Cooked stems can be cut in small pieces and puréed in a blender with a little chicken stock and cream.

VEGETABLE	QUANTITY NEEDED FOR 2 PEOPLE	AVAILABLE SEASON
Brussels sprouts	¾ pound	September–February. Peak is fall months.
Cabbage, green or purple	½ pound	Available year round. Peak is summer and fall.
Carrots	2 to 3, depending on size	Year round. Peak is summer and fall.
Cauliflower	¼ to ½ head, depending on size	Available almost year round. Peak is late summer and fall.
Celery	½ bunch	Year round.
Corn, sweet	2 to 4 ears, depending on appetites	Available May through September. Peak for freshly picked in cool climates is July and August.
Cucumbers	1 or 2, about ½ pound	Year round. Peak is summer months.

BUYING TIPS

Select firm green buds free of yellow or brown leaves.

Choose a head with loose rather than tightly closed leaves.

Choose fresh, straight, firm carrots.

Look for snowy white head with as little yellow discoloration as possible. Leaves should be firm and green.

Select straight, crisp stems. Do not buy cracked, brown, or limp stems.

Choose the freshest (picked only hours before, if possible), with tightly closed outer leaves. Pull a leaf back and prick a kernel with a thumbnail to make sure it is moist and milky.

Choose seedless variety if available. Look for long, firm, dark green cucumbers.

PREPARATION AND COOKING

• Soak in salted cold water. Discard limp outer leaves. Cut a cross in base at stem end. Cover and simmer in salted water for 5 to 6 minutes, or until just tender. Drain, season, and serve with butter. Also cook by steaming.

• Cut cabbage into quarters and remove heavy stem. Discard outer leaves. Tie quarters with string in two places to retain shape while cooking. Steam for 8 minutes, or until just tender. Season and serve.

• Scrape with vegetable peeler. Cut in julienne strips or slice or dice. Simmer covered in salted water for 8 to 10 minutes, depending on size. Taste for doneness. Drain, season, and serve. Baby carrots can be cooked and served whole; larger ones can be cut up, simmered with a little onion until tender, and mashed with butter.

• Remove outer green leaves and tough bottom stems. To cook whole, steam or simmer in boiling water 12 to 20 minutes, depending on size, until flowerets and stems are just tender. Drain. Cauliflower can also be broken into flowerets and simmered 3 to 5 minutes or steamed. Creamed cauliflower and cauliflower in butter and crumbs are delicious. (See Index.)

• Store in a plastic bag. Save leaves for salads and soups. Can be stir-fried, or simmered in broth 10 minutes, until tender. Delicious braised. (See Index.)

• Husk or remove leaves just before cooking. Cut off any remaining white stem and cook in rapidly boiling salted water for 2 to 4 minutes, till done to the touch of a sharp fork prong. Serve with butter and salt and pepper. See Index for other methods.

• Can be sautéed or steamed. Remove skin with vegetable parer. To sauté in butter, slice lengthwise, remove seeds, and cut halves into quarters. Cook quickly, season, and serve. To steam, cut into slices and steam about 5 minutes, until translucent or just tender. Serve with butter and salt and pepper. Also can be stir-fried.

VEGETABLE	QUANTITY NEEDED FOR 2 PEOPLE	AVAILABLE SEASON
Eggplants	1 small or ½ medium	Available almost year round. Summer is peak period.
Endives (Belgium)	2 to 4, depending on size	Available in fall, winter, and spring.
Leeks	2 to 4, depending on size	Almost year round. Peak is November–January.
Mushrooms	About 8, depending on recipe	Year round. Peak is November–April.
Okra	½ pound	Available almost year round. Peak period is summer.
Onions, Bermuda, Italian, or Spanish	1 to 3, depending on recipe	Year round. Summer is peak.
Onions, white or yellow	3 to 4, depending on appetites and recipes	Year round.

BUYING TIPS

PREPARATION AND COOKING

Choose firm, well-rounded, uniform-colored eggplants, free of blemishes and soft spots.

Choose firm, white endives with tightly closed leaves. Tips should be yellow—*not* slightly green.

Select firm white bulb with fresh green tops. Do not buy limp or dry-looking leeks.

Select white, tightly closed caps with moist stems.

Choose firm, small pods.

Choose all onions free of blemishes.

• Cut in ½-inch to 1-inch slices but do not peel. Sprinkle slices with salt to draw out bitter juices. Let drain on wire rack 15 minutes. Pat dry with paper towels. Pan- or stir-fry in hot butter or oil for a few minutes on each side, or deep fry. Used in moussaka and ratatouille (see Index) and other dishes.

• Braising is the most popular cooking method. Slice off the very end of the stem and the tip of the outer leaves. Parboil endives for 5 minutes, put in buttered baking dish, cover with chicken stock, and bake, covered, in 300-degree oven for 30 to 40 minutes, until tender. Drain, season, and sprinkle with parsley.

• Discard small end root and remove outer white leaves and green tops. Soak in water to remove sand. Cut white part into slices for soups and stews and sautéeing. Good braised in oven: Parboil slices 5 minutes, drain, cover with chicken stock. Bake, covered, in 300-degree oven for 30 to 40 minutes. Drain and serve. Also good in cream. (See Index.)

• Wipe with a damp cloth. Slice into quarters or cook whole. As a vegetable course, mushrooms are good sautéed quickly in butter for 3 to 5 minutes, or stir-fried. For delicious stuffed mushrooms, see Index.

• Remove stem ends and wash carefully to remove sand. Cook whole or cut large okra into slices. Fry, deep fry, stir-fry, or simmer covered in salted water for 15 minutes, until tender. Drain and season.

• Bermuda, a large white onion, is a sweet onion and is famous as deep-fried rings and in salads. Italian (red) and Spanish (purple) onions are sweet, decorative, and used in salads and cold dishes.

• Remove skins. White are delicious boiled for 10 minutes or until tender. Drain and season. Also excellent braised. Parboil first 5 minutes, drain, put in baking dish, and cover with chicken stock. Bake, covered, in 300-degree oven for 30 to 40 minutes, or until tender. Drain and season. A superb dish for onion lovers is creamed onions (see Index.) Small yellow onions can be boiled or braised. Larger yellow onions are generally used to flavor dishes, for example, when chopped onion is required. Slices can be stir-fried, and whole yellow onions also can be baked.

VEGETABLE	QUANTITY NEEDED FOR 2 PEOPLE	AVAILABLE SEASON
Parsnips	¾ pound	Fall and winter.
Peas, green	1 pound	March to July. Peak is May, June, and early July.
Peas, snow	¼ to ½ pound, depending on appetites	March until September in certain areas. Peak period is spring and summer.
Peppers, bell	About 2, depending on recipe	Year round. Peak is April–October.
Potatoes, all-purpose, for boiling, mashing, salad, frying, etc.	2 to 4 for boiling or mashing; 6 for salad	Year round.
Potatoes, baking	2	Year round, but good baking potatoes are scarce in late spring and early summer.
Potatoes, new	6 to 8, depending on appetites	April–October.

BUYING TIPS

PREPARATION AND COOKING

Select fat-topped parsnips; do not buy long, thin ones.

• Difficult to peel, so best to simmer or steam and then peel. To simmer, cook in salted water 20 to 45 minutes, depending on size and age. Test for doneness with sharp fork. Drain and peel when cool, discarding tough ends. Slice thin, season, and serve with butter. (See Index for steamed julienne parsnips.)

Fat pods hold old overripe peas, and flat pods contain immature peas. Ideally should be picked just hours before eaten. Choose uniformly filled pods.

• Shell, saving 1 or 2 pods. Cooking pods with peas is a trick that helps peas retain a fresh green color. Bring small amount of salted water (enough to cover) to a boil, add pods and peas. Simmer 1 or 2 minutes, or until just tender. Drain and season.
• Steam, stir-fry, or sauté (see Index).

Either green or red, peppers should be firm and well shaped.

• Remove stem; discard inside ribs and seeds. To parboil for stuffing, simmer 5 minutes or until just tender. To serve cold or as a seasoning, chop raw into strips, circles, or dice. Can also stir-fry.

Choose firm, clean potatoes of uniform size, free of blemishes.

• Peel potatoes and soak in cold water until ready to use. For boiling, mashing, or salad, cook potatoes in salted water to cover. Boil 20 to 25 minutes, depending on size, until tender. Drain, return to pan, and let dry out over low heat, shaking pan. To mash, use a potato masher and beat until pulpy. Then, either continuing with the hand masher or switching to an electric hand-held beater, add ¼ cup warm milk or light cream, beat in 2 pats butter, and season. For richer mashed potatoes you can add an egg yolk at the last minute and a teaspoon of ground nutmeg. See Index for French-fried potatoes.

Choose firm, clean potatoes of uniform size, free of blemishes. Many people prefer mealy, dry ones for baking, usually grown in inland states such as Idaho and Colorado.

• Wash and scrub skin with a wire vegetable brush. Rub with vegetable oil. With a sharp fork, poke a few holes in the skin to let steam escape while baking. Bake in preheated 400-degree oven for 1 hour, or until done to touch of a sharp fork.

Choose firm, clean potatoes of uniform size, free of blemishes.

• Wash and scrub skin of each. Put potatoes in saucepan, cover with boiling water, and simmer 8 to 10 minutes, or until tender. Drain and serve with minced fresh parsley, butter, and salt and pepper.

VEGETABLE	QUANTITY NEEDED FOR 2 PEOPLE	AVAILABLE SEASON
Spinach	1 pound	Available year round. Peak seasons are spring and early fall.
Squash, summer (both yellow and green, or zucchini)	¾ pound	Available almost year round. Peak period is June–September.
Squash, winter (acorn or butternut)	1 large	Readily available September–February. Fall is peak time.
Sweet potatoes	1 to 2, depending on recipe	Available September–March. Peak period is October–December.
Tomatoes	1 to 2, depending on recipe; 1 if broiled or sliced raw	Ideally should be bought only when locally ripe. Supermarkets make available year round but result is tasteless out of season. Summer is peak period in most areas.
Turnips and rutabagas	1	Available fall and winter.

BUYING TIPS

PREPARATION AND COOKING

Choose fresh, crisp, dark green leaves.

• Discard heavy stems and soak in at least 2 soakings of cold water to remove grit. Lift out of water after each soaking and put in a colander so that sandy water runs off. Cook without water in a covered pan over low heat for 5 minutes, until wilted. Drain well. Can be chopped or served whole. Add butter and season. Also can be stir-fried or creamed.

Choose small, firm squash, free of blemishes.

• Wash and cut into ½-inch slices. Steaming takes about 5 minutes, as does sautéing in butter. Can also be grated and sautéed (see Index) or stir-fried.

Choose firm, evenly colored squash with no blemishes.

• Cut in half and remove seeds. Add butter, nutmeg, salt, pepper, and a spoonful of maple syrup or brown sugar, if desired. Bake on foil-lined cookie sheet in 350-degree oven for 40 to 45 minutes, or until tender. Can also be peeled, cubed, and simmered for 25 minutes, then mashed with butter and seasonings.

Choose uniformly sized potatoes with as few blemishes as possible. Do not buy any with soft spots or frost blemishes.

• Can be baked, boiled, and mashed like white potatoes. See Index for candied sweet potatoes.

Buy firm, unblemished, bright red tomatoes.

• Peel by immersing in boiling water for a minute or two; let cool and remove skin with sharp knife. Tomatoes are delicious stewed, broiled, baked, or raw. To stew, peel, cut in quarters, squeezing out the seeds by hand, put in a saucepan with onion and green pepper, and cook over low heat for 30 minutes. Season and serve in small bowl. To broil or bake, cut tomato in half, sprinkle with a little sugar, salt, pepper, herbs, and broil for 10 minutes, or bake in 350-degree oven for 20 minutes.

There are two types of turnip. One is the small white turnip with the purple top; the other is called rutabaga and is large and yellow. Look for small white turnips and small or medium rutabagas, as the large ones tend to be pithy and spongy.

• Peel, slice, and simmer white turnips in salted water for 20 minutes, or until tender. Drain and season. Can also be parboiled for stews, sautéed, or braised in broth. Rutabagas are generally peeled, diced, and simmered in salted water for 20 minutes, or until done, and then drained and mashed with butter. Both turnips and rutabagas can be julienned, parboiled, and sautéed.

OTHER GENERAL VEGETABLE HINTS

• To avoid losing valuable nutrients when cooking vegetables, adhere to four simple rules:

1. When cutting, do not expose to air for long—cut directly before use.
2. Cook in as little water as possible.
3. Steam vegetables in a pot with a tight-fitting lid.
4. Do not overcook. Vegetables lose firmness and flavor as well as nutrients.

• Peeling and cutting onions is a teary task for most cooks. Here are a few ideas for washing away the tears:

1. Wear safety goggles or a skin-diving mask. (This is no joke!)
2. Put a piece of soft bread between your teeth. The moisture in the bread absorbs the onion's fumes or smell.
3. Hold the root end of the onion and slice toward the opposite end.
4. Slice under running water, carefully and with a firm grip—don't slip!

• Add a peeled potato to an oversalted soup or stew. It will absorb some of the excess salt.

• To perk up tired carrot or celery sticks, soak them in ice water, or refrigerate them in a jar filled with water. You may lose some nutrients, but it is useful in an emergency.

• Do not cook cauliflower in an aluminum pot, as it will become discolored. Use stainless steel or tin-lined pots.

• Boil several cloves in a cup of water to eliminate odors due to cooking such foods as seafood, cabbage, and onions.

• Keep tomatoes longer by storing them stem end down.

• For succulent, flavorful tomatoes, keep them at room temperature. They tend to lose flavor if refrigerated for more than 1 or 2 hours.

• Avocados and tomatoes will ripen faster if stored in a closed paper bag.

• If you change the water twice when soaking dried beans you will reduce their flatulent effect.

• To keep mushrooms fresh, store in a brown paper bag in the refrigerator. They will keep for 3 or 4 days. For optimum freshness, store in a sealed plastic container in the refrigerator. Do not wash mushrooms; always wipe clean with a damp cloth.

◆

RED CABBAGE AND APPLES
Serves 4

1 small head red cabbage	2 tablespoons sugar
¼ cup (½ stick) butter	1 teaspoon salt
½ cup red wine vinegar	2 teaspoons caraway seeds
2 small green or other tart apples, peeled, cored, and sliced	1 clove
	Red wine

Choose a firm, compact head of cabbage. Remove wilted leaves. Cut in half and remove core. Shred. Melt butter in a large skillet. Add cabbage and remaining ingredients. Stir to blend. There should be enough red wine to keep cabbage from sticking. Cover and cook over low heat, stirring occasionally, for about 30 minutes, or until cabbage is tender, adding more wine as needed to prevent sticking. Serve immediately.

◆

BROCCOLI WITH LEMON BUTTER SAUCE

Serves 4

1 bunch broccoli
½ cup (1 stick) butter or
  margarine, melted

Juice of 1 lemon
Salt and pepper

Trim ends of broccoli. Cut thick ends into 1-inch slices. Cut large broccoli flowerets in half lengthwise. Steam about 5 minutes, or boil in salted water for 3 to 5 minutes, until tender. Drain and put in serving dish. Heat butter in a small skillet and add lemon juice. Add salt and pepper to taste. Pour over broccoli and serve.

◆

BRUSSELS SPROUTS WITH CHESTNUTS

Serves 4

1 pint Brussels sprouts
¼ cup (½ stick) butter
1 can (11 ounces) chestnuts,
  drained

⅛ teaspoon ground nutmeg
Salt and pepper to taste

Trim outer leaves of Brussels sprouts and trim ends. Cut off bottoms. Steam or simmer in salted water 5 to 6 minutes, or until sprouts are just tender but still crisp. Drain and stir in remaining ingredients. Heat until butter melts, and serve.

◆

GLAZED ORANGE CARROTS

Serves 4

1 bunch young slender carrots
¼ cup (½ stick) butter)
2 tablespoons firmly packed
  brown sugar

⅛ teaspoon ground cloves
2 teaspoons grated orange rind
2 teaspoons chopped fresh mint
  or ½ teaspoon crumbled dried

Scrape or peel carrots. Cut into thin strips. Put in a saucepan and cover with ⅓ cup of water and add remaining ingredients. Bring to a boil and simmer, uncovered, about 8 to 10 minutes, or until just tender. Serve at once.

◆
CREAMED CAULIFLOWER
Serves 4 to 6

1 medium head cauliflower   1 cup Mornay Sauce (see Index)

Cut off green leaves and heavy stem of cauliflower. Wash the cauliflower well. You can either cook it whole, stem down, or break it into flowerets. Simmer in salted water in a large pot. A whole cauliflower will take 12 to 20 minutes, depending on size; flowerets require 3 to 5 minutes. (Both will take longer in a steamer.) Be sure not to overcook. It should be just tender. Drain thoroughly in a colander. Put cauliflower in a buttered baking dish. Top with warmed Mornay sauce. Bake in a preheated 350-degree oven for 10 minutes. Serve immediately. (You can complete the dish up to the final baking time, set aside, and bake just before serving.)

◆
CAULIFLOWER IN BUTTERED CRUMBS
Serves 4 to 6

1 medium head cauliflower   2 tablespoons white bread
3 tablespoons butter   crumbs

Cauliflower can be steamed or simmered, either whole or in flowerets. Steaming whole will take 12 to 20 minutes, depending on size. Flowerets require 3 to 5 minutes. Count on a little less time for simmering. Drain well and put in a serving dish. Melt butter in a small frying pan and add bread crumbs. Stir. Pour over cauliflower and serve immediately.

◆
FRENCH CHESTNUT PURÉE
Serves 4

2 pounds chestnuts   ¼ cup (½ stick) butter or
2 to 3 cups chicken stock or   margarine
   canned broth   Salt and pepper
1 cup hot milk or cream
   (approximately)

Choose large round chestnuts that feel firm when pressed. Slit chestnuts with a sharp knife. Put in a single layer in a shallow pan and add water to a depth of ½ inch. Bake in a preheated 400-degree oven for 10 to 15 minutes. Remove chestnuts and peel off heavy outer skin and thin inner skin while they are still warm. Cover chestnuts with stock in a saucepan and cook until they are easily pierced. Drain and press through a ricer or food mill. Gradually beat in milk and butter until consistency is that of a smooth purée. Season to taste with salt and pepper. Serve as a change from potatoes.

◆

CORN ON THE COB
Allow 1 or 2 ears per person

In addition to the basic cooking suggestion in the vegetable chart, corn can be cooked by the following methods. In the first, the corn is not actually cooked on the stove.

1. To boil ears of corn, remove husks and silk. Wash ears and put them in a pot of hot water with 1 tablespoon sugar. Do not add salt to corn until it is cooked. (Salt toughens corn during cooking.) Bring water to a boil, remove from heat, and let stand for 2 minutes. Serve immediately.
2. To steam corn, put shucked ears in a steamer with boiling water. Cover and steam for 15 minutes.
3. To roast corn, turn back husks and remove silk. Butter the corn and replace the husks. Tie each husk together at end with string. Put corn in a shallow pan in a single layer and roast at 350 degrees for 30 to 35 minutes.
4. Corn can be prepared on a barbecue as roasted corn is prepared, leaving unshucked or shucking and wrapping ears in foil. Roast over gray coals 15 to 20 minutes, turning ears occasionally.

◆

CORN PUDDING
Serves 6

This sumptuous dish, an old American favorite, monopolizes the oven. Plan the rest of the meal so it can be prepared on top of the stove or quickly broiled.

¼ cup all-purpose flour
Salt and pepper to taste
3 eggs
3 cups corn kernels, either
  fresh and cut from about 6
  ears or frozen and defrosted

2 cups light cream
4 tablespoons butter, melted
  and cooled

Mix flour and salt and pepper in a small bowl. In a large mixing bowl beat eggs until frothy, using a whisk or beater. Stir in corn and gradually sift in the flour and seasonings. Add the cream and butter and blend well for a minute or so. Pour the corn mixture into a 1½-quart baking dish that has been generously rubbed with butter. Put the baking dish in the center of a large shallow pan (a roasting pan will do well) and place on the middle shelf of a preheated 325-degree oven. Add enough boiling water to the shallow pan to come up at least 1 inch on the sides of the baking dish. Replenishing any water that boils away in the shallow pan, bake the pudding for 1½ hours, or until a knife inserted in the middle comes out clean. Serve immediately.

◆

BRAISED FENNEL
Serves 6

3 to 4 fennel bulbs
1 cup boiling chicken or beef
   stock or canned broth

¼ stick butter
Garnish: 2 tablespoons finely
   chopped fresh parsley

Cut fennel bulbs in half lengthwise. Put in a saucepan and cover with boiling water. Parboil for 5 minutes. Drain and put in a baking dish. Add the stock and butter. Cover and bake in a preheated 300-degree oven for 15 minutes, or until tender. Remove fennel from the baking dish with a slotted spoon. Serve garnished with parsley.

◆

CREAMED ONIONS
Serves 4

Many cooks forget how good creamed onions are and think of them only as a fall holiday treat.

1¼ pounds small white
   onions
2 tablespoons butter
2 tablespoons all-purpose
   flour

¾ cup milk
¼ cup heavy cream
Salt and pepper to taste
¼ teaspoon nutmeg, freshly
   grated if possible

Bring water to a boil in a large saucepan. Drop in the onions and blanche for about half a minute. Drain in a colander and let cool, then remove the skins with a small, sharp paring knife. (Nip off the root end and the outer skin should slide off easily.) Trim the top so that it looks neat. Simmer the peeled onions in salted water, just enough to cover them. They should take about 10 minutes and resist slightly when pierced with a fork. Drain the onions in a colander set over a bowl and reserve 1 cup of the liquid. Melt butter in a large heavy saucepan and add the flour, mixing the roux well. Gradually pour in the reserved onion liquid, stirring constantly with a spoon or whisk. Then add the milk and cream and cook, stirring constantly, until sauce thickens. Blend in salt and pepper and nutmeg. Butter a large casserole or baking dish. Put the onions in the casserole and pour the cream sauce over them, making sure all onions are coated with sauce. Bake in a preheated 350-degree oven for 30 minutes. You can prepare creamed onions in advance.

◆
LEEKS AU GRATIN
Serves 6

Leek lovers become addicted to this tantalizing recipe. It is also most impressive at a dinner party.

3 pounds leeks (about 8 small ones)	Ground pepper
	1 cup heavy cream
2 tablespoons butter	½ cup freshly grated
⅛ teaspoon ground nutmeg	Parmesan cheese

Trim off the stem end of each leek. Cut off enough of the green part to leave a main section of about 6 inches. Split leeks in half lengthwise. Cut the split leeks crosswise into 1½-inch pieces. There should be about 8 cups, loosely packed. Rinse thoroughly in a colander under cold water and drain. Melt butter in a heavy frying pan. Add leeks, nutmeg, and pepper. Sauté, stirring for about 1 minute. Add cream and bring to a simmer. Cover and cook for 15 minutes. Preheat broiler to high. Spoon hot leeks into a fireproof gratin dish. Smooth top with a spatula. Sprinkle with cheese and put under broiler until nicely browned and glazed. Serve piping hot.

If dish is to be reheated, put it in a preheated 350-degree oven for 20 minutes.

◆
STUFFED MUSHROOMS
Serves 2

4 to 6 large mushrooms, depending on appetites	3 tablespoons freshly grated Swiss cheese
2 tablespoons butter	Salt, pepper, and nutmeg to taste
1 small onion, finely chopped	1½ cups beef stock or canned
1 tablespoon minced fresh parsley	broth or consommé
½ cup bread crumbs	

Wipe mushrooms clean with a damp cloth. Remove stems (use in another dish). Melt butter in a small frying pan and sauté onion. When onion is golden and wilted, add parsley, bread crumbs, and cheese. Mix together and season to taste. Put a teaspoon or so of the bread crumb stuffing in each cap and arrange caps side by side in a shallow baking or gratin dish so that all mushrooms fit in one layer. Gently pour stock around caps to a depth of about ⅛ inch, and spoon a little over each cap. Bake in a preheated 350-degree oven about 20 minutes, or until crumb mixture looks toasted. From time to time, check stock level (it evaporates quickly) and baste caps. Serve mushrooms piping hot.

SNOW PEAS
Serves 2

¼ pound snow peas　　　　*1 tablespoon butter*
Salt to taste

Trim off string side of each snow pea. In a saucepan bring to a boil enough water to cover peas. Add salt and peas and let simmer about 30 seconds, or until just crisp; do not overcook. Drain. Heat butter in a frying pan and add peas. Quickly toss them in butter and serve immediately.

SAUTÉED PARSNIPS
Serves 4

1½ pounds parsnips　　　　*1 teaspoon sugar*
¼ cup (½ stick) butter, melted　*Salt and pepper to taste*

Choose small, firm young parsnips. Steam 15 to 20 minutes, or until tender. Peel and cut into julienne strips. Toss with butter and seasonings.

FRENCH-FRIED POTATOES
Serves 4

A deep-fat fryer is needed for this recipe.

4 large Idaho potatoes,　　　*Fat or oil for deep frying*
washed　　　　　　　　　*Salt*

Cut potatoes into ½-inch slices. Then cut slices into ½-inch-wide strips. Soak potatoes in cold water to cover for 1 to 2 hours, to remove excess starch. This will help keep potatoes dry and crisp. Drain potatoes and dry thoroughly to keep fat from spattering when potatoes are added. Put a layer of potatoes, not more than 2 inches deep, in the frying pan or basket. To prevent spattering, lower potatoes very slowly into fat heated to 375 degrees. Cook for a few minutes. If using a basket, lift it from the fat and shake sideways to loosen potatoes. Continue frying and shaking until potatoes are golden brown. Lift basket from fat or remove potatoes with a slotted spoon. Put potatoes on brown absorbent paper to drain excess fat. Sprinkle with salt and serve at once.

◆
POTATO PANCAKES
Serves 6 to 8

4 large Idaho potatoes, peeled	2 tablespoons oil
1 medium onion	½ cup all-purpose flour
2 eggs, well beaten	½ teaspoon baking powder
1 teaspoon salt	Oil for frying
¼ teaspoon pepper	Applesauce or sour cream

Using a hand grater, finely grate potatoes into a bowl of ice water. Let stand for a few minutes. Grate onion into another bowl and beat into it all the remaining ingredients except oil and applesauce. Drain potatoes and squeeze dry to remove excess water and starch. Beat potatoes into onion batter. Heat oil in a skillet, about ½ inch deep, and spoon in 2 tablespoons potato mixture for each pancake. (Mixture will make about 16 small pancakes.) Fry over medium heat until golden brown. Turn and brown on the other side. Drain on paper towels. Serve hot with applesauce or sour cream.

◆
CANDIED SWEET POTATOES
Serves 4

This is a popular fall vegetable and a must at holiday meals.

4 medium-size sweet potatoes	⅓ cup brown sugar
¼ cup butter	

In a large saucepan bring to a boil enough water to cover the sweet potatoes. Simmer sweet potatoes 20 to 25 minutes, or until tender. Drain, peel, and cut into oval or medallion shapes. Put sweet potatoes in a greased baking dish and pour sugar and butter mixture over. Bake in a preheated 350-degree oven for about 15 minutes, or until hot.

◆
SCALLOPED POTATOES
Serves 4

This is a popular potato dish at both buffets and winter and fall meals.

3 cups thinly sliced peeled potatoes	3 tablespoons butter
	Salt and pepper to taste
3 tablespoons minced onion or chives	1½ cups warm milk
	Paprika

Butter a 1½-quart baking dish. Put a layer of potatoes in the bottom of the dish. Sprinkle with onion and dot with bits of butter. Add salt and pepper to taste. Repeat layering until potatoes, onion, and butter are used up. Pour milk over the potatoes and sprinkle paprika on top. Bake, covered, in a preheated 350-degree oven for 45 minutes. Remove cover and bake for another 15 minutes, or until potatoes are tender. Serve piping hot.

◆

SPINACH-STUFFED TOMATOES
Serves 4

4 large tomatoes
1 pound fresh or 1 package
   (10 ounces) frozen
   spinach, cooked, drained,
   and chopped
½ cup freshly grated
   Parmesan cheese

1 hard-cooked egg, chopped
Salt
¼ cup dry bread crumbs
¼ cup (½ stick) melted
   butter

Scoop out tomato pulp, leaving a shell about ½ inch thick. Chop ½ cup of the pulp and add spinach, cheese, egg, and salt to taste. Use mixture to stuff tomatoes. Mix crumbs and butter. Sprinkle stuffed tomato tops with crumb mixture. Put tomatoes in a greased shallow pan. Bake in a preheated 350-degree oven for 15 to 20 minutes, or until tomatoes are easily pierced.

◆

GRATED ZUCCHINI
Serves 2

This is a wonderful, light, refreshing way to serve summer squash. It can be stir-fried in a wok or quickly sautéed in a skillet.

1 pound small zucchini
1 teaspoon salt
2 tablespoons vegetable oil
2 tablespoons butter

1 tablespoon lemon juice
Ground pepper to taste
1 tablespoon minced fresh
   parsley

Wash zucchini. Cut off each end. Using the coarsest side of a hand grater, grate the zucchini into a colander. Sprinkle salt over it and mix it in. (This draws water out of the squash.) Let the salted zucchini rest about 12 minutes. With your hands, squeeze the zucchini as dry as you can. Heat oil and butter in a heavy skillet or wok. Add the zucchini and cook quickly, stirring with a wooden spoon. It should be crisp and just barely done. Stir in the lemon juice and pepper. Add parsley and serve immediately. The whole cooking process takes just minutes.

RATATOUILLE
Serves 4

A delicious combination of summer vegetables, ratatouille can be served as a hot vegetable dish or cold with sliced meats.

3 tablespoons olive oil
1 small onion, finely chopped
2 garlic cloves, finely chopped
1 cup diced eggplant
2 small zucchini, sliced
1 tomato, peeled, seeded, and chopped

½ cup chopped cucumber
½ cup chopped black olives
1 bay leaf
½ teaspoon dried oregano
½ teaspoon salt
2 tablespoons finely chopped fresh parsley

Heat the oil in a large frying pan. Add the onion and garlic and sauté for 3 minutes. Add the eggplant and zucchini and sauté over high heat until lightly browned. Add all the remaining ingredients and simmer over moderate heat for 20 minutes. Discard the bay leaf.

Other fresh vegetables, such as chopped green pepper and sliced mushrooms, can be added to the ratatouille. If it is served hot, the ratatouille can also be sprinkled with freshly grated Parmesan cheese.

Fruit

There is no healthier snack or end to a meal than fresh fruit. Fruit contains important vitamins, such as vitamin C, and fruit also is low in calories.

Because of the marvels of transportation, Americans now enjoy year round a wealth of fruit that their parents either never ate or tasted only on rare occasions. To make these vast choices available, many fruits are picked by the growers when the fruit is mature, which means that the fruit has developed its full sugar content but still needs to soften and become ripe. As a result, a good many fruits—melons, peaches, pears, and plums, to name a few—are generally not found in retail stores ready to eat. These fruits must be taken home and given time to ripen at room temperature. Sometimes the ripening process can be forced or hurried along by putting fruit in a plastic bowl especially designed and sold to help ripen fruit, or simply in a sealed paper bag. These devices trap the fruit's own gases to quicken the ripening process.

There are, of course, some fruits in retail stores that can be used or eaten immediately. But the number of them is far less. Included in the ready-to-eat or -use group are oranges, grapefruits, apples, lemons, and limes.

The chart that follows is a guide to fruit buying and use; it tells you exactly what to look for in making a selection and how to treat and store the fruit at home.

Guide to Buying and Using Fruits

FRUIT	QUANTITY NEEDED FOR 2 PEOPLE	AVAILABLE SEASON
Apples	2	Year round. Peak period is fall.
Apricots	2	Available in spring and summer. Peak period is June and July.
Avocados	1	California avocados are available year round, but peak period is winter and spring. Florida avocados' peak period is fall; they are not available in spring and early summer.
Bananas	2	Year round.
Berries: strawberries, raspberries, blueberries, blackberries	Sold only in baskets.	Spring and summer is the peak period.
Cantaloupes	Some stores sell by quarters and halves, but mostly by the melon.	Available spring through fall. Peak is summer.
Cherries	½ pound	Late May into August.
Coconuts	Depends on recipe.	Available all year. Peak months are September through January.

BUYING TIPS	CULINARY USE AND TIPS
• Should be firm and unblemished.	Can be cored and baked whole or used in pies, tarts, puddings, and in applesauce and apple butter. Many people prefer green or unripe apples for cooking.
• Should be plump, relatively soft, and of good, even, orange-yellow color, without blemishes. Keep cold.	Can be stewed, used in jam, or used in soufflés and shortcakes.
• California avocados have rough dark green skin and should be unblemished; Florida avocados have a smooth skin, are a lighter green, and tend to be more "watery." Ripen at room temperature. When ripe and soft, refrigerate and eat as soon as possible.	Used raw in salads, first courses, soups, and added to some casseroles and dishes as an exotic accent.
• Should be plump. Color varies from green to yellow with brownish flecks. Ripen at room temperature and use within a few days. Avoid gray-yellow-looking fruit, which indicates a chilling injury.	Chiefly used in desserts, breads, and salads. Also eaten with cold cereals with milk or cream.
• Choose plump, firm, full-colored berries. Avoid baskets showing signs of bruised or leaking fruits. Use within a few days.	Chiefly used raw, in jellies and jams, and in desserts and muffins.
• Should be free of any stem and should "give" when pressed gently. Hold at room temperature for a few days. They will take on a yellowish appearance and a distinct aroma. Then refrigerate and use as soon as possible.	Chiefly raw and in salads.
• Select fresh, firm, unsticky fruit. Color can range from bright red to black. Immature cherries are light red and small. Avoid decayed fruit. Keep cold and use in 2 to 3 days.	Chiefly in desserts, salads, jams, and jellies, as well as raw.
• Select coconuts that are heavy for their size and full of liquid. Shake to make sure the milk sloshes around. Avoid ones with moldy or wet eyes. Keep cold and use as soon as possible.	Chiefly grated and used in desserts or as a condiment for curry.

FRUIT	QUANTITY NEEDED FOR 2 PEOPLE	AVAILABLE SEASON
Cranberries	Depends on recipe.	September through December.
Dates	Depends on recipe.	Year round.
Figs	Depends on appetites.	In small amounts in some stores, mainly August to October.
Grapefruit	1	Year round, but quality is poor off season. Peak is October through April.
Grapes	1 medium-size bunch	Year round. Peak is summer and early fall.
Honeydew melon	Sold in quarters and halves in some stores, but mostly by the melon. Quantity depends on use and appetites.	Year round. Peak season is June through October.
Kiwis	2	Year round. Imported from New Zealand but also grows in California.
Lemons	Depends on recipe.	Year round.
Limes	Depends on recipe.	Year round. Peak months are June through August.

BUYING TIPS

CULINARY USE AND TIPS

• Look for shiny, plump berries, red to reddish-black. Refrigerate and use in a week or two.

Chiefly in sauce, juice, and desserts.

• Prepackaged; sold either pitted or with pits. Fruit should be lustrous, brown, and soft. Reject dried and shriveled-looking fruit.

Chiefly in desserts.

• Look for soft-ripe fresh fruit with color ranging from greenish yellow to purple or black, depending on variety. A sour aroma is detected when overripe. Extremely perishable. Keep cold and use immediately.

In desserts, as fresh fruit, and in preserves.

• Select firm, springy-to-touch fruit, not soft, wilted, flabby, or loose-skinned. Should be well shaped and heavy for its size, as heavy fruits are thin-skinned and contain more juice than thick-skinned fruit. Grapefruits come in pink or white flesh; the white is usually more pronounced in flavor. Color preference is a matter of personal taste.

Chiefly fresh and raw, but used in salads, as juice, and in desserts.

• Look for those firmly attached to the stem. Should be plump, fresh, and not sticky. All grapes are as ripe when bought as they will ever be, so do not buy with thought of holding to ripen. Keep cold and eat in a week or 10 days.

Chiefly as fresh fruit or in salads, but also in desserts, jams, and jellies, and with some fish and chicken dishes.

• Look for a creamy yellow color and velvety surface; avoid dead-white ones with a greenish tinge. A ripe honeydew rind will have a soft and velvety feel to it. Hold a few days before serving. When ripe, keep cool and use as soon as possible.

Chiefly raw and fresh and in fruit salad. Chilled pulp can be puréed with ice cubes and a squeeze of lime in a blender to make a fruity thick cold drink.

• Look for fuzzy-looking skin, resembling brown suede. Size is about that of an extra-large egg.

Chiefly raw and fresh and in fruit salad and pies.

• For juicy fruit, select those with a rich, yellow color, fine-textured skin, moderately firm, and heavy for their size. Lemons are best if used within a week or 10 days.

Juice and garnish, also in desserts and other dishes.

• Limes should be bright green and heavy for their size, except those imported from Mexico, which are light yellow when ripe. Any limes with purple or brown spots are

Juice and garnish, pies.

FRUIT	QUANTITY NEEDED FOR 2 PEOPLE	AVAILABLE SEASON
Mangoes	Depends on appetites.	Peak period is May through August.
Nectarines	Depends on appetites.	Peak period is June into September.
Oranges	Depends on use and appetites.	Year round, but best fruit is available December into June.
Papayas	Depends on use and appetites.	Year round, but peak months are June through December.
Peaches	2	Peak is June through September.
Pears	2	On market mainly August through March.

BUYING TIPS

CULINARY USE AND TIPS

affected with scald and should be avoided. Keep at room temperature for the few days before use.

• Smooth outer skin has traces of green, red, and yellow. As fruit ripens, the red and yellow predominate. Pass up mangoes that have a grayish look or black spots, are wilted, or have any signs of decay. Keep at room temperature until very soft and then consume as quickly as possible.

Chiefly as fresh fruit or in desserts or fruit salad. To remove flesh, cut off the two halves of fruit on either side of flat center pit. Score flesh with crossed lines to form cubes. Bend back skin and slice off cubes.

• Select plump, smooth, unblemished fruit. Avoid shriveled, hard, dull-looking fruit. Do not buy fruit with any green. Give them time to soften and then refrigerate and use quickly.

Chiefly as fresh fruit or in fruit salads.

• The best oranges have a firm, heavy, fine-textured skin according to variety. Some have color added, but dye is harmless. Reject any oranges that are puffy, spongy, or light, as they will lack juice. Can be kept at room temperature or refrigerated.

Famous for their juice but eaten whole fresh, in salads, and used as a flavor in many desserts, dishes, and sauces.

• Look for papayas that are bigger than a large pear. Also look for fruit that is at least half yellowish, with no huge amounts of green. Skin should not appear shriveled or be bruised. Ripen until soft at room temperature and use as quickly as possible.

Chiefly consumed as fresh fruit or in fruit salads.

• Never buy green peaches. Look for good yellow-red color and hold fruit at room temperature until soft and ripe. Then use as soon as possible. If any brown spots or rot appear, use quickly, as rot spreads. There are also white peaches; fruit and skins are paler than regular ones.

Used fresh in fruit salads, in desserts, sauces, and preserves.

• Look for those free of blemishes and scars, firm and unwilted. The plump ones are the best. There are many varieties and colors. Ripen at room temperature. They ripe from the inside out and it is hard to tell when ready. If soft on the outside, they are too ripe. Bartlett variety has a perfume when ripe. Refrigerate and eat quickly when ripe.

Used fresh, in fruit salads, and in desserts.

FRUIT	QUANTITY NEEDED FOR 2 PEOPLE	AVAILABLE SEASON
Persimmons	Depends on use.	Mostly October through December.
Pineapples	Depends on use—1 is enough for most recipes.	Year round. Peak is March through July.
Plums	2	Mainly June into September.
Pomegranates	Depends on use and recipe.	Late September into November. Peak month is October.
Pumpkins	Depends on whether you are eating or decorating!	Peak month is October, but available in small quantities year round.
Rhubarb	Depends on use. 1 pound stewed makes 4 servings.	Mainly January through June.
Tangerines	2	Mainly November through January.
Watermelon	1 is usually ample for most recipes. Can be bought in smaller pieces in some stores.	May into September is prime period.

BUYING TIPS	CULINARY USE AND TIPS
• Select plump, smooth, unblemished fruit. Green cap should be in place and color should be bright orange. Keep at room temperature until very soft; then when ripe, refrigerate and use quickly.	As fresh fruit or in desserts.
• Select heavy, large fruit, which has more edible flesh. Crown leaves should be dark green and fresh-looking. Avoid those with soft spots or discoloration. You cannot further ripen the fruit. Keep cold and use quickly.	Mainly used as fresh fruit, in salads and desserts, but also with some meat dishes.
• Look for plump fruit that is beginning to soften. Plums take 3 or 4 days to ripen at room temperature. Once ripe, keep cold and use quickly. They come in many colors.	Fresh raw, also in desserts and sauces.
• Rind should be pink or bright red. It should be tough and thin. Avoid those that appear dry and hard. Keep cold until used.	In special dishes and desserts.
• Look for those with a good orange color and a hard rind, and heavy in relation to size. There should be no bruises. Keep cool.	Famous in pies, but also made into soup and cooked and mashed as a vegetable.
• Select fresh, crisp, tender stalks that are not thin. Color ranges from pink to red depending on variety. Younger stalks, with immature leaves, are generally more delicate and tender. Big stalks are tough, and flabby ones indicate stringiness.	Chiefly stewed and eaten as a fruit or in pie. To stew, wash well, cut in 1-inch lengths, and put in saucepan with 2 or 3 tablespoons water (it gets watery as it cooks) and 1 cup sugar. Cook, covered, on very low heat about 20 to 25 minutes, until tender.
• Look for those that are heavy for their size. A puffy appearance is normal, as skin peels off easily. Color is deep orange into red. Avoid any fruit with mold or soft areas. Highly perishable, so keep refrigerated.	Eaten raw but also used in fruit salads and desserts.
• Hard to determine maturity. Ripe ones are usually firm, well shaped, with good color. Lower side should be yellowish where melon lay on its side. If the underside is white or pale green, the melon is probably not mature. Since many retailers sell them in slices, you can tell if a precut one is ripe, as it will have reddish flesh and black seeds. Can be chilled or kept at room temperature.	Chiefly as fresh fruit and in fruit salad. Rind is pickled.

SOME GENERAL FRUIT HINTS

- When cooking with lemon and lime juice, use only stainless steel, tin-lined copper, or heatproof glass saucepans. Pans made of iron, aluminum, or carbon steel will give the food a less desirable color and flavor.
- To keep lemons and limes from shrinking, put them in a bowl of water, cover with a plate to hold underwater, and refrigerate.
- Roll citrus fruit on a table to loosen up juices; or warm them in the oven for a few minutes.
- To keep apple, pear, peach, and banana slices from turning brown when exposed to air, sprinkle them with lemon juice.
- When preparing jam or jelly, add a small slice of butter to keep foam from developing at the top.
- To unwax fruit like apples (vegetables, too), run hot water over the fruit to melt the wax, then scrub it with a plastic brush. Wax is added to fruit and vegetables for cosmetic reasons—to make the produce shiny—and also to prolong their shelf life.
- Do not put bananas in the refrigerator; it turns their skins black and reduces their flavor.
- If crystals form on dried fruit (a natural process), dissolve them by heating the fruit in a 325-degree oven.
- After opening dried fruit packages, store fruit in plastic bags or other airtight containers to keep fresh.

PASTA

Every day Americans are discovering new pleasure and fun in eating pasta—all that joy that Italians have known for generations. The wonderfully imaginative and odd-shaped noodles that were once only the province of Italy are becoming almost commonplace all over the United States. Americans are also learning that you do not have to eat your pasta hot—that many dishes are served at room temperature, such as pesto sauce and pasta, and many pastas are the base of salads.

Over the centuries hundreds of pasta shapes have been created. They can be baked, boiled, or deep fried. Following are some of the varieties available:

cannelloni: These are large noodle tubes. They are usually stuffed with ground beef, veal, or chicken mixed with spinach or cheese, then baked.

capellini: This is an extra-thin variety of spaghetti—so light and gossamer it resembles its nickname—angels' hair.

conchiglie: This pasta is shaped like conch or sea shells and is most decorative.

fettuccine: These are flat noodles that resemble ribbons. This pasta, mixed with butter, cream, and cheese, is famous as Fettuccine Alfredo.

fusilli: This pasta resembles small spirals.

lasagne: These noodles are long, broad, and flat. They are famous layered and baked with meat, tomato sauce, cream sauce, and cheese.

linguine: The noodles are flat and thin. The pasta is well known served with clam sauce.

manicotti: These are large noodle tubes, similar to cannelloni, but usually stuffed with a mixture of ricotta and mozzarella cheeses and eggs, and topped with a tomato sauce.

orzo: This pasta resembles rice and can be used as a substitute or in soups.

ravioli: These are distinctive pasta squares, often stuffed with meat or with spinach and ricotta cheese.

rigatoni: This pasta resembles large grooved tubes and is popularly served with a fresh tomato sauce.

spaghetti: This pasta is familiar to almost everyone. It is a long, very thin round noodle.

tagliatelli: These are noodles that resemble ribbons and are similar to but wider than fettuccine.

tortellini: These are distinctively shaped small dumplings that look like ears. In Italy they are often referred to as "the navels of Venus." They are popular in a salad, or with cream sauce.

vermicelli: This is an extra-thin variety of spaghetti.

ziti: This is a long, large macaroni-like noodle tube. It is served in salads or baked with meat or cheese and tomato sauce.

Homemade Pasta

Today a large number of gourmet shops are selling their own freshly homemade pasta in response to the tremendous new interest in pasta. Once you have tasted the freshly made variety (or made your own), you will want to have it as often as possible! For those who want to try a hand at making their own, there are many machines on the market today, from simple hand-cranked pasta machines to dazzling automatic devices. Simply follow the instructions given for the machine. Here is a recipe for the basic dough.

BASIC PASTA
Serves 4

This recipe can be stretched in any direction. The basic formula is ¾ cup flour to every egg and 1 egg per serving. If you get overenthusiastic and make too much pasta, let it dry and either store it loosely, covered, in a dry place, where it will keep for at least 30 days, or freeze the extra batch.

3 cups all-purpose flour,   *Salt to taste*
* unsifted*   *4 eggs*

Choose a large flat surface where you can work. Put the flour and salt in the middle and mix together with your hands. Take a rubber or metal spatula and neatly push the flour into a small mound. With your hand, make a well or hole in the middle of the mound. One at a time, crack the eggs and drop them into the well. With your hands, mix the flour and eggs together, and keep mixing until the resulting dough is stiff and all the flour is mixed in. If it seems too sticky, add just a bit more flour. Form the dough into a ball and knead the dough (see Index for instructions) until it is fairly smooth, which should take about 5 minutes. If you want to use a food processor for all the foregoing steps, combine the flour, salt, and eggs in it and process until a dough ball is formed; no further kneading is necessary. If the dough is too stiff, add 1 or 2 tablespoons water. Now you are ready to make your pasta.

• VARIATIONS •
Spinach Pasta. Defrost and squeeze the water from a 10-ounce package of frozen chopped spinach. Mince it finer with a chopping knife. Add spinach to the dough when you add the eggs. You may have to add extra flour, as the dough will tend to be sticky.

Tomato Pasta. Add 4 tablespoons of tomato paste when you add the eggs.

Cooking and Serving Pasta

Fresh pasta cooks faster than store-bought. Use this formula as a rule of thumb for cooking either: For 4 to 6 servings use 1½ pounds of pasta of your choice. Bring 4 quarts of water to a boil in a large kettle to which a tablespoon of vegetable oil has been added to keep the pasta from sticking. Add a dash of salt, if you use salt. Add pasta, a few strands at a time, quickly pushing it under the water so as not to lose the rolling boil. As the pasta cooks, stir with a wooden spoon to prevent sticking to the bottom and the sides. Cook, uncovered, until *al dente*, or just tender but still firm. (Do not overcook as pasta continues to cook after it is removed from the heat.) Drain thoroughly in a colander. Fresh pasta takes about 2 to 3 minutes; store-bought will need an extra minute or two.

To serve pasta, tongs or a multipronged pasta fork is the easiest device. Put pasta in a large bowl and ladle sauce over. Each person can toss his pasta and sauce together. Most sauces are enhanced by a sprinkling of Parmesan cheese before being tossed. The cheese also gives the sauce extra body.

You can invent almost any dish you want with pasta. You can use a classic sauce (see Index), such as tomato sauce, or simply butter or olive oil. Make sure the cheese is always freshly grated; use the pre-grated cheese only in emergencies.

BOLOGNESE SAUCE
Serves 6

This is one of the favorite and classic sauces in Italy, and a hit with almost everyone. It can be served on spaghetti, vermicelli, fettuccine, or linguine, or in a casserole with conchiglie.

2 tablespoons oil	2 cups tomato purée
1 onion, finely chopped	1 tablespoon tomato paste
1 garlic clove, mashed	1 tablespoon chopped fresh
1 carrot, diced	oregano or 1 teaspoon
1 thin stalk celery, diced	dried
1 pound ground beef	¼ teaspoon salt
3 mushrooms, finely chopped	Freshly ground black pepper
1 tablespoon flour	2 tablespoons finely chopped
1 cup beef stock or canned	fresh parsley
broth	1 cup freshly grated
½ cup red wine	Parmesan cheese

Heat the oil in a large skillet and fry the onion, garlic, carrot, and celery over low heat for 5 minutes. Add ground beef and mushrooms and cook for 10 minutes, until beef has browned. Pour off accumulated fat and stir in the flour. Add stock, wine, tomato purée, tomato paste, oregano, salt, pepper, and parsley. Stir to combine ingredients. Simmer, uncovered, over low heat for 45 minutes, until the sauce is fairly thick. Serve with cooked and drained pasta of your choice. Pass a bowl of Parmesan cheese at the table.

♦

GARLIC AND PARSLEY SAUCE
Serves 4

½ cup olive oil
2 garlic cloves, minced

1 cup minced fresh parsley
Salt and pepper to taste

In a small heavy frying pan, heat the oil until hot but not smoking. Add the garlic and sauté until golden brown. Toss the cooked and drained pasta of your choice with the sauce, parsley, and seasonings. Serve immediately.

♦

SAUCE ALFREDO
Serves 4

½ cup (1 stick) butter,
  softened
1 cup heavy cream
1 cup freshly grated
  Parmesan cheese

2 egg yolks
Salt and pepper to taste
½ teaspoon nutmeg

In a heavy saucepan, heat the butter and cream almost to a simmer; do not let it bubble. Remove from heat and pour over cooked and drained pasta of your choice. Toss with cheese, egg yolks, salt and pepper, and nutmeg. Serve immediately.

♦

MARINARA SAUCE
Serves 6

This is another classic Italian sauce for pasta. It is simple, straightforward, and always good.

¼ cup olive oil
2 garlic cloves, chopped
5 cups whole, seeded, and
  drained fresh tomatoes or
  canned Italian tomatoes

¼ cup chopped fresh oregano
  or 1 teaspoon dried
Salt and pepper
½ cup freshly grated
  Parmesan cheese

In a large heavy skillet heat oil until hot but not smoking. Add garlic and sauté until golden brown. Add tomatoes, parsley, and oregano. Simmer 35 to 40 minutes, adding salt and pepper to taste. Serve over cooked and drained pasta of your choice and toss with freshly grated Parmesan cheese. Serve immediately.

CLAM SAUCE
Serves 6

Linguine and clam sauce are linked like two lovers, but feel free to experiment. Try vermicelli, spaghetti, and similar pastas with the sauce.

1¼ cups (2½ sticks) butter
4 garlic cloves, minced
¾ cup chopped fresh parsley

4½ cups minced fresh or
   canned clams
1 tablespoon fresh oregano or
   1 teaspoon dried

Heat butter in a large, heavy skillet, add garlic, parsley, clams (including any clam juice), and oregano and heat just to a simmer. Immediately remove from heat, ladle over cooked and drained pasta of your choice, and serve.

PESTO SAUCE
Serves 2

The basis of this popular pasta sauce is fresh basil. Make the sauce in summer, when this wonderful herb is abundant and inexpensive. Most Italian groceries stock it, if your supermarket does not. A food processor or blender is necessary, although the old-fashioned way was to make the sauce with a mortar and pestle.

2 cups fresh basil leaves
2 garlic cloves, coarsely
   chopped
¼ cup Italian or flat parsley
¼ to ½ cup peanut or olive oil

¼ cup pine nuts
Salt to taste
¼ cup freshly grated
   Parmesan cheese

Put all ingredients except the cheese in a blender or food processor and blend or process; add more oil if necessary, to make a smooth paste. Add cheese and blend or process for a few seconds. Serve on cooked and drained pasta of your choice. Spaghetti and vermicelli are nice. Any pasta with pesto should be served at room temperature. Walnuts can be substituted for the pine nuts.

Pesto sauce freezes well, but do not add the cheese to the portions you intend to freeze. Add cheese when the sauce has thawed. Before storing or freezing, put a ¼-inch layer of olive oil over sauce to seal it further from the air.

• VARIATIONS •
Pesto is also sensational served on grilled fish, chicken, or on poached eggs or in an omelet.

◆
PRIMAVERA SAUCE
Serves 2

This is a fresh and light meatless sauce and is delicious in spring and summer, when fresh vegetables become abundant. You can make up your own vegetable combination.

¼ cup butter	1 cup tiny broccoli flowerets
¼ cup olive oil	12 snow peas, trimmed
2 garlic cloves, minced	8 mushrooms, sliced
2 shallots, minced	2 teaspoons fresh chopped
2 large ripe tomatoes, seeded	basil or 1 teaspoon dried
and chopped	Salt and pepper to taste
2 small carrots, cut into	¼ cup freshly grated
julienne strips	Parmesan cheese

In a large heavy skillet heat butter and oil until hot but not smoking. Add garlic and shallots and sauté until golden brown. Add all the vegetables and basil and cook quickly so that they are heated through but crisp. It should take about 5 minutes. Spoon the sauce over cooked and drained pasta of your choice. Linguine is a nice selection, but capellini, spaghetti, and vermicelli are nice, too.

Other Pasta Combinations

◆
STRAW AND HAY
Serves 4 to 6

This pasta dish got its name because it is made with both white and green noodles—colorful and delicious.

2 eggs	2 cups fresh or frozen peas
½ cup freshly grated	8 ounces linguine
Parmesan cheese	8 ounces spinach linguine
½ cup heavy cream	Ground pepper
1 cup chopped prosciutto	

In a small mixing bowl, beat eggs with the cheese. In a small saucepan, heat cream and prosciutto. Cook peas in rapidly boiling water until just tender. Drain and keep warm. Cook and drain pasta and put in a large bowl. Ladle over it the egg-and-cheese mixture, cream-and-prosciutto, and the peas. Toss and add pepper to taste. Toss again and serve immediately.

SPINACH TAGLIATELLI
Serves 4 to 6

2 eggs
¼ cup freshly grated fontina
   cheese
¼ cup freshly grated
   Parmesan cheese
½ cup heavy cream

½ cup chopped prosciutto
2 tablespoons butter
½ cup sliced mushrooms
16 ounces spinach tagliatelli
Ground pepper

In a small mixing bowl, beat eggs with the cheeses. In a small saucepan, heat cream and prosciutto. In a small skillet, heat butter and sauté mushrooms until just wilted and soft. Cook and drain tagliatelli and put in a large bowl. Spoon over it the egg-and-cheese mixture, cream-and-prosciutto, and mushrooms. Toss, add pepper to taste, and toss again. Serve immediately.

LASAGNE
Serves 8 to 10

This is a great, inexpensive party dish and is always a hit with guests.

2 cans (8 ounces each)
   tomato sauce
1 can (1 pound) tomatoes
3 tablespoons fresh oregano
   or 1½ teaspoons dried
1 tablespoon fresh basil or
   ½ teaspoon dried
4 tablespoons olive oil
1 garlic clove, minced

1 pound ground round steak
Salt
8 ounces lasagne noodles
½ pound ricotta cheese
½ pound mozzarella cheese,
   shredded
1 cup freshly grated
   Parmesan cheese

In a saucepan, combine tomato sauce, tomatoes, oregano, and basil. Bring to a boil, lower heat, and simmer. Heat 2 tablespoons oil in a skillet. Add garlic and ground meat. Break up lumps of meat with a spoon and cook until it just loses its red color. Stir tomato sauce into meat and drippings. Add salt to taste and simmer, uncovered, about 1 hour, stirring occasionally.

Cook noodles according to directions on package, adding remaining 2 tablespoons oil to the water to keep noodles separate. Separate noodles and place strips on waxed paper.

Spoon some of the sauce into the bottom of a 13 × 9 × 2-inch pan. Spread a layer of noodles over the bottom, trimming them with scissors to fit the pan. Spoon some of the ricotta over noodles and sprinkle with some of the mozzarella and Parmesan.

Spoon some of the meat sauce over all. Repeat layering of noodles, cheese, sauce, ending with Parmesan cheese. Bake in a preheated 350-degree oven for 40 minutes. Remove from oven and let stand for 15 minutes so it has a chance to set and is easier to cut. Cut into squares and serve with additional tomato sauce and Parmesan cheese.

MANICOTTI
Serves 6

2 cups (1 pound) ricotta cheese
1 cup freshly grated
    Parmesan cheese
½ cup shredded mozzarella
    cheese
1 egg
2 tablespoons chopped fresh
    parsley

1 small onion, grated
Salt and pepper
8 ounces manicotti
2 cups (two 8-ounce cans)
    tomato sauce
½ cup water
Freshly grated Parmesan
    cheese

In a mixing bowl mix cheeses with egg, parsley, and onion. Add salt and pepper to taste. Cook manicotti according to directions on package. Do not overcook. Drain thoroughly. Stuff manicotti with cheese mixture, using a teaspoon to push mixture into tube. Put filled manicotti in a shallow casserole. Pour over tomato sauce mixed with water. Sprinkle with Parmesan cheese. Bake in a preheated 350-degree oven for 25 to 30 minutes, or until sauce is bubbly and manicotti are tender. Serve immediately.

CHICKEN TETRAZZINI
Serves 6

This is a very good basic version of a famous dish. You can make it in a large quantity because it freezes well.

2 2½-pound chickens
2 cups chicken stock or
    canned broth

2 onions, finely chopped
2 carrots, diced
2 stalks celery, sliced

1 bay leaf
3 tablespoons butter
6 mushrooms, sliced
3 tablespoons all-purpose
    flour
½ cup heavy cream
2 tablespoons white
    vermouth or dry sherry

½ tablespoon salt
Freshly ground black pepper
1 pound thin spaghetti,
    broken into 2-inch pieces
    and cooked al dente
¾ cup freshly grated
    Parmesan cheese

Put the chickens in a large casserole and add the stock, onions, carrots, celery, and bay leaf. Cover and simmer over low heat for 50 minutes. Remove the chickens and discard the skin and bones. Cut the chicken meat into thin strips. Heat 2 tablespoons butter in a saucepan. Add the mushrooms and sauté over moderate heat for 3 minutes. Stir in the flour and add the strained stock from the casserole. Add the cream, vermouth, chicken meat, salt, and pepper. Put the hot cooked spaghetti in a baking dish. Put the chicken and sauce in the center of the dish. Sprinkle with cheese and dot with remaining 1 tablespoon of butter. Bake, uncovered, in a preheated 350-degree oven for 20 minutes. Serve immediately.

• VARIATIONS •

The chicken mixture can be served on a bed of green noodles or rice instead of spaghetti. Or you can serve it on a bed of cooked broccoli spears.

EGGS

Many busy people consider Sunday breakfast or brunch their favorite meal. It is a meal made for lingering and relaxing, and, of course, wonderful different dishes must help to start the day right. What follows are basic recipes that you can call upon repeatedly to quickly give you ideas and remind you of the number of simple but delicious treats that breakfasts and brunches can hold in store. (Omelets are not included here, but can be found in the section containing hearty casseroles and economical dishes.)

Here are a few valuable tips on buying and storing eggs and keeping leftover yolks and whites.

• Eggs are graded in varying sizes. Large sizes are best for the breakfast table, but the smaller (and usually cheaper) sizes can be used in cooking and baking.

• The yolks of brown-shelled eggs may have a yellower appearance; otherwise, brown- and white-shelled eggs are the same.

• Fresh eggs when broken have a firm, well-rounded yolk surrounded by a thick, slightly cloudy white with a small amount of thin white around the edge. In less fresh eggs you will find the yolk is not well rounded and tends to spread out. The white is clearer, since much of the carbon dioxide in very fresh eggs has escaped.

• Store them in the coldest part of the refrigerator, but not the freezer compartment.

• If eggs are to be separated into yolks and whites, break them open when they are cold. This makes separation much easier.

• If you want the foamiest of egg whites, beat them after they have warmed to room temperature.

• Leftover yolks with a film of water over them can be stored in a tightly covered jar in the refrigerator. Whites can be stored in the refrigerator or frozen as is. Do not keep either in a refrigerator for more than 5 days.

• Yolks and whole eggs should be mixed with 1 tablespoon sugar or 1 teaspoon salt per cup before freezing (depending, of course, on whether you plan to use them for a sweet or nonsweet dish).

• If you have forgotten whether an egg is raw or hard-cooked, spin it on a flat counter. A cooked egg will spin; a raw one will wobble.

• Most professional chefs advise beating egg whites with a wire whisk in a copper bowl, as the electrostatic interaction allows for smoother, more rapid whipping. If you use an electric mixer, use only one beater, for greater aeration.

• To remove any bits of yolk from egg white, use a piece of the eggshell to fish them out. If you do not remove the bits of yolk, the whites will not whip to stiffness.

• Refrigerate eggs upright with the large end up and the narrow end down; this will retard spoilage.

• To keep yolks from crumbling when you slice hard-cooked eggs, dip the knife in water periodically.

112

◆
SOFT- OR HARD-COOKED EGGS

Forget you ever heard the word "boiled" in connection with eggs. Eggs should be cooked gently in order to keep the egg white tender. When cooking eggs in the shell, let them warm to room temperature to prevent cracking when they are put in boiling water.

METHOD I
Bring water to boil in a saucepan. Depending on appetites, count on 1 or 2 eggs per person. Add eggs carefully with a slotted spoon, lower heat, and simmer 3 to 5 minutes for soft-cooked eggs, 12 to 15 minutes for hard-cooked eggs.

METHOD II
This is a slightly gentler method of cooking eggs in the shell. Carefully place eggs in a single layer in a saucepan, cover with cool water, and bring just to a boil. Lower heat and simmer 2 to 5 minutes for soft-cooked eggs, and 10 to 12 minutes for hard-cooked eggs.

Overcooking eggs causes a harmless, unattractive green tinge to form on the outside of the yolk. This is caused by iron and sulfur compounds, which unfortunately flavor the egg.

To serve a soft-cooked egg, break the shell through the middle with a knife and with a teaspoon scoop the egg out of each half into a small cup or dish. If you like to eat your eggs out of an egg cup, cut off the end of the egg with a knife and eat your egg directly from the shell with a small teaspoon. Add salt, pepper, and butter to taste. If a soft-cooked egg has to keep for a few minutes, put it in a bowl of lukewarm water.

Hard-cooked eggs should be plunged immediately into cold water as soon as done. To remove the shell, roll the egg on a hard surface until shell is cracked all over. Peel off shell and attached membrane. Rinse. When eggs are very fresh, they are difficult to shell.

◆
SCRAMBLED EGGS

Serves 2

Perfectly scrambled eggs are a delicious dish. The secret is to cook them *slowly* over low heat. That way they come out moist and creamy.

2 tablespoons butter	*1 tablespoon water or light cream*
4 eggs	*Salt and pepper to taste*

METHOD I (FRYING PAN)
Melt butter in an 8-inch frying pan. Crack eggs into a small mixing bowl. The French add water to scrambled eggs to make them light; Americans prefer cream or

113

milk. Add whichever you prefer to the eggs and lightly beat with a fork or whisk. Add salt and pepper. Pour eggs into the frying pan and cook over low heat, stirring constantly with a fork or wooden spoon, until they are thickened but moist. Remove from heat when slightly underdone, as the eggs will continue to cook from their own retained heat. Serve immediately. Chopped parsley or chives make a pretty garnish for the plate.

METHOD II (DOUBLE BOILER)

The advantage of this method, and it is a great advantage when preparing scrambled eggs for a hungry crowd, is that you do not have to stand over them and stir constantly.

Fill the bottom of a double boiler about one-third full of water and bring to a boil. Melt butter in the top of the double boiler set directly on the stove. Beat eggs with water or cream, season, and pour into hot butter and stir for a few moments. Lower heat under water to a gentle simmer. Put the eggs over the gently bubbling water in the bottom of the double boiler. Give them an occasional stir. When eggs achieve a creamy consistency, remove from the heat and serve immediately. Another advantage of this method is that the eggs can keep warm over the hot water until you are ready to serve them.

• VARIATIONS •

Scrambled Eggs with Ham. Add ⅓ cup diced ham to eggs just before they begin to thicken.

Scrambled Eggs with Cheese. Add ⅓ cup diced Cheddar or Swiss cheese to eggs just before they begin to thicken.

Scrambled Eggs with Herbs. Add 1 teaspoon each minced fresh parsley, chives, and tarragon to eggs just before they begin to thicken.

Scrambled Eggs with Curry. Add a dash of curry powder to the beaten eggs before you put them in the frying pan.

Scrambled Eggs in Pita Bread. Cut a piece of pita bread in half. Add 2 minced olives, 1 tablespoon green pepper, and 1 tablespoon chopped tomato to eggs just before they begin to thicken. When eggs are done, spoon a portion into each pita pocket and eat as a sandwich.

◆

CODDLED EGGS

As the name implies, coddled eggs are given much love and protection, but they are also one of the easiest and most delicate and delicious ways to serve morning or brunch eggs. Basically, they cook slowly by just sitting for a period of time in very hot water.

Put the eggs in a bowl of lukewarm water when you take them from the refrigerator. Fill a saucepan with enough water to cover the eggs by about 1 inch. Bring water to a rapid boil. Lower eggs, one by one, into the water with a slotted spoon. Immediately take the pan off the heat and cover with a tight-fitting lid. After 20 minutes the yolk and white of a medium-size egg will be nicely set; adjust your time up or down by a minute or so depending on egg size and how well set you prefer yolks and whites. Remove eggs from water and serve as you would soft-cooked eggs.

FRIED EGGS

There are two basic methods for frying eggs. Whichever you prefer, fry the eggs at a low temperature to avoid toughening the whites.

METHOD I

For 2 eggs use a 10-inch frying pan and heat enough butter or bacon fat to coat the bottom of the pan. Carefully break an egg directly into the pan. Immediately reduce heat to low. Baste eggs with some of the butter or fat; if you want the yolks sunny side up, keep basting until they are set. If you prefer them browned on both sides, flip them over with a spatula for a few seconds. Season to taste with salt and pepper and serve immediately.

METHOD II

For 2 eggs use a 10-inch frying pan and heat enough butter or bacon fat to coat the bottom of the pan. Carefully break each egg directly into the pan. Immediately reduce heat to low and fry until edges turn white (about 1 minute). Add 2 teaspoons water and cover the frying pan with a tight lid to hold in the steam. Cook to desired degree, salt and pepper to taste, and serve immediately.

POACHED EGGS
Serves 2

Eggs must be strictly fresh for use in poaching. Eggs are usually poached in water, but they can be cooked in any liquid—chicken stock, tomato juice, milk, cream, or wine. Poached eggs are the basis for some of the tastiest and best brunch dishes.

2 or 4 eggs, depending on appetites	*1 teaspoon vinegar*

Fill a frying pan about three fourths full of water. Bring to a boil and lower heat so that water is just simmering. Add vinegar. Break each egg—first onto a saucer if you feel your hand is not steady—and slip it into the gently simmering water. Repeat until all eggs are in the pan. Do not try to poach more then 4 eggs at a time. The water should just about cover the yolk; if it does not, gently spoon a little hot water over the yolk to produce a protective film. Poach the eggs until the whites set, about 3 to 4 minutes. Lift each egg out with a slotted spoon. Drain and serve immediately on a slice of buttered toast.

115

If you need to hold eggs a few minutes, remove to paper towels to drain. To rewarm eggs, slip back into simmering water for a few seconds.

• VARIATIONS •

Eggs Benedict. For each egg, sauté a slice of Canadian bacon or ham and toast and butter half an English muffin. Make ½ cup of Hollandaise Sauce (see Index) for 4 eggs. To assemble, put a slice of bacon or ham on each toasted muffin half, add a poached egg, and top with a dollop of hollandaise sauce.

Eggs Blackstone. For each egg, fry 2 slices of bacon until crisp and sauté 1 slice of tomato in a little butter until soft. Toast and butter 1 slice of bread per egg. Make ½ cup of Hollandaise Sauce (see Index) for 4 eggs. To assemble, drain bacon on paper towels and crumble. Put crumbled bacon on toasted bread. Add a slice of tomato, then a poached egg, and top with a spoonful of hollandaise sauce. Dust with paprika.

Poached Eggs with Sausage. For 4 eggs, make ½ pound of sausage meat into 4 cakes, fry, and drain. Make ½ cup of Hollandaise Sauce (see Index). Top each sausage cake with a poached egg and cover with hollandaise sauce.

Poached Eggs with Spinach. For 4 eggs, cook 1 pound fresh (or 2 10-ounce packages frozen) spinach and thoroughly drain. Sauté 4 slices of ham in a little butter in a frying pan. Serve each poached egg on a slice of ham and cover with spinach. Top with Mornay Sauce (see Index).

◆

EGGS EN COCOTTE

Eggs *en cocotte* are a dainty and decorative dish, but do not just spoil guests with eggs cooked by this method—treat yourself to them often. A cocotte is any small earthenware or china saucepan that has a handle and is deep enough to hold 1 egg plus some tasty garniture, such as crumbled bacon, vegetable purée, or creamed seafood or chicken. An individual soufflé dish can be used as a cocotte.

Preheat oven to 350 degrees. Butter individual cocotte or soufflé dishes. Spoon in your garniture. Garniture should fill dish about one third full. Very carefully crack an egg over the garniture and spoon enough cream over the egg to cover it. Using a cookie sheet, transfer dish or dishes to the oven, and bake until the egg white and yolk are set to desired doneness. Garnish with a sprinkle of minced fresh parsley.

◆

SHIRRED OR BAKED EGGS

Shirred and baked are basically the same method of cookery. The main difference is that shirred eggs are started on the top of the stove over direct heat and transferred to the oven to finish cooking.

SHIRRED EGGS

For each egg, melt 1 tablespoon butter in an individual baking dish over low heat on a stove-top burner. (Be sure you use a dish that can withstand direct flame under it.)

Do not brown the butter. Carefully crack 1 or 2 eggs (depending on dish size) into it and season with salt and pepper to taste. Pour another tablespoon of hot melted butter over the eggs and put the dish in a preheated 350-degree oven for about 15 minutes, or until whites are firm and yolks are set to desired firmness. Serve immediately in the dish.

BAKED EGGS

For each serving, butter a custard cup or slightly larger ramekin. Carefully crack 1 or 2 eggs, depending on dish size and appetite, into the dish. Season with salt and pepper to taste. Spoon 1 tablespoon light cream over the eggs and dot with butter. Put dish in a preheated 350-degree oven for about 15 minutes, or until the yolks and whites are set to your taste. Serve immediately in the dish.

BACON

When one thinks of eggs, one also thinks of bacon. Here are two basic ways to cook bacon. The never-fail oven method produces less fatty bacon, golden brown and crisp. If you use the frying-pan method, store the drippings in a covered can or jar in the refrigerator and use it for frying eggs.

OVEN METHOD

Preheat the oven to 400 degrees. Remove your broiler rack and pan and lay slices of bacon side by side across the broiler rack. Put rack and pan in the oven. (The fat automatically drains into the pan.) Bake for about 15 minutes, or until crisp and brown. Check from time to time to make sure bacon does not overcook.

FRYING-PAN METHOD

Preheat frying pan and arrange bacon strips in one layer. If bacon is too cold to separate into strips easily, put a chunk of it in the pan and it will separate as it heats up. Fry over low to moderate heat until brown and crisp, turning occasionally. Watch carefully so bacon does not burn. As fat accumulates, pour it off into a container. Drain on paper towels.

CASSEROLES, ONE-DISH MEALS AND ECONOMICAL DISHES

There are a vast number of tasty and attractive one-dish meals that are ideal for the two of you as well as for party fare. A good many stretch the food budget a long way, but in a most delicious manner. To these hearty and robust dishes add a simple tossed green salad and a dessert of fruit or cheese, or perhaps sherbet, and you have a menu your guests will long remember. You will find yourself going back to these basic casseroles, soufflés, crêpes, quiches, and omelets time and time again, because they are simple and fit a busy schedule. Beans, rice, and other cereal grains are a part of this section because they, too, are economical.

PAELLA
Serves 8 to 10

Paella is a dramatic and particularly attractive party dish. You can serve it over and over.

½ cup olive oil
½ pound Spanish or Italian sausages, cut into ½-inch slices
1 chicken (about 3 pounds), cut up
½ teaspoon crumbled dried thyme
2 garlic cloves, mashed
1 cup chopped onions
1 can (4 ounces) pimientos, drained and chopped
2½ cups converted rice
½ cup chopped tomato
1½ teaspoons saffron threads

4 to 5 cups chicken stock or canned broth
1 tablespoon vinegar
Salt and pepper
2 pounds shrimps, shelled and deveined
4 frozen rock lobster tails (6 ounces each)
1 package (10 ounces) frozen peas, thawed
1 package (9 ounces) frozen artichoke hearts, thawed
2 dozen mussels, scrubbed and debearded
2 dozen littleneck clams, scrubbed

Heat oil in a large skillet and cook sausages until golden brown. Remove and put into a 4-quart casserole or roasting pan. Rub chicken with thyme and brown in oil in skillet. Put chicken in casserole. Add garlic, onions, and pimientos to oil in skillet and cook until onions are golden brown. Add rice, tomato, and saffron. Stir and pour into casserole. Pour stock and vinegar over rice. Add salt and pepper to taste. Bake, uncovered, in a preheated 350-degree oven for 20 minutes. Add shrimps. Cut rock lobster tails into 1-inch crosswise slices, shell and all, and add to casserole. Stir slightly to mix. Add more stock, if necessary to keep from drying and sticking, and bake another 20 minutes. Add peas and artichoke hearts and stir to blend. Push in mussels and clams and, if necessary, add more stock to keep mixture moist. Bake for another 10 to 15 minutes, or until shells open. Serve paella hot.

◆

STUFFED GREEN PEPPERS
Serves 2

An economical supper and a good way to use small quantities of leftover meat. Serve the peppers with a fresh tomato sauce (see Index).

2 large green peppers, blanched
⅓ cup cooked rice
2 scallions, finely chopped
1 teaspoon tomato paste

¼ cup beef stock or canned broth
¼ teaspoon dried marjoram
½ cup diced leftover lamb, beef, or chicken
¼ teaspoon salt

Slice off the top of each green pepper. Scoop out the seeds and membranes, taking care not to pierce the shells. Combine all the remaining ingredients, adding only enough stock to moisten the rice. Stuff the peppers and replace the lids. Put in a baking dish and fill to a depth of ½ inch with hot water. Bake in a preheated 350-degree oven for 50 minutes, until the peppers are soft.

◆

EGGPLANT MOUSSAKA
Serves 6 to 8

¾ cup (½ stick) butter
1 pound ground chuck
1 small onion, chopped
1 can (8 ounces) tomato sauce
3 tablespoons chopped fresh parsley
1 cup dry white wine
1 cup tomato juice
3 medium-size eggplants, unpeeled

Salt
Fat for deep frying
4 cups white sauce (see Index)
2 eggs, well beaten
Pepper
Ground nutmeg
½ cup dry bread crumbs
1 cup grated Romano cheese

Melt butter in a skillet and brown the meat, chopping at it with the edge of a wooden spoon so it crumbles. Add onion, tomato sauce, parsley, wine, and tomato

119

juice. Cover and simmer over very low heat, stirring occasionally, for 1 hour. After removing stem end, cut eggplants lengthwise into ½-inch slices. To remove excess water, sprinkle slices with salt, put on a platter, and place a heavy can on top. Let eggplant sit about 30 minutes, then drain. Dry well, or the water will make the hot fat spatter. Fry in deep fat until pieces are golden. Make sure your white sauce is warm but not hot, and add the beaten eggs to it slowly. Season to taste with salt, pepper, and nutmeg. Stir half the bread crumbs and half the cheese into the meat sauce. Butter a 2-quart shallow baking dish and fill with eggplant slices. Top with meat sauce. Spoon white sauce evenly over meat sauce, covering it completely. (Alternatively, make several layers of eggplant, meat sauce, and white sauce in a casserole.) Sprinkle with remaining bread crumbs and cheese. Bake in a preheated 350-degree oven for 20 to 25 minutes, or until bubbly and brown.

◆

HOMEMADE PIZZA
Serves 4

Pizza is no more complicated than making a salad. Just follow the recipe. After you have made it the first time, you will think nothing of pizza for twenty people. The crust is made with a yeast dough. When it is baked it is light, crisp, and flaky. It can be used for other pies, too.

CRUST

½ package yeast	*¼ teaspoon salt*
2 tablespoons lukewarm	*2 tablespoons butter*
water	*1 egg*
1¼ cups all-purpose flour	*¼ cup cold water*

Sprinkle the yeast over the lukewarm water. Stir once and let stand for 10 minutes. Measure the flour and salt into a bowl. Cut the butter into small pieces and blend into the flour with your fingertips or a pastry blender until the pieces are the size of small peas. Stir the egg with the water and add to the flour mixture, along with the yeast. Stir with a fork and form into a ball. Knead the pastry for a minute or two (see Index) and put in a buttered clean bowl. Cover with a kitchen towel and leave for 2 hours to double in bulk. Roll the pastry into a 10-inch circle and fit it into a flan ring or shallow tart tin.

FILLING

3 tablespoons oil	*4 tomatoes, peeled, seeded,*
2 onions, finely chopped	*and chopped, or one*
2 garlic cloves, finely	*1-pound can of tomatoes*
chopped	*with their juice*

1 tablespoon tomato paste
1 tablespoon fresh oregano or
   1 teaspoon dried
½ teaspoon sugar
½ teaspoon salt
Freshly ground black pepper
1 cup sliced cooked Polish sausage

1 cup freshly grated
   Parmesan cheese
1 2-ounce can anchovy fillets,
   cut in half lengthwise
12 black olives, pitted
Freshly grated Parmesan
   cheese

Heat oil in a skillet and fry the onions and garlic for 5 minutes. Add the tomatoes, tomato paste, oregano, sugar, salt, and pepper. Cook, uncovered, over low heat until almost all of the juice from the tomatoes has evaporated and the mixture is a thick purée. Spread on top of the unbaked pastry shell. Scatter sausage slices and grated cheese on top and bake in a preheated 350-degree oven for 30 minutes. Decorate the pizza with a crisscross pattern of anchovies and with olives. Serve with a bowl of Parmesan cheese.

◆

BOUILLABAISSE
Serves 10 to 12

This is an easy basic recipe for a fish soup that makes a hearty one-dish meal.

1 small red snapper (about
   1½ pounds), cleaned, head
   and tail removed
1 small sea bass (about 1½
   pounds), cleaned, head and
   tail removed
¾ pound cod fillets or 1
   package frozen cod fillets
¾ pound perch fillets or 1
   package ocean perch fillets
2 small mackerels (about 3
   pounds), cleaned, head and
   tail removed
2 lobsters, split while raw

1½ pounds shrimps, fresh or
   frozen and thawed, peeled
   and deveined
½ cup olive oil
3 leeks, chopped
2 onions, chopped
4 ripe tomatoes, peeled and
   chopped
2 garlic cloves, mashed
1 teaspoon crumbled saffron threads
1 bay leaf
3 tablespoons chopped fresh parsley
1 tablespoon salt
¼ teaspoon black pepper
Chicken stock

Wash fish. Cut red snapper, sea bass, cod, perch, and mackerel into 1-inch crosswise slices. Break off claws and legs of lobsters and cut lobsters into 1½-inch crosswise pieces, cutting through shell. Wash shrimps, and let defrost if frozen. Heat oil in large kettle and sauté leeks, onions, tomatoes, garlic, saffron, bay leaf, parsley, salt, and pepper until soft. Add lobster, snapper, sea bass, and mackerel. Add enough stock to cover. Cover kettle and bring to a boil. Lower heat, uncover, and simmer for 10 minutes. Add cod, perch, and shrimps and more broth to cover. Simmer for 10 minutes more. Pour into a large tureen. Serve at once with hot French bread.

121

◆
QUICHE LORRAINE
Serves 6

Quiche Lorraine is a basic and classic quiche, and you may come to know the recipe by heart. It was first made in the Alsace-Lorraine region of France.

PASTRY

1¼ cups sifted all-purpose
   flour
¼ teaspoon salt
4 tablespoons butter

2 tablespoons shortening or
   margarine
About 4 tablespoons water

Sift the flour and salt together into a bowl. Cut the butter into small pieces and blend into the flour with your fingertips or a pastry blender. When the pieces are about the size of small peas, blend in the shortening or margarine. Stir in the water with a fork, a little at a time. Add more water if necessary to form the mixture into a ball. (Different flours absorb different amounts of water.) Wrap the dough in waxed paper and refrigerate for 20 minutes. Roll out and fit into a 9-inch pie pan. Cover the pastry with a piece of oiled foil (oiled side down), weight the foil with a single layer of dried beans, and bake in a preheated 375-degree oven for 10 minutes. Remove the beans and foil.

CUSTARD

4 eggs
¾ cup milk
¾ cup heavy cream
2 tablespoons melted butter
½ teaspoon salt
⅛ teaspoon cayenne pepper

⅛ teaspoon nutmeg
1 cup grated Swiss or
   Gruyère cheese
½ pound bacon, fried until
   crisp and crumbled

Stir together the first seven ingredients. Sprinkle the cheese and bacon into the pie shell and pour in the custard slowly. Bake in a preheated 375-degree oven for 40 minutes, until the custard is firm, puffy, and lightly browned. Serve warm or cold.

• VARIATIONS •
Quiche can be varied in many ways. Prepare the crust and the custard, keep the cheese, but leave out the bacon and add one of the following: ¾ cup cooked asparagus tips; ¾ cup crab meat or other shellfish; 2 teaspoons tomato paste and 1 tablespoon cocktail sherry; ¾ cup sliced mushrooms, sautéed in 2 tablespoons butter; ¼ pound smoked salmon, cut into small pieces, and 4 chopped scallions simmered for 5 minutes in ¼ cup dry vermouth; ¾ cup sliced cooked Polish sausage and 2 teaspoons prepared mustard; one 10-ounce package frozen, cooked, and drained chopped

spinach; ¾ cup chopped tomatoes and ¼ cup diced boiled ham; ½ cup cooked broccoli flowerets and 2 tablespoons minced sweet red pepper.

The possible combinations are limitless. Herbs can be added to the basic custard, and part of the milk can be replaced with wine.

Crêpes

A crêpe is a simple batter made of flour, milk, eggs, and butter, but it is dramatic in its effect. It is also very international. The Russians fold the batter differently and call it a blintz; the Chinese substitute water for milk and call it an egg roll; the British call it a pancake; and the French, of course, coined the name crêpe. Crêpes can be served as both main courses and desserts, the latter being slightly sweetened. Recipes for those can be found in the Index or in the dessert section of this book.

You might consider entertaining with a crêpe party; it is a good deal of fun. A variety of fillings can be kept hot in chafing dishes or similar warming contraptions. If either of you fancies yourself a showman, make the crêpes in front of your guests so they can eat them hot from the pan. Everyone will soon want to get in on the act and make his or her own. You can just relax and be a charming host and hostess!

SEASONING THE CRÊPE PAN

It is the crêpe pan that makes the crêpes. The cook is there merely to add the batter and remove the completed crêpes.

The best crêpe pans are made of black iron, 5 or 6 inches in diameter at the base, with shallow flaring sides. Once seasoned, the pan must never be washed or the smooth surface will be ruined, at least temporarily. The crêpe pan is a tool for the crêpe specialist and should not be used for any other purpose. When the pan is not in use, hide it under the bed, or a night-prowling visitor may find it and cook up a batch of bacon and eggs. If the integrity of the pan is violated in this manner, rub it gently with a combination of oil and salt. If the surface is not restored you will have to reseason the pan. Otherwise, it usually is necessary to season a pan only once, and it will last for your lifetime and that of your heirs, who will fight to inherit it.

Wash the pan in soapy water and scrub it with a nylon pad. Rinse it in clear water, dry it, and fill it three quarters full of vegetable oil. Put over low heat for 20 minutes. Remove the pan from the heat and let stand for 24 hours. Tip out the oil. Wipe with paper towels. Cover with transparent wrap and paste a label on the wrap saying, "To be used *only* for crêpes." Between uses wipe the pan with paper towels.

BATTER
. . . .
Makes 14 Crêpes

¾ cup sifted all-purpose flour
¼ teaspoon salt
1 cup milk
3 eggs

1 egg yolk
3 tablespoons melted butter
Vegetable oil

Put all the ingredients in the blender and blend for 10 seconds, until smooth. Let batter rest in the refrigerator 1 to 2 hours. It will thicken as it stands, so you may need to add another tablespoon or two of milk. Pour about a tablespoon of oil into the pan. Put the pan over moderate heat and swirl the oil to coat the bottom and sides. Tip out the oil. Using a large shallow-bowled kitchen spoon, ladle into the pan a spoonful of batter, sufficient to make a paper-thin layer. Tip out any excess batter; the crêpe itself will remain, clinging to the bottom of the pan. Cook the crêpe until it looks dull and no longer shiny. This will take about 1½ minutes. Small bubbles will appear around the edges of the crêpe, and the underside will be lightly browned. Slide a metal spatula under the crêpe and flip it onto the other side. Cook for about 1 minute on the second side.

Cover a wire cooling rack with a folded kitchen towel. Stack the cooked crêpes on the towel, second side up. The second side is never as beautiful as the first, but it will not be visible when the crêpe is filled.

If the batter forms a clump in the center, the pan is too hot. Wave it about like a flag until it cools slightly. Add a teaspoon of oil and carry on. It is not necessary to add oil to the pan before making each crêpe, as there is sufficient butter in the batter.

If the batter does not cover the base of the pan evenly but forms holes, fill in the spaces with more batter.

Remember, batter will thicken as it stands. Thin it with additional milk. The batter should be the consistency of light cream. If, disastrously, you add too much milk, pour it back into the blender and add more flour and another egg yolk.

Cooked crêpes, either filled or unfilled, can be kept refrigerated in a plastic bag. They can also be frozen. Frozen crêpes keep best when they are filled. Unfilled, they tend to become dry and to break when rolled around a filling. Leftover crêpe batter can be used to make batter-fried chicken, French-fried onions, or fruit fritters.

Almost any creamed food can be enfolded in a crêpe. Always garnish the finished crêpes with a little of the filling and a sprig of fresh parsley or dill. What follows are a few ideas for fillings.

◆
CHICKEN CRÊPES
Serves 12

¼ pound (1 stick) butter
¾ cups all-purpose flour
1½ cups rich chicken stock
2 cups half-and-half or light cream
½ cup white wine
Salt and pepper
2 pounds diced cooked chicken

2 tablespoons each minced fresh chives, parsley, and tarragon, or 1 tablespoon each dried
24 crêpes
1 cup Mornay Sauce (see Index)
1 cup Hollandaise Sauce (see Index)
2 cups heavy cream, whipped

Melt butter in a large heavy saucepan. Add flour and cook, stirring, until mixture bubbles. Gradually stir in stock, half-and-half, and wine. Stir constantly until sauce thickens. Season to taste with salt and pepper. Add the chicken and herbs. Put a large spoonful of the chicken mixture on each crêpe, roll into a cylinder, and arrange in shallow buttered baking dishes. Combine the Mornay and hollandaise sauces and fold in whipped cream. Spoon over the crêpes in a wide ribbon and put under the broiler until sauce is bubbling and slightly browned.

◆

SMOKED SALMON AND DILL CRÊPES

Serves 4

8 crêpes (add ¼ cup fresh
   snipped dill to batter)
¾ cup crème fraîche (see
   Index)

8 slices of marinated salmon
   (see Index) or smoked
   salmon
Garnish: dill sprigs

To fill crêpes, spread 1 tablespoon crème fraîche over each crêpe, place 1 slice salmon on top. Roll each crêpe loosely in cigar fashion. Put a dollop of crème fraîche and a sprig of dill on each crêpe. Serve immediately.

◆

CHEESE SOUFFLÉ

Serves 4

Do not just wait for holidays, parties, and other special occasions to serve a soufflé. Treat yourself or a few friends to the excitement and goodness of this wonderful concoction that the French introduced to us. The secret of a soufflé is in the beating of the eggs and folding of the beaten whites into the basic mixture. The whites must be mixed into the yolk mixture as gently as possible to retain the air beaten into them. A large metal spoon is the best tool to use. One or two whites can be added to give a soufflé greater height. Soufflés must always be served *immediately*. It is possible to hold a soufflé for 1 hour before baking, but you must cover the dish with a large pan to keep drafts away.

A soufflé can be made in any dish, but it is best made in a soufflé dish, because part of the beauty of a soufflé lies in its appearance. A good soufflé should rise 2 inches above the rim of the dish. A spectacular soufflé will rise 6 inches above the rim. In order to perform this magic (achieved merely by adding more egg whites), the soufflé will have a little support in the form of a waxed paper or foil collar tied around the dish.

Soufflé dishes come in various sizes, ranging from miniature ones to 2-quart dishes for serving six hearty adults. If you are contemplating buying only one dish, a 1½-quart dish will be perfect for four people. To make a soufflé for two, cut the recipe in half, use individual soufflé dishes, and reduce the cooking time to 25 minutes.

2 tablespoons butter	Dash of dry mustard
3 tablespoons all-purpose flour	Salt and pepper to taste
1 cup hot milk	4 egg yolks
1 cup freshly grated Swiss or Cheddar cheese	6 egg whites
	⅛ teaspoon cream of tartar

Butter the soufflé dish and sprinkle with flour. Tear off a piece of waxed paper large enough to encircle the dish and allow a 2-inch overlap. Fold the paper in half lengthwise and make a ½-inch fold at the folded edge, for additional rigidity. Butter the top third of the paper, including the overlap, and sprinkle with flour. With a piece of string, tie the paper around the outside of the dish.

Heat the butter in a saucepan. Stir in the flour and add the milk gradually to obtain a smooth sauce. Add the cheese and stir until melted. Remove from heat and beat in mustard and salt and pepper. Beat in egg yolks, one at a time. Set aside to cool slightly. Put egg whites in a large bowl and add cream of tartar. Beat whites until they stand in stiff peaks. Gently fold the egg whites into cheese mixture. Do not stir, or the air that has been beaten into the whites will escape. Carefully transfer the mixture to the prepared soufflé dish and bake in the center of a preheated 375-degree oven for 30 minutes, without disturbing. To test for doneness, shake the dish gently. If the center appears firm, it should be done. If the center is still creamy, it should cook for 5 minutes longer.

To serve, remove the paper collar and, if you want to be fancy, tie a white napkin around the dish. Carry the soufflé to the table; everyone will gasp with awe. Promptly take up two serving spoons, hold them back to back, and enter the top center of the soufflé. Pull the spoons toward the sides to allow the steam to escape, and serve immediately. Each minute of delay diminishes the airiness of the soufflé, for it is merely a castle in the air and you cannot linger to admire the architecture!

• VARIATIONS •

Soufflés are a wonderful way to use leftovers.

Chicken Soufflé. Substitute 1 cup diced cooked chicken for the cheese. A teaspoon or two of curry powder adds a piquant taste.

Herb Soufflé. Substitute ¾ cup finely chopped fresh parsley, ½ cup finely chopped fresh chives, and 3 teaspoons finely chopped fresh tarragon for the cheese.

Ham Soufflé. Substitute 1 cup minced cooked ham for the cheese.

Mushroom Soufflé. Substitute ½ pound fresh mushrooms, sliced and sautéed in butter, for the cheese.

Green Vegetable Soufflé. Substitute 1 cup puréed cooked vegetables, such as broccoli, spinach, or asparagus, for the cheese. A dash of nutmeg added to sauce gives it zest.

Seafood Soufflé. Substitute 1 cup cooked minced shrimp, crab meat, tuna, salmon, or lobster for the cheese. Add a dash of curry powder, 1 teaspoon minced fresh parsley, and 1 teaspoon lemon juice.

◆

◆
OMELETS
. . . .
Makes 1

The most perfect omelet is made in less than 3 minutes. If you have a few eggs, you can feed yourself and your friends or neighbors quickly and triumphantly at any time of the day or night.

In addition to eggs, it is essential to have an 8- to 10-inch omelet pan with rounded shoulders, to help the omelet slide out easily onto a plate. The pan should have a nonstick surface, or season the pan as you would a crêpe pan (see Index). Just as with a crêpe pan, an omelet pan should be reserved for making omelets *only*. Never wash a seasoned pan. Simply wipe it out with paper towels, to preserve its oily surface. If any egg adheres, rub it clean with salt and coat the spot with a few drops of oil. Store in plastic wrap.

The best omelets are cooked one at a time. When you have guests you can form an informal assembly line: Put one person to work cooking, another cracking and beating eggs, and the third putting in a hot filling when the eggs form a smooth layer in the pan.

1 tablespoon butter	*Salt to taste*
3 eggs	*Freshly ground black pepper*

Heat the butter in the omelet pan. As it heats, large bubbles will appear and then subside, to be replaced with tiny bubbles about the size of a heady champagne bubble. At this point the butter is almost ready to burn. Add the eggs immediately, sprinkle with salt and pepper, and stir rapidly with a fork. Hold the fork parallel with the bottom of the pan, as though making scrambled eggs. As the eggs begin to form curds, stop stirring and spread the eggs over the bottom of the pan to form a smooth layer.

Put a spoonful of the filling across the pan on the side opposite the handle. Tilt the pan away from you and slide a spatula under the unfilled portion of the omelet. Fold this half over the filled half.

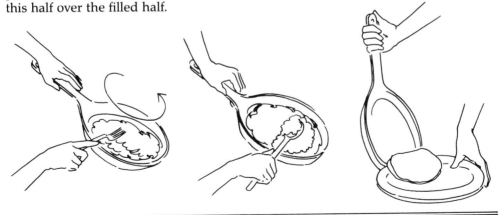

Slide the omelet back to the center of the pan and let the underside brown slightly for a minute.

To get the omelet safely out of the pan, reverse your grip on the handle of the pan so your thumb is on top. Hold the pan at a 45-degree angle to the plate. Quickly run your rubber spatula around edge of the omelet and under the far side, to make sure it is not stuck to the pan. Invert the pan over the plate, and the omelet—rounded, golden, and beautiful—will slide happily onto the plate.

Brush the top of the omelet with melted butter, to make it even shinier, and garnish with parsley sprigs, cherry tomatoes, black olives, or any other colorful, good-tasting things you can think of. To be very fancy, top it with caviar and sour cream.

· VARIATIONS ·

Herb Omelet. Add 2 tablespoons combined fresh herbs (for example, 1 tablespoon chopped parsley, 2 teaspoons chopped chives, ½ teaspoon tarragon) or half the quantity of dried herbs. Dill, basil, marjoram, and oregano may also be used.

Cheese Omelet. Fill with ¼ cup grated Cheddar, combined Swiss and Parmesan, or other hard cheese. If using soft cheeses, cut into tiny cubes.

Ham and Spinach Omelet. Heat 1 teaspoon butter in a small saucepan and add ¼ cup cooked chopped spinach, 1 slice boiled ham chopped into small pieces, a sprinkle of nutmeg, and 1 teaspoon lemon juice.

Mushroom Omelet. Saute ¼ cup sliced mushrooms and 1 tablespoon finely chopped onion in 1 tablespoon butter until soft and tender.

Smoked Salmon Omelet. Mix ¼ cup finely cut smoked salmon with 2 tablespoons softened cream cheese. (This filling is not heated before being added to the omelet.)

Pesto Omelet. Fill with 1 tablespoon room-temperature Pesto Sauce (see Index). Top omelet with sour cream.

Tomato Omelet. Peel, seed, and dice a small ripe tomato. Cook tomato in 1 tablespoon butter until hot and reduced to a thick moist purée.

◆

MEXICAN FRIJOLES
Serves 4 to 6

This is another inexpensive meatless meal. When guests come, double or triple the recipe.

½ cup (1 stick) butter or margarine	1 can tortillas
1 can (1 pound) kidney beans	1 cup grated Cheddar or Monterey Jack cheese

Melt half the butter in a skillet. Add beans with liquid in can and mash with a potato masher. Cook until thick. Open can of tortillas and put a spoonful of beans on each. Fold over tortillas and fasten with toothpicks. Put on a greased cookie sheet. Melt remaining butter and use to brush tortillas. Sprinkle with cheese and bake in a preheated 400-degree oven for 10 to 15 minutes, or until golden brown and crisp.

◆

PASTA E FAGIOLI
Serves 4

Another meatless dish for you or when you are entertaining.

½ pound dried pinto beans	*1 onion, chopped*
3 cups beef stock or boullion	*1 cup ditali macaroni*
1 cup canned tomatoes	*Salt and pepper*

Put beans in stock with tomatoes and onion in a large saucepan and bring to a boil. Cook for 2 minutes, remove from heat, and let stand for 1 hour. Reheat to a boil, lower heat, and simmer until beans are tender and all liquid has been absorbed, about 30 to 40 minutes. Cook macaroni until tender. Mix macaroni with beans and reheat. Season to taste and serve hot.

◆

NEW ENGLAND BAKED BEANS
Serves 8

These baked beans can be prepared ahead of time, refrigerated, and reheated at serving time. They are a most economical dish.

3 cups navy beans	*2 teaspoons dry mustard*
½ pound salt pork, sliced	*2 teaspoons Worcestershire*
1 large onion, chopped	*sauce*
¼ cup dark molasses	*1 teaspoon salt*
¼ cup catsup	

Cover beans with water in a large saucepan and bring to a boil. Simmer for 5 minutes. Remove from heat and let stand for 1 hour, to allow beans to swell gradually without bursting their skins. Add enough water to amply cover beans and bring to a boil again. Lower heat and simmer until beans are tender, about 1 hour. Drain and reserve liquid. Put half the salt pork slices in the bottom of a 2-quart casserole or bean pot. Mix beans with onion, molasses, catsup, mustard, Worcestershire sauce, and salt. Pour into a casserole or bean pot. Top with remaining salt pork. Pour reserved bean liquid over top until beans are covered. Cover with a lid or foil. Bake in a preheated 300-degree oven for 2 to 3 hours, adding more bean liquid if necessary. Uncover during the last hour of baking. They are even better reheated next day for 1 hour.

Rice

There are many different tastes and textures of rice. The following is a guide to some of the textures on the market:

Brown rice comes almost in its natural state, with only the outer husk removed. The tan coloring is bran, which gives the rice a nutlike flavor and chewy texture. You can enjoy it sautéed with mushrooms and pieces of scallion, or topped with yogurt, walnuts, and raisins for a healthy lunch. As the cooking directions on the package indicate, it takes slightly longer to cook than white rice, but it is worth the wait for its natural goodness and nutrients.

Enriched white rice has less natural goodness and nutrients than brown rice; it is therefore less wholesome. It does afford a nice change from brown rice, and with certain foods and in casseroles its softer texture is more desirable.

Converted rice has been specially treated to retain most of its natural vitamins and minerals. All rice, incidentally, is a good source of B vitamins, and rice is also easily digested.

Wild rice, not truly rice but an aquatic edible grain, is harvested straight from the paddies where it grows. It is expensive because production is limited. Wild rice is brownish-gray-white in color and has a slightly crunchy taste. It is delicious mixed into the Thanksgiving stuffing, served with pheasant and game dishes, or with trout and other fish.

Precooked or instant rice is strictly for emergencies. It can be cooked in a few minutes, but has little of the taste, texture, or nutrients of regular rice.

In cooking rice, keep in mind that rice "grows" as it cooks and therefore you will need a large pot or pan to cook it in. It should have a heavy bottom so the rice will not scorch. Cooking methods suggested on rice packages have been well tested and can be followed with full confidence.

◆

BOILED RICE
Serves 2

Some people prefer boiled rice; others like baked rice. Try both and see which you prefer.

1 cup water
½ tablespoon butter

Salt to taste
½ cup rice

Bring the water, butter, and salt to a boil in a saucepan and add the rice. Bring the water to a simmer, cover, and cook for 20 minutes or until all the water is absorbed.

◆

BAKED RICE
Serves 4

2 tablespoons butter
⅓ cup minced onion
1 cup rice
2 cups chicken stock or broth,
    heated to a boil

Salt and pepper
Bouquet garni: 2 parsley
    sprigs, 1 bay leaf, ⅛ tea-
    spoon dried thyme

In a large flame-proof casserole, melt butter and sauté the onion for 5 minutes, or until soft and golden. Add rice and stir over moderate heat for 3 or 4 minutes, until the rice looks milky white. Stir in the boiling stock, season to taste, and add the herbs, either tied in a piece of cheesecloth or by themselves. Stir and bring to a simmer. Bake, covered, in a preheated 400-degree oven for exactly 17 minutes; do not stir rice during the cooking. When done, fluff with a two-pronged long fork and remove the parsley and bay leaf (if added loose) or cheesecloth bag. Serve immediately.

WILD RICE
Serves 4

5 cups water   Butter
1 cup wild rice   Salt and pepper to taste

In a colander, run water over the wild rice until it looks clear and clean. Bring the 5 cups of water to a boil in a large heavy pan. Add the wild rice and stir once or twice with a fork. After the water returns to a boil, lower the heat to a simmer, cover, and cook about 20 to 25 minutes, for crunchy wild rice. When wild rice has cooked it will puff up and you can see the white interior of the grain. Taste to make sure it is cooked the way you like it. Drain thoroughly and toss well with butter and salt and pepper.

• VARIATIONS •
Wild Rice with Walnuts. Add ½ cup of finely chopped walnuts to cooked and drained wild rice, then toss with butter and season.
Wild Rice with Scallions. Add ½ cup finely chopped scallions to cooked and drained wild rice, then toss with butter and season.

BARLEY
Serves 3 or 4

This is a nice change from rice and potatoes. It complements lamb dishes to perfection.

1 tablespoon vegetable oil   1 cup pearl barley
1 medium onion, chopped   1 tablespoon fresh thyme or 1
1¼ cup chicken stock or   teaspoon dried
   canned broth   Salt and pepper to taste
¾ cup water   1 tablespoon chopped fresh parsley

Heat oil in a large, heavy saucepan and sauté onion until tender, about 5 minutes. Add stock, water, barley, and thyme. Stir with a wooden spoon a couple of times. Cover and simmer for about 30 minutes, or until stock has been absorbed and barley is tender. Season, sprinkle with parsley, and serve immediately.

MINTED COUSCOUS WITH YOGURT
Serves 4

Another tasty and popular accompaniment to poultry and lamb dishes.

1 cup couscous
2 tablespoons chopped fresh
 mint
1 small onion or 3 scallions,
 minced finely
1 tablespoon lemon juice
Salt and pepper to taste
1 cup yogurt

Put couscous in a cheesecloth-lined steamer and steam for 25 minutes, or until soft. Put couscous in a bowl and add mint, onion, lemon juice, salt, and pepper. Stir in yogurt and coat couscous evenly. Serve immediately.

BULGUR PILAF
Serves 6

Bulgur, or cracked wheat, is a grain prized by the people in the Near East and North Africa. Try this pilaf at your next party.

½ cup butter
1 medium onion, finely
 chopped

Salt and pepper to taste
2 cups bulgur
1 quart chicken stock or
 water

In a heavy, flame-proof 2-quart casserole, melt the butter until foaming and sauté the onion until golden brown. Season with salt and pepper and stir in the bulgur. Cover and cook over low heat for 10 minutes. Add stock and bake, covered, in a preheated 350-degree oven for 30 minutes. Remove lid, fluff with a long-handled fork, recover, and bake for an additional 15 minutes, or until liquid has been fully absorbed. The bulgur will be moist and fluffy.

FIRST COURSES

It is nice to start off dinner for yourselves or guests with something to spark the appetite. The subject of this chapter is just that—fish, vegetables, pâtés, and fruit that make especially attractive first courses. Portions should be small, of course, but garnishes, sauces and dressings can be more lavish to create a special touch.

◆

ARTICHOKES VINAIGRETTE
Serves 6

It has been said that the world is divided into those who are addicted to artichokes and everybody else. Cold artichokes are also marvellous with rémoulade dressing (see Index).

> 6 artichokes
> 1½ cups Vinaigrette Dress-
>   ing (see Index)

Cut off the artichoke stems very close to the bottom so they can stand without tipping. Remove any blemished outer leaves. Snip off the point of each leaf with a pair of scissors, cutting about ¼ inch down each leaf. Put artichokes into a steamer, cover, and steam for 40 minutes, or until a leaf pulls away easily. Serve at room temperature or cold with sauce in individual small containers.

◆

CHICKEN LIVER PÂTÉ
Makes 1½ cups

Chicken liver pâté makes a nice, delicate starter. It is usually served with freshly made toast, but it is also good at cocktail time served on crackers, or used for sandwiches made with whole-wheat bread.

> 1 stick butter
> 1 small onion, finely chopped
> ½ pound chicken livers
> ⅓ cup thinly sliced apples
> ½ cup chicken stock or
>   canned broth
>
> 1 tablespoon apple brandy or
>   lemon juice
> ¼ teaspoon allspice
> ¼ teaspoon salt
> Garnish: 1 hard-cooked egg,
>   finely chopped

133

Melt the butter and pour into the blender. Put all remaining ingredients except the egg in a small saucepan. Remove any membranes from chicken livers first. Cover and simmer for 10 minutes. Pour into the blender and blend with the butter until smooth. Chill and garnish with chopped egg. The pâté may be frozen.

◆

SHRIMP PÂTÉ
Serves 6

1 pound medium shrimps,
   cooked, peeled, deveined,
   and diced
1 stick butter, melted
¼ teaspoon salt

Dash of cayenne pepper
¼ teaspoon mace
2 teaspoons lemon juice
¼ cup chili sauce
Watercress

Put all ingredients except the watercress in blender and blend until smooth. Transfer to an oiled bowl. Chill the pâté for 4 hours before serving. Unmold and cut into small wedges. Serve on a bed of watercress leaves on individual serving plates.

◆

MARINATED SALMON
Serves 6

Salmon devotees relish this appetizer. The fish is "cooked" in lemon juice in the refrigerator. It seems to take a large quantity of dill, but it will be fine. There is no such thing as too much. Leftover salmon can be used in quiches, crêpes, and omelets.

1 pound fresh salmon steak,
   as thick as possible
1 bunch dill
2 tablespoons salt

1 tablespoon sugar
1 tablespoon cracked
   peppercorns
1 teaspoon fresh lemon juice

Cut the salmon in half horizontally to form two pieces. Cut a piece of aluminum foil large enough to enclose the salmon. Put a third of the dill on the foil. Cover with one of the salmon pieces, cut side up. Combine the salt, sugar, and peppercorns and spread half the mixture on the salmon. Cover with half the remaining dill and top with the other piece of salmon, cut side down, thus reassembling salmon as it was originally. Cover with remaining salt mixture, sprinkle with lemon juice, and top with remaining dill. Seal the edges of the foil and put in a loaf pan or dish. Weight with food cans and refrigerate for 48 hours, turning the package every 12 hours.

Open the package and scrape off the salt mixture. Drain off the liquid that has accumulated. Discard the dill. Slice the salmon as thinly as possible, holding the knife almost horizontally. Give each person a few slices on a small plate. Serve with freshly made toast.

OYSTERS ROCKEFELLER
Serves 6

This is expensive, as oysters are high in price, but a treat for oyster lovers.

36 oysters, freshly opened
and on the half shell
1 pound fresh or 1 10-ounce
package frozen spinach,
cooked and chopped
6 scallions
1 cup snipped fresh parsley

1 garlic clove
4 strips bacon
½ cup dry bread crumbs
1 cup (2 sticks) butter, melted
Salt and cayenne pepper to
taste
Few drops of Tabasco sauce

Have your seafood shop open the oysters for you and pack them on a bed of ice for the trip home. Refrigerate immediately; they will keep fresh for 3 hours. If you want to tackle opening your own, scrub oysters and open with an oyster knife, pushing it into the back of each oyster and cutting the muscle at the back until the shell opens. Oysters are stubborn and difficult to open. Drain spinach in a strainer and press out all moisture with the back of a spoon. Chop scallions: Cut off roots, bundle scallions, and cut across into thin slices. After removing all thick stems, use scissors to snip parsley into a bowl, and snip again while in bowl to get finer pieces. Mash garlic in a garlic press. Fry bacon in a skillet until crisp and drain on paper towel. Crumble until fine. Mix spinach, scallions, parsley, garlic, bacon, and bread crumbs with melted butter. Add salt and cayenne pepper and Tabasco sauce. Spoon about 1 tablespoon of the spinach mixture onto each oyster. Do not worry if it does not cover the oyster; heat will melt the topping. Make a bed of rock salt, or crumple foil, and set shells on it. Bake in a preheated 450-degree oven for 10 to 12 minutes, or until oysters crinkle slightly around the edges. Serve at once.

AVOCADO VINAIGRETTE
Serves 2

1 ripe avocado

¼ cup Vinaigrette Dressing
(see Index)

Halve the avocado, remove the pit, and fill the center with vinaigrette dressing. Serve on individual salad plates and pass the extra dressing in a small bowl. Prepare avocado at the last minute, as it turns brown if left standing for any length of time.

• VARIATION •
Avocado halves can be filled with a few cooked shrimp and served with vinaigrette dressing.

◆

CELERY RÉMOULADE
Serves 4

This is another delicious French invention. It is a light starter and takes the place of a green salad course.

1 small celeriac or celery root
1 teaspoon lemon juice

½ cup Rémoulade Sauce (see
   Index)
Finely chopped fresh parsley

Wash celeriac, peel, and cut into long thin julienne strips, or shred in a food processor. Place in a bowl with lemon juice. Mix well and let sit for 15 minutes. Rinse the celeriac, drain, and pat dry with paper towels. Put in a bowl and mix in enough rémoulade sauce to moisten. Sprinkle with chopped parsley before serving on individual dishes.

◆

PROSCIUTTO WITH MELON
Serves 2

This is a refreshing first course when melon is available. You may substitute papaya, dates, or figs when in season.

2 melon wedges
2 slices imported prosciutto
  or Virginia ham

Ground pepper

Cantaloupe, honeydew, or cranshaw melon are all good in this recipe. Cut the melon you prefer, seed, and cut into wedges, according to the size of the melon. Peel the rind off each wedge. Drape wedges with prosciutto and serve on individual plates with a knife and fork. Have a pepper mill on hand, as pepper enhances the flavor of both the ham and the melon.

◆

LEEKS VINAIGRETTE
Serves 2

This is a good way to serve leeks. It makes an unusual and impressive starter to any meal.

4 small to medium-size leeks

½ cup Vinaigrette Dressing
  (see Index)

Cut off green tops of leeks. Run cold water over white part to remove any dirt or hidden sand. Put white part of leeks in a steamer and steam for 15 minutes, or until tender. Cool for at least 1 hour. Put leeks on individual serving plates, dress with a few tablespoons of vinaigrette, and serve immediately.

· VARIATION ·
Asparagus Vinaigrette: Substitute leftover or freshly cooked asparagus for leeks.

◆

AVOCADO STUFFED WITH SHRIMP
Serves 4

This is a classic way to serve avocado as a first course.

2 ripe avocados
16 shrimps, cooked, peeled,
   and cleaned (see Index)

1 cup Russian Dressing (see
   Index)

Halve the avocados, remove the pits, and put each half on an individual serving plate. Put 4 shrimps in the center of each avocado half and top with a generous portion of Russian dressing. Pass the extra dressing in a small bowl.

◆

STUFFED CLAMS
Serves 4

24 cherrystone clams on the
   half shell, freshly opened
   (see Index)
8 tablespoons (1 stick) butter
½ cup finely chopped onions
1 cup fresh bread crumbs

3 tablespoons chopped fresh
   parsley
1 tablespoon chopped fresh
   thyme or 1 teaspoon dried
Salt and pepper

Put clams through the coarsest blade of a food grinder into a small bowl. Let 2 tablespoons of the butter soften and spread with a pastry brush over the inside of clam shells. In a heavy medium-size frying pan, melt 4 tablespoons butter and cook onions over moderate heat for about 5 minutes, until soft and wilted. Add ground clams and stir for about 2 minutes. When clams shine with the butter, add bread crumbs and cook until crumbs are golden brown. Remove from the heat and stir in parsley, thyme, and seasonings to taste. Spoon the clam mixture into the buttered shells, dividing it evenly. Cut the remaining 2 tablespoons butter into small bits and scatter on top. Arrange shells on a cookie sheet, put in the upper third of a preheated 400-degree oven, and bake for 10 to 12 minutes, or until crumbs are a light golden brown. Serve immediately.

◆

SHRIMP COCKTAIL
Serves 2

This is a hit beginning course with almost everyone.

4 to 6 cooked shrimps per
   person (see Index)
Lettuce leaves
½ cup chili sauce
1 tablespoon fresh lemon
   juice

1¼ tablespoons prepared
   horseradish
1 teaspoon Worcestershire
   sauce
¼ teaspoon Tabasco sauce

Put shrimp on lettuce leaves on individual serving plates or in small bowls or sherbet dishes. Combine remaining ingredients to make a seafood cocktail sauce and pass the sauce in a small bowl. If you like a hotter cocktail sauce, add a bit more horseradish and Tabasco sauce.

◆

MARINATED MUSHROOMS
Serves 6

Make this delectable starter at least a day before you intend to serve it, as the flavor greatly improves with time.

1 pound mushroom caps,
   about 1 inch in diameter
About 1 cup dry white wine
1⅔ cups olive oil
Salt and pepper to taste
1 teaspoon Tabasco sauce
3 tablespoons finely chopped
   onion

1 tablespoon minced garlic
1 lemon
3 whole cloves
1 bay leaf
Garnish: 3 tablespoons
   minced fresh parsley

Remove stems from mushrooms and use in another dish. Wipe mushroom caps with a dampened kitchen towel and put in a bowl. Cover with wine. Cover the bowl with foil or plastic and refrigerate for 1 hour. In a small mixing bowl, mix the olive oil, salt and pepper, Tabasco sauce, onion, and garlic. Slice the lemon thinly and add, along with the cloves and bay leaf. At the end of the hour, drain the wine from the mushrooms and in its place add the olive oil mixture. Turn the mushrooms gently to coat evenly. Transfer the contents of the bowl to a wide-mouthed 1-quart jar or crock with a tight-fitting cover. Cover and refrigerate for 24 hours. To serve, put a few mushrooms on each plate and sprinkle with parsley. Marinated mushrooms will keep in the refrigerator for 2 weeks.

SOUPS

Among the most versatile foods available to any household are soups. Hot or cold, meaty or fishy, in tiny cups or a giant, meal-in-a-soup tureen—ways to enjoy soups are limited only by your imagination.

◆

VICHYSSOISE
Serves 4 to 6

This famous French soup, a mixture of leeks and potatoes, adds elegance to any dinner or lunch party, style to picnic or tailgate gathering.

4 medium-size leeks
2 tablespoons butter
1 medium-size onion,
    chopped
4 medium-size potatoes,
    sliced thin

4 cups chicken stock or
    canned broth
Salt and pepper to taste
1½ cup heavy cream
Garnish: Finely chopped
    fresh chives

Use the white part of the leeks only. Wash thoroughly to remove any sand and chop fine. Melt butter in a frying pan and sauté leeks and onion for about 3 minutes. Put the leeks and onion in a large saucepan or stockpot and add the potatoes, stock, and seasonings. Simmer, covered, for 15 minutes, or until vegetables are tender. Put soup in a blender, or through a food mill or fine strainer, and stir in the cream. Vichyssoise can be served piping hot or chilled in the refrigerator and served cold. Sprinkle with chives as the crowning touch.

◆

GAZPACHO
Serves 6 to 8

1 cucumber, peeled and
    chopped
2 cans (1 pound each)
    tomatoes or 1 pound fresh
    tomatoes
1 can (4 ounces) pimientos,
    drained

1 onion, chopped
1 garlic clove, mashed
⅓ cup chopped fresh parsley
2 tablespoons chopped fresh
    chives
⅓ cup olive oil
¼ cup fresh lemon or lime juice

2 cups chicken stock or
    canned broth
Salt
Paprika

Ice cubes
Garnish: Chopped fresh
    parsley, seasoned croutons

Process cucumber and tomatoes in a blender until smooth. Pour into a bowl and set aside. Put pimientos, onion, garlic, parsley, chives, oil, and lemon juice in blender jar and blend until smooth; pour into bowl with tomatoes. Stir in stock. Add salt and paprika to taste. Chill. To serve, put 2 ice cubes in each bowl, pour in gazpacho, and sprinkle with parsley and croutons.

◆

MINESTRONE
Serves 6

A thick soup that is so substantial only a light dessert is needed to complete the meal. Peas, zucchini, and other vegetables may be added. If you do not have any macaroni, substitute broken spaghetti.

2 tablespoons oil
1 onion, finely chopped
1 carrot, peeled and diced
1 small turnip, peeled and
    diced
2 celery stalks, chopped
2 garlic cloves, finely
    chopped

8 cups chicken stock or
    canned broth
¼ teaspoon saffron
1 cup macaroni shells
3 tomatoes, peeled, seeded,
    and chopped
½ teaspoon oregano
1 cup freshly grated
    Parmesan cheese

Heat the oil in a large saucepan. Add the onion, carrot, turnip, celery, and garlic and fry over low heat for 5 minutes. Add the stock and saffron and simmer for 15 minutes. Add the macaroni, tomatoes, and oregano. Simmer for 10 minutes, until the macaroni is cooked to your taste. Serve the Parmesan cheese separately.

◆

ONION SOUP
Serves 2

A bowl of steaming onion soup is perfect for a cold winter night.

1 tablespoon oil
1 tablespoon butter
2 small onions, thinly sliced
2 teaspoons all-purpose flour

2½ cups beef or canned broth
2 slices French bread
2 tablespoons brandy
    (optional)

¼ cup freshly grated Swiss
  or Gruyère cheese

1 tablespoon freshly grated
  Parmesan cheese

Heat the oil and butter in a saucepan. Add the onions and stir over low heat for 5 minutes, until softened. Stir in the flour and add the stock. Cover and simmer for 20 minutes. Meanwhile, toast the bread on a cookie sheet in a preheated 250-degree oven for 20 minutes, until completely dry and crisp. Add the brandy to the soup and ladle into broiler-proof bowls. Top with bread and combined cheeses. Put under the broiler for 4 minutes, until the cheese has melted and is bubbling and lightly browned.

If the bowls will not fit under the broiler, put the bread and cheese in the bowls before adding the soup. The heat of the soup will melt the cheese.

◆

BLACK BEAN SOUP
Serves 8

This stick-to-the-ribs soup is great on a winter's day or when picnicking in a chilly stadium.

2 cups dried black beans
⅓ cup diced celery
1 large carrot, scraped and
  diced
1 large onion, sliced
1 ham hock or bone or bits of
  leftover ham

Salt and pepper to taste
Dash of cayenne pepper
2 tablespoons sherry
  (optional)
Garnish: Thin slices of hard-
  cooked egg or lemon

Put beans in a large kettle, cover with 2 quarts of cold water, and bring to a boil. Lower heat and simmer 10 minutes. Cover and let stand for 1 hour. Add celery, carrot, onion, and ham. Simmer for 3 or 4 hours, or until beans are tender. Add additional water, if necessary, as the soup will start to thicken. There should be about 1½ quarts. Remove ham and cut into bite-size pieces. Blend soup in a blender or rub through a food mill or fine sieve. Add seasonings and sherry. Reheat and decorate each bowl or cup with a slice of hard-cooked egg or lemon.

◆

SPLIT PEA SOUP
Serves 6

A full-bodied soup for a cold winter day. Diced cooked ham can be added to make it even more substantial. If you cannot find quick-cooking dried peas, cover peas with water and bring to a boil. Remove from heat and let soak in the water for 1 hour before beginning the recipe.

½ pound quick-cooking dried
  split peas
6 cups chicken stock or
  canned broth
4 tablespoons butter
2 onions, finely chopped
1 carrot, chopped
2 celery stalks, chopped

1 teaspoon sugar
½ teaspoon salt
Freshly ground black pepper
½ cup heavy cream
3 slices bread, cut into
  croutons
1 tablespoon oil

Wash the peas and put in a saucepan. Add the stock and simmer for 1 hour. Melt 2 tablespoons butter in a skillet and fry the onions, carrot, and celery for 5 minutes. Add to the peas and stock. Add the sugar, salt, and pepper and continue cooking for 20 minutes. Purée the soup in a blender. Return to a clean saucepan and add the cream. Cook until hot. To make the croutons, heat the remaining 2 tablespoons butter with the oil and fry the bread over moderately low heat until lightly browned. Drain on paper towels and add to the soup after it is ladled into soup bowls.

◆

CAPE COD CLAM CHOWDER
Serves 6

36 cherrystone or 24 large
  chowder clams
4 ounces salt pork, diced
2 tablespoons oil
1 large onion, peeled and
  chopped
4 potatoes, peeled and cubed

3 tablespoons butter
3 tablespoons all-purpose
  flour
1 quart milk
Garnish: Minced fresh
  parsley, butter

Most seafood stores will open clams for you if you are buying them for a chowder; it is lots easier if they do. But it is also good to know how to open clams yourself: Scrub clams with a stiff brush to remove dirt and grit. Insert the blade of a clam knife into the back of the clam and cut across the back muscle. When the shell opens, pry open top and remove the clam. Chop clams and collect juice from the shells in a large bowl, as this liquid is what gives the chowder its flavor. Set clams aside.

Dice salt pork (cut into slices, cut slices into strips, then into dice) and fry in oil in a kettle until almost crisp. Add onion and cook over low heat until onion is golden brown. Add enough water to the reserved clam juice to measure 4 cups. Add this liquid and potatoes to the onion in the kettle. Cover, bring to a boil, lower heat, and simmer for 10 or 12 minutes, or until potatoes are tender and done. In a saucepan, melt butter and stir in flour. Gradually stir in milk. Bring to a boil over low heat, stirring constantly. Pour into the kettle with potatoes. Add clams and reheat but do not boil. Serve chowder sprinkled with parsley and a dot of butter.

◆

SALADS AND DRESSINGS

Americans have sometimes been referred to as the greatest salad consumers in the world. The wonderful thing is that salads can be served at any point in a menu. California-style, salads often comprise the first course in a luncheon or dinner. The only salad generally served after the main course is the simple tossed green salad; and many times in less formal meals it is presented at the same time as the entrée. A fruit salad can also be served as a simple dessert after a rich meal.

Salads can be basic and uncomplicated or dramatic and elaborate. The range is fantastic—from tossed green salad to a decorative chicken-vegetable aspic ring. Select a salad to fit the menu and the weather. Always use a large bowl to prepare your salad, and make sure the individual salad plates or bowls are slightly chilled. One word of caution: Dressings should be used sparingly—only to coat the ingredients. Wash greens and dry thoroughly so the dressing will cling.

◆

TOSSED GREEN SALAD
Serves 6 to 8

One or several greens can be used in basic tossed green salad. Varieties include lettuce (Boston, Bibb, leaf, iceberg, and others), romaine, Belgian endive, curly endive or chicory, young raw spinach, cabbage, mustard greens, dandelion greens, watercress, escarole, fennel, and young Swiss chard.

1 large head Boston lettuce	½ cup Vinaigrette Dressing
1 bunch watercress	(see Index)

Wash lettuce and watercress thoroughly in cold water. Cut off and discard coarse stems of the watercress, reserving only the tender leaves and stems. Discard any blemished lettuce leaves. Dry greens in a salad spinner or put in a colander, let drain, and pat dry with paper towels or a dish towel. Tear greens into bite-size pieces. Refrigerate. Immediately before serving, toss with just enough dressing to coat evenly. Serve immediately. Green salad can be washed and put in the refrigerator up to 2 hours before serving; dressing is always applied at the last moment.

• VARIATIONS •
Any of the following can be added to the basic salad just before it is dressed: croutons; canned or cooked artichoke hearts, cut into small pieces; flowerets of quickly blanched broccoli or cauliflower; fresh tomatoes cut in wedges; hard-cooked egg, quartered; avocado or cucumber in thin slices; raw mushrooms in thin slices;

Spanish onion rings; julienne carrot strips; crumbled blue or Rocquefort cheese; thin radish slices; asparagus tips or diced hearts of palm.

ENDIVE AND WATERCRESS SALAD
Serves 6 to 8

4 cups watercress, washed
  and trimmed
3 medium-size Belgian
  endives

½ cup Vinaigrette Dressing
  (see Index)

Wash and dry watercress according to preceding recipe. Cut off base and ½ inch of top leaves of each endive. Separate leaves, wash, and dry. Endive leaves can be cut in thin strips or served whole, depending on size. Mix greens in salad bowl and toss with dressings just before serving.

• VARIATION •
A cup of cooked beets, cut in julienne strips, can be substituted for the watercress to make an interesting cold beet and endive salad for a first course.

COLE SLAW
Serves 8

This has been a favorite salad with generations of Americans. It is excellent with simple seafood dishes, a nice change from the eternal green salad, and a must at picnics. For variety, substitute red or Chinese cabbage for the standard green cabbage.

1 head firm cabbage
1 cup mayonnaise
Salt and pepper to taste

½ cup grated carrot or shredded green pepper (optional)

Discard limp outer leaves of cabbage and cut head in two. With a large chopping knife or in a food processor, finely shred cabbage. Add carrot or pepper, mix with mayonnaise, and season to taste.

• VARIATIONS •
A number of dressings can be substituted for mayonnaise, and a number of different ingredients can be added to basic cole slaw to add variety and different taste sensations. Among substitute dressings are yogurt, Vinaigrette Dressing (see Index), or a cream dressing of half mayonnaise and half sour or heavy cream. Among additions for variety are minced onion, caraway or celery seeds.

◆

CAESAR SALAD
. . . .
Serves 6

1 garlic clove, chopped
½ cup salad oil
1 small head romaine,
   washed, trimmed, cored
1 bunch watercress, washed
   and trimmed
4 heads Belgian endive, ends
   trimmed off, broken into
   leaves

2 teaspoons Worcestershire
   sauce
1 raw egg
Juice of 1 large lemon
2 ounces Roquefort cheese (¾
   cup crumbled)
2½ cups croutons

Add garlic to oil and let stand for several hours. Remove garlic and pour oil into salad bowl. Break greens into bite-size pieces and add to oil. Add Worcestershire sauce, egg, and lemon juice. Toss to blend well. Add cheese and croutons. Toss again and serve at once.

◆

CHEF'S SALAD
. . . .
Serves 6

1 head lettuce, washed and
   trimmed
½ bunch chicory, washed and
   trimmed
1 bunch watercress, washed
   and trimmed
1 cup ½-inch strips Swiss
   cheese
1 cup ½-inch strips boiled or
   cooked smoked ham

1 cup ½-inch strips cooked
   breast of chicken
1 cucumber, peeled and sliced
4 hard-cooked eggs, peeled
   and sliced
3 tomatoes, cored and cut
   into wedges
½ cup sliced radishes
1½ cups Vinaigrette Dressing
   (see Index)

Break greens into bite-size pieces and put in salad bowl. Arrange strips of cheese, ham, and chicken on top of greens. Surround with cucumber slices, egg slices, tomato wedges, and radish slices. Chill until time to serve, then toss with dressing.

◆

SPINACH SALAD
. . . .
Serves 6 to 8

A small handful of croutons can be added to the salad just before tossing to give it a delightful crunchiness.

2 pounds fresh spinach, thoroughly washed and dried
½ pound fresh mushrooms, thinly sliced
6 slices crispy fried bacon, crumbled
½ cup Vinaigrette Dressing (see Index)
4 hard-cooked eggs, cut in quarters

Trim off coarse stems of spinach. Put in a large salad bowl with mushrooms and bacon. Toss with dressing immediately before serving. Decorate with the hard-cooked egg quarters.

◆

TOMATO ASPIC
Serves 8 to 10

4½ cups tomato juice
3 envelopes unflavored gelatine
2 teaspoons Worcestershire sauce
Dash of Tabasco sauce
6 tablespoons fresh lemon juice

Bring 2½ cups of tomato juice to a boil in a saucepan. Put gelatin in a large bowl. Put ¼ cup cold tomato juice in the bowl with the gelatin. Let stand for 5 minutes. Pour in remaining hot tomato juice and stir until gelatin is completely dissolved. Add remaining ingredients. Pour into an oiled 6-cup ring mold or decorative serving bowl. Chill until firm to the touch. If a ring mold is made, unmold it (see directions on page 148) on a bed of lettuce leaves and fill the center with any fish, chicken, or meat salad. The center can also be filled with plain cooked shrimps, diced avocado, or cottage cheese and served with or without dressing.

◆

GREEK SALAD
Serves 4

This salad is built in layers to create a striking color contrast. It has a wonderful piquant flavor and makes a surprise starter or a lunch dish.

1 large Spanish or Bermuda onion, cut in rings
2 green peppers, cut in julienne strips
4 tomatoes, peeled and sliced
½ pound feta cheese
24 Greek olives, pitted
½ cup chopped Italian or flat-leaf parsley
Salt and pepper
½ cup Vinaigrette Dressing (see Index)

Make layers of the onion rings, green peppers, tomatoes, cheese, olives, and parsley in a large serving bowl. Sprinkle with salt and pepper to taste. Chill. Pour dressing over the layers and serve immediately.

◆

TUNA, CRAB, SHRIMP, OR LOBSTER SALAD
Serves 4

Fish salad can be served simple and unadorned, or it can be presented with pomp and circumstance. Often crab, shrimp, and lobster are combined and called "seafood salad." In warm weather, fish salads make a fancy lunch or satisfying dinner.

2 cups cold cooked fish or
   shellfish, fresh, canned, or
   frozen
¾ cup diced celery
1 tablespoon chopped fresh
   dill
¾ cup mayonnaise, or
   enough to moisten salad
1 tablespoon lemon juice

Salt and pepper to taste
Garnish: Lettuce leaves,
   hard-cooked egg quartered,
   capers, sweet pickle,
   olives, radishes, carrot
   strips, tomato wedges (all
   optional)

If tuna fish is used, drain the oil or water in which it is packed. Cut or break fish into bite-size bits. Put in a large bowl with the celery and green pepper and mix thoroughly with mayonnaise. Add lemon juice and mix again. Season to taste. Serve on a bed of lettuce leaves, plain or garnished.

• VARIATIONS •
Any of these fish salads can be stuffed into a fresh tomato case from which the seeds and flesh have been removed (drain tomato upside down for a few minutes before filling).

◆

CURRIED CHICKEN SALAD
Serves 4

3 cups cooked chicken
1 green apple, cored and
   thinly sliced
½ cup chopped walnuts
½ cup yellow raisins
½ red pepper, cut into
   julienne strips

1 teaspoon lemon juice
2 teaspoons curry powder, or
   to taste
1 cup mayonnaise (see Index)
1 head Boston lettuce

Cut the chicken into bite-size pieces. Combine the chicken, apple, walnuts, raisins, and pepper in a bowl. In another bowl combine the lemon juice, curry powder, and mayonnaise. Toss the chicken with the curry-mayonnaise. Line a large, attractive bowl with lettuce leaves. Arrange the chicken salad on the lettuce and keep cool until serving.

147

◆

CHICKEN TARRAGON AND VEGETABLE ASPIC RING

Serves 10 to 12

A spectacular party or buffet offering any time of year.

2 cups fresh, cooked vegetables	½ cup chopped celery
3 envelopes unflavored gelatin	1 tablespoon capers, drained
	1 tablespoon finely chopped fresh tarragon leaves
3 cups chicken stock or canned broth	1 cup Green Goddess Dressing (see Index)
3 cups cooked chicken cut into bite-size bits	Garnish: Cherry tomatoes or tomato wedges, watercress

Select colorful vegetables such as peas, carrots, or flowerets of broccoli or cauliflower. Put gelatin in a large bowl. Heat stock to boil. Put ¼ cup of the stock in the bowl with the gelatin. Let sit for 5 minutes, then pour in remaining boiling stock and stir until gelatin is completely dissolved. Add chicken, celery, and cooked vegetables and stir. Add capers and tarragon and pour mixture into a 10-cup oiled ring. Chill until firm. To unmold, loosen edge with a sharp knife. Dip bottom and sides of mold in lukewarm water for a few seconds. Put a serving plate on the mold, turn upside down, and shake to get air under the gelatin. (Air pushes the gelatin out of the mold.) Serve with dressing. Garnish with tomatoes and watercress.

◆

NIÇOISE SALAD

Serves 6

This salad originated in the South of France and adds a gay and carefree touch to summer lunches and picnics.

1 head washed Boston lettuce, torn into bite-size pieces	1 can anchovies, drained and coarsely chopped
2 7-ounce cans tuna, drained	2 hard-cooked eggs, quartered
¾ cup cooked green beans, cut in ¼-inch pieces	½ cup small black olives
	½ to ¾ cup Vinaigrette Dressing (see Index)
1 cup diced cooked potatoes	Garnish: Tomatoes cut in wedges
½ cup Spanish onion rings	

Put lettuce in a salad bowl and put the tuna, string beans, potatoes, onion, anchovies, eggs, and olives on top. Toss with salad dressing to just coat ingredients. Decorate with tomato wedges around the top of the bowl.

◆
FRESH FRUIT SALAD
. . . .
Serves 2

This refreshing salad can be served as an ending to a full and satisfying meal or as a light summer dish on a hot day.

1 banana, sliced
1 medium-size apple,
*   unpeeled, diced*
12 cantaloupe or honeydew
*   melon balls*
½ cup sliced strawberries, or
*   blueberries*

1 medium peach, sliced
2 tablespoons confectioners'
*   sugar, or to taste*
Garnish: Fresh mint

Combine fruits in a large bowl. Dust with confectioners' sugar, toss gently, and taste. Add more sugar to taste. Fresh fruit salad can be eaten without any dressing, or you can moisten with Apricot Fruit Salad Dressing (see Index). Serve immediately on individual plates or as a buffet item.

Salad Dressings

◆
VINAIGRETTE DRESSING
. . . .
Makes 1 cup

This is a classic dressing for salads, one that you will use time after time—for the simplest tossed salad or an elaborate Niçoise salad. Vinaigrette is a blend of oil, vinegar or lemon juice, and seasonings.

¼ cup vinegar or fresh lemon
*   juice*
Salt and pepper to taste

¼ teaspoon dry mustard or 1
*   teaspoon Dijon-type*
¾ cup olive or other vegetable oil

Put vinegar in a small mixing bowl. Add salt and pepper and mustard. With a whisk or fork, beat until seasonings are blended in. Gradually, slowly, whisk or fork-beat in the oil. Set aside until ready to use. Whisk again lightly before pouring over a salad or using in a recipe.

• VARIATIONS •
Garlic Vinaigrette. In the mixing bowl, mash and bruise 1 peeled and split garlic clove, with a pestle or the back of a spoon. Discard the clove after the vinegar and seasonings are blended. This method gives the dressing a faint but heavenly hint of garlic.

149

Herb Vinaigrette. To 1 cup dressing add 2 tablespoons each chopped fresh parsley, tarragon, and chives just before serving.

To 1 cup of basic dressing you can also add any of the following: ½ teaspoon curry powder, 1 chopped hard-cooked egg, ¼ cup crumbled Roquefort cheese, or ¼ cup of watercress. Make additions when the dressing is finished, just before serving.

◆

MAYONNAISE
Makes 1¾ cups

Nothing tastes better than homemade mayonnaise, and once you get the hang of making it, you will never want the commercial kind again. Mayonnaise is made by mixing egg yolks, mustard, oil, and lemon juice or vinegar into a stable emulsion. Mayonnaise can also be made in a blender (recipe follows).

2 egg yolks	*1 tablespoon lemon juice or*
½ teaspoon Dijon mustard	*wine vinegar*
1½ cups vegetable oil	*Salt to taste*

Beat egg yolks and mustard in a small bowl with a whisk or electric hand mixer until yolks are thick. *Very* slowly beat in the oil, drop by drop, until the mixture starts to thicken. Then beat in the remaining oil more rapidly, but making sure each addition is thoroughly absorbed before adding more. When all the oil has been beaten in, stir in the lemon juice and salt to taste. Mayonnaise will stay fresh up to a week in a covered container in the refrigerator.

◆

BLENDER MAYONNAISE
Makes 1¼ cups

Blender mayonnaise is thicker and consequently a little heavier than mayonnaise made by hand or in an electric mixer. It is absolutely foolproof and takes just 2 minutes to make.

1 egg	*½ teaspoon mild Dijon*
1 egg yolk	*mustard*
¼ teaspoon salt	*2 teaspoons lemon juice*
	1 cup vegetable oil

Put the egg, yolk, salt, and mustard in the blender. Turn on the motor and add the lemon juice. Add all the oil in a slow, steady stream of droplets. Turn off the motor. Taste the mayonnaise and add more salt or lemon juice if necessary.

If you add the oil too quickly, the egg yolks will get indigestion, a condition that will make itself immediately apparent to the naked eye. Stop the blender at once. Put another egg yolk in a clean, dry bowl. Beat the curdled mayonnaise into the egg yolk, a little at a time, and it will straighten itself out.

• VARIATION •

Russian Dressing. Add 2 tablespoons prepared chili sauce to ¾ cup mayonnaise.

◆

RÉMOULADE SAUCE
Makes 1½ cups

1½ cups mayonnaise (see
   Index)
1¼ tablespoons minced
   gherkin pickles
1 teaspoon Dijon mustard
1 teaspoon capers

1½ teaspoons chopped
   parsley
1 teaspoon finely chopped
   chives
½ teaspoon finely chopped
   tarragon

Mix ingredients together in a bowl and serve.

◆

GREEN GODDESS DRESSING
Makes 2 cups

1 cup mayonnaise (see Index)
1 clove garlic, finely minced
3 anchovies, chopped
¼ cup finely chopped chives
   or green onion tops

¼ cup chopped parsley
1 tablespoon lemon juice
1 tablespoon vinegar
½ cup sour cream
Salt and pepper to taste

Blend all ingredients together except the sour cream. Fold in sour cream and serve.

◆

APRICOT FRUIT SALAD DRESSING
Makes 1½ cups

1 package (3 ounces) cream
   cheese
⅓ cup mayonnaise

¾ cup apricot nectar
2 teaspoons lemon juice
Salt

Mash cream cheese until soft. Gradually beat in mayonnaise, apricot nectar, and lemon juice. Add salt to taste. Chill until ready to serve.

STOCKS, GRAVIES, AND SAUCES

Stocks

There are four basic stocks that all cooks should be able to produce. All are simple and can be frozen for future use. The word *stock*, by the way, simply refers to the liquid that results from simmering meat or fish and vegetables in water. Below is a basic recipe for beef stock, which can be adjusted for veal, chicken, and fish stock.

◆

BEEF STOCK
Makes 1 quart

This produces a classic brown stock.

2 pounds beef bones
1 large yellow onion,
  quartered (reserve skin)
1 carrot, scraped and chopped
1 celery stalk

1½ quarts cold water
3 parsley sprigs
1 tablespoon fresh thyme or 1
  teaspoon dried
1 bay leaf
1 teaspoon peppercorns

Put the bones, vegetables, and onion skin in a roasting pan and put it in a preheated 425-degree oven for 15 minutes, until bones and vegetables are browned. Transfer them to a large saucepan or stockpot and add the water. There should be sufficient water to cover the bones by a depth of 1 inch. Add herbs and pepper. Adjust the lid to cover three quarters of the pan or pot. Simmer over low heat for 6 hours. Strain and chill the stock, or use immediately.

• VARIATIONS •

Chicken or Veal Stock. This produces a classic white stock. Prepare same way as beef stock, substituting chicken or veal bones; all other ingredients remain the same. Do not, however, brown the bones or vegetables. Just put them in the pan or pot, cover with cold water, add the remaining ingredients, and simmer for 4 hours.

Fish Stock. Substitute the head, bones, and trimmings from a fresh fish. Do not use an oily fish, such as tuna, mackerel, or bluefish. Cover the fish parts with cold water to a depth of 1 inch above the bones. Add the same remaining ingredients and simmer for 20 minutes. Pour the stock through a strainer before using in fish sauces and stews. In an emergency, bottled clam juice can be substituted for homemade fish stock, but it tends to be salty and does not have the rich taste of the stock you make yourself.

Gravies

PAN GRAVY
Makes 1 cup

Old-fashioned cooks would never think of serving any kind of roast meat without a good thick gravy made of the meat juices and flour. Pan gravy is always a treat.

3 tablespoons meat drippings
   from the roasting pan
2 tablespoons all-purpose flour

1 cup meat stock, milk, or
   water
Salt and pepper to taste

Remove meat from roasting pan and keep warm. Pour drippings from pan into a bowl or plastic container; remove excess fat by laying a paper towel on the surface of the drippings. The fat will be immediately absorbed by the paper. Measure 3 table-spoons drippings back into roasting pan and sprinkle flour evenly over drippings. Pour liquid over this and blend thoroughly. (Milk is substituted for stock or water when making chicken or turkey gravy.) Heat on top of stove just to the boiling point, stirring constantly. Lower flame and continue to simmer for 2 minutes, until thickened. Stir in seasonings.

• VARIATION •
Unthickened Gravies. These gravies are much more popular with today's fitness- and weight-conscious cooks. The gravy is simply made by adding 2 tablespoons hot water to the juices or scrapings left in the roasting pan after the fat is poured out. Scrape the pan well to blend scrapings with the water. For variety, 2 teaspoons of a fresh herb, such as tarragon or dill, or ½ teaspoon dried herbs can be added to gravy for chicken or turkey; 2 tablespoons wine can be added to gravy for beef, veal, or lamb.

Sauces

Many gourmet dishes and tantalizing desserts owe their fame to the sauces that make them so sumptuous. There are also many simple, straightforward sauces. What follows is an assortment of the classics and basics, with a number of interesting variations.

WHITE SAUCE
Makes 1 cup

This is one of the so-called mother sauces, classic and basic to great chefs the world over. You will find it again and again as the basis of many creamed dishes, scalloped dishes, casseroles, curries, etc. After a while, you will not have to look up the recipe.

153

2 tablespoons butter	1 cup slightly warmed milk
2 tablespoons all-purpose flour	Salt and pepper to taste

Melt butter over low heat in a heavy-bottomed saucepan. Blend in flour, stirring constantly for 2 to 3 minutes. Gradually stir in the warm milk. Increase heat to medium flame and continue stirring until the sauce is thick and smooth. Do not let it boil. Lower heat and simmer for 4 or 5 minutes longer, stirring constantly. Add seasonings.

• VARIATIONS •

Mornay Sauce. Stir in ¼ cup freshly grated Parmesan, Gruyère, or Swiss cheese plus a pinch of dried mustard. Simmer for a few minutes until dissolved.

Cream Curry Sauce. Add 2 teaspoons curry powder and ¼ teaspoon of ground ginger to finished sauce. Simmer a few minutes to blend.

Parsley Sauce. Add 3 tablespoons minced fresh parsley to the finished sauce.

Caper Sauce. Add 2 tablespoons drained capers to the finished sauce.

Mustard Sauce. Add 1 teaspoon mild prepared mustard to the sauce, of ¼ teaspoon hot dried mustard. Blend well.

Sherry Sauce. Add 1 tablespoon sherry to the finished sauce and stir well.

Velouté Sauce. Substitute 1 cup rich homemade chicken stock for the milk. This sauce is particularly delicious over fish fillets.

Mushroom Velouté Sauce. Add ¼ cup sliced fresh mushrooms to Velouté Sauce and simmer for 5 minutes.

◆

BÉCHAMEL SAUCE
Makes 2 cups

Béchamel, another mother sauce, is similar to white sauce but a bit more tasty.

2 cups milk	3 tablespoons butter
1 small onion, sliced	3 tablespoons all-purpose flour
Salt to taste	
4 peppercorns	

In a medium-size saucepan heat milk, onion, salt, and peppercorns until hot but not boiling. Melt butter in a heavy-bottomed saucepan over low heat and add flour gradually, stirring constantly. Cook for 3 to 4 minutes over low heat. Remove from heat and add hot milk after straining it to remove onion and peppercorns. Blend hot milk into flour-and-butter mixture and return to heat. Cook over moderate heat until sauce is smooth and thickened. Reduce heat to simmer and cook another 5 minutes, stirring constantly.

The French use this as the basis of a good many creamed dishes. The variations suggested for white sauce can be used with this sauce.

◆

BROWN SAUCE
Makes 2 cups

This is another mother sauce and is indispensable to all cooks. It can be left simmering while you go about your work and does not require constant attention. The sauce can be frozen, so it is worth making a large amount at one time. Herbs such as tarragon or thyme (1 tablespoon fresh each or 1 teaspoon dried) can be added at the last moment, or 1 tablespoon butter can be added to enrich the sauce and make it shine. Brown sauce is particularly good with leftover beef, lamb, and veal dishes.

2 tablespoons butter
1 onion, finely chopped
1 carrot, finely chopped
1 celery stalk, finely chopped
4 mushrooms, finely chopped
3 tablespoons all-purpose flour
4 cups homemade beef stock
1 bay leaf

1 tablespoon fresh thyme or 1
    teaspoon dried
3 parsley sprigs
1 teaspoon peppercorns
½ teaspoon salt
2 teaspoons tomato paste
2 tablespoons Madeira
    (optional)

In a large kettle or stockpot heat the butter and fry the onion, carrot, celery, and mushrooms for 5 minutes over moderate heat. Stir in the flour and cook for 2 minutes. Add all the remaining ingredients except the Madeira. Simmer the sauce, uncovered, for 2 hours, until the quantity is reduced to 2 cups. Stir in the Madeira.

◆

FOOLPROOF HOLLANDAISE SAUCE
Serves 4

Hollandaise is delicious on fresh vegetables and with different kinds of eggs and fish. Do not be afraid of hollandaise; the only thing that can possibly go wrong is if the eggs get too hot and curdle and become lumpy. If this should happen—and it will not if you are careful—break an egg yolk into a bowl and beat in the curdled sauce a little at a time, and it will become smooth.

1¼ sticks butter cut into
    ½-inch pats
3 egg yolks

2 teaspoons lemon juice
¼ teaspoon salt
Dash of cayenne pepper

Put egg yolks and one pat of butter in a saucepan over low heat. Stir constantly with a wire whisk until the butter has melted. Immediately add the second pat of butter and continue whisking until butter has melted. Repeat, adding pats and whisking, until all butter is used and sauce has thickened. Remove pan from heat. Add lemon juice and seasoning.

155

It is not necessary to serve hollandaise sauce piping hot. In fact, the hotter it is, the greater the danger of curdling. Serve it at room temperature; the heat of the food will warm it slightly.

· VARIATION ·

Mousseline Sauce. This is a lighter version of hollandaise. Fold in ⅔ cup heavy cream, whipped until stiff, to the finished sauce just before serving.

◆

BÉARNAISE SAUCE

Makes ¾ cup

1 tablespoon each fresh
   chopped parsley, tarragon,
   and chervil
1 shallot, chopped
1 bay leaf
6 peppercorns

4 tablespoons wine vinegar
2 egg yolks
8 tablespoons (1 stick) butter,
   softened
Salt and pepper to taste

In a heavy-bottomed saucepan combine herbs, shallot, and peppercorns with vinegar. Cook over low heat until reduced to 1 tablespoon. Pour through a strainer into a saucepan containing the egg yolks. Put the saucepan in a larger saucepan containing about 1½ inches of hot water. In a small skillet heat the butter until it begins to foam. Pour the butter into the egg yolk mixture in a slow but steady stream. Stir over *very* low heat until the sauce is thick. Taste and correct seasoning with salt and pepper.

◆

HOMEMADE
TOMATO SAUCE

Makes 2 cups

1 tablespoon butter
1 onion, finely chopped
1 garlic clove, finely chopped
1 celery stalk, finely chopped
1 tablespoon all-purpose flour
2 cups chicken stock or
   canned broth

4 large tomatoes, chopped
1 tablespoon fresh basil or 1
   teaspoon dried
1 teaspoon tomato paste
½ teaspoon salt
Freshly ground black pepper

Heat the butter in a large saucepan. Add the onion, garlic, and celery and sauté over low heat for 5 minutes. Stir in the flour and add all the remaining ingredients. Cover and simmer for 15 minutes. Remove the lid and simmer for another 10 minutes. Purée the sauce in a blender and force through a strainer to remove the tomato seeds and skins.

BARBECUE SAUCE
Makes 2 cups

This is a good, tangy sauce for barbecued spareribs or chicken, cooked either outdoors over a charcoal fire or in the broiler.

2 tablespoons oil
1 onion, finely chopped
1 garlic clove, finely chopped
2 teaspoons Dijon mustard
¼ cup honey

1 cup catsup
1 cup chili sauce
1 tablespoon soy sauce
Dash of Tabasco sauce

In a large saucepan heat the oil and sauté the onion and garlic for 5 minutes. Remove from the heat and stir in all the remaining ingredients.

Marinate spareribs or chicken in the barbecue sauce for at least an hour; the longer the better. Baste periodically with the sauce while cooking, and serve any extra sauce with the cooked ribs or chicken. (See Index for broiled chicken and ribs recipes.)

CURRY SAUCE
Makes 2 cups

This basic curry sauce can be used with meat or fish and makes a good party dish.

4 tablespoons butter
½ cup chopped onion
½ cup peeled and chopped
  tart apple
1 tablespoon chopped celery
2 garlic cloves, minced

2½ tablespoons all-purpose
  flour
1 cup chicken stock or canned
  broth
1 cup heavy cream
1½ tablespoons curry powder

Melt butter in a large frying pan and slowly sauté the onion, apple, celery, and garlic until tender. Sprinkle in the flour and stir until well blended in. Stirring constantly, slowly add the stock and then the cream. Cook slowly over low heat and continue stirring until sauce thickens. Add the curry powder.

About 1 cup of any of the following leftover or cooked meats or fish can be added to the sauce: lamb, beef, chicken, turkey, shrimps, etc. The mixture is then traditionally served on rice with such condiments as chopped peanuts, minced hard-cooked egg yolks, shredded coconut, and chutney. This recipe serves 3 people generously, so just double sauce and meat for 6 servings.

◆

GARLIC SAUCE
Makes 1 cup

Southern France has made this sauce famous. It adds zest to such delicate fish as flounder, cod, and halibut. The fish can be served either hot or cold.

8 garlic cloves, mashed in a press
2 egg yolks

Salt and pepper to taste
1 cup good imported olive oil
Juice of 1 lemon

In a small bowl mix together garlic, egg yolks, and seasonings. Add 3 tablespoons olive oil very slowly, drop by drop. Then stir in the lemon juice, again slowly. Add the remainder of the oil, *very* slowly, until all is blended in to form a smooth, mayonnaise-textured sauce.

◆

HORSERADISH SAUCE
Serves 6 to 8

This is a famous English sauce, served traditionally with roast beef.

½ cup freshly grated horse-radish root or ⅓ cup drained prepared horseradish

1 tablespoon lemon juice, if fresh root is used
1 pint heavy cream, whipped

Blend horseradish and lemon juice together. Fold in whipped cream. Put in a glass bowl and serve.

MINT SAUCE
Makes 1 cup

The traditional sauce for roast lamb is mint. What you make yourself you will find far superior to store-bought bottled sauce, and your guests will never fail to compliment you.

¼ cup sugar
½ cup vinegar

½ cup chopped fresh mint leaves

In a small heavy-bottomed saucepan heat sugar and vinegar until sugar is totally dissolved. Pour over the mint leaves in a small bowl. This sauce acquires greater flavor if made an hour or so before serving.

Dessert Sauces

These are basic sweet sauces you will use again and again as a festive touch to end a gracious meal. The sauces can be served with a number of desserts, elaborate or as simple as a scoop of ice cream.

◆

HOT FUDGE SAUCE

Makes 1 cup

6 ounces semisweet chocolate
2 tablespoons butter
¼ cup water

¼ cup sugar
½ cup heavy cream
1 teaspoon vanilla extract

Put the chocolate, butter, and water in a small, heavy saucepan. Stir over low heat until the chocolate has melted. Add the sugar and cream and simmer for 15 minutes. Remove from the heat and stir in the vanilla.

◆

HOT CHOCOLATE SAUCE

Makes 1 cup

½ cup sugar
¾ cup water

2 ounces unsweetened
  chocolate
1 teaspoon vanilla extract

In the top part of a double boiler over simmering water cook sugar and water to a thick syrup. Meanwhile, melt chocolate in a small saucepan, making sure it does not boil. Add chocolate to the thickened sugar syrup and beat in vanilla. If sauce is too thick, thin it with a tablespoon of rum, brandy, or cream. Keep sauce hot in the double boiler. (It can be served cold as well.)

◆

BUTTERSCOTCH SAUCE

Makes 1¼ cups

2 cups brown sugar
¾ cup heavy cream
4 tablespoons butter

⅛ teaspoon salt
1 teaspoon vanilla extract

Put the sugar, cream, butter, and salt in a small, heavy saucepan. Set over low heat, stir occasionally until the sugar has dissolved, and simmer for 20 minutes, until thick. Stir in the vanilla.

MELBA SAUCE
Makes 1 cup

1 cup raspberries
¼ cup superfine sugar

1 teaspoon lemon juice

Purée all the ingredients in a blender. Force through a fine strainer to remove the seeds. Serve in a gravy boat or spoon over individual servings.

• VARIATIONS •
Strawberry and other berry sauces are made in the same way. Orange juice or fruit-flavored liqueur can be substituted for lemon juice.

BREAD, ROLLS, AND MUFFINS

Bread is one of the most satisfying of all foods to make, to eat, and to share. More and more, people are making their own bread, searching out health-food stores and little specialty-food stores to find whole-grain, cracked-grain, and rye flours. The results of bread making are usually good, for little can go seriously wrong. If you are armed with a few facts, your bread will be spectacularly good. These are the things to know.

YEAST

Yeast consists of small plants that begin to work in the presence of moisture, like seeds coming to life after being planted. The ideal condition for growth is a medium of milk or water at a temperature of 105 to 115 degrees Fahrenheit. This is slightly above body temperature, a cool "lukewarm." If the yeast is put into a liquid below this temperature, it will still work, but slowly and reluctantly. If the temperature is too high, the yeast is killed and will not work at all.

Active yeast will soften in the liquid, making it cloudy, and create a slight bubbling effect as gas is released. If there is no action, either the liquid was too hot or the yeast was too old. Check the expiration date on the package.

Sugar increases the action of the yeast, and salt slows·it down. Both sugar and salt are added to almost all yeast doughs. Too much sugar makes bread rise too rapidly, creating air pockets; too much salt inhibits the action of the yeast, making for a dense and poorly risen bread.

Fresh, or compressed, yeast is grayish white and crumbly. It can be refrigerated for up to 2 weeks in a jar with a tightly fitting lid, or frozen for 2 months. Thaw frozen yeast at room temperature and use immediately. One ½-ounce package of fresh yeast can be substituted for 1 package (1 tablespoon) of active dry yeast.

Baking powder is used instead of yeast for making quick breads, such as biscuits and corn bread. Baking soda is sometimes added to breads containing highly acid fruits to neutralize their effect.

FLOUR

Bread flour is a "hard" flour, high in gluten. This enables the flour to absorb liquid and retain the gases produced by the yeast. This gives the dough greater elasticity when it is kneaded, and the bread rises better and has a finer crumb and crust than bread made with "soft" or all-purpose flour. Kneading helps to develop the gluten in the flour.

All-purpose flour is a blend of hard and soft wheat. The proportions vary throughout the country.

Cake flour and pastry flour are made from soft wheat and are not recommended for bread making. The bread does not rise well or slice well. Bread made with these flours lacks taste and body.

Whole-wheat flour and graham flour are both high in gluten. They are excellent for bread making and retain all the natural vitamins and minerals. These flours require little kneading and produce a firm, well-textured bread. Whole-wheat and graham flours can replace some or all of plain bread flour in any recipe.

Enriched flour has had the outer part of the grain removed to extend its shelf life. The nutrients that are removed are replaced with synthetics, but though they are not in any way harmful and may even be good for your health, enriched flour does not produce as good-tasting a loaf as the natural flours.

The Five Basic Steps in Making Bread

1. Sprinkle fresh or dry yeast over lukewarm water or milk. Water makes a coarse "French bread" type of crumb; milk gives a soft crumb. Except for French and Italian breads, add sugar or honey to feed the yeast and salt to control the action of the yeast. You can add oil or butter to enrich and soften the dough and the crumb. The yeast mixture is combined with a minimum quantity of flour to form a soft dough. As the dough is kneaded, small amounts of flour are worked in, until the dough is soft and elastic and no longer sticky.

2. As the dough is kneaded it becomes firm and smooth; it seems to acquire "body." Fold the dough toward you and press it down firmly and authoritatively with the heels of your hands. Turn it a quarter of a circle. Gradually a rhythm will develop: Turn and fold and press.

    Gather more flour into the dough if it feels sticky, but do not add too much or the bread will be heavy. When you have the dough in front of you, you will get the feel of how much flour to add. When the dough has absorbed as much flour as it wants, it does not pick up any more, so do not force it. When small air blisters appear beneath the surface of the dough and it is smooth and firm, let the dough, and yourself, rest.

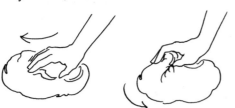

3. Put the dough in a buttered large bowl. Brush the dough surface with butter to keep it from drying out and cover with a cloth to exclude any possible drafts. Leave the dough to rise until it has doubled in size and formed a smooth dome. This can take from 1 to 4 hours, depending on the type of dough, but probably will take around 2 hours.
4. Punch the dough down in the bowl and knead again for 2 to 3 minutes. Then shape it into loaves or rolls and put in buttered and floured loaf pans or on baking sheets. Cover and let rise for an hour, until it has again doubled in bulk.
5. The dough may or may not be brushed with a glaze made from an egg yolk combined with milk, with beaten egg white, or with water. The top of the dough may be slashed with two or three cuts to make a more attractive appearance. Bake the dough in a preheated oven. It is done when it begins to shrink from the sides of the pan. When it is tapped it emits a hollow, empty sound. The sound is hard to interpret; one can never be quite, quite sure. However, if you stick closely to the time given in the recipe, you cannot go too far wrong.

If you have to leave the kitchen for several hours, put the dough in the refrigerator. It will continue to rise, but very slowly. You can bring it back to room temperature, let the dough double in bulk, and bake it when you are ready.

Unbaked bread dough can be frozen. It will spring back to life when it reaches room temperature. Baked breads freeze very successfully.

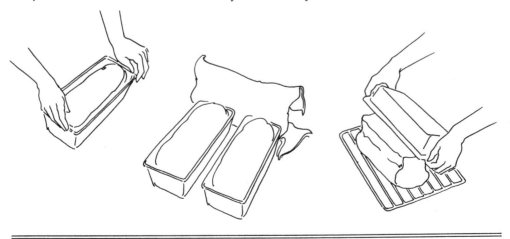

◆

WHITE BREAD
. . . .
Makes 2 loaves

As you will see from the following recipes, white and all other breads follow the same basic pattern. Either the total quantity of white flour is used or half of the white flour is replaced with whole-wheat, rye, or graham flour. These flours all absorb more water than white flour does, so breads made with them call for slightly less flour. The quantity of sugar can be varied by up to ¼ cup, according to taste, and sugar can be substituted for honey in white breads and molasses in date breads. Also, the salt can be varied, from 1 teaspoon to 1 tablespoon, according to taste; do not add more than 1 tablespoon. Instead of butter, you can use margarine or oil. The more butter that is added, the softer will be the crumb when the bread is sliced.

1 package dry yeast
1 cup lukewarm water (110
  degrees)
1 cup milk
3 tablespoons butter

2 tablespoons sugar or honey
2 teaspoons salt
5 cups sifted unbleached flour
Glaze: 1 egg yolk combined
  with 1 tablespoon milk

Sprinkle the yeast over the water. Stir and set aside for 10 minutes. Heat the milk to a simmer. Cut the butter into small pieces and add to the milk. Add the sugar and salt and stir to dissolve. Let cool to 110 degrees. Pour the yeast and milk mixtures into a large bowl and add sufficient flour to form a dough—approximately 4 cups. Turn the dough out on the counter and knead for 5 minutes, adding more flour as necessary to keep the dough from sticking to your hands and the counter. Knead until the dough is smooth and firm. Small bubbles will appear beneath the surface, and as the dough is kneaded it springs back on itself, expanding when pressure is applied and bouncing back when the pressure is released. Put the dough in a buttered bowl and turn it so that the entire surface is buttered. Cover with a kitchen towel and leave in a warm, draft-free spot in the kitchen for 2 hours, until doubled in size.

Punch the dough with your fist to release the gases. Cut the dough into two pieces. Knead each for 3 to 4 minutes. Shape dough into two loaves to fit 9 × 5 × 3-inch buttered loaf pans sprinkled with flour. (The bread can also be made into round loaves or rolls and baked on prepared cookie sheets). Cover the dough and leave for 1 hour, until again doubled in bulk.

Preheat the oven to 375 degrees. Brush the dough with egg yolk–milk glaze. Bake the loaves for 45 minutes and rolls for 30 minutes. Remove the bread from the oven and leave in the pans for 5 minutes. If possible, turn loaves out to cool on wire racks for at least an hour before slicing.

Note: To obtain a coarser crumb, use 2 cups water instead of 1 cup each water and milk, and reduce the butter to 1 tablespoon.

• VARIATIONS •
Whole-Wheat Bread. Substitute whole-wheat flour for half the white flour.

Rye Bread. Substitute rye flour for half the white flour. Try these variations: (1) Use dark molasses instead of sugar or honey. (2) Add 2 teaspoons caraway, fennel, or dill seeds to the dough. (3) Powdered milk can replace whole milk. Dissolve 1 cup powdered milk in 1 cup of water. There will then be a total of 2 cups water and 1 cup powdered milk to replace 2 cups liquid in white bread recipe. (4) Use 1 cup sour cream instead of milk.

Spiced Bread. When the milk has cooled to 110 degrees, stir in 2 lightly beaten eggs. Add to the flour 1 teaspoon cinnamon, ¼ teaspoon nutmeg (freshly grated, if possible), and 1 teaspoon allspice. The grated rind of 2 oranges and 1 lemon can also be added. Dust the baked bread with sifted confectioners' sugar.

Cheddar Cheese Bread. Substitute 2 cups beer for the water and milk. After the dough's first rising, punch it down and knead in 1 cup grated Cheddar cheese and ½ cup minced fresh dill or 1½ tablespoons dried dill. Other ideas: (1) Chop 1 onion finely, fry for 5 minutes in 2 tablespoons butter, and add to the dough at the same time as the cheese. (2) Dredge ½ cup chopped walnuts in flour and add to the bread at the same time as the cheese.

The variations on bread recipes are endless. Sour cream, cottage cheese, water, or beer can replace the milk. Herbs do not change the texture of the bread but improve the flavor. Add up to ½ cup finely chopped fresh herbs or 1 to 2 tablespoons dried herbs to 5 cups of flour.

◆

SAFFRON BREAD WITH RAISINS
Makes 2 loaves

Soak ½ teaspoon saffron threads in ¼ cup boiling water for 5 minutes. Soak 1 cup raisins in 1 cup boiling water for 5 minutes. Drain the raisins and pat dry on paper towels. Dredge the raisins in flour. Follow recipe for white bread but sprinkle the yeast over ¾ cup lukewarm water. Stir and set aside for 10 minutes, then add the saffron with its soaking water. Add the raisins after dough's first rising.

• VARIATIONS •
Use ½ cup raisins and ½ cup chopped nuts. Dredge the nuts, too, in flour, to prevent them from sinking to the bottom of the bread.

Substitute 1 cup chopped glacéed fruit for the raisins. Dredge the fruit in flour.

◆

OATMEAL BREAD
Makes 2 loaves

This is another wonderful variation of basic white bread.

1 package dry yeast	*3 tablespoons butter, melted*
2 cups lukewarm water (110 degrees)	*2 tablespoons honey*

165

2 teaspoons salt
2 cups sifted white flour
1½ cups rolled oats

1½ cups (approximately)
whole-wheat flour

Sprinkle the yeast over the water. Stir and set aside for 10 minutes. Stir in the butter, honey, and salt. Pour into a large bowl and add the flour and oats. Add ½ cup whole-wheat flour. Turn the dough out on a counter and knead. Continue adding whole-wheat flour until the dough sticks to neither your hands nor the counter but is smooth and firm. Continue with the directions for white bread.

ROLL
DOUGH
Makes 2 to 3 dozen rolls

Nine different and delightful kinds of dinner, lunch, and breakfast rolls can be made from this basic recipe. After the dough is shaped into the rolls of your choice, count on at least 1 hour for it to rise before baking. If you like, the dough can be prepared ahead and refrigerated.

1 package active dry yeast or
   1 cake compressed yeast
¼ cup lukewarm water
¾ cup lukewarm milk (110
   degrees)
½ cup vegetable shortening
   or butter

½ cup sugar
2 teaspoons salt
2 eggs, well beaten
5 to 6 cups sifted all-purpose
   flour

In a small bowl sprinkle yeast over lukewarm water. Let stand 2 minutes and then stir to dissolve. In a large mixing bowl mix milk, shortening, sugar, and salt with a wooden spoon. Stir until shortening melts. Stir in eggs. Let cool in lukewarm and stir in dissolved yeast. Beat in flour and continue beating until dough pulls away from spoon. Knead dough, put in a greased bowl, cover and set in a warm place. Let rise until doubled in bulk. Punch down and knead again. (At this point, if you like, dough can be refrigerated for 3 to 4 days.) Divide and form into desired shape. Let rolls rise until doubled in bulk. Bake in a preheated 375-degree oven for 10 to 12 minutes. Remove from pan and serve warm.

Here are nine different rolls—of all different shapes—that can be made from this basic recipe.

PAN BUNS
Put balls of dough about the size of small plums side by side, just touching each other, in two well-greased 9-inch layer cake or pie pans. Brush tops heavily with melted butter. Let rise and bake as directed.

CLOVERLEAF ROLLS

Roll dough into small balls about the size of a large olive and put three in each well-greased muffin-pan cup. Let rise and bake as directed.

BOWKNOT ROLLS

Cut dough into walnut-size pieces. With your fingers, roll each piece into a rope about 6 to 7 inches long. Lift the rope and tie it in a knot. Put on a greased cookie sheet and let rise. Bake as directed.

CLOTHESPIN ROLLS

Cut dough into pieces the size of a small plum. Shape into ropes 8 inches long and ¼ inch in diameter. Grease peg-type clothespins and wrap dough loosely around clothespins. Put on greased cookie sheet and let rise. Bake in a preheated 375-degree oven for 10 to 12 minutes. Let cool slightly on a rack. Twist clothespin to remove from roll.

CINNAMON BUNS

Roll out dough to an oblong 16 × 18 inches, ¼ inch thick. Brush with melted butter. Sprinkle with sugar mixed with cinnamon. Sprinkle with raisins or chopped nuts. Roll up, starting at long side. Using a sharp or serrated-edge knife, with a sawing motion cut dough into 12 slices and put side by side in a well-greased 13 × 9-inch pan. Let rise and bake as directed.

SEEDED ROLLS

Add 1 tablespoon caraway seeds, poppy seeds, or toasted sesame seeds to dough when beating in flour. Shape as desired and brush tops with slightly beaten egg white. Sprinkle tops of rolls with additional seeds. Let rise and bake as directed.

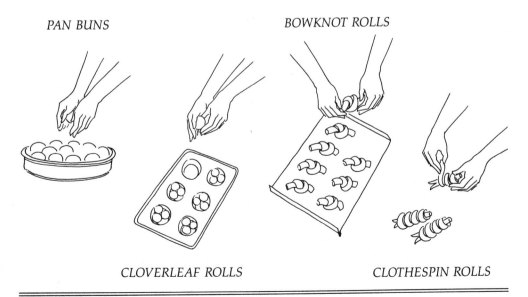

PAN BUNS

BOWKNOT ROLLS

CLOVERLEAF ROLLS

CLOTHESPIN ROLLS

HOT CROSS BUNS

Add ½ cup raisins to dough when it is kneaded. Shape dough into balls about the size of plums. Snip a cross in the top, making one cut straight across and then cutting each half. Let rise on cookie sheets. Bake as directed. When baked and cool, spoon 2 cups confectioners' sugar mixed with 3 tablespoons milk into the cuts.

CRESCENT ROLLS

Cut dough into 3 equal pieces. Roll each piece into a circle 12 inches in diameter and ¼ inch thick. Cut the circle into 12 wedges. Brush dough with melted butter and roll up each wedge, starting at the wide end. Put on a well-greased cookie sheet, point side down, and shape into a crescent. Let rise and bake as directed.

FANTANS

Roll dough into an oblong ½ inch thick. Cut into 1½-inch-wide strips. Brush strips with melted butter. Stack six strips, one on top of another. Cut stack crosswise into 1½-inch pieces. Put pieces, cut side up, in well-greased muffin pans. Let rise and bake as directed.

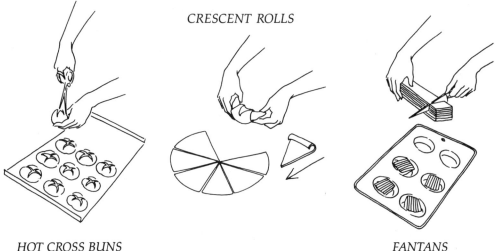

CRESCENT ROLLS

HOT CROSS BUNS

FANTANS

◆

COFFEE CAKE

Makes 1 large cake

1 cake yeast
¼ cup lukewarm water
4 cups sifted all-purpose
   flour
4 tablespoons sugar
1 teaspoon salt
1 cup (2 sticks) butter

8 egg yolks
½ cup lukewarm milk
¼ cup melted butter
1 cup light brown sugar
¾ cup chopped almonds
Garnish: Candied fruit, almonds, confectioners' sugar

Put yeast in a small bowl, add water, and set aside to soften. Combine flour, sugar, and salt in a large mixing bowl. Add butter and with your fingers work it into the dry ingredients until finely crumbled. Add egg yolks and yeast to the bowl and mix until the dough is fairly stiff. Add milk and blend thoroughly. Turn dough out on a floured board or marble slab and knead until smooth and elastic. With a rolling pin, roll dough out into a rectangle about 18 inches long. Brush with some of the melted butter and sprinkle with brown sugar and ¾ cup almonds. Roll the dough lengthwise so it looks like a thick sausage and then form a circle with it. Press ends together and put the dough circle in a 12-inch round cake pan. Brush with the remaining melted butter. Using kitchen shears, cut deep slanting slashes about halfway through the circle at 2-inch intervals. Put coffee cake in a warm place and let rise for about 1 hour. It should double in size and puff up. Bake in a preheated 350-degree oven for 40 minutes, or until a lovely golden brown. Remove cake from tin to a cake rack while still warm.

If you like, while the coffee cake is still warm, mix a little warm water with some confectioners' sugar to make icing. Frost the coffee cake and garnish with fruit, almonds, and confectioners' sugar.

◆

BACON BISCUITS
Makes 16

2 cups sifted all-purpose
    flour
1 tablespoon baking powder
½ teaspoon salt

¼ cup vegetable shortening
¾ cup milk or light cream
6 strips crisp bacon,
    crumbled

In a large mixing bowl mix flour, baking powder, and salt. Cut in shortening with two knives or a pastry blender until mixture resembles course cornmeal. Add milk and bacon all at once and stir until dough follows spoon around the bowl. Turn out dough and knead (see Index for instructions) a few times until smooth. Roll out on a lightly floured board to ½ inch thick. Cut out biscuits with a floured cutter; press cutter straight down so biscuits will rise evenly. Put biscuits on an ungreased cookie sheet and bake in a preheated 450-degree oven for 12 to 15 minutes. Bake biscuits apart for crusty sides, together for soft sides. Serve hot from the oven.

◆

SCONES
Makes 16

Scones are traditionally served at teatime with butter and jam, but there is no reason not to serve them at brunch or breakfast.

Omit bacon in preceding recipe. Add 2 tablespoons sugar to flour. Use 6 tablespoons butter instead of vegetable shortening, and use 1 egg and ⅔ cup light cream for liquid. Roll out dough into two 8-inch rounds. Cut each round into six wedges. Bake as directed in preceding recipe.

◆

FRENCH BLUEBERRY MUFFINS
Makes 12 to 14

2 cups sifted all-purpose
   flour
2 tablespoons sugar
1 tablespoon baking powder
½ teaspoon salt
1 egg
½ cup milk

⅓ cup peanut oil
1 cup blueberries
½ cup melted butter or
   margarine
½ cup sugar mixed with 1
   teaspoon ground cinnamon

In a large mixing bowl mix flour, 2 tablespoons sugar, baking powder, and salt. In a smaller bowl mix egg, milk, and oil. Add wet ingredients all at once to dry ingredients and stir just to moisten dry ingredients. Do not leave batter lumpy, or muffins will be tough. Fold in blueberries. Spoon batter into well-greased muffin pans, filling cups two thirds full. Bake in a preheated 400-degree oven for 20 to 25 minutes. Remove from pan and while hot dip tops in melted butter and then in cinnamon sugar. Serve warm.

◆

ZUCCHINI BREAD
4 large or 8 small loaves

This has long been a favorite bread in summer, when zucchini is at its peak. The walnuts in this recipe give a special taste.

6 eggs
3½ cups sugar
1¾ cups vegetable oil
5 cups grated unpeeled
   zucchini
5 teaspoons vanilla extract
6 cups sifted unbleached flour

2 teaspoons salt
2 teaspoons baking soda
½ teaspoon baking powder
6 teaspoons cinnamon
2 cups chopped walnuts
¼ cup walnut oil

In a large mixing bowl beat eggs until light. Add the sugar, mixing well. Add the vegetable oil, zucchini, and vanilla and mix thoroughly. Sift together the dry ingredients in another small bowl. Add mixed dry ingredients by the cupful to the egg mixture. Stir well after each addition. Add nuts and walnut oil. Butter 4 large loaf pans (9 × 5 inches) or 8 small (7¼ × 3¾ inches). Spoon batter into the pans and bake in a preheated 350-degree oven for approximately 1 hour. Cool on cake racks.

• VARIATION •
Substitute grated carrots or sweet potatoes for the zucchini to make either carrot or sweet potato bread.

DESSERTS

Here is a wealth of desserts—cakes, pastries, custards, mousses, ice creams, meringues, soufflés and other tempting creations. It goes without saying that fresh fruit and cheese are always good foods to end a meal, but occasionally it is fun to indulge yourselves and friends with a beautiful and irresistible dessert.

Cakes

A cake is often the center of interest at a party or a special meal. Here are some favorite basic cakes that you will find yourself making over and over, for birthdays, anniversaries, and holidays. Included are instructions for frosting and decorating tips.

To test a cake for doneness, insert a small knife, or a clean toothpick, or a straw in the center. If it comes out clean, the cake is done. If it comes out with wet batter clinging to it, the cake needs further baking.

◆

DEVIL'S FOOD CAKE
Serves 8

Almost everyone likes chocolate cake. Few chocolate lovers can resist this one.

1 cup vegetable shortening
2 cups firmly packed light
    brown sugar
1 teaspoon salt
2 teaspoons vanilla extract
4 squares (4 ounces) un-
    sweetened chocolate

5 eggs
3 cups sifted all-purpose
    flour
1½ teaspoons baking soda
1¾ cups milk plus 2 table-
    spoons vinegar, or 1¾
    cups buttermilk

In a large mixing bowl cream shortening until light and fluffy. Gradually stir in brown sugar, salt, and vanilla. Put chocolate in the top part of a double boiler and melt over hot water. Stir melted chocolate into shortening-sugar mixture. Beat in eggs, one at a time. Beat until smooth after each addition. In a smaller bowl, blend flour and baking soda. Stir in one third of the flour, then half the milk, a third of flour, remaining milk, and remaining flour. Beat until smooth after each addition, and scrape sides of bowl and spoon often during mixing. If you use an electric beater, add ingredients using low speed and then beat at medium speed. Pour batter into three greased and floured 9-inch layer cake pans. (To grease and flour pans, brush bottom and sides thickly with vegetable shortening. Sprinkle 1 tablespoon flour into pan. Rotate pan so every part is covered with flour. Turn pan upside down and tap to remove all excess flour.) Spread batter evenly in pans, pushing batter so it is slightly lower in the center. Put filled pans on oven racks in the center of the oven. If you are using two racks, arrange the pans so one isn't directly above the other. Bake in a preheated 350-degree oven for 20 to 25 minutes, or until cake springs back when touched lightly and sides have shrunk in a little. Loosen edges of cake with a sharp knife. Tap each pan on its sides to loosen cake. Put cake rack on pans and turn upside down. Cool layers on the rack and then spread 1½ cups apricot jam between layers and frost top and sides of cake with Seven-Minute Frosting (see Index).

◆

ANGEL FOOD CAKE
Serves 8

This is a feathery-light cake, a dramatic dessert. Some cooks believe that angel food cakes taste better if they age for a day before being eaten. Try it both ways and decide which you prefer. You will need a 10-inch tube pan to bake this cake.

1½ cups egg whites (from approximately 10 large eggs)
1½ teaspoons cream of tartar
1 teaspoon vanilla extract
1 teaspoon almond extract
½ teaspoon salt

1 cup sifted cake flour
½ cup confectioners' sugar
Garnish: Fresh strawberries and other fruit and a dollop of whipped cream

Put egg whites, cream of tartar, vanilla and almond extract, and salt in a large mixing bowl. With an electric beater, beat until mixture is stiff but not dry and appears shiny or glossy. Put flour in a medium-size bowl. Add confectioners' sugar and then sift and resift combined flour and sugar six times. Using a rubber spatula, fold the flour-and-sugar mixture, 2 tablespoons at a time, into the egg whites.

With a rubber spatula transfer the batter to a 10-inch ungreased tube pan. To break up any air bubbles, run a knife through the batter in widening circles. Bake in a preheated 375-degree oven for 15 minutes. Reduce heat to 250 degrees and bake about 15 minutes more, or until done. Invert cake on a cake rack and let cool completely. Remove from pan; you may have to run a knife around the side of pan to help the cake drop away. Dust with confectioners' sugar. Garnish and serve.

◆

LEMON SPONGE CAKE
Serves 8

This cake provides both a light and pleasing end to a meal and a special sweet treat with a cup of tea or coffee. You will need a 10-inch tube pan.

1½ cups sugar
1¼ cups sifted cake flour
½ teaspoon baking powder
½ teaspoon salt
½ cup egg yolks (about 6)
2 tablespoons lemon juice

1 teaspoon vanilla extract
1 tablespoon grated lemon
  rind
½ cup egg whites (about 4)
¼ teaspoon cream of tartar

Sift 1 cup of the sugar, the flour, baking powder, and salt into a medium-size mixing bowl. Add the egg yolks, lemon juice, vanilla, and lemon rind, but do not stir in yet. In a large mixing bowl beat the egg whites until fluffy. Add cream of tartar and continue beating for a few moments. Then slowly add the remaining ½ cup of sugar and beat until whites form stiff peaks. Beat the flour-and-yolk mixture until well mixed, about 1 minute. With a rubber spatula gently fold—do not stir—the egg yolk mixture into the beaten egg whites, about a quarter at a time. When yolk mixture is completely folded in, carefully transfer into an ungreased 10-inch tube pan. Bake in a preheated 350-degree oven for 40 to 50 minutes. A sponge cake should spring back to the touch when it is done. Invert the tube pan on a cake rack and let the cake cool completely before turning out of the pan. Cake can be dusted with confectioners' sugar or iced with a fruit glaze.

◆

SOUTHERN FRESH COCONUT CAKE
Serves 8

Coconut cake is a traditional Southern favorite.

To prepare fresh coconut milk, pierce coconut in the three dark depressions (eyes) at the end. Drain the milk; if necessary, add water to make 1 cup. Heat the coconut in a 350-degree oven for 20 minutes. Let cool. Break shell with a hammer and remove the coconut meat. Pare off the brown rind. Grate coconut on a fine grater.

½ cup (1 stick) butter or
  margarine, softened
¾ cup sugar
2 eggs

1½ cups sifted all-purpose flour
1½ teaspoons baking powder
1 cup coconut milk
1 cup grated fresh coconut

In a large mixing bowl cream butter until light and fluffy. Gradually beat in sugar. Beat in eggs, one at a time. Mix flour and baking powder in a small bowl. Stir half the flour mixture into the batter-sugar-egg mixture. Stir in coconut milk. Stir in remaining flour and coconut. If using an electric mixer, add ingredients at low speed and then beat at medium speed. Pour batter into two greased and floured 8-inch layer cake pans. Bake in a preheated 350-degree oven for 25 to 30 minutes, or until cake is firm to the touch.

Let layers cool for 5 minutes, then tap to loosen and unmold on a rack. Spread cooled layer with Coconut Filling (see Index). Top with second layer. Frost sides and top with Seven-Minute Frosting (see Index) and cover with more grated coconut.

◆

ITALIAN RUM CAKE
Serves 8

A wonderful surprise ending to a meal with Italian food or a festive dinner party.

6 eggs, at room temperature
1 cup sugar
1 cup instant flour

½ cup (1 stick) unsalted
   butter or margarine, melted
1 teaspoon vanilla extract
¼ cup rum

With a mixer beat eggs in a bowl at high speed until thick and lemon-colored. Gradually, at high speed, beat in sugar, 1 tablespoon at a time, and beat for 10 minutes, or until mixture has tripled in volume. Fold in flour gradually with a wooden spoon. (Instant flour gives a smooth, fine-grained cake that is easy to handle.) Melt butter in a small skillet and let stand for a few minutes to cool. Pour clear melted butter slowly into batter, leaving milky residue behind in the pan. Fold butter into batter. Fold in vanilla. Grease bottoms only of two 9-inch layer cake pans. Line bottoms with foil and grease foil. Pour batter into pans and spread evenly. Bake in a preheated 350-degree oven for 25 to 30 minutes, or until cake feels springy to the touch. Cool layers in pans for 10 minutes. Cut sides of cake away from pan with a sharp knife. Tap cake to loosen. Remove layers from pans, remove foil, and let layers cool on racks. Sprinkle layers with rum. Spread Rum Butter Frosting (see Index) between layers and over sides and top of the cake.

◆

PEACH UPSIDE-DOWN CAKE
Serves 8

This cake is best made just before serving time and served warm.

¼ cup firmly packed brown
   sugar
3 tablespoons butter, melted
⅓ cup pecan halves
9 fresh peach halves or 9
   canned halves, well
   drained
1⅓ cups sifted all-purpose
   flour

2 teaspoons baking powder
½ teaspoon salt
⅔ cup white sugar
¼ cup vegetable shortening
1 egg
½ cup milk
1 teaspoon vanilla extract
½ teaspoon almond extract

Butter a 9 × 9 × 2-inch pan. In a small bowl mix brown sugar and butter. Sprinkle evenly over bottom of pan. Sprinkle pan with pecans and put peaches, hollow side down, on brown sugar. Mix flour, baking powder, salt, and sugar together in a bowl;

add remaining ingredients and beat until smooth and creamy. Pour batter evenly over peaches. Bake in a preheated 350-degree oven 35 to 40 minutes, or until golden brown. Immediately loosen edges with a knife and turn upside down on a platter. Remove cake while hot, or peaches will stick to pan. Serve warm.

GINGERBREAD
. . . .
Makes 9 squares

This fragrant warm bread-cake can be served for dessert or with tea or hot chocolate.

2 eggs
1 cup sugar
½ cup (1 stick) butter, cut
*   into small pieces*
1 cup boiling water
¼ cup dark molasses
2 cups sifted all-purpose
*   flour*

Grated rind of 1 orange
2 teaspoons ginger
1 teaspoon allspice
1 teaspoon baking soda
½ teaspoon baking powder
Garnish: Whipped cream

In a large mixing bowl beat the eggs and sugar until very thick. Put the butter in a small bowl and add boiling water. Stir to dissolve the butter and add the molasses. Combine all the remaining dry ingredients in another bowl. Fold the butter mixture and dry ingredients alternately into the eggs and sugar. Pour into a buttered 8 × 8 × 2-inch baking pan and bake in a preheated 350-degree oven for 45 minutes, or until a toothpick inserted in the center of the cake comes out clean. Let the gingerbread cool for 15 minutes before cutting. Garnish with whipped cream.

CHEESECAKE
. . . .
Serves 8

This makes one 9-inch cheesecake with a wonderful lemony flavor that melts in your mouth. You will need a springform pan.

CRUST

1 6-ounce box of graham
*   crackers, finely crumbled*
*   (about ¾ cup)*

2 tablespoons sugar
½ teaspoon cinnamon
6 tablespoons butter, melted

Put the cracker crumbs, sugar, and cinnamon in a mixing bowl and stir in the melted butter. When well mixed, heavily butter a 9-inch, 3-inch-deep springform pan.

With the back of a spoon (or your fingers), pat an even layer of the crumb mixture on the bottom and sides of the pan to form a pie shell. Keep refrigerated while you prepare the filling.

FILLING

3 8-ounce packages cream
   cheese, softened
1¼ cups sugar
6 egg yolks.
1 pint sour cream
3 tablespoons all-purpose
   flour

1 tablespoon lemon juice
1 tablespoon grated lemon
   rind
2 teaspoons vanilla extract
6 egg whites

In a large mixing bowl beat the cream cheese with a wooden spoon until it is smooth and creamy. Slowly beat in the sugar and the egg yolks, one by one. Continue to beat until yolks are thoroughly blended in. Add the sour cream, flour, lemon juice, lemon rind, and vanilla, stirring thoroughly after each addition. Beat egg whites in a separate bowl until they form stiff peaks. With a rubber spatula, gently fold the egg whites into the cream cheese mixture. Pour the filling into the lightly chilled pie shell and bake in a preheated 350-degree oven for 1 hour. Turn off the oven and let the cheesecake sit in the oven with the door open for 15 minutes. Remove and let cool. Remove sides of pan before serving.

HOW TO FROST A LAYER CAKE

Wait until the cake layers are thoroughly cooled and feel firm to the touch. Brush all crumbs from the surface of the cake. If a layer is uneven, it may be necessary to trim a piece from the top to make it flat. If it is necessary to cut a cake layer into thinner layers, mark the cut at intervals with toothpicks. Use a sharp or serrated-edge knife longer than the diameter of the cake, to make sure you are cutting clear across the layer. Follow the toothpicks, cutting with a sawing motion.

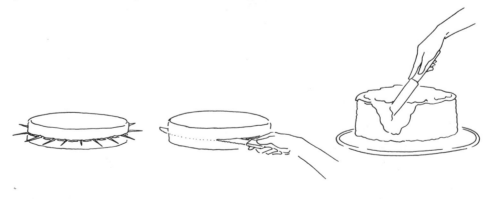

To begin frosting a cake, put an outspread hand under the layer to support it when transferring it to a platter. For a very large layer, use two spatulas to lift the layer onto a platter. (Put four small squares of wax paper on the platter first. After the cake is frosted these pieces can be pulled away, leaving a clean platter.) Put one layer, top down, on the platter. Spread filling or frosting and cover with the other layer, top up.

Cover the entire cake with a thin layer of frosting, starting with sides and ending with top, and refrigerate or freeze for 10 minutes. (This thin layer holds crumbs in place and keeps them from being pulled off and mixed into the frosting.) Then frost the cake a second time, using a flat knife or spatula. Start at the top, making casual and fluffy swirls then frost the sides. Run the frosting up to the top edge of the cake.

◆

UNCOOKED FUDGE FROSTING
Makes enough for the top and sides of a 9-inch tube cake

This icing is quick and requires no cooking.

*2 cups sifted confectioners'
    sugar
¼ teaspoon salt
6 egg yolks
6 tablespoons milk
6 tablespoons vegetable
    shortening*

*4 squares (4 ounces)
    unsweetened chocolate,
    melted in a double boiler
    over hot water
2 teaspoons vanilla extract*

Combine all ingredients in a bowl. Set bowl in ice water and beat with an electric beater until frosting is the right spreading consistency.

◆

RUM BUTTER FROSTING
Makes enough for the top and sides of a 9-inch two-layer cake

*½ cup (1 stick) butter,
    softened
1 package (1 pound) confec-
    tioners' sugar, sifted*

*1 egg, well beaten
1 teaspoon vanilla extract
2 tablespoons dark rum*

Cream butter until soft and fluffy. Gradually beat in some of the sugar. Beat in egg, vanilla, and rum. Add remaining sugar gradually until frosting is a good spreading consistency. Spread on cake and refrigerate to harden frosting (this makes it easier to cut neat thin slices).

◆
SEVEN-MINUTE FROSTING
Makes enough for the top and sides of an 8- or 9-inch two-layer cake

This is a glamorous, delicious, and reliable frosting for cakes. There are many variations of this icing; a few suggestions follow. It must be prepared just before the cake is frosted.

2 egg whites	¼ teaspoon cream of tartar
1½ cups sugar	1½ teaspoon vanilla extract
½ cup water	

Put egg whites, sugar, water, and cream of tartar in the top of a double boiler over boiling water. Beat with an electric beater at high speed until mixture is thick and creamy, about 8 minutes. Remove from heat and continue beating until very smooth and glossy. Add vanilla and beat again to blend. Spread on cake.

• VARIATIONS •
Seven-Minute Sea Foam. Substitute 1½ cups firmly packed brown sugar for the white sugar.

Seven-Minute Lemon. Substitute 3 tablespoons water, 2 tablespoons lemon juice, and ¼ teaspoon grated lemon rind for the ½ cup water.

Seven-Minute Peppermint. Just before spreading Seven-Minute Frosting, add a few drops of peppermint extract or 1 crushed stick peppermint candy.

Seven-Minute Nut. Spread Seven-Minute Frosting over cake and sprinkle with ½ cup chopped nuts (pecans, walnuts, etc.).

Seven-Minute Orange Coconut. Spread Seven-Minute Frosting over cake and sprinkle with 1 cup fresh coconut mixed with 1 teaspoon grated orange rind. Rub the coconut first with the orange rind to work the flavor of the rind into the coconut.

◆
BASIC
BUTTERCREAM
Makes enough for top and sides of 8- or 9-inch cake

This recipe can be doubled or tripled.

5 egg yolks	16 tablespoons (2 sticks)
⅔ cup sugar	butter, softened
3 tablespoons water	

Put the egg yolks in a bowl and with a handheld electric beater beat a low speed. In a saucepan boil the sugar and water until sugar reaches the softball stage, 236 degrees on a candy thermometer. Immediately pour the boiling syrup into the yolks in a thin stream of droplets, simultaneously beating at medium speed. When syrup is completely incorporated, turn beater to high speed and beat for about 10 minutes, until mixture has the consistency of marshmallow sauce and is cool. Beat in the butter, 1 tablespoon at a time. Add desired flavor (see following variations). Beat until smooth and thick. If the buttercream looks lumpy and curdled, add a little more softened butter. Chill until firm and spreadable.

• VARIATIONS •

Chocolate Buttercream. Add 2 ounces melted semisweet chocolate to basic recipe.

Lemon Buttercream. Add grated rind of 2 lemons and 2 tablespoons fresh lemon juice to basic recipe.

Mocha Buttercream. Add 3 tablespoons strong coffee to basic recipe.

Liqueured Buttercream. Add 2 to 3 tablespoons any liqueur to basic recipe.

◆

ORANGE OR LEMON BUTTER GLAZE

Makes ¾ cup, enough for the top of a 10-inch tube cake

2 tablespoons frozen orange or lemon juice concentrate	2½ cups sifted confectioners' sugar
1 tablespoon heavy cream	½ teaspoon grated orange or lemon rind
1 tablespoon butter	

Mix orange juice, cream, and butter in a saucepan. Heat until butter melts. Stir in sugar and rind. If desired, thin with a little orange juice. Spoon over cake.

◆

COCONUT FILLING

Makes enough filling to go between two 9-inch layers

2 egg whites, at room temperature	1½ cups fresh grated coconut (see recipe for Southern Fresh Coconut Cake)
¼ cup confectioners' sugar	

Beat egg whites with an electric beater at high speed until they hold soft peaks. Gradually beat in confectioners' sugar, 1 tablespoon at a time. Beat until stiff and glossy. Fold in coconut and spread between layers.

CAKE DECORATING

Decorating cakes is not only great fun, it brings out all your creativity. Decorations always add a glamorous touch to any cake, no matter how simple. You will need a plastic-lined pastry bag with a variety of tips to make decorations. Some of the most

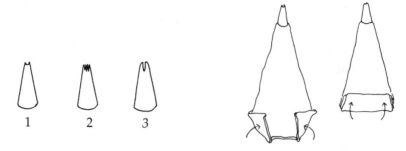

1   2   3

useful tips are (1) writing tip—used for writing names and letters, for stems of flowers; (2) star tip—used for making rosettes, borders, and fancy letters; and (3) leaf tip—used for borders and leaves.

Large star tips can be used for piping mashed potatoes, whipped cream, sweet potatoes, choux paste, etc. Make sure the frosting to be pressed through the tip is smooth and soft, yet stiff enough to hold its shape. Fill the pastry bag half full. Turn down the corners of the top and then fold the top down. Keep folding the top of the bag with the right hand and pressing out frosting. Guide the tip with the left hand. Hold the tip about ½ inch above the surface of the cake. Allow the frosting to flow onto the cake; keep the tip moving smoothly and evenly. Practice makes perfect.

Pastry, Pies, and Tarts

Here are a few basic rules that should help all cooks make perfect pastry:
1. Always cut in shortening with a pastry blender or with two knives drawn through the pastry mixture at right angles to each other.
2. Get a feeling for when the pastry is damp enough to handle. Too damp won't work; neither will too dry. "Just right" comes from experience. Add liquid cautiously, almost drop by drop, until you have learned exactly how much to add.
3. Try not to roll or reknead dough too much.
4. Roll out pie dough from the center of the piece of dough to the outside edge, in order to maintain an even thickness.
5. If you have to mend a tear in the dough or piece out a scanty crust, moisten dough slightly along both edges to be joined and pinch them together lightly.

Use these methods of mixing, shaping, and rolling also when using packaged piecrust mix.

◆

PIECRUST
Makes two 8- or 9-inch pie shells or eight 4-inch tart shells

2 cups sifted all-purpose flour
½ teaspoon salt

⅔ cup vegetable shortening
5 to 6 tablespoons cold water

In a large bowl, mix flour with salt. Cut in shortening until consistency of very small peas. Sprinkle water over top of crumbs. (A water-sprinkler stopper on a bottle is an excellent device for sprinkling the water.) It is difficult to specify a definite amount of water, since flours vary in moisture content. Stir with a fork and push the moistened particles to one side. Sprinkle the surface of dry flour again with water and mix again until some particles are moistened. Continue until all flour is moistened. Gather moistened particles together in the bowl with your hands.

Turn out on a lightly floured board. Knead on the board until dough is smooth. To knead, fold dough over. Press together firmly with heel of hand. Turn and fold again. Repeat three steps several times. At this point the dough should be soft and elastic. Do not overhandle, as heat melts the fat and makes the piecrust less flaky. Chill for 30 minutes.

Shape the dough into a small round flat cake. Roll out on a lightly floured pastry canvas. (A pastry canvas keeps dough from sticking and lessens the need to add flour, which would toughen the piecrust.) Roll dough evenly from the center out, lifting the rolling pin as you reach the edge, to keep the dough an even thickness throughout. Roll out dough to a circle 2 inches larger than the diameter of the pie pan. To lift dough into ungreased pan, roll around rolling pin and unroll in pan. Do not stretch dough into pie pan (this causes shrinkage), but ease it in.

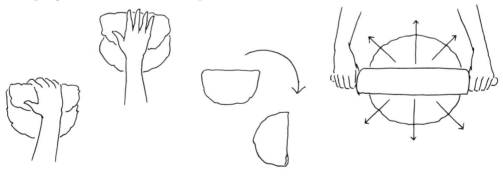

For a one-crust pie shell, which is baked and then filled, line the pan with dough. Fold over edge of dough and stand up edge. Flute by pinching dough between fingers, or snip with scissors for a frilly edge. Prick sides and bottom of pie shell with a fork to allow air to escape and keep crust flat while it is baking. Chill for 30 minutes. Bake in a preheated 450-degree oven for 10 to 15 minutes, or until browned. Cool thoroughly on a rack and then fill.

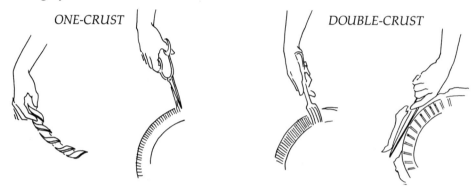

ONE-CRUST   *DOUBLE-CRUST*

For a double-crust pie, roll out the bottom crust and fit it into the pan. Pour in the filling. Roll out the top crust into a round 1 inch larger than the diameter of the top of the pie. Roll dough over rolling pin and unroll over filling. Moisten edge of bottom crust with water for a tight seal. Press edges of pastry together with the tines of a fork. Trim off excess dough with a sharp knife and prick top with a fork to allow steam to escape. Bake as directed in recipe.

For a lattice-top pie, roll out bottom crust and fit into pan. Pour in filling. Roll out remaining piecrust into a round 1 inch larger than the diameter of the top of the pie. With a pastry jagger or sharp knife, cut piecrust into ½-inch strips. Lay strips on pie, 1 inch apart, and lay other strips over pie in a diamond or square pattern. These strips of piecrust can also be woven while on the pie—lift strips to weave other strips over and under. Trim lattice piecrust even with bottom crust. Fold bottom piecrust over strips and press or flute edges. Bake as directed in recipe.

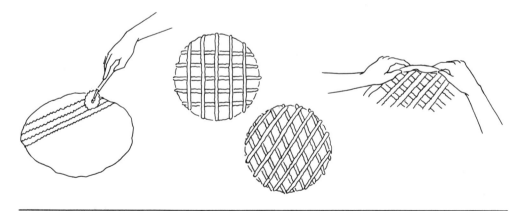

· PIECRUST VARIATIONS ·

Add ¼ cup finely chopped nuts to the flour before mixing pastry.

Add ½ cup finely grated sharp Cheddar cheese to the flour before mixing pastry.

Add 1 teaspoon grated orange rind to the flour before mixing pastry. Use orange juice instead of water.

Add 1 teaspoon ground cinnamon to the flour before mixing.

TART SHELLS
Makes 8

Make piecrust (as in preceding basic recipe) and roll out into an oblong 10 × 20 inches and cut into eight 5-inch rounds. Fit rounds into ungreased tart pans or over the backs of custard cups. Edges can be fluted or pressed with a fork if desired. Prick with a fork on sides and bottom. Bake in a preheated 450-degree oven for 10 to 20 minutes, or until golden brown. Cool in pans, then loosen, remove, and fill as desired.

· VARIATION ·

Petal Tart Shells (makes 8). Roll out piecrust and for each ungreased custard cup or muffin pan cut six 2¼-inch circles of piecrust with a cookie cutter. Put one circle at bottom of cup and five circles overlapping around the edge of cup. Moisten edges that touch with water, so they will stick together after they are baked. Prick and bake as for tart shells. Let cool in cups. Loosen, remove, and fill.

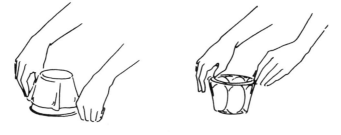

PUFF PASTRY
SHELLS
Makes 12 3-inch patty shells

Make puff pastry only on a cool day—the butter softens in hot, humid weather. The dough and butter should have the same consistency. Puff pastry is made of many layers of dough and butter. During baking, the butter melts and crisps dough layers and creates steam, causing the dough to puff.

4¼ cups (1 pound) sifted all-
purpose flour
1 pound (4 sticks) cold butter
1 teaspoon salt

1 cup ice water
2 tablespoons lemon juice
Beaten egg

Pour flour into a bowl. Add 2 sticks butter and salt and cut in with a pastry blender in a chopping motion until particles are the size of small peas. Add ice water and lemon juice and stir with a fork to moisten flour. Turn dough out on a lightly floured board or pastry cloth and knead (see recipe for piecrust) until smooth and elastic, moistening hands with water to keep dough moist. Chill for 30 minutes.

Cut remaining butter into ¼-inch pats. Chill. Roll out dough on a lightly floured surface into a 12 × 18-inch oblong. Place butter pats over a 12 × 12-inch square of dough, pressing butter into dough. Work quickly to keep butter cold and firm. Fold uncovered dough over butter. Fold butter-covered dough over. Fold into thirds again, making an oblong 4 × 6 inches. Roll out to an oblong 12 × 18 inches. Fold into thirds and into thirds again. Chill for 30 minutes.

Roll to a 12 × 18-inch rectangle, fold into thirds and again into thirds, and chill for 30 minutes.

Repeat this three more times. After the last folding, chill pastry for 2 hours.

Roll out half of the puff pastry ⅛ inch thick. Cut out twelve 3-inch rounds. Put rounds on a cookie sheet. Brush with beaten egg. Make sure egg does not drip down the sides, as this interferes with the rising. Top with a second round that has a 2-inch round cut out of the center. Brush top with egg. Press a 2-inch cookie cutter partway into third round, not all the way through. Put this on top of the ring and brush top with egg. Chill for 30 minutes.

Bake in a preheated 450-degree oven for 10 minutes, then reduce heat to 350 degrees and bake 20 minutes longer, or until golden brown. With a sharp knife, remove the 2-inch pastry round on top. Replace shells in oven for 5 minutes to dry completely. Fill patty shells with a creamed food, topping each serving with the pastry round removed from patty shell.

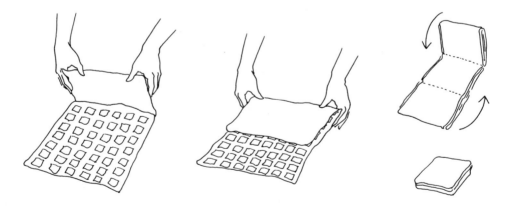

◆
GRAHAM CRACKER CRUST
Makes one 9-inch pie shell

This is a great shortcut to crust making and is easy and tasty.

> 1½ cups graham cracker
> crumbs (approximately 10
> to 12 crackers)

> 6 tablespoons butter, melted
> ¼ cup confectioners' sugar

Put a few graham crackers at a time between two sheets of waxed paper and roll over them with a rolling pin to crumble. Put crumbs in a mixing bowl and repeat until all crackers are reduced to crumbs. Stir in butter and sugar. Pat mixture with the palm of your hand or with the back of a spoon against sides and bottom of a pie pan to form a shell. The crust can be used baked or unbaked. If unbaked, refrigerate for an hour or more to firm it up. If you need to use it immediately, firm it up by baking in a preheated 375-degree oven for 15 minutes. Let cool slightly before filling.

◆
LEMON OR LIME
MERINGUE PIE
Serves 6 to 8—makes one 9-inch pie

This must be prepared ahead of time and allowed to stand until filling sets.

> ½ cup cornstarch
> 2 cups sugar
> ¼ teaspoon salt
> 4 egg yolks
> ½ cup fresh lemon or lime
> juice
> 1½ cups water

> 1 teaspoon grated lemon or
> lime rind
> 1 9-inch pie shell, baked and
> cooled (see Index)
> 4 egg whites, at room
> temperature
> ¼ teaspoon cream of tartar

In a saucepan, mix cornstarch, 1½ cups sugar, and salt. Stir in egg yolks and lemon juice. Gradually stir in water. Cook over low heat, stirring constantly, until mixture bubbles and thickens. Remove from heat and stir in grated rind. Let cool. Pour into baked pie shell. Beat egg whites with cream of tartar until stiff. Gradually beat in remaining ½ cup sugar, 1 tablespoon at a time, beating until stiff and glossy. Feel meringue between fingers to make sure sugar grains are dissolved. Spread meringue over top of pie, making sure meringue is touching pastry all around pie (to keep it from shrinking during baking). Bake in a preheated 325-degree oven for 15 minutes, or until lightly browned. Let cool at room temperature for several hours before cutting.

◆

BLUEBERRY PIE
Serves 6 to 8—makes one 9-inch pie

6 cups fresh blueberries
¼ cup cornstarch
2 tablespoons water
1½ to 2 cups sugar (depending on sweetness of berries)
1 tablespoon fresh lemon juice

Pastry for a double-crust 9-inch pie (see Index)
3 tablespoons butter
1 egg, beaten and mixed with 1 tablespoon water

Wash berries in a sieve or colander under cold running water and pick over, removing stems and any blemished berries. Dry berries on paper towels. In a mixing bowl, dissolve cornstarch in water. Add berries, sugar, and lemon juice and toss lightly to coat berries. Roll out bottom piecrust, fit into pie pan, and spread berries evenly over the bottom. Dot with small pieces of butter. Cover filling with top crust, press edges of pie together according to basic crust directions, and brush top with beaten egg mixture. Prick the top crust with a fork in several places to allow steam to escape. Bake in a preheated 450-degree oven for 15 minutes; then reduce heat to 350 degrees and bake for 25 to 30 minutes, or until golden brown. Serve slightly warm or at room temperature.

• VARIATION •

Blackberry Pie. Substitute blackberries for blueberries.

◆

CHOCOLATE CREAM PIE
Serves 6 to 8—makes one 9-inch pie

2 ounces semisweet chocolate
½ cup sugar
3 tablespoons cornstarch
¼ cup cold milk
1½ cups hot milk
½ cup heavy cream
3 egg yolks, lightly beaten

1 teaspoon vanilla extract or 1 tablespoon rum
Pastry for one 9-inch pie shell, baked and cooled (see Index for basic piecrust or graham cracker crust)
Garnish: ½ cup heavy cream, whipped

In the top of a double boiler over simmering water, melt the chocolate; do not let it burn. Remove from heat and set aside. In a heavy-bottomed saucepan mix sugar with the cornstarch. Slowly stir in cold milk. Add hot milk gradually and put mixture over moderate heat, stirring constantly. Cook until mixture thickens. Blend in the melted chocolate, cream, and egg yolks. Cook for about 2 minutes over moderate heat, stirring vigorously. Remove from heat. Beat in vanilla and pour into baked pie shell. When filling has cooled, garnish with whipped cream and serve immediately.

◆

APPLE PIE

Serves 6 to 8—makes one 9-inch pie

8 tart apples, peeled, cored,
  and cut into ½-inch slices
2 tablespoons fresh lemon juice
1 cup sugar
¼ teaspoon nutmeg

1 tablespoon vanilla extract
Pastry for a double-crust
  9-inch pie (see Index)
4 tablespoons butter
1 egg, beaten and mixed with
  1 tablespoon water

Mix apples, lemon juice, sugar, nutmeg, and vanilla together in a bowl. Roll out bottom piecrust, fit into pie pan, and fill with the apple filling. Dot apple with the butter, cut into small bits. Roll out remaining piecrust to a round 1 inch larger than the diameter of the top of the pie. Transfer top crust to cover filling, press edges together according to directions, and brush top with beaten egg mixture. Prick the top crust with a fork in several places to allow steam to escape. Bake in a preheated 425-degree oven for 45 minutes, or until crust is golden brown. Serve slightly warm.

• VARIATION •

Peach Pie. Substitute peaches for apples. Use less sugar if the peaches are sweet.

◆

CHERRY ALMOND LATTICE-TOP PIE

Serves 6 to 8—makes one 9-inch pie

Pastry for a double-crust
  9-inch pie (see Index)
2 cans (1 pound each) pitted
  tart cherries, drained
⅓ cup syrup drained from
  cherries
3 tablespoons quick-cooking
  tapioca

¼ teaspoon almond extract
½ cup slivered blanched
  almonds
1 cup sugar
2 tablespoons butter or
  margarine

Roll out half the pie dough and use to line the bottom and sides of a 9-inch pie pan. Combine remaining ingredients except butter and pour into pie pan. Cut butter into pieces and put on top of pie filling. Cover pie with lattice top (see basic piecrust) and bake in a preheated 425-degree oven for 40 to 45 minutes, or until crust is golden brown.

187

PECAN PIE
Serves 6 to 8—makes one 9-inch pie

Pastry for one 9-inch piecrust
  (see Index)
3 eggs, well beaten
¾ cup sugar
⅛ teaspoon salt

1¼ cups corn syrup
2 tablespoons melted butter
  or margarine
1 teaspoon vanilla extract
¾ cup shelled pecan halves

Roll out piecrust and line the bottom and sides of a 9-inch pie pan, fluting the edge. Mix eggs with sugar, salt, corn syrup, melted butter, and vanilla. Put pecans in pie shell and pour egg mixture over. Bake in a preheated 325-degree oven for 45 to 50 minutes, or until filling is set.

Other Desserts

In addition to cakes and pies, dessert can mean puddings, ice cream, mousses, sherbets, meringues, soufflés, crêpes, and roulades or rolls.

CRÈME BRÛLÉE
Serves 6

This is a famous and elegant French custard with a most unusual burned-sugar flavor. It is always a hit with guests. This recipe can be doubled.

7 egg yolks
1 tablespoon cornstarch
4 tablespoons white sugar

3 cups heavy cream
2 teaspoons vanilla extract
1 cup light brown sugar

Put egg yolks in a mixing bowl and beat in cornstarch and white sugar until mixture appears thick and pale-colored. In a large heavy-bottomed saucepan heat cream to a simmer. Gradually pour hot cream into the egg yolk mixture, beating constantly. Return cream-and-egg mixture to the saucepan and cook over moderate heat, stirring constantly and rapidly. When bubbles appear around edge of the mixture it will start to increase in volume and rise up in the pan. Do not let it boil. Stir as hard as you can. Immediately take off the heat and continue to stir vigorously so the cream will cool and stop cooking. If the mixture is not as thick as a pudding, repeat cooking and stirring process. Once it is cooled off, add vanilla and pour into a heat-proof serving bowl. Chill for several hours, or overnight if possible.

To serve, sprinkle brown sugar thickly and evenly over top of custard. Run under the broiler, keeping door open, and broil just until sugar forms a crust and begins to carmelize, or melt. Do not let sugar burn. This should take only 2 or 3 minutes. Serve immediately, or chill custard again and serve later.

ZABAGLIONE
Serves 6

This wonderful Italian dessert is light and ever so frothy, a dramatic ending to any meal.

8 tablespoons sugar
8 egg yolks

½ cup sherry, Madeira, or
other sweet wine

In a mixing bowl beat sugar and egg yolks together until very light. Transfer mixture to the top of a double boiler over simmering water. Make sure the simmering water in the bottom section does not touch the top. This is imperative. With a whisk, beat the sugar-and-egg mixture until foamy. Gradually add the wine, and continue to beat until the custard doubles or triples in bulk and starts to thicken. Immediately remove from the heat. Serve at once in large wine or sherbet glasses.

BROWN BETTY
Serves 4

Apple lovers have enjoyed this famous pudding for generations.

1½ cups graham cracker
    crumbs or stale white
    bread crumbs
2½ cups peeled and sliced
    apples
¾ cup brown sugar
¼ teaspoon nutmeg

¼ teaspoon ground cloves
1 teaspoon cinnamon
1 teaspoon grated lemon rind
2 tablespoons lemon juice
Whipped cream or vanilla ice
    cream

Line the bottom of a lightly buttered square oven-proof baking dish with a third of the crumbs. Put half the apples in the baking dish. In a small mixing bowl mix together the sugar, spices, and lemon rind. Sprinkle the layer of apples with this sugar mixture. Then sprinkle with 1 tablespoon lemon juice. Sprinkle 2 tablespoons water over the mixture and add another crumb layer, using another third of the crumbs. Add remaining apples to make another layer and sprinkle as before with the sugar mixture, lemon juice, and water. Top with the last third of the crumbs. Cover dish and bake in a preheated 350-degree oven for about 40 minutes, or until apples are tender. Remove the cover and increase the oven temperature to 400 degrees. Leave the pudding in another 15 minutes to brown. Serve warm with whipped cream or vanilla ice cream.

◆

VANILLA BAVARIAN CREAM
Serves 4

This is another hard-to-resist dessert. It can be made in a number of flavors.

2 tablespoons water
1 envelope gelatin
½ cup sugar
4 egg yolks

1 cup hot milk
1 teaspoon vanilla extract
1 cup heavy cream, whipped

Put water in a small dish, sprinkle gelatin over it, and let dissolve. In a heavy-bottomed saucepan beat sugar with egg yolks until smooth and creamy. Stir in hot milk, a little at a time. Put pan over moderate heat and cook, stirring constantly, until mixture becomes smooth and thick enough to coat a spoon. Make sure mixture does not boil. Remove from heat, stir in the gelatin and vanilla, and stir until gelatin is completely dissolved. Let cream cool, stirring occasionally so that a crust does not form on the top. When thick and cool but not set, fold in the whipped cream and pour into a quart mold or dish. Chill until firm. When ready to serve, unmold by running a knife around the edge and cover mold with a dish towel rinsed in hot water, to warm sides of mold and ease out the cream. Invert onto a serving plate.

• VARIATIONS •
Coffee Bavarian Cream. For vanilla substitute 1 teaspoon instant coffee dissolved in 3 tablespoons hot water.

Chocolate Bavarian Cream. For vanilla substitute 2 ounces unsweetened chocolate, melted.

Liqueur Bavarian Cream. For vanilla substitute ¼ cup of your favorite liqueur.

◆

BLACKBERRY COBBLER
Serves 4

Some blackberry lovers sneak seconds of this summer treat.

1 pint blackberries
4 tablespoons sugar
1 cup all-purpose flour
2 teaspoons baking powder
1 cup sugar
2 eggs

¾ cup milk
1 teaspoon vanilla extract
1 teaspoon grated lemon rind
Topping: Whipped cream
    sweetened with confec-
    tioners' sugar

Wash and dry berries. Put berries in a 2-quart oven-proof dish and sprinkle with 4 tablespoons sugar. Sift together flour and baking powder in a mixing bowl. Add 1 cup sugar, eggs, milk, vanilla, and lemon rind. Beat with a wooden spoon until combined. Pour over berries and bake in a preheated 350-degree oven for 1 hour. Remove from oven and let rest for 10 minutes. Top servings with sweetened whipped cream.

• VARIATION •

Blueberry Cobbler. Substitute blueberries for blackberries.

Ice Cream

Homemade ice cream is an inspired and beautiful dessert. The first time the making seems to take forever and you wonder why on earth you did not go to the store and buy some. But after the second or third batch it is easy and relatively effortless. Homemade ice cream, brimming with fresh, ripe, pure fruit flavor nestled in sweet cream and eggs, richness begetting richness, is a sensual delight of incomparable ecstasy. This is how to go about it with an electric ice cream maker:

1. Read the manufacturer's directions carefully.
2. Prepare the ice cream mixture and pour it into the can. Do not fill the can more than *two thirds* full or the top part will not freeze.
3. Crush the ice finely. Finely crushed ice gives a smooth, creamy texture to the ice cream.
4. Add three layers of crushed ice, each with a single, thin layer of coarse salt. Too much salt causes the ice to freeze in blocks and alters the texture of the ice cream. The ice and salt should come 2 inches above the level of the top of the ice cream in the can. You will need at least one large bag of ice and 1 cup coarse salt.

◆

VANILLA ICE CREAM
Makes 1½ quarts

4 cups light cream, or 2 cups milk and 2 cups heavy cream	¾ cup sugar
	¼ teaspoon salt
	1 tablespoon vanilla extract
4 egg yolks	

In a large saucepan heat 2 cups of the cream to a simmer. In the meantime, in a small bowl stir together the egg yolks, sugar, and salt. Pour the simmering milk into the egg yolk mixture and return to the saucepan. Stir continuously over low heat until the custard has thickened slightly. Do not let it boil. Remove from the heat and stir in the remaining cream. Add the vanilla extract. Let cool and pour into the freezer can.

This quantity of ice creams fits into a standard ice cream maker. To adapt it for the small machine that fits right in the freezer, cut the recipe in half.

191

◆
CHOCOLATE ICE CREAM
Makes 1½ quarts

4 egg yolks
½ cup sugar
6 ounces sweet or semisweet
   chocolate

3½ cups light cream, or 1½
cups milk and 2 cups
heavy cream

Beat the egg yolks in an electric mixer until thick and light in color. Put the sugar in a small heavy saucepan. Add ¼ cup water and stir over low heat until the sugar has dissolved. Boil the syrup until it reaches 218 degrees on a candy thermometer. The syrup will be extremely hot, so be very careful. Continue beating the egg yolks and add the boiling syrup *very* slowly in a continuous fine stream of drops. Continue beating at high speed. The eggs and syrup will triple in quantity. Meanwhile, put the chocolate in a small saucepan. Add ¼ cup water and stir over low heat until the chocolate has just melted. Stir the chocolate and the cream into the egg yolk mixture. Pour into the freezer can.

• VARIATIONS •
Mocha Ice Cream. Follow recipe for chocolate ice cream but substitute 1 cup triple-strength coffee (3 teaspoons instant coffee to 1 cup boiling water) for 1 cup cream. Add 2 tablespoons coffee liqueur, if you wish.

Chocolate Chip Ice Cream. Follow recipe for vanilla ice cream. Break 6 ounces semi-sweet or sweet chocolate into small pieces and put on a plate suspended over a pan of simmering water. Cover with another plate. Maintain over low heat until the chocolate has melted. Line a cookie sheet with waxed paper and spread the chocolate over the paper in a thin layer, using a metal spatula. Put in the freezer for 10 minutes, until the chocolate is cold and brittle. Crumple the paper and the chocolate will break into tiny pieces. Stir the chocolate chips into the completed vanilla ice cream.

Strawberry, Raspberry, Blackberry, or Other Berry Ice Cream. Follow the recipe for vanilla ice cream, using 2 cups cream only. Purée 2 cups berries in the blender and force the purée through a strainer to remove the seeds. Replace the remaining 2 cups cream in the recipe with the fruit purée. Let cool and pour into the freezer can.

Butter Pecan Ice Cream. Follow the recipe for vanilla ice cream. Add 1 cup finely chopped pecans, 4 tablespoons melted butter, and ½ cup maple syrup. Chop the nuts finely, or they may become wedged between the dasher and the sides of the freezer can and prevent the dasher from turning.

Pistachio Ice Cream. Follow the recipe for vanilla ice cream. Add 1 cup ground pistachio nuts, 1 teaspoon almond extract, and 4 drops green food coloring.

• OTHER ICE CREAM IDEAS •
Quick Chocolate Ice Cream Pie (serves 6 to 8). Use chocolate wafers to line the sides and bottom of a 9-inch pie plate. Fill with softened ice cream. Spread with sweetened whipped cream and top with crushed peppermints. Freeze until ready to serve. Thaw thirty minutes before serving.

Chocolate Cups with Ice Cream. Melt semisweet chocolate over hot water. Spread melted chocolate thickly into individual crinkly paper cupcake liners. Put liners in muffin pans. Chill until chocolate hardens. Remove cupcake liners carefully. Fill cups with scoops of ice cream.

 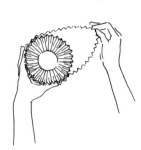

Quick Biscuit Tortoni (serves 8). Soften 1 quart vanilla ice cream and stir in ½ cup chopped candied fruits, ½ cup seedless raisins, ⅓ cup macaroon crumbs, and 1 tablespoon rum extract. Spoon into serving dishes and sprinkle tops with macaroon crumbs. Freeze until ready to serve.

Baked Alaska (serves 8 to 10). Unwrap a 1-quart block of hard ice cream. Put ice cream on a sponge or chocolate cake layer (or brownies before they are cut) and put in freezer. Beat 5 egg whites with ¼ teaspoon cream of tartar until stiff. Gradually beat in ⅔ cup sugar, 1 tablespoon at a time, until stiff and glossy. Put cake and ice cream on a wooden board or cookie sheet. Completely cover cake and ice cream with meringue. Leave no holes, or heat will melt ice cream. Bake in a preheated 450-degree oven for 5 to 6 minutes, or until meringue is lightly browned. Serve at once.

◆

CHERRIES JUBILEE
Serves 8

This famous dessert always brings a round of applause for the chef. It should be prepared just before serving time.

2 pounds red Bing cherries	*1 cup brandy*
1 cup sugar	*1 quart vanilla ice cream*
2 cups orange juice	

Wash cherries and remove stems. Remove pits, using a cherry pitter or opened paper clip, and put cherries in a saucepan. Add sugar and orange juice, bring to a boil, and simmer for 5 minutes. Pour mixture into a chafing dish and keep warm. Add brandy and warm for a few minutes. Set aflame with a lighted match. Spoon flaming cherries over scoops of vanilla ice cream.

◆

STRAWBERRY SORBET
Serves 6

Sorbet or sherbet is easy to make in the freezer. Other berries can be substituted for the strawberries.

1 cup water	2 tablespoons lemon juice
¾ cup sugar	6 tablespoons Cointreau
1 quart strawberries	

Put the water and sugar in a small saucepan. Bring slowly to a boil and boil gently for 5 minutes. Remove from the heat. Purée the strawberries in a blender and strain to remove the seeds. Add the strawberry purée and lemon juice to the syrup. Cool and put in the ice cream maker or pour into two 9-inch layer cake pans. Put in the freezer. Stir sorbet in the cake pan vigorously every hour until it is thick. Transfer to individual parfait dishes. Insert a chopstick or similar implement in the center of the sorbet and fill the hole with Cointreau or other fruit-flavored liqueur.

◆

CHOCOLATE MOUSSE
Serves 6 to 8

This sinfully rich dessert can be made several days ahead of a party and sit in the freezer.

10 ounces semisweet chocolate, broken into bits	4 egg whites
	Pinch of salt
4 egg yolks	Garnish: ⅔ cup heavy cream,
12 tablespoons (1½ sticks) butter, softened	whipped with ½ teaspoon vanilla extract and 2 table-
⅔ cup sugar	spoons confectioners' sugar

In a heavy-bottomed saucepan, melt the chocolate with ¼ cup water over low heat. Remove from heat and beat in egg yolks, one at a time. Return pan to low heat and warm mixture until it is slightly thickened. Remove from heat and beat in butter, tablespoon by tablespoon, until smooth. Set aside. In a small saucepan boil the sugar and ¼ cup water for a few minutes, until it forms a thread; the syrup should run in a slightly sticky stream from the end of a spoon. While the sugar mixture is cooking, put the egg whites and salt in a mixing bowl and beat until they form soft peaks. Then take the hot syrup and pour it into the egg whites in a steady stream, beating at high speed. Beat whites until shiny, firm, and cool. You can aid the cooling process by setting the bowl over cracked ice. When the whites are ready, gently fold in the lukewarm chocolate mixture. Turn mixture into a lightly greased 2-quart mold. Chill in freezer for 4 to 5 hours, at the least. To serve, run a knife around edge of mold and invert on serving dish. Garnish with flavored whipped cream.

◆

MERINGUES
Makes 6 shells

Shells can be prepared ahead of time and stored in an airtight container, but they must be filled just before serving time.

2 egg whites, at room	*⅛ teaspoon cream of tartar*
temperature	*½ cup granulated sugar*

In a large bowl beat egg whites and cream of tartar to stiff peaks. Gradually beat in sugar, one tablespoon at a time, until mixture is stiff and glossy. Feel a bit of the meringue between the fingers to make sure all the sugar has dissolved. (This will keep meringue shells from becoming sticky while standing.) Line a cookie sheet with foil and spoon 6 mounds of meringue onto foil. With the back of a spoon, hollow out center. Bake in a preheated 250-degree oven for 1 hour and 20 minutes, or until shells feel dry and tops are cream-colored. Remove from foil and let cool on a rack.

• FILLINGS •
Orange Melba. Fill with mandarin orange slices and a small scoop of ice cream. Press frozen or fresh sweetened raspberries through a sieve and spoon over ice cream.

Peaches and Cream. Fill with sweetened fresh sliced peaches and top with a dab of sweetened whipped cream.

Ice Cream and Chocolate Sauce. Fill with a scoop of ice cream topped with Hot Chocolate Sauce (see Index).

Ice Cream and Butterscotch Sauce. When shells cool, fill with a scoop of ice cream topped with hot Butterscotch Sauce (see Index).

◆

CREAM PUFFS OR CHOUX PASTE
Makes 10 large puffs or 14 éclairs

½ cup (1 stick) butter or	*1 cup sifted all-purpose flour*
margarine	*¼ teaspoon salt*
1 cup boiling water	*4 eggs*

Add butter to boiling water in a sauce pan. Stir with a wooden spoon until butter melts. Add flour and salt all at once and continue cooking while stirring over high heat until mixture forms a ball. Let cool off heat for 5 minutes. Beat in eggs, one at a time, making sure dough is smooth and well blended before adding next egg. Dough will be shiny and hold its shape. Drop dough by spoonfuls onto an ungreased cookie sheet, about 3 inches apart. To make éclairs, press dough through a pastry tube, making dough ¾ inch wide and 4 inches long. Bake in a preheated 450-degree oven for 15 minutes; lower heat to 325 degrees and bake an additional 25 minutes. Remove puffs from oven and prick with a fork to allow steam to escape. Replace in oven, turn off heat, and let dry in oven for 20 minutes. Cool thoroughly before filling. Split and fill puffs or éclairs with ice cream (see Index). Top with Hot Chocolate Sauce (see Index).

◆

LEMON SOUFFLÉ
Serves 4

This is a basic dessert soufflé recipe to which lemon flavoring has been added. There are a host of different delicious soufflé flavors; the variations that follow offer some of the tantalizing tastes available. But before undertaking any dessert soufflé, see the Index for Cheese Soufflé and read how to test for doneness and how to tie a collar around the soufflé dish before baking.

2 tablespoons butter
3 tablespoons all-purpose
    flour
¾ cup hot milk
¼ cup sugar
4 egg yolks

Grated rind of 3 lemons
5 tablespoons fresh lemon
    juice
7 egg whites
Confectioners' sugar
½ cup whipped cream

In a large saucepan melt butter and stir in flour, stirring until mixture gently bubbles. Remove from heat and add hot milk, stirring rapidly with a whisk or wooden spoon until smooth and blended. Add sugar and return mixture to heat. Cook over moderate heat, stirring all the while, until thick and smooth. Remove from heat and beat for 1 or 2 minutes, until slightly cooled. One at a time, beat in the egg yolks. Add the lemon rind and juice. Beat egg whites until they form stiff peaks but are not dry. Fold about one fourth of the beaten egg whites into the mixture. Gently fold the remaining whites into the mixture. Butter a 1-quart soufflé dish and sprinkle inside with a little white sugar. Transfer the soufflé to the dish and set in a preheated 400-degree oven. Immediately reduce oven to 375 degrees and bake for 30 to 35 minutes, or until set. When soufflé is done, sprinkle with confectioners' sugar and serve immediately with whipped cream.

• VARIATIONS •

Orange Soufflé. Omit lemon and substitute grated rind of half an orange and 3 tablespoons fresh orange juice before folding in egg whites.

Liqueur Soufflé. Omit lemon and substitute 2 tablespoons of any tasty liqueur, such as Grand Marnier, Cointreau, curaçao, or Benedictine.

Strawberry Soufflé. You will need a larger, 1½-quart soufflé dish for this recipe. Omit lemon flavor and add 1 teaspoon vanilla extract before folding in egg whites. Before preparing soufflé itself, mix together 2 cups fresh sliced strawberries, ½ cup orange juice, ½ cup of curaçao, and 2 tablespoons sugar. Put in soufflé dish and gently pour in the soufflé mixture. If there is any fruit juice left over, add to the whipped cream topping for added color and flavor.

◆

CHOCOLATE ROULADE
Serves 8 to 10

This is an impressive dessert; even dieters are tempted to ask for seconds. It has the delicateness of a soufflé—but it is really a fallen one!

6 egg yolks	*6 egg whites*
½ cup sugar	*Confectioners' sugar*
3 tablespoons strong coffee	*Cocoa*
6 ounces semisweet chocolate	*1½ cups heavy cream,*
1 teaspoon vanilla extract	*whipped and sweetened*

Butter an 11 × 14 jelly roll pan, line it with waxed paper, and generously butter the waxed paper. Beat egg yolks until light and gradually beat in the sugar. Put the coffee and chocolate in a small saucepan under very low heat, or in the top of a double boiler over simmering water, and melt. As soon as chocolate has cooled slightly, beat into the egg-and-sugar mixture. Add vanilla. Beat egg whites until they form stiff peaks but are not dry. Gently fold whites into the chocolate mixture. Pour batter into the jelly roll pan and spread evenly with a spatula. Bake in a preheated 350-degree oven for about 15 minutes, or until a toothpick or knife inserted in mixture comes out clean. Remove roll from oven, cover with a slightly damp dish towel, and let stand 20 minutes. Meanwhile, arrange two lengths of waxed paper, about 14 inches each, side by side, slightly overlapping, on a working table or area. Sprinkle paper with sugar and cocoa. Run a spatula around edges of the roll and invert it carefully onto the waxed paper. It should come out easily. Gently peel off the waxed paper on which it was baked. With a spatula, spread whipped cream evenly over the roll. Then, by lifting the edge of the waxed paper under the roll, coax the end of the roll to fold inward, just as a jelly roll begins rolling up. This motion starts the roll rolling. Continue lifting the waxed paper and roll up ever so gently and quickly onto a large serving platter. To serve, slice thickly on the diagonal with a saw-toothed knife.

SOME GENERAL DESSERT HINTS

• For a super flambé, you must preheat the alcohol to approximately 130 degrees before lighting it so that the flame will catch. *Never* ignite the alcohol while you are in the process of pouring from the bottle. Before setting the dessert ablaze, turn the room lights off or down to get the full, dramatic impact of the flaming dish.
• Sprinkle a light dusting of flour or confectioners' over the tops of cakes to prevent the icing from running off as it is applied.
• For stick-free baked desserts, rub cookie sheets and loaf pans with butter or shortening, then coat with flour.

• To keep nuts or fruits from settling to the bottom of a dessert batter, sprinkle them with flour first.

Cookies

Everyone loves the smell and taste of homemade cookies. To keep cookies fresh, store them in a moisture-proof cookie jar with a slice of fresh bread. The cookies will stay soft and fresh for a week. The same bread trick works with cakes.

◆

PEANUT BUTTER COOKIES
Makes 48

Peanut butter lovers adore these.

1 cup (2 sticks) butter or
   margarine
1 cup white sugar
1 cup brown sugar
1 cup peanut butter

2 eggs
2½ cups sifted all-purpose
   flour
¾ teaspoon salt
2 teaspoons baking soda

Soften the butter in a large mixing bowl. Gradually cream in the white and brown sugar. Thoroughly blend in the peanut butter. Add eggs and beat in well. Sift the flour, salt, and baking soda together into a small mixing bowl. Gradually add the flour to the sugar-butter mixture. When batter is well mixed, shape into small balls, put on a buttered cookie sheet, and press down to flatten with the tines of a fork dipped in flour. Press fork in two directions to make a pretty design. Bake in batches in a preheated 375-degree oven 10 to 12 minutes, or until golden brown. Remove from cookie sheet with a spatula and let cool on a cake rack. Store in an airtight container.

◆

DATE NUT BARS
Makes 36

2 eggs, lightly beaten
1 cup sugar
1 cup sifted all-purpose flour
1 teaspoon baking powder
½ teaspoon salt

1 box dates cut up in small
   pieces (about 1 cup)
1 cup chopped pecans or
   walnuts

In a large mixing bowl, mix ingredients in order given. Bake in a buttered 12 × 7½ × 2-inch pan in a preheated 350-degree oven for 35 minutes, or until done.

Use a straw or knife to test for doneness; it should come out clean when inserted in the middle of the batter. Cut into small squares, remove with a spatula, and let cool on a cake rack. Store in an airtight container.

◆

CHOCOLATE CHIP (TOLL HOUSE) COOKIES
Makes 100

These famous cookies were invented by Ruth Wakefield, owner of the Toll House in Whitman, Massachusetts. Many chocolate and cookie companies have copied Mrs. Wakefield's world-famous recipe and made the cookies famous under their own name. But it is Mrs. Wakefield to whom we are indebted for these delicious cookies that have been favorites of generations of Americans.

1 cup (2 sticks) butter, softened
¾ cup brown sugar
¾ cup white sugar
2 eggs, lightly beaten
1 teaspoon baking soda
1 teaspoon hot water

2¼ cups sifted all-purpose flour
1 teaspoon salt
2 packages semisweet chocolate bits
1 cup chopped pecans or walnuts
1 teaspoon vanilla extract

Put butter in a large mixing bowl and gradually cream in brown and white sugar. When thoroughly blended, gradually stir in the beaten eggs and mix until well blended. Dissolve the baking soda in the hot water and add, alternately with the flour and salt, to the egg-and-sugar mixture. When all the flour is mixed in, add chocolate and nuts and stir in vanilla. You will find batter becomes thicker and thicker. Drop by half teaspoons onto a lightly buttered cookie sheet. Bake in batches in a preheated 375-degree oven for 10 to 12 minutes, or until golden brown. Use a spatula to remove cookies and transfer to a cake rack to cool. The cookies are delicious slightly warm.

◆

OATMEAL-CARROT COOKIES
Makes 24

The combination of oatmeal and carrot makes particularly good cookies.

¾ cup (1½ sticks) butter
¾ cup sugar
1 egg
1 cup grated carrots
2 teaspoons grated lemon rind

1¼ cups sifted all-purpose flour
½ teaspoon salt
2 teaspoons baking powder
1 cup oatmeal (not the 1-minute instant variety)

Soften butter in a large mixing bowl. Cream in the sugar. Beat in the egg, carrots, and lemon rind. Mix in the flour, salt, and baking powder, and finally blend in the oatmeal. Put about a teaspoon of batter for each cookie on a lightly buttered cookie sheet and bake in batches in a preheated 375-degree oven for 10 to 12 minutes, or until golden brown. With a spatula carefully remove to a cake rack for cooling. Store in an airtight container.

BROWNIES

Makes 16

Brownies taste like cake. They should be chewy and never dry.

2 squares unsweetened chocolate	½ teaspoon salt
¼ cup (½ stick) butter	1 cup sifted all-purpose flour
2 eggs, well beaten	½ teaspoon baking powder
1 cup sugar	1 teaspoon vanilla extract
	1 cup chopped walnuts

In the top of a double boiler over the hot water, melt chocolate and butter together. Remove from heat and add all remaining ingredients, blending thoroughly. Pour batter into a buttered 8-inch square cake pan and bake in a preheated 350-degree oven for about 25 to 30 minutes. When a straw or knife poked into the center comes out clean, brownies are done. Let cool slightly, cut into squares, and remove with a spatula to a cake rack for further cooling. Store in an airtight container.

CHOCOLATE-VANILLA PINWHEELS

Makes 36

These are pretty cookies to serve with fruit at the end of a meal or with tea or coffee on a cold afternoon.

½ cup (1 stick) butter	½ teaspoon baking powder
½ cup sugar	⅛ teaspoon salt
1 egg yolk	1 square (1 ounce) un-
3 tablespoons milk	sweetened chocolate
1½ cups sifted all-purpose flour	

In a large mixing bowl soften butter and gradually cream in sugar. Add the egg yolk and beat well. Stir in the milk. Thoroughly blend in the flour, baking powder, and salt. Remove half of this dough to a floured board and set aside. Melt the chocolate and add to the remaining dough in the bowl. When chocolate is thoroughly mixed in, set aside. Roll the white dough into a thin rectangle. Carefully transfer to a sheet of waxed paper. On the same floured surface, roll out the chocolate dough into a same-size rectangle. Gently lay chocolate dough over white dough. Taking the long side of the rectangle, slowly roll up, jelly roll fashion. You should end up with a roll about 2 inches in diameter. Refrigerate roll on a piece of waxed paper to harden for about 4 hours. Cut in thin, ⅛-inch slices with a sharp or serrated knife and put cookies on a lightly greased cookie sheet. Bake in a preheated 350-degree oven for about 6 to 8 minutes, or until just lightly browned.

◆

APRICOT CHOCOLATE THUMBPRINT COOKIES
Makes 36

½ cup vegetable shortening
¼ cup sugar
½ teaspoon salt
1 egg yolk
1 square (1 ounce) un-
   sweetened chocolate,
   melted

½ teaspoon ground mace
1 cup sifted all-purpose flour
1 egg white
1 cup finely chopped pecans
⅓ cup apricot preserves

In a large mixing bowl cream shortening until light and fluffy. Beat in sugar, salt, egg yolk, chocolate, and mace. Stir in flour. Wrap dough in foil and chill for 30 minutes. Roll dough with your hands into balls 1 inch in diameter. Beat egg white until slightly foamy. Roll balls in egg white and then in chopped nuts. Put about 2 inches apart on greased cookie sheets. Press center of each cookie with your thumb. Bake in a preheated 350-degree oven for 8 minutes. Remove from oven and quickly press centers down again. Replace in oven and bake another 8 minutes, or until they feel firm. Remove from oven and let cool on a rack. Fill centers with small spoonfuls of apricot preserves.

◆

VIENNESE ALMOND CRESCENTS
Makes 48

These cookies are nice to have on hand at holiday times. The almonds must be grated, so they will be dry and mealy; grinding them would make the cookies oily.

1 pound confectioners' sugar
1 vanilla bean
1 cup (2 sticks) butter or
   margarine
¼ teaspoon salt

1½ cups finely grated
   blanched almonds
2 cups sifted all-purpose
   flour

About a week ahead of time, open sugar package and push vanilla bean down into sugar. Reclose package tightly. After a week the vanilla bean can be removed and used to season other sugar or syrup.

When ready to prepare cookies, cream together butter, 1 cup of the vanilla sugar, and salt in a large mixing bowl. Beat in almonds and flour. Chill dough for 1 hour. Pinch off a ball of dough about the size of a large olive. With your fingers, roll the dough on a lightly floured board into a log and shape it into a crescent. Put on ungreased cookie sheets and bake in a preheated 325-degree oven for 12 to 15 minutes, or until cookies are pale beige. Let cool overnight on the cookie sheets, so they have a chance to harden thoroughly. Roll in vanilla sugar.

◆

LACE WAFERS
Makes 48

These are particularly dainty cookies and are perfect to serve at a special dinner or lunch as accompaniments to fruit, ice cream, or sherbet. They must be prepared ahead of time, and can be stored in an airtight container.

½ cup light corn syrup
½ cup (1 stick) butter
*⅔ cup firmly packed dark
    brown sugar*
1 cup sifted all-purpose flour

1 cup grated walnuts
1½ cups heavy cream
2 teaspoons instant coffee
⅓ cup confectioners' sugar

In a large saucepan, mix corn syrup, butter, and brown sugar. Stir mixture constantly over low heat until it starts to boil. Remove from heat and beat in flour and walnuts. Using 1 level teaspoon of dough per cookie, put cookies on a greased cookie sheet, about 3 inches apart. Put no more than five or six cookies on each sheet. Bake in a preheated 375-degree oven for 5 to 6 minutes. Let cookies cool for a few minutes. Lift off with a spatula. Wrap each cookie around the handle of a wooden spoon. Let cool until set. Repeat with remaining cookies. If cookies cool and cannot be rolled, replace in oven for a minute to soften again. Repeat, using remaining cookie dough. Just before serving, whip cream with coffee and confectioners' sugar. Use a pastry bag with a round writing tip to fill rolls with whipped cream. Serve immediately.

◆

GREEK KOULOURIA
Makes 48

¾ cup sugar
*2 eggs, one whole and one
    separated*
1 teaspoon vanilla extract
1 teaspoon grated lemon rind

*1½ cups sifted all-purpose
    flour*
½ teaspoon baking soda
½ teaspoon salt

In a large mixing bowl cream butter until soft and light. Stir in ½ cup of the sugar. Add whole egg, egg yolk, vanilla, and lemon rind and stir until well blended. Mix together flour, baking soda, and salt in another bowl. Add dry ingredients to first mixture and stir. When stiff, turn out on a lightly floured board and knead dough until smooth. Wrap in foil and chill for 1 hour. Pinch off pieces of dough about the size of a large olive. With your fingers, roll on a lightly floured surface to shape like a pencil, 6 inches long. Twist into a figure eight and put on a greased cookie sheet. Beat egg white and remaining ¼ cup sugar until foamy and use to brush tops of cookies. Bake in a preheated 350-degree oven for 15 minutes, or until pale golden brown. Remove from cookie sheet while hot and let cool on a rack.

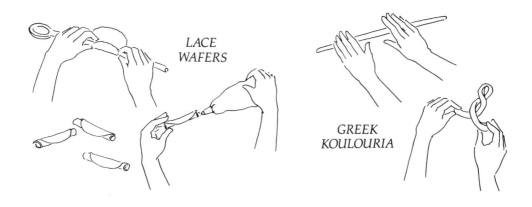

LACE
WAFERS

GREEK
KOULOURIA

◆

SPICE COOKIES
Makes 30

4 cups sifted all-purpose flour	¾ cup honey
1 teaspoon baking powder	1 cup dark corn syrup
1 teaspoon ground cloves	¾ cup sugar
½ teaspoon allspice	2 tablespoons butter
½ teaspoon cinnamon	1 tablespoon lard

In a large mixing bowl combine the flour, baking powder, cloves, allspice, and cinnamon and set aside. In a heavy 6-quart saucepan, bring honey, corn syrup, and sugar to a boil over moderate heat, stirring until the sugar dissolves. Reduce heat and simmer, uncovered, for 5 minutes. Remove from the heat, add butter and lard, and stir until melted. Beat in the flour mixture, a cup or so at a time. When the batter is smooth, drop it by teaspoonfuls onto a greased cookie sheet, at least 1 inch apart. Bake in a preheated 400-degree oven for 15 minutes, or until light brown and firm to touch. Transfer to a cake rack with a spatula. Proceed with the next batch. Cookies keep for 6 to 8 weeks in tightly sealed jars or tins.

COCKTAIL PARTY FOOD

Cocktail parties can be great fun, because they have the right degree of informality to allow people to mix easily and engage in conversations on all levels. Cocktails also are an ideal way to solve certain entertaining obligations when you find that you have a large number of people you must invite. Furthermore, cocktail parties require less space than a sit-down dinner party. The best part of all is that cocktail parties need only a few manageable finger foods and an ample stock of wine and spirits.

Here are a few tasty treats guaranteed to produce a sensational party.

◆

TAPENADE
Makes 1 cup

This tangy dip originated in the Mediterranean.

1 8-ounce can pitted black
   olives, drained
1 7-ounce can albacore tuna
   packed in oil, drained
1 2-ounce can flat anchovy
   fillets, drained

3 tablespoons capers, rinsed
   and drained
¼ cup fresh lemon juice
4 parsley sprigs
2 large garlic cloves
1 cup olive oil
Freshly ground pepper

Combine first seven ingredients in food processor or blender and mix until smooth. Slowly add oil, blending thoroughly. Season to taste with pepper. Serve with crudités (assorted raw vegetables).

◆

MEXICAN DIP
Serves 8

1 pound lean ground beef
1 large onion, chopped
½ cup catsup
1 teaspoon chili powder
1 teaspoon garlic powder
½ teaspoon salt

1 teaspoon ground cumin
1 teaspoon crushed dried
   oregano
Hot pepper sauce to taste
1 24-ounce can kidney beans,
   undrained

1 2-ounce jar pimiento-
  stuffed green olives, sliced,
  at room temperature

½ pound Cheddar cheese,
  freshly grated, at room
  temperature
4 scallions, chopped
Tortilla chips

Cook beef and onion in a 2-quart casserole over high heat for 5 minutes, stirring once to crumble beef. Add catsup, chili powder, garlic powder, salt, cumin, oregano, and hot pepper sauce, and blend well. Purée beans in a blender and stir into beef mixture. Cover and cook over high heat for 10 minutes, stirring once halfway through cooking time. Blend in about three quarters of the olive slices. (The dip can be prepared ahead to this point and reheated just before serving.) Sprinkle cheese over top and garnish with scallions and remaining olives. Serve immediately with chips.

CURRY DIP
Makes 1¼ cups

1 cup mayonnaise
¼ cup chili sauce (optional)
2 teaspoons lemon juice
1 teaspoon minced onion
1 teaspoon curry powder, or
  to taste

½ teaspoon Worcestershire
  sauce
½ teaspoon hot pepper sauce,
  or to taste
Salt and freshly ground
  pepper

Combine all ingredients. Cover and chill. Serve with crudités.

RUMAKI
Makes 16

Rich and crisp—a classic party favorite.

8 slices bacon, cut in half
8 canned water chestnuts,
  drained and cut in half

¼ pound chicken livers,
  trimmed and cut into 16
  pieces
Chinese mustard or plum sauce

Cook bacon briefly, about 5 minutes. Stop cooking while it is still soft. Drain on paper towels. Place water chestnut half and liver piece on bacon and roll up, securing with a plain wooden toothpick. (Rumaki can be prepared ahead to this point and refrigerated.) Arrange rumaki on a cookie sheet. Bake in a preheated 400-degree oven for about 3 or 4 minutes until bacon is crisp. Serve with mustard or plum sauce on the side.

◆

CHEESE AND SPINACH MUSHROOMS
Makes about 30

2 pounds medium
  mushrooms
1½ cups red wine vinegar
1 garlic clove, sliced
3 ounces blue-veined cheese
2 10-ounce packages frozen
  chopped spinach

½ teaspoon white pepper
1 teaspoon salt
1 medium onion, finely
  minced
¼ cup olive oil

Wipe mushrooms with a damp cloth to remove any soil and pat dry with paper towels. Remove stems and use in another dish. Put caps in a large bowl, add vinegar and garlic, and marinate at room temperature for 6 hours, tossing occasionally. Put cheese in a medium-size bowl, add ¼ cup vinegar from the marinade, and mash with a fork until cheese is crumbled. Thaw spinach and squeeze out all liquid. Add spinach and all remaining ingredients to cheese mixture. Mix thoroughly and use to stuff caps. Put mushrooms on plates or a tray, cover tightly with aluminum foil, and refrigerate until serving.

◆

FRIED WALNUTS
Makes 2 cups

3 cups water
2 cups whole shelled walnuts
¼ cup sugar

Vegetable oil
¼ teaspoon salt

In a large saucepan bring water to boil over high heat. Add walnuts and cook for 1 minute after the water returns to a boil. Rinse in a strainer under hot running water and drain. Put sugar in a large bowl, add walnuts, and toss. In an electric or stove-top skillet heat about 1 inch of oil to 350 degrees. With a slotted spoon add about half the walnuts to the oil. Fry for about 5 minutes, or until golden, stirring often. Remove walnuts from oil with the slotted spoon and drain in a sieve. Sprinkle with salt and toss lightly to keep walnuts from sticking together. Spread out on waxed paper to cool and fry the second batch of nuts. Store in a tightly sealed container until serving time.

◆

TINY MEATBALLS
Makes 60 to 75

2 tablespoons butter
½ cup minced fresh parsley

2 tablespoons minced onion
2 pounds freshly ground steak

1 to 2 tablespoons Wor-
cestershire or steak sauce,
or to taste
Salt and pepper

2 eggs plus 2 egg yolks
Catsup and mustard
(optional)

In a large skillet melt butter and sauté parsley and onion until onion is golden brown. Put meat in a large mixing bowl and add cooked onion mixture to it. Season with Worcestershire sauce. Add salt and pepper to taste. Beat eggs together and add to meat mixture. Knead mixture with your hands to keep it light. Wet hands so meat will not stick to them and proceed to make small balls from the meat. Sauté meatballs in batches in the skillet, to which you can add a little more butter if necessary. Meatballs will puff up. Drain on paper towels and serve immediately, plain or with a small dish of steak sauce, mustard, or catsup.

◆

DOLMADES (STUFFED GRAPE LEAVES)
Makes approximately 36

These hors d'oeuvres can be served hot or at room temperature.

1 jar grape leaves
1 pound ground chuck or
lamb
1 cup raw rice
1 medium onion, chopped
Salt and pepper to taste

1 teaspoon dried mint
1 egg, lightly beaten
1 cup stewed tomatoes
1½ cups beef stock or canned
broth
Juice of 1 lime

Wash grape leaves, pat dry, and put on paper towel. In a bowl, mix all remaining ingredients except stock and lime and stuff each grape leaf with a teaspoon of meat mixture. Wrap each leaf envelope-fashion around meat and put, seal side down, in a single layer in a skillet. You will have enough wrapped grape leaves to fill two large skillets. Heat stock and pour about an inch into each skillet. Simmer, uncovered, adding more stock when necessary, for about 25 minutes, or until rice inside leaves feels tender to the touch of a fork. Serve with a squeeze of lime juice.

◆

HAM ROLLS
Serves 36

This is a pretty hors d'oeuvre to serve at Christmastime, but it is a hit anytime.

6 slices lean boiled ham
1 8-ounce package cream
cheese, softened

12 stalks cooked asparagus

Spread each slice of ham with cream cheese. Put 2 asparagus stalks at the end of each piece of ham and roll up ham around the stalks. Put toothpicks in each roll to hold it together and put rolls in freezer for 1 hour to get firm. When ready to serve, remove from freezer, slice with a serrated knife, and serve immediately.

◆

ENDIVE STUFFED WITH CHEESE
Makes 18

18 Belgian endive leaves
  (about 2 large heads)
1 8-ounce package cream
  cheese, at room
  temperature

10 ounces Roquefort or other
  blue-veined cheese, at room
  temperature
½ cup finely chopped
  walnuts
Garnish: Watercress

Separate the endive leaves, wash carefully, and crisp in cold water for 5 minutes. Mash the cheeses in a bowl until well blended, then fold in the walnuts. Drain and dry the leaves. Fill the bottom third of each with the cheese-and-nut mixture. Garnish each with a small sprig of watercress.

◆

NEW POTATOES STUFFED WITH CAVIAR
Makes 12

More elegance than expense, these little jewels add a touch of class to any party.

12 unpeeled new potatoes,
  the smaller the better
¼ cup sour cream

1 tablespoon chopped fresh
  chives
2-ounce jar caviar

In a large pot, bring to a boil enough salted water to cover potatoes. Add the potatoes and return water to a boil. Lower the heat to medium and boil the potatoes until tender but still firm—about 8 to 10 minutes, depending upon their size. Drain the potatoes and immediately drop into cold water to stop the cooking. When they are cool, cut a thin slice from the bottom of each so they won't tip over when served. Use a small spoon or a melon baller to scoop out a cavity in each potato. Mix the sour cream and chives together and spoon into each potato; top with a dollop of caviar. Refrigerate, covered with aluminum foil. Remove from refrigerator ½ hour before serving.

PART III

Menus

Food and entertaining are great pleasures to share. Today's life-styles allow you to serve a variety of foods and to entertain in any fashion you please. You can invite friends for anything from a casual breakfast to a leisurely picnic to a dinner party with your finest china, crystal, and silver. The most important thing is that your food and the way you entertain reflect your personal style. On the following pages are ideas for entertaining themes and menus. These should be taken as suggestions only; substitute your own recipes to meet your needs and likes.

Most recipes can be prepared in one or more stages, with hours or even days between one step and the next. It is particularly important to pace the cooking for a party so that you both do not feel exhausted or harassed when guests arrive.

Work out the menu carefully to eliminate as many last-minute steps as possible. If you are preparing an entrée that requires close attention to timing, do not serve an appetizer that takes an unpredictable amount of time to eat—for example, artichokes vinaigrette followed by sherried crab soufflé. With a menu like that, you would find yourself nervously checking your watch as guests enjoyed the first course. Keep foods reasonably simple. It is triumph enough to cook asparagus, carrots, or potatoes to perfection without having to complicate everything with sauces and fancy garnishes.

It goes without saying that each meal should be balanced in color, flavor, and texture. Otherwise, the total effect will be lost in a blur of sameness.

All of the following recipes can be easily reduced or increased to serve your needs.

Photographs

FLORAL FANTASY
LUNCHEON

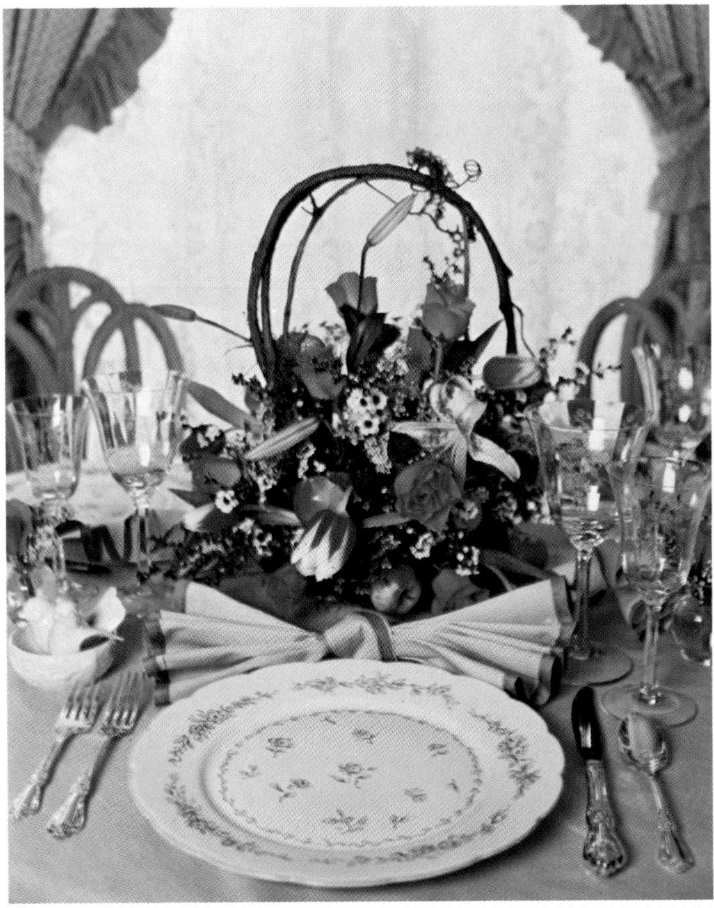

. . . . .▲. . . . .
CONTEMPORARY
COMBINATIONS

THE ULTIMATE
LUXURY

· · · · · ▲ · · · · ·
BOUNTIFUL
BREAKFAST
· · · · · ▼ · · · · ·

A FEAST
FOR FRIENDS

LEISURELY
GARDEN LUNCH

· · · · ▲ · · · · ·
A CREATIVE
RECEPTION
· · · · · ▼ · · · · ·

MIDSUMMER REPAST
EUROPEAN STYLE

*AUTUMNAL
TAILGATE FÊTE*
· · · · · ▼ · · · · ·

Monday-Night Football

....

*D*uring the football season, everyone likes to gather for parties. A bracing "bowl o' red" is perfect for an exciting Monday-night game. The menu suggested offers chili, which most likely originated around cowboys' campfires in El Paso at the turn of the century. Whether you root for the Dallas Cowboys or not, there is nothing better than chili with a tang.

.......▲.......

FIRESIDE CHILI
CHEESY NACHOS
GUACAMOLE
CRÈME BRÛLÉE (See Index)
BEER

.......▼.......

FIRESIDE CHILI
Serves 10 to 12

3 pounds coarsely ground
  chuck
2 pounds hamburger-grind
  chuck
2 large onions, coarsely
  chopped
6 medium cloves garlic,
  finely chopped
1 teaspoon cayenne pepper
1 tablespoon ground hot red
  chili pepper

5 tablespoons ground mild
  red chili pepper
3 tablespoons ground cumin
2 tablespoons dried oregano
3 teaspoons salt
3 cups water
2 15-ounce cans tomato sauce
2 28-ounce cans peeled whole
  tomatoes
2 16-ounce cans pinto beans,
  drained

Put meat, onions, and garlic in a heavy 5-quart stockpot pot or Dutch oven. Break up any lumps and cook over medium heat, stirring occasionally, until meat is evenly browned. Stir in the cayenne pepper, hot and mild chili pepper, cumin, oregano, and salt, blending well. Add water, tomato sauce, and tomatoes, mashing them with a fork. Bring to a boil, lower the heat, and simmer, uncovered, for about 1½ hours. Stir occasionally. Taste and adjust seasonings. Stir in the beans and simmer, uncovered, for another ½ hour. Taste it and adjust seasonings. If you've gone light on the chili until now, you may decide to add more, but then be sure to simmer another ½ hour so the flavors can blend. Since chili improves with rest, age, and reheating, try to make it a day ahead of serving. It also freezes well, so why not make enough for a future meal.

◆

CHEESY NACHOS
Makes 24 chips

24 tostados
⅔ cup canned bean dip
24 small squares of Monterey
  Jack, sharp Cheddar, or
  jalapeño cheese

3 jalapeño chilies, thinly
  sliced into rings
4 scallions, finely chopped

Put the tostados on a cookie sheet. Top each with a dollop of bean dip and cover with a square of cheese, chili rings, and scallion. Broil for 6 minutes, or until the cheese bubbles. Serve hot.

◆

GUACAMOLE
Serves 12

4 large, very ripe avocados,
  peeled and seeded
Juice of 2 limes
1 cup chopped sweet green
  chilies
4 tablespoons finely chopped
  red onion

2 large tomatoes, peeled,
  seeded, and chopped
½ teaspoon crushed dried red
  pepper
2 garlic cloves, minced

Cut the avocados into pieces, put them in a blender, add lime juice, and process at high speed until smooth. Pour into a bowl and stir in the remaining ingredients. Cover with plastic wrap, making sure the wrap directly touches the guacamole. (This keeps the guacamole from turning brown.) Serve as a dip with tortilla chips.

Breakfast in Bed

*E*ntertain yourselves with a cozy breakfast in bed. It is a lovely, languorous morning—you can hardly get out of bed and are too lazy to fix breakfast even though your stomachs are rumbling. What do you do? Toss a coin to see who makes breakfast. The winner gets to stay in bed. The suggested menu will pamper you with tastes of an international morning meal.

· · · · · · · ▲ · · · · · · ·

FRESH BLUEBERRIES IN PAPAYA CUPS
CREAMED EGGS IN BRIOCHE (STORE-BOUGHT)
BRAZILIAN CHOCOLATE COFFEE

· · · · · · · ▼ · · · · · · ·

FRESH BLUEBERRIES IN PAPAYA CUPS

Serves 2

1 ripe papaya
½ cup fresh blueberries

Garnish: 2 lime wedges

Cut papaya in half lengthwise. Scoop out seeds and discard. Fill with blueberries and garnish with lime.

◆

CREAMED EGGS IN BRIOCHE

Serves 2

1½ ounces cream cheese
1 tablespoon butter
½ cup heavy cream
¼ teaspoon salt

½ teaspoon dried chervil
4 eggs
2 brioches

Melt cream cheese and butter in the top of a double boiler over simmering water. Scald the cream and stir it in. Add the salt and chervil. Break in the eggs. Before the egg whites are firm, stir the eggs gently with a fork and cook until thick. Slice the tops off the brioches, partially hollow out the centers, fill with creamed eggs, and replace the tops.

◆

BRAZILIAN CHOCOLATE COFFEE

Makes 2 servings each

1 ounce semisweet chocolate
¼ cup sugar
1 cup boiling water
½ cup hot milk
½ cup hot cream

1½ cups freshly made hot
   strong coffee
1 teaspoon vanilla extract
Pinch of cinnamon

In the top of a double boiler over hot water, melt the chocolate together with the sugar. Stir in the boiling water. Continue to cook for 3 to 5 minutes. Add the milk, cream, and coffee. Beat well and add the vanilla. After pouring into cups, dust with cinnamon. Serve immediately.

Food and Fun Italian Style

· ·

*T*hemes are fun for parties. Why not create a merry all-out Italian night. Capture the Italian passion for robust food, and be sure to include good wines and mood-evoking background music, such as the rich, operatic tones of Pavarotti.

· · · · · · · ▲ · · · · · · ·

ANTIPASTO
INSALATA DI MARE (COLD SEAFOOD SALAD)
FRIED ZUCCHINI
FOCACCIA (FLAT BREAD)
ZABAGLIONE (SEE INDEX)
WINE: PINOT GRIGIO

· · · · · · · ▼ · · · · · · ·

ANTIPASTO

Serves 6

1 large jar roasted peppers
2 small cans anchovies
1 pound thinly sliced salami
1 large can black olives
1 medium-size jar or can
  each marinated artichoke
  hearts and mushrooms

½ pound sliced mozzarella
  cheese
½ pound raw fennel, sliced
  thinly
Olive oil

Arrange ingredients on a large, attractive platter, drizzle with a touch of olive oil, and serve.

◆

INSALATA DI MARE (COLD SEAFOOD SALAD)

Serves 6

When you buy the squid and octopus, ask the fish market to do any cleaning needed.

1 medium onion, quartered
2 celery stalks, with tops
1 large lemon, quartered
3 quarts water
1 pound squid, cut in rings

1 pound octopus, cut in
  pieces
1 pound fresh shrimps
1 garlic clove
½ cup olive oil

Juice of 2 lemons
¼ cup chopped fresh parsley

½ teaspoon salt and freshly
   ground black pepper to
   taste

Put onion, celery, lemon, and water in a stockpot. Bring to a boil; plunge in squid and octopus and boil gently until tender, 40 to 50 minutes. Drop in shrimps and boil until shrimps turn pink, about 2 minutes. Drain and let cool. Shell and devein shrimps. Discard onion, celery, and lemon. Rub a bowl with the cut garlic and put the seafood in it. Blend remaining ingredients together in a small bowl, mince the garlic and add, and mix with seafood. Marinate in the refrigerator for 2 to 3 hours before serving.

◆

FRIED ZUCCHINI
. . . .
Serves 6

½ cup all-purpose flour
½ cup cornstarch
1 teaspoon salt
1 egg, beaten
⅔ cup water

Vegetable oil for frying
4 medium-size zucchini, cut
   in half crosswise, then each
   half cut into ¼-inch strips

In a mixing bowl combine flour, cornstarch, salt, egg, and water. Stir until the batter is blended but slightly lumpy. Chill the batter in the refrigerator, or add 4 ice cubes and stir until it is very cold. Discard any unmelted ice. Heat 4 inches of vegetable oil to 360 degrees in a deep fryer. A few pieces at a time, toss zucchini into the cold batter and then remove to the hot oil with tongs. The change in temperature will make the coating puff up. Do not crowd the zucchini in the pan, which would lower the oil temperature and make the zucchini stick together. Cook each batch briefly, no more than 2 minutes. Test a few pieces to see if crisp and done. Drain in paper towels. Serve on a warm plate.

◆

FOCACCIA
. . . .
Serves 6

1 package active dry yeast
1 cup lukewarm water (110
   degrees)
2 teaspoons sugar
½ teaspoon salt

½ cup olive oil
About 3 cups sifted all-
   purpose flour
Dried oregano

Sprinkle yeast over warm water in a large bowl and let stand for 5 minutes to soften. Stir in sugar, salt, and 2 tablespoons of oil. Add 2 cups flour; mix together. With a heavy-duty mixer or wooden spoon, beat about 5 minutes, or until dough is elastic.

Add ⅔ cup more flour to make a soft dough. Turn dough out on a board sprinkled with the remaining ⅓ cup flour; knead 10 to 15 minutes, or until dough is smooth and springy. Put in a large bowl, add 2 tablespoons oil, and turn dough to grease on all sides. Cover with a clean tea towel and let rise in a warm place about 1 hour, or until doubled. Punch dough down; knead again briefly on a lightly floured board to release air. With a rolling pin, roll and stretch dough to fit bottom of a well-greased 10 × 15-inch shallow baking pan. With your fingers or any tool, poke holes in dough at 1-inch intervals. Brush dough with remaining oil and sprinkle generously with oregano. Let dough rise, uncovered, for 15 to 20 minutes, or until almost doubled. Bake in a preheated 450-degree oven for 12 to 15 minutes, or until well browned. Serve bread warm or at room temperature.

Sunday Brunch with the Neighbors

*B*runch, that delicious combination of breakfast and lunch, is an easy and informal way to entertain. Brunch reportedly originated with the hunt breakfast in England, when ravenous riders returned from chasing the fox. Now a weekend institution in this country, brunch is a terrific way to catch up with friends after a busy workweek.

······▲······

VEGETABLE FRITTATA
GOAT CHEESE AND ARUGULA SALAD
PROSCIUTTO BREAD
ORANGE AND GRAPEFRUIT IN MARSALA

······▼······

VEGETABLE FRITTATA
Serves 6 to 8

4 tablespoons olive oil
1½ onions, thinly sliced
1 12-ounce can artichoke
  hearts, rinsed, drained,
  and quartered
2 small zucchini, sliced
1 small red pepper, seeded
  and sliced

1 cup freshly grated Gruyère
  cheese
2 tablespoons chopped fresh
  parsley
Salt and pepper to taste
10 eggs, lightly beaten with
  ¼ cup light cream

Pour oil into an 8-inch pie plate and arrange onion slices in the bottom. Bake for 5 minutes in a preheated 450-degree oven. The onion should be slightly cooked.

Remove from oven and arrange the artichoke hearts, zucchini, and red pepper over the onions. Sprinkle with cheese and parsley. Season with salt and pepper. Reduce oven temperature to 400 degrees. Pour egg mixture over the vegetables and cheese. Bake for approximately 10 minutes, until the eggs have puffed and the center of the omelet is set. Do not overcook. Serve in wedges.

◆

GOAT CHEESE AND ARUGULA SALAD

Serves 6 to 8

3 bunches arugula, washed
  and dried
8 ounces goat cheese,
  crumbled

¾ cup Vinaigrette Dressing
  (see Index)

In a large bowl combine arugula and cheese. Add dressing and serve.

◆

PROSCIUTTO BREAD

Makes 2 loaves

1 package active dry yeast
¼ cup warm water (about
  110 degrees)
1 cup warm milk (about 110
  degrees)
1 tablespoon sugar

½ teaspoon salt
2 tablespoons olive oil
3 to 3½ cups sifted all-
  purpose flour
1 cup thinly sliced and
  chopped prosciutto

In a large bowl, sprinkle yeast over warm water and let stand for 5 minutes to soften. Stir in milk, sugar, salt, and oil. Add 1 cup of flour and blend thoroughly; stir in 1½ cups more flour. With a powerful mixer or a wooden spoon, beat until dough is smooth and elastic, about 5 minutes. Stir in ½ cup more flour to make a soft, pliable dough. Turn out onto a lightly floured board or pastry cloth. Knead until dough is smooth and resilient and develops small bubbles just under the surface, about 15 minutes. Put in a greased bowl and turn dough to grease all sides. Cover and let rise in a warm place until doubled, about 1 hour. Punch dough down, turn out onto a floured surface, and divide in half. Roll each half out to a long strip about 12 × 6 inches; arrange half the prosciutto evenly down the center of each. Roll each up tightly to make a long slender loaf, pinching along the length to seal. Transfer to a greased cookie sheet, cover lightly, and let rise until nearly doubled, 30 to 40 minutes. Bake in a preheated 375-degree oven for 20 to 25 minutes, or until loaves are a rich golden brown. Slide out onto wire racks to cool before slicing. Serve warm or at room temperature.

◆
ORANGE AND GRAPEFRUIT IN MARSALA
Serves 6 to 8

3 navel oranges   2 tablespoons sugar
3 grapefruits   4 tablespoons sweet marsala

Remove skins and pith from the oranges and grapefruits. Slice fruit thinly and arrange in a serving dish. Sprinkle with sugar and marsala and refrigerate for at least 4 hours.

Boss Home for Dinner

Only the finest cuisine will do when you invite the boss to dinner. A roast with a tantalizing sauce and the finale of a rich, royal dessert is a meal that should win you praise.

. . . . ▲ . . . .

POTTED SHRIMP IN ARTICHOKE BOTTOMS
HONEY-MUSTARD-GLAZED ROAST VEAL
CRISPY MINIATURE POTATO MEDALLIONS
STEAMED FRESH ASPARAGUS (SEE INDEX)
CHOCOLATE ALMOND TORTE
WINE: CHARDONNAY

. . . . ▼ . . . . . .

POTTED SHRIMP IN ARTICHOKE BOTTOMS
Serves 4

You can save the artichoke leaves for another meal—steam, chill, and dip in vinaigrette.

½ pound cooked shrimps   Cayenne pepper
4 tablespoons butter, softened   4 artichokes
2 ounces cream cheese,   Lettuce
    softened   Garnish: Lime slices
¼ teaspoon salt

Put the shrimp, butter, cream cheese, salt, and cayenne pepper in a food processor and whirl until well combined. With a heavy knife cut through each artichoke, leaving only about ½ inch of the leaves attached to the bottom. Trim the bottoms, removing the stems. Cook the bottoms in boiling salted water until tender. Let cool, remove the choke with a spoon, and trim again around the edge. Wrap in plastic and chill. With a pastry bag and a large star tip, pipe the shrimp mixture into the artichoke bottoms. Put each on a lettuce leaf on an individual serving plate and garnish with lime. Keep refrigerated until 15 minutes before serving.

◆

HONEY-MUSTARD-
GLAZED ROAST VEAL

Serves 4

Salt and pepper to taste
1 2-pound veal loin
½ cup soy sauce
2 tablespoons honey

2 tablespoons Dijon mustard
1 teaspoon chopped fresh
  ginger (optional)

Salt and pepper the veal. Mix the remaining ingredients and rub over the roast. Set in a roasting rack in a pan and let rest for 30 minutes. Put in a preheated 350-degree oven for 45 minutes, occasionally basting with pan juices. Remove from the oven and let rest for 20 minutes. Slice and serve with pan juices.

◆

CRISPY MINIATURE
POTATO MEDALLIONS

Serves 4

1 pound potatoes
2 tablespoons heavy cream
1 egg yolk
1 tablespoon chopped fresh
  parsley
1 teaspoon dried tarragon
1 tablespoon dried chervil

4 tablespoons butter
Salt and pepper
Nutmeg
2 tablespoons all-purpose
  flour, plus flour for
  dusting

Peel and quarter potatoes. In a large pot, cover potatoes with water and boil about 15 minutes, or until tender. Put the potatoes through a ricer or food mill until puréed. Beat in cream and egg yolk. Mix herbs and butter into the purée and season to taste with salt and pepper and nutmeg. Put on a work surface dusted with flour. Add 2 tablespoons flour to the purée and mix thoroughly. Chill for 30 minutes. Make the purée into medallions the size of a silver dollar and about ¼ inch thick. Put on a buttered cookie sheet. Melt the remaining 2 tablespoons butter, heat until brown, and use to brush the medallions. Bake in a preheated 375-degree oven for 20 minutes, until crisp and brown.

CHOCOLATE ALMOND TORTE

Serves 8

6 tablespoons unsalted butter, softened	5 eggs
1½ cups almonds, skins on	6 tablespoons very fine bread crumbs
6 1-ounce squares semisweet chocolate	½ tablespoon instant espresso
1 cup sugar	1 tablespoon coffee liqueur
	Glaze (recipe follows)

Butter the bottom and sides of a 9-inch round cake pan thoroughly, then line the bottom with waxed paper and butter it, too. In a blender grind the almonds as fine as possible and set aside. Melt the chocolate in the top of a double boiler over barely simmering water. If the chocolate should tighten, becoming excessively thick or tough (caused by moisture getting into chocolate), add 1 or 2 tablespoons vegetable shortening and work the mixture until smooth. Cream the remaining butter with an electric beater or in an electric mixer until very soft and light. Very gradually add the sugar, beating continuously. After all sugar is included, add the eggs, one at a time, beating vigorously after each addition. Blend in the chocolate, ground nuts, bread crumbs, instant coffee, and liqueur with a rubber spatula. Pour batter into the prepared pan and put in the middle of a preheated 375-degree oven for 25 to 35 minutes. Remove and let cool on a cake rack for about 30 minutes, then run a metal spatula around the edge of the cake pan and turn cake onto the rack. If the cake does not drop out easily, bang the pan with your hand. Gently ease off the waxed paper. Let cool completely. Refrigerate overnight.

Remove from refrigerator and let stand 1 hour on a cake rack. Put a piece of waxed paper under the rack and pour chocolate glaze gently over the cake. Tip the cake so the glaze runs evenly over the top and down the sides.

GLAZE

Makes 1½ cups

4 1-ounce squares unsweetened chocolate	½ cup (1 stick) butter, softened and cut up
4 1-ounce squares semisweet chocolate	4 teaspoons honey

In the top of a double boiler combine the unsweetened and semisweet chocolate, butter, and honey and melt over hot water. Remove from heat and let cool, stirring until lukewarm.

Parents for Dinner

....

*A*mong the first you will want to entertain are your parents. The menu here includes a member of the pasta family. In Italy, playful shapes of pasta, such as rings, seashells, hats, and bows, are symbolic of affection. What tastier way to express love for your parents!

. . . . ▲ . . . .

PASTA ALLA CARBONARA
SCALLOPS PROVENÇALE
PURÉE OF BROCCOLI WITH NUTMEG
POACHED PEARS WITH CHOCOLATE SAUCE
WINE: CHARDONNAY

. . . . ▼ . . . .

PASTA ALLA CARBONARA
Serves 4

½ pound mild Italian sausages	½ cup chopped fresh parsley
¼ pound thinly sliced pros-ciutto or cooked ham	4 eggs, well beaten
8 tablespoons (1 stick) butter	½ cup freshly grated Parmesan cheese
½ pound spaghetti	Freshly ground black pepper

Remove sausages from skin and crumble meat. Chop prosciutto in small pieces. In a large frying pan over medium-low heat, melt 2 tablespoons of the butter. Add sausage and half the prosciutto and cook, stirring, for about 10 minutes, until sausage is lightly browned and prosciutto is curled. Stir in remaining prosciutto. Cook spaghetti in a large pot of salted boiling water until *al dente*. Drain well and add to hot meat. Add remaining butter and parsley to spaghetti mixture; mix quickly to blend. Pour in eggs and lift and toss spaghetti to coat well. Sprinkle in the cheese and a pinch of pepper; toss again. Pass additional grated cheese at the table.

◆

SCALLOPS PROVENÇALE
Serves 4

1 pound (about 2 cups) scallops, cut into ½-inch pieces	Lemon juice
	Salt and pepper
	½ cup all-purpose flour

Oil
2 tomatoes, seeded and cubed
2 tablespoons sliced scallions
1 garlic clove, mashed

2 tablespoons butter
2 tablespoons minced fresh
    parsley

Dry the scallops in paper towels, then put on a large platter. Sprinkle with lemon juice and salt and pepper. Dredge with flour and shake in a sieve to dislodge excess flour. Lightly oil a 10-inch frying pan. Heat until oil is almost smoking, then add the scallops. Toss for 4 to 5 minutes, until scallops are lightly browned. Add tomatoes, scallions, and garlic; cook briefly and toss with butter and parsley. Serve immediately.

◆

PURÉE OF BROCCOLI
WITH NUTMEG
Serves 4

1½ pounds broccoli
Salt and pepper

3 tablespoons butter
¼ teaspoon grated nutmeg

Separate the broccoli into stems and flowerets, and cut the stems into large pieces. Peel. Wash the broccoli under cold running water. Plunge the stems into a large quantity of boiling water, adding salt as soon as the water returns to a boil. Boil the stems, uncovered, for 5 minutes, then add the flowerets and simmer 3 to 5 minutes longer, until a sharp knife easily pierces the stalks. Rinse the broccoli in cold water and let drain. Melt butter in a large pan, add broccoli, and toss to coat with butter. Season with salt and pepper to taste. Sauté, tossing every few minutes, until the broccoli is heated through. Purée in a blender or food processor, return the purée to the pan, and heat gently, adding nutmeg and more butter if desired.

◆

POACHED PEARS
WITH
CHOCOLATE SAUCE
Serves 4

½ cup sugar
Peel from 1 lemon
4 medium-size firm pears,
    peeled

Chocolate Sauce (see Index)
Garnish: 4 mint leaves

Put sugar, lemon peel, and 4 cups water in a saucepan. Bring to a boil, lower the heat, and add pears. Simmer for 15 to 20 minutes, or until pears are easily pierced with a fork but still hold their shape. Remove pears from pan and chill. Drizzle with warm chocolate sauce and garnish with mint.

Candlelight Supper for Two to Eight

This delicately herbed poultry entrée combined with the romantic ambience of candlelight will be a memorable supper just for the two of you or for many more. At points in history, poultry was such a luxury that it was covered by sumptuary laws.

······▲······

SLICED TOMATOES AND MOZZARELLA WITH BASIL
CHICKEN BREASTS WITH WHITE WINE AND TARRAGON
STEAMED SNOW PEAS AND JULIENNE CARROTS
BUTTERED NOODLES
ALMOND CREAM PUFFS
CHOCOLATE TRUFFLES
WINE: CHARDONNAY

······▼······

SLICED TOMATOES AND MOZZARELLA WITH BASIL

Serves 8

4 beefsteak tomatoes, cored
   and cut in ¼-inch slices
8 ounces fresh mozzarella
   cheese, thinly sliced

Fresh basil leaves
Olive oil

Arrange tomato slices and cheese on individual salad plates and top with basil leaves. Drizzle with oil.

◆

CHICKEN BREASTS WITH WHITE WINE AND TARRAGON

Serves 8

8 chicken breasts
1 onion, sliced
1 carrot, sliced
1 small celery stalk, sliced
¼ cup dry white wine
½ teaspoon salt
5 tablespoons butter
4 tablespoons all-purpose
   flour

⅛ teaspoon cayenne pepper
2 tablespoons heavy cream
1 egg yolk
1 tablespoon milk
3 tablespoons fresh tarragon
   leaves
Garnish: Tarragon sprigs

Wash chicken and pat dry. Remove the skin and trim the bones neatly. Put the breasts in a large pot with the onion, carrot, celery, and wine. Add just enough water to cover the chicken and the salt. Bring to a boil, cover, and simmer very gently for 15 minutes. Reserve 1½ cups of liquid in which chicken has cooked. To make the sauce, melt 4 tablespoons butter in a saucepan. Remove from the heat, stir in the flour, and season with salt to taste and cayenne pepper. When blended, strain in the reserved liquid. Stir over low heat until the sauce comes to a boil. Gradually stir in the remaining 1 tablespoon butter and the cream. Simmer the sauce gently for 5 minutes. Blend egg yolk and milk together, then stir into the sauce. Add the tarragon. Put the chicken breasts on a platter, coat with the sauce, and garnish.

◆

STEAMED SNOW PEAS
AND
JULIENNE CARROTS
Serves 8

1 pound carrots, peeled and
   cut in julienne strips
1½ pounds snow peas,
   trimmed

4 tablespoons (½ stick) butter
Salt
White pepper

Put the carrots in a steamer basket and put the basket over boiling water in a pot with a tight-fitting lid. Steam for 5 minutes. Add the snow peas, replace the lid, and cook for 3 to 4 minutes longer. While the vegetables are still hot, transfer them to a serving dish, toss lightly with butter, and season to taste with salt and pepper. Serve immediately.

◆

BUTTERED
NOODLES
Serves 8

Salt
1¼ pound broad noodles
6 tablespoons butter, melted

Freshly ground black pepper
¼ to ½ cup heavy cream
   (optional)

In a large pot bring 3 quarts of water to a boil. Add salt. Add the noodles and stir well. When the water returns to a boil, lower the heat. The noodles must not be overcooked—test after a few minutes. Drain the noodles quickly and toss them with butter; season with salt and pepper. Add cream and toss again lightly. They can wait for 15 to 20 minutes in a tightly covered pot or serving dish.

◆

ALMOND CREAM PUFFS
Serves 6

3 egg yolks
¼ cup sugar
3 tablespoons cornstarch
1 cup milk
½ teaspoon almond extract
3 tablespoons ground
    almonds

2 tablespoons amaretto
    liqueur
½ cup heavy cream, cold
6 cream puffs (see Index)
6 fresh strawberries or Choc-
    olate Sauce (see Index)

In a mixing bowl, whisk together the egg yolks, sugar, and cornstarch until light and creamy. Scald the milk in the top of a double boiler and pour into the egg yolk mixture, whisking constantly to keep the yolks from cooking. Continue to whisk until the mixture is foamy, then pour into the top of the double boiler. Cook slowly over simmering water, beating all the while, for about 10 minutes, until it has thickened to the consistency of custard. Set the double boiler top in a bowl of ice and whisk the custard continuously until it has cooled completely. Stir in the almond extract, ground almonds, and amaretto. Whip the cream in a mixing bowl until it forms soft peaks. Gently fold the custard into the whipped cream until it is thoroughly combined. Using a pastry bag with a small plain tip, puncture the bottoms of the cream puffs and fill with the custard mixture. Decorate with sliced strawberries or drizzle with chocolate sauce.

◆

CHOCOLATE TRUFFLES
Makes about 30

These are perfect served after dinner, with coffee.

10 ounces semisweet
    chocolate
3 egg yolks
3½ tablespoons heavy cream
2½ tablespoons anisette
    liqueur

2 ounces unsalted butter,
    softened
Cocoa for dusting

Melt chocolate in the top of a double boiler over simmering water. Remove from heat and add egg yolks. Whisk until smooth. Add cream, a tablespoon at a time, and whisk until smooth. Add the anisette and whisk until smooth. Put back over hot water to heat through. When it is warm, whisk in the butter, a tablespoon at a time. Refrigerate until firm. Roll into small balls and dust with cocoa.

Chinese New Year

Chinese food is good any time of year, but it is especially fitting for a midwinter party around the time of the Chinese New Year. Evoke the mood of the Orient by including fan-folded napkins, chopsticks, and flowers floating in a low bowl.

·······▲·······

SHRIMP BALLS
WONTON SOUP
CASHEW CHICKEN
SPICY SZECHWAN BEEF
STIR-FRIED BROCCOLI
CHINESE WHITE RICE
SPICED PEANUT NOODLES
ALMOND COOKIES
WINE: GEWÜRZTRAMINER

·······▼·······

◆

SHRIMP BALLS
·············
Makes 20

Shrimp balls can be made in advance and refried before serving.

*½ pound fresh or frozen
  shrimp, thawed*
*2 tablespoons pork fat
  (optional)*
*4 water chestnuts, finely
  chopped*
1 scallion, finely chopped
1 egg white, lightly beaten

½ teaspoon garlic salt
1 teaspoon sesame oil
1 to 2 teaspoons cornstarch
Dash of white pepper
Dash of sugar
1 cup fine bread crumbs
4 cups oil

Shell, devein, and mince shrimp. Combine shrimp, pork fat, water chestnuts, and scallion in a blender or food processor and process for 3 to 5 minutes. Add remaining ingredients except bread crumbs and oil and blend well. Turn out on a board and knead until slightly elastic. Form 20 balls from the mixture. Roll balls in bread crumbs. Deep fry in hot oil over medium-high heat until golden brown and floating on top of the oil. Serve hot.

◆
WONTON SOUP
Serves 6

6 cups chicken broth
2 tablespoons soy sauce
2 tablespoons scallions,
 chopped
2 tablespoons Chinese or
 regular parsley, chopped

1 tablespoon rice wine
1 teaspoon sesame oil
½ teaspoon salt
¾ pound spinach or escarole,
 washed and trimmed
36 wontons (store-bought)

Combine broth, soy sauce, scallions, parsley, rice wine, sesame oil, and salt in a large pot. Bring to a boil and add spinach or escarole and cook 2 minutes. Keep warm. Cook wontons according to package instructions. Place wontons in individual soup bowls and pour hot broth over them.

◆
CASHEW CHICKEN
Serves 6

2 whole chicken breasts,
 boned
1¼ teaspoons salt
1½ teaspoons sugar
1 teaspoon light soy sauce
1 tablespoon oyster sauce
Dash of pepper
2 tablespoons cornstarch
2 scallions, slivered
3 thin slices ginger root,
 slivered

1 cup plus 3 tablespoons oil
½ cup raw cashew nuts
15 small Chinese mushrooms,
 fresh or dried
3 celery stalks
½ cup canned bamboo shoot
 tips
10 canned water chestnuts
1 yellow onion, thinly sliced
1½ cups chicken stock
2 tablespoons water

 Cut the chicken into bite-size pieces. Arrange chicken in a single layer in a baking dish. In a small bowl mix ¾ teaspoon salt, ½ teaspoon sugar, soy sauce, oyster sauce, pepper, and 1 tablespoon cornstarch. Sprinkle over chicken, add scallions and ginger, and set aside for 1 hour. Heat 1 cup oil to 325 degrees in a wok and fry the nuts for 5 minutes. Drain on paper towels and lightly salt. Remove oil from wok. In a saucepan with water, boil the mushrooms for 10 minutes; rinse, squeeze dry, and cut off and discard stems. Cut the celery into 1½-inch pieces, then cut each piece lengthwise into julienne strips. Cut the bamboo shoot tips into thin slices. Heat the wok, add 1 teaspoon oil, and stir-fry the bamboo tips for 1 minute. Remove the bamboo tips and set them aside. Add 1 teaspoon oil and ½ teaspoon sugar to the hot wok and stir-fry the water chestnuts for 1 minute. Remove and set aside. Add 1 teaspoon oil and the remaining ½ teaspoon salt and ½ teaspoon sugar to the hot wok and stir-fry mushrooms, celery, and onion for 3 minutes. Remove and set aside. Add the remaining 2 tablespoons oil and stir-fry the chicken for 3 minutes. Add the stock, cover, and cook for 10 minutes over medium heat. Add the cooked vegetables and bring to a fast boil. Dissolve the remaining 1 tablespoon cornstarch in water and stir in. Cook for 1 minute and turn off the heat. Add nuts, mix thoroughly, and serve.

◆

SPICY SZECHUAN BEEF
Serves 6

1 pound flank steak, thinly
   shredded
3½ tablespoons soy sauce
2 teaspoons cornstarch
2 tablespoons oil
3 tablespoons rice wine
   vinegar
3 teaspoons sesame oil
2 tablespoons chili sauce
½ teaspoon sugar
¼ teaspoon black pepper
½ teaspoon cornstarch
   dissolved in 1 tablespoon
   water

5 tablespoons peanut oil
3 slices ginger root, thinly
   shredded
3 garlic cloves, chopped
1 medium carrot, thinly
   shredded
2 celery stalks, thinly
   shredded
⅔ cup chicken stock

Put beef in a bowl. Add 2 tablespoons soy sauce, 2 teaspoons cornstarch, 2 tablespoons oil, 1 tablespoon vinegar, and 1 teaspoon sesame oil. Marinate for 30 minutes. Combine chili sauce, remaining 1½ tablespoons soy sauce, sugar, remaining 2 tablespoons vinegar and 2 teaspoons sesame oil, pepper, and cornstarch dissolved in water. Mix well and set aside. Heat peanut oil, ginger, and garlic in a wok over high heat for 10 seconds. Add the beef and stir-fry for 1 to 2 minutes, then remove from the wok. Add the carrot, celery, and stock. Stir-fry quickly for 1 minute. Add the hot sauce and stir for 30 seconds. Add the beef and stir again. Serve hot.

◆

STIR-FRIED BROCCOLI
Serves 6

1¼ pounds broccoli
1 teaspoon salt
1 teaspoon sugar
1½ teaspoons light soy sauce
1 scallion, slivered

3 thin slices ginger root,
   slivered
1 tablespoon peanut oil
⅓ cup chicken stock

Wash broccoli and trim stems. Cut into bite-size pieces and put in a large bowl. Add ½ teaspoon salt, ½ teaspoon sugar, 1 teaspoon soy sauce, scallion, and ginger and mix well. Heat a wok, add oil, and stir-fry the broccoli for 2 minutes. Add the remaining ½ teaspoon salt, ½ teaspoon sugar, and ½ teaspoon soy sauce and the stock. Bring to a boil and cook, uncovered, for 2 to 3 minutes. (Covering the wok keeps the broccoli bright green and crunchy.) Serve hot.

CHINESE WHITE RICE
Makes 2 cups

This is stickier than ordinary rice.

2 cups long-grain rice *3 cups water*

Wash and drain rice several times until the water runs clear. Drain well. Combine rice and water in a saucepan. Bring to a boil over high heat, uncovered. Reduce heat and simmer until almost all the water has evaporated and craterlike holes appear in the rice. Cover saucepan and simmer for about 20 minutes. Remove from heat and let stand 8 to 10 minutes to complete final cooking. Fluff the rice and serve hot.

SPICED PEANUT NOODLES
Serves 6

½ teaspoon salt
½ pound vermicelli
1 tablespoon plus 2½ teaspoons sesame oil
2 tablespoons ground peanuts
2 tablespoons white vinegar
2 teaspoons chili oil

½ teaspoon sugar
2 tablespoons creamy peanut butter
2 teaspoons chicken stock
¼ pound cooked pork or chicken, thinly shredded
1 cup bean sprouts, roots snapped off
2 scallions, cut into 1½-inch strips

Bring a large pot of water to a boil and add salt. Stir in the vermicelli; when the water returns to a boil, cook for 1½ minutes. Drain vermicelli and toss with 1 tablespoon sesame oil and refrigerate. Make the dressing: Mix together in a bowl the peanuts, the remaining 2½ teaspoons sesame oil, vinegar, chili oil, sugar, peanut butter, and stock. Put noodles in a large serving bowl. Toss to blend with meat, bean sprouts, scallions, and dressing.

◆
ALMOND COOKIES
Makes 24 cookies

⅔ cup shortening
1⅓ cups sugar
½ teaspoon almond extract
4 cups sifted all-purpose
   flour

1½ teaspoons baking powder
½ teaspoon baking soda
1 egg yolk, beaten
24 almonds

Beat the shortening with an electric mixer. Add sugar and almond extract and beat until creamy. Sift the flour, baking powder, and baking soda into the shortening, little by little, beating after each addition. Turn out on a floured board and knead well. Divide into 24 balls. Flatten the balls into ¼-inch thick rounds. Brush egg yolk over the surface. Press an almond on each cookie. Put on a nonstick-surface cookie sheet and bake in a preheated 375-degree oven for about 15 minutes.

Valentine's Day

One of the most romantic of times that a couple can share is Valentine's Day. Slip a little heartfelt gift (perhaps a poem you have specially written for your valentine) onto the dinner plate before the rhapsody begins!

· · · · · · ▲ · · · · · · ·

RED CAVIAR WITH TOAST TRIANGLES
FILET MIGNON WITH COGNAC
SAUTÉED MUSHROOM CAPS
BUTTERED PARSLEY POTATOES
COEUR À LA CRÈME WITH STRAWBERRY SAUCE
WINE: RED BORDEAUX

· · · · · · ▼ · · · · · · ·

RED CAVIAR WITH TOAST TRIANGLES
Serves 2

Salmon caviar
Thinly sliced toast triangles,
   crusts removed

Sour cream

Chill caviar. Just before serving, spoon caviar on toast points. (An optional idea is to cut out heart shapes from the toast.) Serve with a side dish of sour cream.

◆

FILET MIGNON WITH COGNAC
Serves 2

4 tablespoons butter
2 tablespoons shallots, finely
    chopped

1 tablespoon Worcestershire
    sauce
2 6-ounce filets mignons
2 ounces Cognac

Heat 2 tablespoons butter in a skillet, add shallots, and sauté over medium heat for 5 minutes. Increase heat to high, add Worcestershire sauce, and put filets in pan. Cook 3 minutes on each side, turning once for slightly rare. Transfer filets to a warm dish. Deglaze pan with Cognac, and then ignite with a kitchen match. Remove pan from heat, swirl in remaining butter to thicken sauce, and pour over filets. Serve immediately.

◆

SAUTÉED MUSHROOM CAPS
Serves 2

¼ pound mushroom caps
1 tablespoon butter
½ tablespoon vegetable oil

1 garlic clove
2 tablespoons Madeira

Wipe mushroom caps with a damp cloth. Remove stems and save for another use. Melt the butter and oil in a skillet over moderately high heat. Add mushroom caps and shake the pan so they are coated and do not stick. Drop in the garlic and continue to cook, uncovered, over moderately high heat, shaking pan frequently. Add Madeira and continue to shake the pan over heat for 3 to 4 minutes, depending on the size of the caps. Do not cover, as this will draw out the juices. Serve at once.

◆

BUTTERED PARSLEY POTATOES
Serves 2

6 small new potatoes
1 tablespoon butter

Garnish: 1 tablespoon fresh
    parsley chopped

In a saucepan, bring to a boil enough water to cover potatoes. Add potatoes. When water returns to a boil, cook for 8 to 10 minutes, or until tender. Drain water from pot, toss potatoes with butter in the saucepan. Serve hot, garnished with parsley.

◆
COEUR À LA CRÈME WITH STRAWBERRY SAUCE
Serves 2

Heart-shaped porcelain and straw baskets are made especially for this dessert. The porcelain has holes in bottom so the whey can seep out.

5 tablespoons cottage cheese
4 ounces cream cheese
¼ cup sour cream
½ tablespoon confectioners'
    sugar
¼ cup heavy cream

1 pint (or one 10-ounce pack-
    age frozen) strawberries
½ cup sugar (¼ cup if using
    sweetened frozen berries)
1 tablespoon kirsch
Garnish: Whole strawberries
    (optional)

In the bowl of an electric mixer, combine the cottage cheese, cream cheese, and sour cream. Beat until completely smooth. Add the confectioners' sugar. Whip the cream separately and fold into the cheese mixture. Line a 1- to 1½-cup heart mold with cheesecloth, letting the cloth hang over the edges. Spoon in the mixture, fold the cheesecloth over the top, put the mold on a dish, and refrigerate overnight.

To make strawberry sauce, mash the berries with sugar, press through a fine sieve, add kirsch, and chill. (If using whole fresh berries, reserve a few for garnish.) To serve, unfold cheesecloth and turn mold onto a serving plate. Peel off cheesecloth. Garnish with strawberries and pour some sauce around the heart. Serve additional sauce on the side.

Promotion Celebration

T he promotion you have been working so hard for has come through. Nothing can hold you back. Celebrate—call up your dearest, closest friends for a gala dinner. Break open a bottle of bubbly champagne. You deserve it!

· · · · · · ▲ · · · · · · ·

CREAM OF WATERCRESS SOUP
ROASTED DUCK WITH PINK PEPPERCORNS AND BRANDY FLAMBÉ
STEAMED GARDEN VEGETABLES
WILD RICE (SEE INDEX)
COUPE AUX MARRON PARFAIT
WINE: RED BURGUNDY

· · · · · · ▼ · · · · · ·

◆
CREAM OF WATERCRESS SOUP

Serves 4

4 tablespoons butter
½ cup minced onions
2 bunches watercress
¼ teaspoon salt
4 cups chicken stock, boiling

3 egg yolks
1 cup heavy cream
2 tablespoons sherry
Salt and pepper to taste

Melt butter in a heavy 2- to 3-quart saucepan and cook the onion for 10 minutes, or until tender. Trim, wash, and dry the watercress, saving a few leaves for garnish. Add watercress to the onion. Sprinkle with salt. Cover and cook over medium-low heat for 5 to 10 minutes. Add the boiling stock and cook 5 minutes longer. Purée mixture in a blender or food processor. Set aside, uncovered, until ready to serve. To serve, reheat the soup in a saucepan to a simmer. Beat the egg yolks into the cream and sherry in a bowl. Add the soup very slowly to the egg-cream mixture, whisking vigorously. Return the mixture to the saucepan and heat, but do not allow to simmer or the soup will curdle. Season with salt and pepper. Garnish with reserved watercress.

◆
ROASTED DUCK
WITH PINK PEPPERCORNS
AND BRANDY FLAMBÉ

Serves 4

1 4-pound duckling
Salt and freshly ground black
    pepper
1 onion stuck with 3 cloves

1 tablespoon pink
    peppercorns
½ cup chicken stock or
    canned broth
½ cup brandy

Wash duckling inside and out and dry with paper towels. Sprinkle inside and out with salt and pepper. Put the onion in the body cavity, tie the legs together, and turn the wings under. Put the duckling on a rack in a shallow, foil-lined roasting pan. Prick the duckling all over with a fork to allow the fat to escape. Roast the duckling in a preheated 350-degree oven until the leg moves loosely, about 2 hours. In a saucepan, mix peppercorns and stock and heat until bubbly. About 20 minutes before the duckling is done, spoon some of the mixture over the duckling and roast for 10 minutes. Repeat. After the second glazing and roasting, heat brandy, pour over duck, and flame with a long kitchen match, letting juices fall into roasting pan; then remove the duckling to a large platter and spoon the remaining glaze over it. Let meat sit for 20 minutes to allow juices to settle and then serve with pan juices (skim off the fat) and peppercorns.

◆

STEAMED GARDEN VEGETABLES

Serves 4

2 carrots, peeled and thinly
   sliced
2 summer squash, sliced in
   rounds

½ pound snow peas, caps
   and strings removed
Butter
Salt and pepper to taste

Put carrots in a steamer and steam for 3 minutes. Add squash and steam for another 2 minutes. Add snow peas and steam for 1 minute. Toss with butter and season. Serve immediately.

◆

COUPE AUX MARRONS PARFAIT

Serves 4

1 small jar chestnuts (mar-
   rons), packed in syrup
1 pint vanilla ice cream

½ cup heavy cream, whipped
Fan-shaped sugar wafers

If chestnuts are whole, cut them in pieces. Starting with ice cream, alternately layer ice cream and chestnuts in individual chilled sherbet glasses or large wine glasses. Drizzle each with 1 tablespoon of the chestnut syrup. Top with whipped cream and serve with wafers.

Midnight Dessert Party

There is something mysterious, glamorous, and romantic to midnight partygoing. Invite friends in after a late theater date or after a long civic or political meeting. An assortment of desserts and drinks takes minimum preparation and offers maximum delight.

· · · · · · ▲ · · · · · · ·

CHOCOLATE CHARLOTTE WITH CRÈME ANGLAISE
LEMON DACQUOISE
GRAPE STRIPS
BITTERSWEET CHOCOLATE APRICOTS
DESSERT CAFÉ

· · · · · · ▼ · · · · · · ·

CHOCOLATE CHARLOTTE WITH CRÈME ANGLAISE

Serves 10

You will need a 2-quart charlotte mold with a 7-inch diameter

*½ pound (2 sticks) unsalted
   butter, softened
½ cup sugar
¼ cup orange liqueur
1 teaspoon almond extract
1⅓ cups pulverized blanched
   almonds (pulverize in
   blender)*

*4 ounces semisweet chocolate,
   melted with ¼ cup strong
   coffee
2 cups heavy cream
About 22 ladyfingers
¼ cup orange liqueur mixed
   with ¼ cup water
Garnish: Crème Anglaise
   (recipe follows)*

To make charlotte filling, in a large bowl cream butter with sugar until light and fluffy. Add liqueur and almond extract and beat until very smooth. Stir in almonds and chocolate and mix well. Let cool completely. Whip cream until almost stiff. With a rubber spatula, gently fold cream into chocolate mixture. To assemble, line the bottom of the charlotte mold with a round of waxed paper. Cut ladyfingers into wedges to fit tightly in bottom of mold, curved side down. Arrange whole ladyfingers around the sides of mold, curved sides facing out. Sprinkle ladyfingers with a bit of diluted liqueur. Pour chocolate cream into line mold and arrange leftover ladyfingers, lightly soaked with diluted liqueur, on top. Cover with waxed paper; set a small plate over the paper and put a weight on it. Refrigerate, covered, for at least 6 hours. To serve, unmold charlotte onto serving plate and remove waxed paper. Serve with Crème Anglaise, or with softly whipped heavy cream.

CRÈME ANGLAISE

Makes about 3 cups

*2 cups milk
½ cup granulated sugar
4 egg yolks*

*2 tablespoons Cognac
1½ teaspoons vanilla extract*

In a small heavy saucepan, bring milk to a boil. In a large mixing bowl, beat sugar into the egg yolks until thick and fluffy. Add boiled milk in dribbles, whisking continuously. Pour into a large heavy-bottomed enamel saucepan. Set over low heat and, stirring constantly, cook until sauce thickens and coats the back of a wooden spoon. Do not simmer, or the sauce will curdle. Take off heat, add Cognac and vanilla, whisk for a moment, and strain through a fine sieve. After cooling, refrigerate, covered. Serve in a decorative bowl.

LEMON DACQUOISE
Serves 10

This is a delicious meringue and lemon buttercream dessert.

5 egg whites
Pinch of salt
¾ cup sugar
1 teaspoon vanilla extract

¾ cup ground almonds
1½ cups lemon buttercream
  (see Index)
Confectioners' sugar

Grease two large baking sheets with oil. Trace four 8-inch circles on wax paper or baking parchment. Cut them out, leaving a rim around the traced circles so the meringues can be lifted once they are baked. Beat the whites with salt until stiff. Gradually beat in the sugar and continue to beat until stiff and glossy. Add vanilla. Fold in the ground almonds. Divide mixture among the four wax paper circles. Spread evenly to the circle edges. Bake in a preheated 250-degree oven for 1 hour. Remove meringues to a rack to cool and peel off the wax paper.

To assemble dessert, place one meringue layer on a cake plate and spread with ½ cup of buttercream; place the second layer on top and repeat process until all layers are in place. Refrigerate to firm cake. Remove 1 hour before serving. Sprinkle top heavily with sifted confectioners' sugar.

GRAPE STRIPS
Serves 10

½ pound frozen puff pastry
  (store-bought), thawed
1 egg, beaten
¼ cup sugar
2 tablespoons cornstarch
½ teaspoon salt
1 cup milk

3 egg yolks
½ teaspoon vanilla extract
½ cup apricot preserves
2 to 3 tablespoons brandy
1½ pounds seedless green or
  red grapes

To make the pastry, roll out three quarters of the dough on a floured surface to a rectangle 14 × 4 × ⅛ inch. Put dough on an ungreased cookie sheet. Roll out remaining dough and cut two 14 × ½-inch strips and two 4 × ½-inch strips. With a pastry brush, paint a ¼-inch border of beaten egg around the edges of the large rectangle. Place the cut strips on top of the painted edges. With the tines of a fork, crimp around the outside edge. Prick the bottom of the pastry and refrigerate for ½ hour. Cover dough with waxed paper and weigh the center down with dried beans.

Bake in a preheated 400-degree oven for 20 minutes. Remove beans. Return pastry to oven for 5 to 10 more minutes, until golden brown.

To make filling, combine sugar, cornstarch, and salt in the top of a double boiler set over simmering water. Add ¼ cup milk and mix well. Heat the remaining ¾ cup milk and add gradually, stirring until thick. Beat the yolks and add to mixture, stirring constantly over low heat until thick. Remove from heat. Add vanilla. Cover with plastic wrap and chill.

To prepare the glaze, heat preserves and brandy in the top of a double boiler and cook until thin and very hot. Force through a fine strainer, pushing pulp through. Keep warm.

To assemble the strips, fill the pastry shell with the cream filling and let it set for a few minutes in the refrigerator. Arrange grapes, side by side, on top of the filling. Brush grapes with apricot glaze and allow to set for 10 minutes before serving. If it is not to be served right away, refrigerate.

◆

BITTERSWEET
CHOCOLATE APRICOTS
Serves 6

½ pound bittersweet
   chocolate

20 fresh or dried apricot
   halves

Line a large tray with waxed paper. Chop chocolate and melt in the top of double boiler over gently simmering water. Stir until smooth. Hold each apricot half and dip it in to about two thirds of its length. Let drip and wipe very gently against the rim of the pot. Put the half on the lined tray. Work quickly but carefully. If chocolate becomes too thick, reheat slowly. Put tray of dipped apricots in refrigerator until chocolate is firm. Remove an hour or so before serving.

◆

DESSERT CAFÉ
Serves 12

12 teaspoons sugar
2 large cinnamon sticks,
   cracked
10 whole cloves
Rind of 1 orange

Rind of 1 lemon
1 cup brandy
8 cups extra-strong fresh
   coffee, piping hot

Put all ingredients except coffee in a saucepan with low sides. Heat and stir until all the sugar is dissolved and liquid is hot. With a long wooden kitchen match, ignite the mixture. When the flame dies out, add coffee, blend together, and pour into demitasse cups.

Rites of Spring

Spirits soar and hearts grow light as the deep freeze of winter begins to thaw and daffodils begin to bud. Spring is on its way, and there is no more welcome sight than the fresh foods of the season, such as asparagus and strawberries. Celebrate the arrival of these seasonal treats with friends.

. . . . ▲ . . . .

CREAM OF ASPARAGUS SOUP
ROAST STUFFED SQUABS
BABY NEW POTATOES IN NESTS
FRESH GREEN PEAS (SEE INDEX)
BIBB LETTUCE AND WALNUT SALAD
STRAWBERRY LEMON CURD TARTLETS
WINE: PINOT NOIR

. . . . ▼ . . . .

CREAM OF ASPARAGUS SOUP

Makes about 6 cups

1 pound fresh green
   asparagus
6 cups chicken stock or
   canned broth
¼ cup chopped onion
½ cup chopped celery
3 tablespoons butter
3 tablespoons all-purpose
   flour

½ cup heavy cream
2 egg yolks
2 tablespoons vermouth
Salt, white pepper, and
   paprika
Garnish: Sour cream

Wash the asparagus and remove the tips. Simmer the tips in a small amount of water in a covered saucepan for 3 to 4 minutes, or until tender. Chop the stalks into pieces and put them in a large saucepan. Add the stock, onion, and celery and simmer, covered, for about ½ hour. Strain through a sieve. Melt the butter in the top of a double boiler over simmering water and stir in the flour until blended. Slowly stir in the cream, egg yolks, and vermouth. Add the asparagus-flavored stock. Heat the soup, adding the asparagus tips. Season to taste just before serving. Garnish each serving with a dollop of sour cream.

◆
ROAST STUFFED SQUABS
Serves 6

6 squabs (1 to 1½ pounds
   each)
3 sticks butter
24 chicken livers
12 large white mushrooms,
   chopped
2 apples, peeled, cored, and
   chopped
10 ounces ham, shredded
6 ounces shelled pistachio nuts

Salt and freshly cracked
   white pepper
4 ounces brandy
3 tablespoons all-purpose
   flour
1 tablespoon tomato paste
2¼ cups chicken stock
1½ cups dry white wine
2 sprigs tarragon (or a pinch
   dried)

Thoroughly wash the body cavity of each squab and pat dry. Heat 6 tablespoons butter in a skillet and sauté livers. Remove livers, add 3 tablespoons butter to skillet, and sauté mushrooms and apples until golden. Mix in ham, nuts, and salt and pepper to taste. Stuff squabbs with mixture and tie legs with string. Heat 9 tablespoons butter in a deep pan and brown squabs on all sides. Heat brandy in a small pan, ignite, and pour over squabs. Put squabs in a roasting pan and roast in a preheated 350-degree over for 35 minutes, basting once with the pan juices. Remove from oven and cover with aluminum foil. In another pan, melt 6 tablespoons butter and blend in flour and tomato paste. Add stock and wine and stir until the mixture comes to a boil. Add tarragon and simmer for 5 minutes. Pour over each squab.

◆
BABY NEW POTATOES IN NESTS
Serves 6

This is a beatiful potato creation. First you make delicate potato nests; then you add new potatoes. To make nests, you will need two deep wire ladles (or scoops), separate or hinged together. They can be found where Chinese kitchen equipment is sold.

12 firm boiling potatoes
4½ cups vegetable oil
Salt
2 pounds new potatoes,
   peeled and sculpted to the
   size of small eggs

6 tablespoons butter, melted
3 tablespoons coarsely
   chopped fresh parsley

Peel and wash the large potatoes. Dry thoroughly and cut into pieces the size of a matchstick. Prepare the first nest: Put a layer of potato sticks in the bottom and sides of one of the ladles. Heat oil in a deep-fat fryer. When the oil just faintly begins to wrinkle, put the second ladle in the first and lower into the fat. Fry for 3 minutes and remove from the fat. The nest will be shaped and almost firm. Remove the nest from the ladle and with a slotted spoon put it back in the fat for just a few seconds, to make it firm and golden. Set the nest on a paper towel to drain. Repeat this procedure until you have used up all the potatoes. (The nests can be made ahead to this point and reheated in an oven preheated to 250 degrees and then turned off.)

Cover the new potatoes in a saucepan with lightly salted water and boil for about 8 to 10 minutes, or until just tender. Drain, pour melted butter over them, and sprinkle with parsley. Put 2 or 3 in each nest.

◆

BIBB LETTUCE AND WALNUT SALAD
Serves 6

1 head Bibb lettuce, washed,
   dried, and torn into bite-
   size pieces
⅔ cup coarsely chopped
   toasted walnuts

½ cup walnut or safflower oil
3 to 6 tablespoons wine
   vinegar
Salt and freshly ground
   pepper

Arrange lettuce in a salad bowl. Sprinkle with walnuts and toss with oil and vinegar. Season to taste with salt and pepper and serve immediately.

◆

STRAWBERRY LEMON CURD TARTLETS
Serves 6

1 cup strained apricot jam
6 4-inch baked tart shells (see
   Index)

¾ cup Lemon Curd (recipe
   follows)
2 pints fresh strawberries,
   washed and hulled

With a pastry brush, paint a small amount of jam on each tart shell. (This keeps them from getting soggy.) Spread about 2 tablespoons of the lemon curd in each shell and fill with whole strawberries, points up. Heat the remaining jam. With the pastry brush, glaze the tarts with hot jam, thinning with hot water if necessary to spread.

◆

LEMON CURD
Makes 1½ cups

½ cup (1 stick) unsalted
   butter

½ cup sugar
4 egg yolks

1 egg	*Grated rind of 3 lemons*
Juice of 4 lemons	

Melt butter and dissolve sugar in the top of a double boiler over gently simmering water. Beat egg yolks and egg thoroughly and add to butter and sugar, along with lemon juice and rind. Cook, whisking constantly, for about 10 minutes, until heavy and thick. Let cool before filling tarts. You can make curd a day or so in advance and refrigerate in a tightly sealed jar.

Picnic Repast

*A*lmost everyone agrees that food tastes and smells more magnificent when enjoyed outdoors. Why not pay back good friends with a charming French country picnic. The menu features crunchy radishes, delicate pastry, earthy sausage, and a fresh, young wine. After you have sampled the treasures of your "movable feast," picnics will never be the same.

· · · · · · · ▲ · · · · · · ·

CHICKEN AND VEGETABLE PESTO SALAD
SAUSAGE IN BRIOCHE
RADISHES WITH SWEET BUTTER
GOAT CHEESE TART
OATMEAL-CARROT COOKIES (SEE INDEX)
ASSORTED FRESH FRUITS
WINE: BEAUJOLAIS

· · · · · · · ▼ · · · · · · ·

CHICKEN AND VEGETABLE PESTO SALAD

Serves 6 to 8

2 pounds skinned and boned chicken breasts	*1 cup blanched broccoli flowerets*
Salt and freshly ground black pepper to taste	*1 cup blanched cauliflower flowerets*
2 cups chicken stock	*1 bunch scallions, thinly sliced*
1 cup Pesto Sauce (see Index)	

Wash chicken, pat dry, and lightly sprinkle with salt and pepper. Put them in a skillet and add the stock. Cover and simmer gently for 10 to 15 minutes, or until tender. Let chicken cool in the stock. Cut chicken into 1½-inch chunks and put in a

241

mixing bowl. Carefully stir in the pesto sauce. Cover and chill. When ready to serve, toss chicken and pesto again. Add the broccoli, cauliflower, and scallions and toss again.

◆

SAUSAGE IN BRIOCHE
Serves 6

This recipe must be made a day in advance of the picnic.

2 tablespoons warm milk
1 package dry yeast
1½ cups all-purpose flour
1 teaspoon granulated sugar
½ teaspoon salt

3 eggs
1 stick (4 ounces) unsalted
  butter, softened
1 large garlic sausage (1½ to
  2 pounds)

Put milk in a small bowl and sprinkle yeast over it to soften. In a large mixing bowl sift together the flour, sugar, and salt and make a well in the center. Put 2 of the eggs in the well and add the yeast. Combine and knead to make a smooth dough. With your hands, work in the butter thoroughly. Shape dough into a ball and put it in a bowl that has been sprinkled with flour. With a sharp knife, cut a deep crosswise incision in the top of the dough. Cover the bowl with a towel and let dough rise in a warm place with no drafts until doubled in size. Punch the dough down, cover again, and refrigerate overnight.

Put the sausage in a roasting pan or other pan large enough for it to lie flat. Cover with cold water and cook over low heat, with the water just simmering, for 45 to 60 minutes. Remove sausage from the water, let cool, cover, and refrigerate.

Turn the brioche dough out on a floured board and roll into a rectangle about ¼ inch thick, working quickly while the dough is still firm and chilled. Remove the casing from sausage and put sausage in the center of the dough. Gather the dough around the sausage without stretching the dough. With fingers moistened in cold water, pinch the edges of the dough together lightly. Put the sausage brioche roll on a buttered baking sheet. Beat the remaining egg with 1 tablespoon water and use to brush top and sides of dough. Bake in a preheated 375-degree oven for 35 minutes, or until the brioche is golden brown. Let the roll rest for about 5 minutes. Use a broad spatula to lift it from the baking sheet. Slice and serve.

◆

RADISHES WITH SWEET BUTTER
Serves 6

2 bunches red or white radishes
Coarse salt

Whipped unsalted butter
Sliced pumpernickel bread

Thoroughly wash the radishes and leave some of the green stems attached for handles. Chill. Serve with salt, along with butter and a platter of sliced bread.

◆
GOAT CHEESE TART
Serves 6

1 unbaked piecrust (see
   Index)
3 tablespoons Dijon mustard
2 cups crumbled goat cheese
5 eggs

2 egg yolks
2 cups light cream
1 teaspoon salt
¼ teaspoon cayenne pepper

Paint piecrust with mustard. Sprinkle with goat cheese. In a bowl, or in a blender or food processor, beat the eggs and yolks with cream and seasonings until well mixed. Pour into the pie shell, over the cheese. It will be short of the top of the crust, to allow for expansion. Bake in the middle of a preheated 375-degree oven for 30 to 35 minutes, or until filling is set and top is browned. Let cool for approximately 15 minutes.

Luncheon in the Shade

W hen it is too hot to cook, indulge yourself in the tempting outdoors. Set a pretty table under a shady tree.

. . . . . . ▲ . . . .

CHILLED CUCUMBER SOUP
MARINATED MONTRACHET BEEF SALAD
CRUSTY FRENCH BREAD (STORE-BOUGHT)
MANGO SUPREME
WINE: CHENIN BLANC

. . . . ▼ . . . .

CHILLED CUCUMBER SOUP
Serves 4

2 cucumbers, peeled and cut
   into chunks
1 tablespoon fresh lemon juice
1 cup chicken stock or canned
   broth
1 cup heavy cream

1 tablespoon chopped fresh
   dill
Salt
Freshly ground black pepper
   to taste

Put all the ingredients except the pepper and 1 teaspoon of the dill in a blender or food processor and process until well blended. A little texture is desirable, so do not overdo the blending. Chill soup until ready to serve. Sprinkle dill on the top of each bowl and, if you like, some freshly ground black pepper.

◆

MARINATED MONTRACHET BEEF SALAD

Serves 4

Cook the beef a day ahead or use cold leftover beef.

2 ¾ *pounds rolled and tied roast beef or 2 pounds leftover beef*
6 *tablespoons red wine vinegar*
1½ *tablespoons Dijon mustard*
3 *sprigs fresh tarragon or 1 tablespoon dried, chopped*

Salt and pepper
1½ *cup safflower oil*
½ *pound Belgian endive*
1 *head radicchio lettuce*
6 *ounces Montrachet or similar goat cheese*
1 *pint cherry tomatoes*

Put ¼ cup water in the bottom of a roasting pan and roast the beef in the preheated 375-degree oven for 17 minutes per pound for rare.

The next day slice beef into thin strips. Put the vinegar, mustard, tarragon, and salt and pepper in a large bowl. Slowly mix in the oil till you have a smooth and blended mixture. Wash the endive, pat dry, and cut in half crosswise. Wash the radicchio, pat dry, and cut leaves in half lengthwise. Put endive and radicchio in the bowl with the sauce, together with the cheese, roast beef, and tomatoes. Toss well. Chill for 2 hours. Serve at room temperature.

◆

MANGO SUPREME

Serves 4

2 *mangos, peeled and sliced*
1 *large orange*
2 *tablespoons brown sugar*

¼ *cup dark rum*
Whipped cream

Put mangos in a bowl. Grate the orange rind; do not include any part of the white membrane. In a heavy bowl, pound together the brown sugar and rind with the back of a wooden spoon. Squeeze the juice from the orange and pour it over the peel and sugar. Stir well and add the rum. Pour the syrup over the mangos, mix well, and let sit for at least 1 hour in the refrigerator. Serve with whipped cream.

Sunset Supper by the Shore

*F*ew changes have altered the preparation of clambakes. Centuries ago, the American Indians steamed clams and mussels on the beaches. With these delectables, enjoy a supper reminiscent of the sea, with the sound of the waves lapping on the shore and a brilliant sun dipping slowly, romantically, over the horizon.

· · · · · · ▲ · · · · · · ·

STEAMERS AND MUSSELS
BOILED LOBSTER (SEE INDEX)
STEAMED NEW POTATOES
CUCUMBER SALAD WITH CRÈME FRAÎCHE
MINTED VODKA WATERMELON
WINE: MUSCADET

· · · · · · ▼ · · · · · · ·

STEAMERS AND MUSSELS

Serves 6

2 quarts steamers, rinsed in sink of cold water at least twice
2 quarts mussels, scrubbed and beards removed

2 cups dry white wine
Salt and pepper
Lemon wedges
Melted butter

Put the steamers and mussels in a large kettle with wine. Cover, bring to a simmer on top of stove, and steam over a moderate flame until shells open. Season broth to taste. Serve in large soup plates with cups of butter and lemon wedges.

◆

STEAMED NEW POTATOES

Serves 6

18 new potatoes (about 2 ounces each)

Melted butter

Scrub potatoes with a brush. Do not peel. Put enough water in a vegetable steamer or saucepan to reach just below the rack or basket. Bring the water to a boil and adjust heat so that steam escapes through the rack. Add the potatoes and cover the pot. Steam for about 15 minutes. Test with a fork; steam for a few more minutes if necessary. Lift out the rack or basket and turn potatoes into a serving dish. Pour melted butter over them.

◆

CUCUMBER SALAD WITH CRÈME FRAÎCHE
Serves 6 to 8

6 long cucumbers
1 teaspoon coarse salt
White pepper

1 teaspoon sugar
2 tablespoons finely chopped
  fresh dill

Peel cucumbers and slice lengthwise. Remove all seeds. Cut into ¼-inch slices. Combine with remaining ingredients. Toss with crème fraîche (recipe follows) and chill 3 hours or overnight.

◆

CRÈME FRAÎCHE
Makes 1 cup

1 tablespoon buttermilk

1 cup heavy cream

Combine buttermilk and cream, cover, and let sit at room temperature for 24 hours, until thick. Refrigerated, it will keep for several days.

◆

MINTED VODKA WATERMELON
Serves 6 plus

You will need to borrow or buy a kitchen hypodermic syringe for this.

1 cup sugar
2 cups water
2 bunches mint

1 large ripe watermelon
Vodka
Garnish: Mint sprigs

Put sugar in a medium-size saucepan and add water. Stir to dissolve the sugar. Bring to a boil and gently boil for 5 minutes. Remove from heat and add mint. Let syrup cool completely. Remove mint. Measure syrup into a mixing bowl. For every cup of syrup, add 2 ounces vodka. Using a kitchen syringe, inject the watermelon with the syrup every 2 to 3 inches. Chill for at least 3 hours. Cut into wedges and serve garnished with mint sprigs.

▼

Afternoon Tea

The civilized ceremony of tea has long been a tradition in the British Empire. We can be grateful that this charming ritual has crossed the ocean to America. Have a tea party and salute the British for passing along this pleasant custom and way of entertaining.

. . . . ▲ . . . .

BUTTERMILK BISCUITS WITH
WESTPHALIAN HAM AND GRUYÈRE CHEESE
STRAWBERRY KIWI TART IN NUT CRUST
RAISIN CHEESE STREUSEL BARS
SELECTION OF FANCY TEAS

. . . . ▼ . . . .

BUTTERMILK BISCUITS WITH WESTPHALIAN HAM AND GRUYÈRE CHEESE

Makes about 12

¾ cup plus 1 tablespoon
   sifted all-purpose flour
½ teaspoon salt
1 teaspoon double-acting
   baking powder
½ teaspoon sugar
¼ teaspoon baking soda
2½ tablespoons lard
6 tablespoons buttermilk

Unsalted butter
Dijon mustard
¼ pound Westphalian ham,
   cut into small pieces
¼ pound Gruyère cheese, cut
   into small pieces
Garnish: Radishes or
   watercress

In a large mixing bowl, sift together the flour, salt, baking powder, sugar, and baking soda. Cut in the lard, add the buttermilk, and mix lightly. Turn the dough out on a floured board and knead gently for ½ minute. Pat the dough to the thickness of ¼ inch. Cut with a biscuit cutter. Bake on a greased cookie sheet in a preheated 450-degree oven for 10 to 12 minutes or until lightly browned. Cool biscuits on a rack. Spread each biscuit with a little butter and mustard and fill with pieces of ham and cheese. Garnish with radishes or watercress.

◆

STRAWBERRY KIWI TART IN NUT CRUST

Serves 6

1 baked Nut Crust (recipe
   follows)

1 pint strawberries, hulled
   and sliced

2 kiwi, peeled and cut in
⅛-inch crosswise slices
6 ounces apricot jam

¼ cup orange-flavored liqueur
½ pint heavy cream, whipped

Let the crust cool. Arrange sliced strawberries in two to three concentric circles from outer edge of tart. Cluster overlapping slices of kiwis in the center. To glaze the fruit, heat the jam in a saucepan. Add the liqueur and stir over low heat until mixture is clear. Spoon or brush glaze over the fruit. Serve with whipped cream.

◆

NUT CRUST
Makes one 9-inch crust

5 ounces finely chopped
walnuts
¼ pound (1 stick) unsalted
butter, softened
2 tablespoons sugar

1½ cups sifted all-purpose
flour
1 egg, beaten
½ teaspoon vanilla

Using electric mixer or a wooden spoon, mix together all ingredients until well blended. Press into a buttered 9-inch springform tart pan. Chill for 30 minutes before baking in a preheated 350-degree oven for 14 to 20 minutes, or until golden brown.

◆

RAISIN CHEESE STREUSEL BARS
Makes 32 bars

1½ cup dark raisins
¾ cup water
1½ cups dark brown sugar
1½ tablespoons cornstarch
½ teaspoon cinnamon
¼ teaspoon each nutmeg,
cloves, ginger

1 teaspoon grated lemon rind
1½ tablespoons lemon juice
1½ cups all-purpose flour
1½ cups sharp Cheddar
cheese, grated
¾ cup (1½ sticks) cold butter,
cut into small cubes

In a large, heavy saucepan combine raisins with water and bring to a boil. In a bowl, combine half the brown sugar, cornstarch, cinnamon, and nutmeg, cloves, and ginger; and stir into boiling mixture. Add lemon rind and juice. Let cool. In a bowl, combine flour and remaining ¾ cup brown sugar. Cut in the cheese and butter to make a crumbly mixture. Butter an 8-inch square cake pan. Pat about two thirds of the cheese mixture on the bottom of the pan. Spread raisin mixture over it. Sprinkle remaining crumbs on top and bake in a preheated 350-degree oven for 40 minutes, till top is crisp. Let cool in pan and cut into bars. Keep at room temperature until teatime.

Enchanted-Evening Anniversary

*E*very year rekindle those "honeymoon" feelings on your anniversary. Make it a really special event with your own private and magical romantic dinner for two. Set aside the evening to escape from the world and indulge yourselves in the interests you share in food, wine, and music.

▲

ENDIVE AND WATERCRESS SALAD (SEE INDEX)
PARSLIED RACK OF LAMB
POTATOES ANNA
JULIENNE OF CARROTS AND ZUCCHINI
FROZEN LEMON SOUFFLÉS
WINE: MERLOT

▼

PARSLIED RACK OF LAMB
Serves 2

1 garlic clove, finely minced
3 tablespoons Dijon mustard
5 tablespoons finely chopped
   fresh parsley
1 tablespoon dried rosemary

2 tablespoons olive oil
Salt and freshly ground
   pepper to taste
1 2-pound rack of lamb

Butter a heavy baking pan. Mix the garlic, mustard, parsley, rosemary, oil, and salt and pepper. Beat into a paste and coat the meaty side of the rack. Put the rack of lamb in the baking pan, coated side up. Roast in a preheated 425-degree oven for 25 minutes, until golden brown outside, pink and rare inside. If the rib bones begin to brown more than desired, shield them with aluminum foil. To serve, carve into individual chops.

◆

POTATOES ANNA
Serves 2

2 cups potatoes
About ⅓ cup melted butter
1 tablespoon vegetable oil
Salt

Grated onion
Freshly grated Parmesan
   cheese

Peel and cut large baking potatoes into even ³⁄₁₆-inch slices. With a small biscuit or cookie cutter, cut the slices into enough rounds to make 2 cups. Put 1½ tablespoons of the butter and the oil in a 6-inch round pan over medium heat on the stove. Add the potato rounds in slightly overlapping spirals until the base of the pan is filled. Shake occasionally while filling to make sure the potatoes are not sticking. Add a sprinkling of salt, grated onion, and Parmesan cheese. The butter will bubble. Coat this first layer of potatoes with additional melted butter. Repeat, layering potatoes with salt, onion, and cheese. It may not be necessary to continue adding butter after you have used about ⅓ cup. The moisture from the cooking potatoes will keep it bubbling. As you add potatoes, continue to shake the pan now and then to prevent sticking. After you have layered all the potato rounds, cover the pan with foil and bake in a preheated 375-degree oven for 45 minutes. Flip pan over and serve turned out on a platter.

◆

JULIENNE OF CARROTS AND ZUCCHINI
Serves 2

2 carrots, cut into thin
   2-inch strips
2 zucchini, cut into thin
   2-inch strips
¼ cup (½ stick) butter
½ teaspoon chopped fresh
   thyme or ¼ teaspoon dried

½ teaspoon dried chervil
1 small onion, peeled and
   grated
Salt and freshly ground black
   pepper

Steam the carrot strips for 5 minutes. Add the zucchini and steam for another minute. Toss immediately with butter, herbs, onion, and salt and pepper. Serve in a warm dish.

◆

FROZEN LEMON SOUFFLÉS
Serves 2 plus

4 egg yolks
½ cup sugar
2 tablespoons fresh lemon
   juice, unstrained
1 tablespoon fresh orange
   juice, unstrained
1 tablespoon lemon rind

1 tablespoon orange rind
2 egg whites
⅛ teaspoon salt
½ cup heavy cream
Garnish: Raspberries or
   strawberries, fresh mint

Combine yolks with sugar in the top of a double boiler and beat until light. Add juices and rinds. Set top of double boiler over simmering water and continue to beat until thick and creamy. Remove from heat and let cool completely. Beat egg whites with salt in a large bowl until stiff. Fold gently into the cooled lemon mixture. Beat cream in another bowl until stiff and fold gently into the lemon mixture. Spoon into 2 or more stemmed glasses and freeze. To serve, decorate with berries and mint and offer extra whipped cream in a separate bowl.

Tailgate Party

The first tailgate picnic was probably born in the back of an old "woody" station wagon. The tailgate was laid open and steaming thermoses of soup, dainty sandwiches, ice-cold cocktails and beer were spread forth. For your own tailgate party, have a celebration with exciting new food. You can improvise on this menu by including convenient gourmet takeout treats. Do not forget the wine if you want to toast your favorite team!

. . . . ▲ . . . .

CHICKEN DIABLE
SAVORY PIE NIÇOISE
NEW POTATO SALAD
ASSORTED CHEESE, FRUITS, AND BREADS (STORE-BOUGHT)
PECAN CRISPS
WINE: SOAVE

. . . . ▼ . . . .

CHICKEN DIABLE
Serves 6 to 8

2 2½-pound broilers, quartered	3 tablespoons finely minced shallots
6 tablespoons melted butter	½ teaspoon dried thyme, basil, or tarragon
2 tablespoons oil	Salt to taste
2 tablespoons red wine vinegar	⅛ teaspoon black pepper
6 tablespoons prepared Dijon mustard	Pinch of cayenne pepper
	3 cups white bread crumbs

Preheat the broiler. Wash chicken and pat dry thoroughly. Coat each piece with a mixture of butter and oil. In a bowl, combine the vinegar and mustard with the shallots, herb, and seasonings. Coat chicken with this mustard mixture. Pour bread crumbs onto a large plate and roll chicken in them, patting them on so they will stick. Put the chicken pieces, skin side down, on a rack in the broiling pan, set 5 to 6 inches below the heat, and dribble leftover butter and oil over them. Broil for 15 to 18 minutes, turning once. Light meat will take less time than dark meat. The chicken is done when the thickest part of the drumstick is tender and the juices run clear when the meat is pricked with a fork.

◆

SAVORY PIE NIÇOISE
Serves 6

Make two of these for hearty appetites.

2 eggs
1 egg yolk
¾ shredded Cheddar cheese
¾ cup heavy cream
Freshly ground pepper
Pinch of nutmeg
1 2-ounce can sliced black
    olives, drained
½ cup minced scallions

2 ounces mozzarella cheese,
    thinly sliced
2 small tomatoes, cut into
    slices ¼ inch thick
1 baked 9-inch piecrust (see
    Index)
Garnish: Fresh basil leaves

In a medium-size bowl beat eggs and yolk lightly. Stir in Cheddar, cream, and spices. Arrange olives, scallions, mozzarella, and tomatoes in the pie shell. Pour in egg mixture. Bake pie in a preheated 375-degree oven for about 25 to 30 minutes until the center is set and the top is golden. Let cool at least 5 minutes before cutting. Decorate with basil.

◆

NEW POTATO SALAD
Serves 6 to 8

The skins are left on in this new version of potato salad.

3 pounds new potatoes
3 bunches scallions, cleaned
    and sliced
3 stalks celery, finely chopped

3 tablespoons seed mustard
3 tablespoons boiling water
1¼ cups vegetable oil
Salt and pepper to taste

Wash and scrub potatoes. Cook, covered, in a large pot of boiling water for 20 minutes, or until just tender. Drain and run under cold water until cool. Quarter potatoes and place in a bowl with the scallions and celery. In another bowl put the mustard. Add the boiling water by the droplet, whisking continuously. When all the water is used, add the oil, also by the droplet, whisking continuously, until all the oil is used, and the sauce has thickened. Pour mustard sauce over potatoes and toss. Season to taste.

◆
PECAN CRISPS
Makes about 40

These cookies must be made a day in advance.

1 stick butter, softened	*¼ teaspoon baking powder*
½ cup brown sugar	*¼ teaspoon baking soda*
½ cup white sugar	*1 teaspoon vanilla extract*
¼ teaspoon ginger	*½ cup chopped pecans*
½ teaspoon cinnamon	*1 egg*
1½ cups sifted all-purpose flour	

In a large mixing bowl, cream together butter and sugar. Add spices, flour, baking powder, and baking soda and blend. Stir in vanilla and pecans. Mix with a wooden spoon for 3 to 5 minutes. When the ingredients begin to form a mass, add the egg and beat the dough until smooth. Shape dough with your hands into a log, 1½ inches in diameter. Roll in waxed paper and refrigerate overnight.

Butter two cookie sheets. Slice cold cookie dough ⅛ inch thick. Put 1 inch apart on cookie sheets. Bake for about 12 minutes, or until golden brown. With a broad spatula carefully transfer to a wire rack to cool. Store in an airtight container.

Open House Buffet

*I*t is always nice as a couple to start a tradition such as inviting family and friends to an annual fall buffet. It is not only a perfect opportunity for everyone to try your new dishes, it is also a good time to ask new acquaintances into your circle and broaden friendships.

. . . . . . ▲ . . . .

ROAST BEEF WITH PEPPERCORN MUSTARD
SEAFOOD MEDLEY WITH GREEN SAUCE
CHARCUTERIE, CHEESE, AND BREAD (STORE-BOUGHT)
MARINATED BROCCOLI AND RED PEPPER SALAD
BLACK FOREST CHERRY SQUARES
WINE: CHABLIS AND CÔTES-DU-RHÔNE

. . . . . . ▼ . . . .

◆

ROAST BEEF
WITH PEPPERCORN
SAUCE

Serves 6

1 3-pound rolled and tied rib   Ground pepper
   roast   Red wine

Put meat in a roasting pan and season with pepper. Pour a little red wine over it. Put the roast in a preheated 350-degree oven and roast 18 to 20 minutes per pound, or until a meat thermometer registers an internal temperature of 130 degrees. Remove roast and let stand 20 minutes before slicing. Arrange sliced beef on a large platter and serve peppercorn mustard sauce in a small separate bowl.

◆

GREEN
PEPPERCORN
MUSTARD SAUCE

Makes about 1 cup

2 egg yolks   2 teaspoons wine vinegar
2 tablespoons green pepper-   ¾ cup vegetable oil
   corn mustard   1 tablespoon finely chopped
1 teaspoon dry mustard   shallots
¼ teaspoon salt   1 tablespoon sour cream
Pinch of cayenne

Put the egg yolks and both mustards in a mixing bowl. Add salt and cayenne pepper and whisk until very thick. Slowly beat in the vinegar. Then gradually beat in the vegetable oil, drop by drop, until the sauce thickens. Mix in the shallots and sour cream. Put sauce in a small decorative bowl.

◆

SEAFOOD MEDLEY WITH GREEN SAUCE

Serves 6 to 8

1 pound medium-size   1 pound mussels
   shrimps   1 cup sour cream
1 pound sea scallops   2 tablespoons freshly grated
1 tablespoon whole pickling   Parmesan cheese
   spice   1 garlic clove, mashed
1 cup dry white wine

3 tablespoons minced
   watercress
2 tablespoons minced spinach
   leaves
1 tablespoon each chopped
   fresh chives, parsley, and
   dill
Salt to taste
Garnish: Lime wedges

In a large pot, bring 2 quarts water to a rolling boil. Add the shrimps, scallops, and pickling spice. Cook over high heat until the water returns to a boil and the shrimps turn pink. Drain in a colander and plunge into a bowl of ice water to stop the cooking. Drain when cool. Fill the pot with wine, add mussels, cover, and steam over low heat until the mussels open. Chill. Shell and devein the shrimps. Cut scallops into thin slices. Combine and chill in a covered dish for at least 2 hours. To make sauce, combine remaining ingredients except lime in a bowl, mix, and chill. To serve, put the shrimps, scallops, and mussels on a serving platter, garnish with lime wedges, and serve the sauce in a bowl.

◆

CHARCUTERIE, CHEESE, AND BREAD

For this selection of food, go to a good takeout food store or department.

1 pound country (roughly
   ground) pâtés
Sausages—French garlic
   (soft), Italian sweet (hard),
   and Italian spicy salami
3 crocks of mustard—herbed,
   green peppercorn, and
   Dijon
1 jar cornichons
1 jar marinated pearl onions
1 pound each herbed Brie,
   sharp Cheddar, and Stilton
   or Roquefort cheese
1 loaf each black bread, sour-
   dough, and crusty French
   bread

Arrange sliced pâtés, sausages, mustards, and garnishes on a large platter, tray, or wooden cutting board. Arrange cheeses and breads on separate servers.

◆

MARINATED BROCCOLI AND
RED PEPPER SALAD
Serves 8

½ cup light olive oil
⅓ cup tarragon vinegar
1 small onion, peeled, halved
   top to bottom and sliced
2 garlic cloves, peeled and
   sliced
½ teaspoon sugar
Salt and pepper to taste
2 bunches of broccoli
3 sweet red peppers

In a large bowl mix together all ingredients except broccoli and peppers to make a marinade. Set aside. Wash the broccoli, remove large stems, and cut into small flowerets. Blanch flowerets in boiling water for about 1 to 2 minutes, until just tender, but still crisp. Instantly drain and plunge into a bowl of ice water. Wash peppers, remove seeds and membranes, and cut into thin strips. Drain broccoli and put it and the peppers in the marinade. Chill for 2 hours, tossing occasionally.

◆

BLACK FOREST CHERRY SQUARES

Serves 12

You can make the cherry filling several days ahead if you wish.

*2 1-pound cans water-packed
    pitted red sour cherries
6 tablespoons sugar
2 tablespoons cornstarch
¼ teaspoon almond extract
½ cup sifted all-purpose flour
⅓ cup unsweetened cocoa
    powder
9 eggs
¾ cup sugar
3 ounces (½ cup) ground
    almonds (blanched or
    unblanched)*

*½ cup fine dry bread crumbs
¼ teaspoon salt
Confectioners' sugar for
    dusting
3 cups heavy cream
6 tablespoons confectioners'
    sugar
1 teaspoon vanilla extract
Kirsch
Shaved chocolate*

Drain cherries thoroughly and reserve ¾ cup of the liquid. In a small saucepan mix the 6 tablespoons sugar and the cornstarch completely. Gradually add the reserved liquid. Stirring constantly with a rubber spatula, cook over moderate heat until mixture comes to a low boil. Reduce heat to a bare simmer and stir gently for 5 minutes. Remove from the heat and add the almond extract. Pour into a bowl, add the cherries, and stir. Let cool, then cover and refrigerate.

Butter a 15½ × 10½-inch jelly roll pan, lined with waxed paper, butter the waxed paper, and dust all over with flour. Turn upside down and tap lightly to shake out excess flour. Sift the flour and cocoa into a mixing bowl and set aside. Separate 8 of the eggs. Put the yolks and the remaining whole egg in the large bowl of an electric mixer. Beat at high speed for 4 to 5 minutes, until pale and lemon-colored. Reduce the speed and gradually add ½ cup of the sugar. Increase the speed to high again and beat for 5 minutes, until the mixture forms a wide ribbon when the beaters are raised. Add the ground almonds and bread crumbs on the lowest speed. Scrape the bowl with a rubber spatula and beat only until everything is incorporated. Set aside. Put the 8 egg whites and the salt in the other large mixer bowl (or transfer egg mixture to another bowl—you need the large one for the egg whites). With clean, dry beaters, beat whites at high speed until they barely hold a soft shape. Reduce the speed to moderate and gradually add the remaining ¼ cup sugar. Then increase the speed and beat until the whites hold a firm shape but are not stiff or dry. Add 2 or 3 large spoonfuls of the whites to the chocolate mixture and stir to lighten the chocolate a bit. Fold in 2 or 3 more spoonfuls, then add all the chocolate to the whites and fold only until blended. Turn into the prepared pan and level the top with a spatula. Bake in a preheated 350-degree oven for 25 to 30 minutes, or until the top springs back when lightly pressed with a fingertip. Immediately cut around the pan sides with a sharp knife to loosen the cake. Invert on a piece of waxed paper dusted with confectioners' sugar. Gently peel off the waxed paper the cake was baked on.

Put cream, 6 tablespoons confectioners' sugar, and vanilla in a chilled bowl and beat until the cream is thick and firm enough to use as filling and icing. It must hold a definite shape.

To assemble, turn the sponge roll right side up on a pastry board or marble. Cut in half lengthwise. Brush one of the strips with kirsch and spread evenly with cherry filling out to ¼-inch from edge. Cover filling with a ½-inch layer of whipped cream. Cover with remaining cake. Brush with kirsch. Spread a ⅓-inch layer of whipped cream over the top layer of the cake; save some whipped cream for final decoration. Sprinkle with chocolate shavings. Chill for 1 to 2 hours. Remove from refrigerator and cut into 2-inch squares. With reserved cream and a pastry tube with a number 5 star tip, pipe a rosette in the center of each square.

Thanksgiving Dinner Country-Style

*I*magine the moment when America's forefathers looked upon their tables overflowing with the bounty of the land and season and gave thanks for their first harvest in the New World. Recreate that proud and glorious time by celebrating this land of plenty with your own family and friends.

. . . . ▲ . . . .

BRANDIED PUMPKIN SOUP
ROASTED TURKEY
CORN BREAD CHILI STUFFING
GIBLET GRAVY (SEE INDEX)
BRUSSELS SPROUTS WITH CHESTNUTS (SEE INDEX)
SWEET POTATO PUFFS
PORT CRANBERRY SAUCE
MINCEMEAT TARTLETS
WHISKEY PRUNE PIE
CORNUCOPIA OF FRUITS, NUTS, AND CANDIES
WINES: CHARDONNAY · CABERNET SAUVIGNON

. . . . ▼ . . . .

◆

BRANDIED PUMPKIN SOUP
Serves 10 to 12

¼ cup (½ stick) butter	¼ teaspoon salt
½ cup finely chopped onion	2½ cups scooped-out
3½ cups chicken broth	pumpkin pulp
¼ teaspoon ginger	1 cup light cream
¼ teaspoon nutmeg	2 tablespoons brandy
¼ teaspoon white pepper	Garnish: Croutons

In a large deep saucepan melt butter, add onion, and cook, stirring occasionally, until transparent. Add chicken broth and seasonings. Bring just to a boil. Blend in pumpkin and cream. Reduce heat, stir occasionally, and cook until soup is thoroughly heated, but do not boil. Blend in brandy. Serve hot with croutons.

◆

ROASTED TURKEY
Serves 8 to 10

12-pound turkey	1 cup dry white wine
Salt and pepper	1 bay leaf
Corn Bread Chili Stuffing	½ teaspoon dried thyme
(recipe follows)	4 parsley sprigs
4 tablespoons butter, softened	

Wash turkey inside and out and pat dry. Rub inside with salt and pepper. Spoon stuffing lightly into body cavity. Do not pack down. Truss legs and wings close to the body of the turkey. (See Index). Rub skin with butter and sprinkle with salt and pepper. Put the turkey, breast down, in a shallow roasting pan or on a rack in a pan. Pour the wine into the pan and add the herbs. Roast turkey in a preheated 350-degree oven for 20 minutes per pound (approximately 3 to 3¼ hours), or until it is a golden brown and juice runs clear when a drumstick is pierced, or until it registers 175 degrees on a meat thermometer. Baste with pan liquid every 30 minutes. If the skin starts to get too brown, shield by covering lightly with a tent of aluminum foil. Save pan liquid for Giblet Gravy (see Index).

◆

CORN BREAD CHILI STUFFING
Makes about 9 to 10 cups

1 cup (2 sticks) unsalted	2 cups chopped onions
butter	4 cups chopped celery

5 cups crumbled corn bread
1 cup cubed dry white bread
1 tablespoon salt, or to taste
2 small cans chopped green
  chili peppers
2 teaspoons freshly ground
  black pepper

1 teaspoon ground marjoram
1 teaspoon ground thyme
2 teaspoons ground sage
4 large eggs, well beaten
1½ to 2 cups chicken or
  turkey broth

Melt butter in a saucepan and cook onions and celery until tender but not brown, about 5 minutes. Set aside. Using a very large bowl, mix the corn bread, white bread, salt, chilies, black pepper, marjoram, thyme, and sage. Add onion-and-celery mixture. Blend in eggs and add 1½ cups broth. If the mixture is dry, use the remaining ½ cup broth. Lightly blend with a fork. To test for seasoning, cook a spoonful in a saucepan for 3 to 4 minutes and taste. Stuff the turkey and bake extra stuffing in a separate pan at 325 degrees (along with the turkey) for 45 minutes. Stuffing is done when bread is dry and fluffy. Cover with aluminum foil. Stuffing can be reheated.

◆

SWEET POTATO PUFFS
Serves 8

2 large ripe bananas
4 cups cooked sweet potatoes
4 tablespoons (½ stick)
  butter, melted
2 egg yolks, beaten

1 teaspoon salt
3 to 4 tablespoons heavy cream
¼ teaspoon each nutmeg and
  ginger
3 egg whites

Peel and mash bananas. Using a ricer, rice sweet potatoes into a large bowl. If you do not own a ricer, you can force potatoes through the holes of a colander to get the same effect. Add the bananas, butter, egg yolks, salt, cream, and nutmeg and ginger, stirring well. In another bowl, beat the egg whites until stiff. Fold whites lightly into the sweet potato mixture. Drop batter in mounds—about 1 tablespoon apiece, set well apart—onto a greased cookie sheet. Bake in a preheated 500-degree oven for about 12 minutes.

• VARIATION •
Bake the mixture in 8 individual buttered ramekins, for about 8 to 10 minutes.

◆

PORT CRANBERRY SAUCE
Serves 8 to 10

2 cups light brown sugar
2 cups port wine

½ teaspoon each ground
  cinnamon, freshly grated
  nutmeg, and ground cloves

1 pound fresh cranberries,
washed and picked over

In a 3-quart saucepan, combine brown sugar, wine, and spices. Bring to a boil over high heat, stirring to dissolve the sugar. Lower the heat slightly, add the cranberries, and boil, uncovered, until the berries begin to pop their skins, not more than 4 to 5 minutes. Remove from the heat and pour into a serving bowl or a lightly oiled mold. Let cool, then refrigerate until ready to serve.

◆

MINCEMEAT TARTLETS
Makes 12

You will need 12 tartlet tins.

1 egg
2½ pounds tart red apples,
unpeeled, cored and
chopped
1 pound ground beef chuck
1 pound dark raisins
¾ pound firmly packed light
brown sugar
¾ pound dried currants
½ pound ground beef suet
¼ pound candied citron,
chopped
¼ pound candied orange and
lemon peels, finely
chopped

2 cups apple cider
2 cups brandy
½ cup dark molasses
1½ teaspoons each ground
cloves, cinnamon, and
nutmeg
1 teaspoon ground mace
1 teaspoon salt
Enough piecrust dough for
12 tartlets (see Index)
Dough crescent moons
1 egg beaten

To make the mincemeat, combine all ingredients except dough and beaten egg in a Dutch oven. Bring to a boil. Reduce heat and simmer, uncovered, for 2 hours. Skim fat and refrigerate until ready to use. Fit dough into tartlet pans. Fill pastry shells with mincemeat. Garnish each with a pastry cutout of a crescent moon and brush crescents with beaten egg. Bake for 20 minutes in a 350-degree oven. Let cool.

◆

WHISKEY PRUNE PIE
Serves 6 to 8

1 pound dried extra-large
pitted prunes
¼ lemon

2 cloves
1 cinnamon stick
½ cup white sugar

¼ cup brown sugar
⅓ cup whiskey
Pastry for a two-crust pie
  (see Index)

Melted butter
1 egg, beaten
Confectioners' sugar

Soak prunes overnight in water to cover. The next day put prunes and soaking liquid in a saucepan, if necessary adding more water, to cover. Over high heat, bring to a boil with lemon, cloves, cinnamon, and white and brown sugar. Reduce heat to low and cook for approximately 20 to 25 minutes, until liquid is syrupy. Remove the lemon, cinnamon, and cloves. Let cool and add the whiskey. Fit the bottom crust into a 9-inch pie pan and brush with melted butter. Add the prune filling. Make a lattice top crust (see Index). Brush crust with beaten egg. Bake in a preheated 400-degree oven for 10 minutes. Reduce the heat to 325 degrees and bake for approximately 40 minutes more, or until it turns golden brown. When the pie is cool, sprinkle with confectioners' sugar.

Family Holiday Breakfast

M ake your holidays extra special and gather the family for a warming country-style breakfast. What better way is there to celebrate a holiday than by starting the day together.

GLAZED GRAPEFRUIT
COUNTRY OMELET
ORANGE YOGURT WAFFLES
HOT COCOA

GLAZED GRAPEFRUIT
Serves 6

3 pink grapefruit, cut in half   6 teaspoons brown sugar

With a small paring knife, cut around each section of grapefruit so that it will be easy to eat. Sprinkle grapefruit with brown sugar. Set, cut-side up, on a cookie sheet close to the broiler. Broil for 3 to 4 minutes, or until sugar begins to bubble. Serve immediately.

◆

COUNTRY OMELET
Serves 6

8 slices Canadian bacon
12 eggs
2 tablespoons water

4 tablespoons bacon
   drippings
¾ cup pecans, chopped
Salt and pepper

In a medium skillet, sauté Canadian bacon slowly until done. Let cool and shred. In a bowl, lightly beat eggs with water. Heat bacon fat until almost sizzling, add eggs, and swirl pan to keep eggs from sticking. When mixture is almost set, add bacon and ½ cup pecans to one half and flip the other half over. Garnish with remaining pecans.

◆

ORANGE YOGURT WAFFLES
Makes 8 4-inch square waffles

You will need a waffle iron for this recipe.

1 cup sifted all-purpose flour
1 teaspoon baking powder
½ teaspoon salt
½ teaspoon baking soda
2 tablespoons sugar
2 eggs, separated

1 cup (½ pint) plain yogurt
½ cup milk
2 tablespoons butter or
   margarine, melted
Orange Cream Custard
   (recipe follows)

Sift dry ingredients into a medium-size bowl. Beat egg yolks in a large bowl until thick; stir in yogurt, milk, and butter. Add dry ingredients and beat until fairly smooth. In another bowl, beat egg whites until they hold soft peaks. Fold into batter carefully but thoroughly. For each 4-inch waffle use about 3 ounces batter. Cook until waffle stops steaming. Serve each with a dollop of Orange Cream Custard.

◆

ORANGE CREAM CUSTARD
Makes about 1½ cups

3 egg yolks
½ cup sugar
1½ teaspoons grated
   orange rind

¼ cup orange juice
½ cup heavy cream

In a small bowl, beat egg yolks and sugar until light and lemon-colored. Pour into top of double boiler. Stir in orange rind and juice. Stirring constantly, cook over simmering water until mixture thickens and coats a wooden spoon. Let cool and chill. Whip cream until stiff. Fold into cold orange custard. Keep refrigerated until needed.

HOT COCOA
Serves 8

2 cups boiling water
1 cup cocoa
6 tablespoons sugar
1 teaspoon cinnamon

¼ teaspoon ground cloves
   and/or grated nutmeg
6 cups scalded milk
2 teaspoons vanilla extract

Combine water, cocoa, and sugar; stir and boil for 2 minutes in the top of a double boiler directly over a low flame. Add cinnamon and cloves. Set the top of the double boiler over boiling water, add the scalded milk, stir, and heat the cocoa. Cover and keep over hot water for 10 minutes more. Add vanilla, beat with a whisk, and serve.

Snowy Winter's Day Buffet

When fluffy cushions of pure white snow are piled outside the window, invite a close circle of friends to your blazing·hearth to enjoy a winter's buffet. The *pièce de résistance* might be a regional French dish, the cassoulet, or one of your own dishes to fortify you against the winter's chill.

· · · · · · ▲ · · · · · · ·

LAMB CASSOULET
TOSSED GREEN SALAD (SEE INDEX)
ASSORTED ZESTY CHEESES, SUCH AS DANISH BLUE, BEL PAESE, AND
MONTEREY JACK, AND CRUSTY BREADS (STORE-BOUGHT)
PEAR TARTS TOPPED WITH CINNAMON SAUCE AND WHIPPED CREAM
WINE: CÔTES-DU-RHÔNE

· · · · · · ▼ · · · · · · ·

LAMB CASSOULET
Serves 6

1 pound dried Great Northern
   or navy beans
1 onion, studded with 2 cloves
Bouquet garni of parsley,
   thyme, and basil
Salt
½ pound slab bacon or salt
   pork, cut into 1-inch pieces

2 pounds garlic sausage, sliced
2 cups leftover lamb, cut into
   cubes
½ cup (1 stick) butter
2 onions, minced
3 garlic cloves, chopped
2 cups plain dry bread crumbs

In a large bowl soak beans covered in water overnight. Drain and put in a large saucepan. Add 6 cups water, studded onion, bouquet garni, and 1 teaspoon salt. Simmer, covered, for 1½ hours, or until beans are tender. Drain and reserve the liquid. Melt half the butter in a frying pan and cook the bacon and sausage until pieces brown. Add minced onions and garlic and sauté for another 5 minutes. Add ½ cup of the reserved bean liquid and simmer for 20 minutes. Put half the beans with bouquet garni in a 4-quart casserole. Cover with bacon, sausage, and lamb. Add the remaining beans and enough bean liquid to cover. Bake for 2 hours, covered, in a preheated 275-degree oven. Melt the remaining ¼ cup butter and mix with crumbs. Sprinkle over beans and bake, uncovered, for 2 more hours, or until top is brown and crusty. Remove bouquet garni before serving.

◆

PEAR TARTS
WITH CINNAMON SAUCE AND
WHIPPED CREAM

Serves 6

2 cups dry white wine	⅔ cup sliced almonds
½ cup sugar	6 puff pastry shells, home-
2 cinnamon sticks	made and baked (see
3 large, firm Bosc pears,	Index) or store-bought
peeled	2 tablespoons cornstarch
	Whipped cream

In a large heavy saucepan combine wine, sugar, and cinnamon. Bring to a boil, lower the heat, and add pears. Simmer, uncovered, until the pears are tender but not mushy, about 10 minutes. Remove from the heat and let cool. Spread out almonds in a skillet and toast over low heat. Stir constantly until the almonds are brown, about 5 minutes. Do not let them burn. Lift the pears from the syrup with a slotted spoon. Slice in half lengthwise and core. Put a half in each pastry shell. Beat cornstarch into the poaching liquid and stir over medium heat for about 6 to 7 minutes, or until the sauce is smooth and thick. Spoon hot sauce over the pears, sprinkle with almonds, and serve right away. Pass a bowl of whipped cream to top the tarts.

Old-Fashioned Christmas Dinner

The season to be merry is also a time to give yourself to your loved ones. Invite family and friends in at Christmas. This sumptuous feast, reminiscent of Grandmother's holiday cooking, is a treasure to share with family and friends.

CREAMED SMOKED OYSTERS ON TOAST POINTS
CROWN ROAST OF PORK WITH CRANBERRY RAISIN STUFFING
BAKED ACORN SQUASH (SEE INDEX)
GLAZED BABY ONIONS
BIBB LETTUCE AND CHERRY TOMATOES WITH LEMON DILL DRESSING
BÛCHE DE NOËL
WINES: RIESLING AND SAINT-EMILION

CREAMED SMOKED OYSTERS ON TOAST POINTS

Serves 8

This recipe takes a few minutes and is ideal when undertaking a large holiday meal. About 15 minutes before serving, make the toast, trim crusts, and cut into triangles.

2 tablespoons butter
2 tablespoons minced shallots
2½ cups heavy cream
2 tablespoons sherry
3 cans (3¾ ounces) smoked
  oysters, drained

8 slices toast, trimmed and
  cut into triangles
Garnish: Chopped parsley

Melt butter in heavy saucepan and add shallots. Sauté for about 5 minutes, or until tender. Add cream and sherry, bring to a boil, and reduce to about 1½ cups. Add oysters and cook to heat through, about 2 minutes. Arrange toast on individual plates; with slotted spoon divide oysters among plates, top with cream sauce, and garnish with parsley. Serve immediately.

◆

CROWN ROAST OF PORK WITH CRANBERRY RAISIN STUFFING

Serves 8 to 10

Buy 16 to 20 paper frills to put on ends of chop bones.

¾ cup (1½ sticks) plus 3
  tablespoons butter
1 cup chopped onions

3 cups chopped peeled green
  apples
1 cup parboiled dark and
  yellow raisins

1 cup coarsely chopped
  cranberries
½ cup chopped celery
  (optional)
4 cups bread crumbs
1 pound sausage meat
½ teaspoon each cinnamon,
  mace, sage, nutmeg, and
  thyme
1 teaspoon salt
¼ teaspoon pepper

2 eggs, beaten
3 to 4 tablespoons oil
1 8-pound crown roast of
  pork (prepared by a
  butcher)
1 cup dry white wine
4 tablespoons chopped
  shallots
½ cup heavy cream
Grated rind of 1 orange
  (optional)

To make stuffing, melt ¾ cup butter in a skillet, add onions and apples, and sauté until soft but not brown. Let cool and combine in a large mixing bowl with the raisins, cranberries, celery, bread crumbs, sausage, herbs, and seasonings. Stir in the beaten eggs. Sauté a bit of the stuffing, taste for seasoning, and adjust if necessary. Put the pork in a shallow round pan. Spoon the stuffing into the center of the crown and drizzle oil over the meat and stuffing. Roast the pork in a preheated 350-degree oven for 2½ to 3 hours, or until a meat thermometer registers 185 degrees. Baste the meat and stuffing frequently during cooking. When done, remove butcher strings and transfer roast to a serving platter. Put a frill on each chop bone. Carve the meat between the chop bones in wedges, so each chop is served with a slice of stuffing.

To make gravy, add the wine, shallots, and remaining 3 tablespoons butter to the pan juices. Boil until reduced to a third the original volume, stirring steadily. Add the cream and orange rind and reheat without boiling. Season to taste and strain into a gravy bowl or boat.

GLAZED
BABY ONIONS
Serves 8

Glazed onions are lighter and a nice substitute for the traditional creamed onions at holiday time.

2 pounds small white onions
½ cup butter, melted
¼ cup honey

Pinch of nutmeg
Salt and pepper to taste

Peel and clean onions. Parboil for 10 minutes. Drain onions and transfer to a buttered baking dish. Mix butter and honey together and pour over. Sprinkle with nutmeg and season. Bake in a preheated 350-degree oven for 20 minutes, or until golden, basting from time to time.

BIBB LETTUCE AND CHERRY TOMATOES WITH LEMON DILL DRESSING
Serves 8

4 heads Bibb lettuce
1 pint cherry tomatoes
¼ cut fresh lemon juice
½ tablespoon sugar
⅔ cup oil

½ teaspoon salt
⅛ teaspoon freshly ground
  pepper
1 teaspoon chopped fresh dill

Wash lettuce and dry in salad spinner or paper towels. Break into bite-size pieces. Wash tomatoes and pat dry. Put lettuce and tomatoes in a large salad bowl and refrigerate. In a small bowl, mix lemon juice and sugar. Whisk together. Add oil very gradually until all is beaten in. Add seasonings and herb and whisk again. Just before dressing salad, give another whisk or two. Toss salad with dressing.

BÛCHE DE NOËL
Serves 8

This French "Christmas log" is always a holiday hit. It can be made the day before.

6 eggs
¾ cup sugar
¾ cup cake flour
¾ teaspoon baking powder
¼ teaspoon salt
8 tablespoons butter, melted
  and cooled

½ teaspoon vanilla extract
Confectioners' sugar
1½ cups rum buttercream
  (see Index)
1½ cups chocolate butter-
  cream (see Index)
Garnish: Fresh holly sprigs

To make the Christmas log, beat the eggs in a large bowl over hot water until foamy and they start to thicken. Gradually add sugar, beating all the time, and continue to beat until mixture becomes thick and has tripled in volume. In another bowl, sift flour, baking powder, and salt together. Gently, but thoroughly, fold flour mixture into egg mixture. Very quickly fold in butter and vanilla. Spread batter evenly on an 11 × 15-inch jelly roll pan lined with buttered wax paper and dusted with flour. Bake in a preheated 375-degree oven for 12 to 15 minutes, or until cake springs back when touched. Remove from oven, cool slightly, and invert onto a dish towel well dusted with confectioners' sugar. Quickly remove wax paper, trim the crust, and gently roll the log lengthwise, jelly roll fashion, in the towel. Chill. Unroll the log and spread rum buttercream from edge to edge. Reroll and chill for at least 1 hour. Remove from refrigerator and spread chocolate buttercream over sides of log. For a decorative effect, draw tines of a fork over log to make a zigzag pattern. Decorate with holly.

267

Reaffirmation Celebration

• •

*R*eaffirmation vows symbolize your continued commitment to a happy, loving relationship. It is almost like getting married all over again. Celebrate this joyful occasion with either a small and intimate or a large and elegant party. Invite family and friends to share the important moment with you.

• • • • • • • ▲ • • • • • • •

SCALLOP MOUSSELINE
BRAISED PHEASANT IN MADEIRA
FRESH SPINACH (SEE INDEX)
OVEN-ROASTED POTATOES
HAZELNUT TORTE
WINE: RIESLING

• • • • • • • ▼ • • • • • • •

SCALLOP MOUSSELINE
• •
Serves 8

2½ cups bay or sea scallops	*Pinch of nutmeg*
1⅔ cups heavy cream	*Honeydew and cantaloupe*
3 eggs	*balls*
Salt and pepper	*Garnish: Chopped coriander*

Butter individual ½-cup ramekins. In a food processor or blender, blend all ingredients except melon and coriander. Pour into the ramekins and put in a pan filled with water that reaches two thirds up the side of the ramekins. Bake for 30 minutes in a preheated 350-degree oven, until set. Remove from oven and let cool. Unmold mousseline from ramekins onto a serving plate. Surround with melon balls and garnish.

◆

BRAISED PHEASANT IN MADEIRA
• •
Serves 8

2 3-pound pheasants, dressed	*3¼ cups Madeira*
3 tablespoons oil	*Bouquet garni of: 3 sprigs*
6 tablespoons butter	*parsley, 2 sprigs thyme,*
1 onion, sliced	*and 1 bay leaf*
2 carrots, peeled and sliced	*½ pound sliced bacon*
2 stalks celery, sliced	*1 cup heavy cream*
Salt and freshly ground pep-	
per to taste	

Wash birds thoroughly. Heat the oil and half the butter in a large heavy casserole or pot and brown the pheasants on all sides. Remove birds, add onion, carrots, and celery, and sauté over moderate heat until the onion begins to color. Return pheasants to the pot, season, add Madeira and bouquet garni. Lay bacon slices over the whole birds. Cover the pot and put in a preheated 350-degree oven for about 1¼ hours, or until juices run clear when pierced with a fork. Transfer birds to a hot serving platter and let rest for 20 minutes before carving. Put cream in a saucepan over medium heat and reduce in half. Add 1½ cups of the strained pan juices to the cream. Reduce cream in half again. Carve pheasants and spoon sauce over them.

◆

OVEN-ROASTED POTATOES
Serves 8

2 pounds boiling potatoes,
   peeled
6½ tablespoons butter
Salt and freshly ground
   pepper to taste

Freshly grated nutmeg to
   taste
Garnish: 2 tablespoons finely
   chopped fresh parsley

With a food processor or a knife, cut the potatoes into medium-size French-fry shapes—about 2 inches long and ¼ inch thick. Cook for 5 minutes in boiling salted water. Drain, plunge into cold water, and pat dry with paper towels. Butter a medium-size baking dish thoroughly and arrange a layer of the potatoes. Dot with butter and season. Repeat layers until potatoes are used up. Roast, uncovered, in a preheated 425-degree oven for 15 to 20 minutes, until the potatoes are very tender. While baking, toss lightly once or twice to evenly coat potatoes with the butter. Serve sprinkled with the parsley.

◆

HAZELNUT TORTE
Serves 8 to 10

1 cup plus 2 tablespoons
   sugar
12 egg yolks
¼ pound hazelnuts
¼ pound pecans
2 tablespoons homemade
   plain bread crumbs (not
   too fine)

8 egg whites
Pinch of salt
Whipped cream flavored with
   vanilla and Bourbon

Sift the 1 cup sugar. In a large mixing bowl, beat the egg yolks for 5 minutes, then add the sugar gradually. Beat well until mixture is very creamy, another 5 minutes.

Grind the hazelnuts and pecans in a nut grinder with the remaining 2 tablespoons sugar, and add to the yolk mixture. Then add the bread crumbs. Whip the egg whites in a large bowl with a pinch of salt until stiff but not dry. Fold whites gently into the yolk mixture. Bake the torte in an ungreased 10-inch springform pan in a preheated 350-degree oven for about 40 minutes or until done. Let cool and serve with flavored whipped cream.

PART IV

Entertaining

Your table never looked more enchanting. The resplendent glow of candlelight casts a magic spell as it sparkles off each facet of cut crystal and reflects the warm radiance of polished silver. Conversation flows, and each guest is replete in the generosity of your attention and your table.

If this is an image you relate to, or however you envision the mood, entertaining is always a special opportunity for both of you to take pride in your home, to enjoy the fulfillment of being partners who together have created your own personal style, and as a way of showing how much you care for your family, friends, and each other.

There is no detail too insignificant to attend to. Be it pristine table linen, flowers artfully arranged, or attentive little touches like flower petals in finger bowls, they all contribute to and enhance your lovingly and skillfully prepared meal, and add to the total enjoyment of your guests.

Use your imagination and be creative. The only rules are those that relate to common sense and common courtesy. Traditions and proper etiquette are important, but life-styles are constantly changing. The goal is to do what is comfortable and correct at the same time.

As you read this section about etiquette and the various principles of entertaining, you will see that there are no stiff, restraining rules, only logical procedures. Interpret these guidelines and creative party-planning ideas to meet your needs and help you offer your guests an atmosphere of gracious hospitality.

PLANNING THE EVENT

The Menu

What is the focal point of any party? It is usually the food! Examine your menu from all viewpoints. It is a good idea to select a menu appropriate to the season, or theme of the occasion. In winter, robust, warming foods are welcomed by most, while cooler, lighter foods are a delight in summer heat. By selecting foods according to the time of year, you can take advantage of the best buys in produce and meats that are in season. For example, you can have a glorious peach tart or parfait in summer, when peaches are plentiful, at their peak of flavor, and also at a good price, the luxury of pomegranates and persimmons when they are available in the fall, fresh rhubarb for homemade pies in winter, or lamb and asparagus at their peak of flavor in the spring.

You also should select dishes that are appropriate for your skills as a chef. Do not try to impress your guests by undertaking complicated meals that you are newly experimenting with. You will be embarrassed if they fail, which can easily happen. Instead, serve a special dish that guests have given rave reviews to in the past. But do not serve your specialty at *every* party, or to the same guests, or they may rightly say, "Oh, I suppose we'll be having your usual chicken casserole." Base the menu on one of your tried and true favorite main dishes, and then plan the vegetables and dessert around it.

Vary the menu in taste, texture, and color. Choose foods that have eye and taste appeal. Do not mix similar dishes, such as two creamed vegetables or foods of the same color. Do orchestrate color and texture, sauces, flavorings, spices, herbs, lightness and richness of dishes, to achieve a harmonious balance. A combination of hot and cold dishes is also welcome. Give palates a refreshing break by serving a chilled appetizer before a hot main course.

In general, plan to serve dishes that have the same or similar cooking temperatures, to avoid competing schedules. A soufflé and a slow-cooking roast, for example, will not fare well at the same temperature. Also, be sure to coordinate your agenda so you do not have to cook two complicated dishes at once: a hollandaise sauce, which can curdle when overheated, and a delicate, time-consuming pastry. Avoid dishes that will keep you in the kitchen doing last-minute sautéing, sauce stirring, or ice cream parfait assembling. It is best to serve dishes that you can prepare in advance, pop in the oven, and present with confidence. Select dishes that can be completely, or at least partially, cooked a day or two ahead of the party and stored in the freezer or refrigerator. This saves you valuable time later and frees you up to be relaxed hosts and enjoy the evening along with your guests.

If you have any questions about whether guests have special dietary needs, it is not impolite to ask when you speak to them about the party. Describe your suggested menu and inquire if they have any preferences. Usually most people who must abstain from certain foods because of allergies, health reasons, or religious obser-vances have learned to accept what they are offered when visiting as a guest and will simply eat whatever foods they can. But, without turning into short-order cooks, gracious hosts should plan to prepare foods that the majority of their guests can enjoy. Usually the key is serving a well-balanced meal based on a variety of nutritious foods, not all of which are highly seasoned.

When planning your entire menu, go light on the hors d'oeuvres and drinks that preface your meal. You do not want to overload your guests with too much food before you have served them your masterpiece. Nor do you want to dull their senses with too many cocktails. A light aperitif, a glass of sparkling wine, or kir (white wine with a touch of crème de cassis—delicious!) is more appropriate than a martini before dinner. Limit the cocktail time to about 45 minutes, certainly never more than an hour.

Before you have even thought about cocktails you must decide on the principal meal. The easiest way to build your menu is to start with the main course, and choose other dishes—vegetables, salad, and dessert—to enhance and complement it in flavor, color, and texture. What follows is a list of courses that are used as a guide by restauranteurs and food experts. Not all are included in every type of entertaining, as will subsequently be explained.

FIRST COURSE

This course is designed to awaken the palate and whet the appetite for what is to follow. A first course can be considered a light treat—something savory and tempt-ing—that is best enjoyed in small portions. Oysters, clams, crudités, fruits, cheeses, pâté with toast triangles, prosciutto and melon—these and many more simple dishes can make an intriguing starter, a counterpoint in weight and taste to the next course.

SOUP

Soup is often served as a first course, and the range is exciting. From bubbling French onion soup topped with golden crusts of cheese (good for winter warm-ups) to a chilled cucumber soup or fresh gazpacho in summer, you can choose a soup that fits into your meal perfectly. Soup can also appear as a main course. You can make a hearty meal with fish chowder or exotic bouillabaisse. A cream of broccoli, cauliflower, or carrot soup can serve as a main course for lunch, a lighter dinner, or late supper.

FISH

At formal dinners with many courses, you may have seen fish served simply and elegantly as a course by itself preceding the main entrée. If you should find yourselves hosting a formal dinner and you want to serve a fish course, you might consider turban of sole; found in a French cookbook. You could also serve a truly American seafood treat such as a small portion of pompano with a cream-and-shrimp sauce or trout with a horseradish sauce. If you are not going the formal route, there are many other ways to include seafood in your dinner menu. If you select seafood as an appetizer, you could serve small portions of steamed mussels, or a few fresh pink shrimps on a colorful bed of lettuce, tomato, and red onion. There are also innumer-able main-course fish dishes to choose from, such as poached salmon with cucumber-dill sauce. Or try a buttery clam linguine.

MAIN COURSE

Your main course will be the focal point of your meal. Whether turkey, trout, or teriyaki the main dish should suit the occasion and the season, and generally contain meat or fish. The possibilities are endless—veal scallopine with lemon and herbs, beef bourguignon or a *confit* of duck with oranges. If you serve a vegetarian meal, there are, of course, many meatless main dishes to choose from—pasta primavera, crêpes filled with spinach and riccotta cheese, an elegant asparagus quiche, or perhaps a piquant and adventurous Chinese dish, such as Szechuan-style vegetables and noodles. Your choice in main courses will be the basis for your wine selection, unless you plan to serve a different wine with each course.

The main course is usually accompanied by one or two vegetables. Here is your chance to design a pretty feast for the eye. Color is an important key, and you will discover that fresh vegetables can provide the prettiest "frame" for your masterpiece, the main dish. Carrots artfully sliced on the diagonal look exotic and taste more exciting, when you lightly steam them and anoint with butter to which you have added a drop or two of cognac. Another eye-catching vegetable offering is bright green steamed asparagus with lemon-yellow butter. Or you might present boiled new potatoes seasoned with dark green fresh basil, or glowing red baby beets with a dot of butter. Try new recipes and experiment with different combinations of ingredients.

SALAD

When it comes to salads, there are two customs to consider: the American style and the European. In this country, particularly in the West, salads are served as a starter course to refresh and cleanse the palate. Europeans offer greens after the main course—for the same reason. They consider the piquant salad dressings too strong to start the meal, and prefer to use vinaigrette dressing to cleanse the palate before dessert. Whatever your preference, there is no reason to feel rigid about either convention. You can serve salads before, after, or along with the main course. For a luncheon, you may choose to turn a fresh garden salad with an array of special touches into the focal point of your meal.

DESSERT

While food styles in every culture vary, in most countries the finale to dinner is a sweet. This delectable course can consist of anything from slices of fresh fruit in season and cheeses to an elaborate whipped-cream-topped torte. There are countless options to suit your meal: plain fresh fruit, hot puddings, soufflés, three-layer chocolate cakes, ice cream topped with liqueurs, nuts, or sauces, sherbets, cookies, and coffee and liqueur. On some occasions, make dessert the main course or the center of attention, such as cold fruit soup for a summer luncheon or a delicious custard tart for a tea. Your imagination is your guide and your only limit.

Themes

Winter, summer, spring, and fall—all offer many seasonal delights to add to your entertaining themes. In winter, have a warm, cozy brunch on a snowy morning and enjoy the bounty of preserves and relishes from summer gardens and produce stands. In spring, fill your baskets with flowers, get out your bright linens, and offer a dinner menu of spring lamb and seasonal vegetables and fruits. In addition to playing on the theme of the season and its special foods, there are dozens of other themes you can choose for entertaining. No matter if you are centering your entertaining event around a big holiday, such as Saint Valentine's Day—or a special birthday, anniversary or promotion—celebrate all momentous occasions with the drama of a shared and very special meal.

People

The basis for a stimulating party atmosphere is the right mix of people who can be interesting to each other. Be sure that you include some guests with outgoing personalities whom you can count on to stir up conversations and excitement. Most of your acquaintances enjoy meeting new faces, so be sure to also include "mystery" guests— friends of friends, or people you are just getting to know. They will provide the unpredictable, and give a sense of adventure to any party.

Tableware

When designing your table, be it a seated meal or buffet, stay true to your theme. Choose serving vessels and accessories that contribute to the mood of your party as well as coordinate and enhance the appearance of the food. For a hearty country-style meal, your stoneware, pewter, wooden bowls, nubby woven linens, and a copper pot with dried field flowers would be most appropriate. If the occasion is more formal, it is *the* time to use your fine china, crystal, and silver; it also is the moment to create a special aura with flowers, candles, fine linen napery, and elegant centerpieces. In addition to using creativity and imagination, keep in mind the contrast of informality versus formality as well as the principles of coordinating color, texture, and mood.

Lighting

Think of lighting as a design element that can have a major effect on the atmosphere of a party. Carefully plan lighting in the rooms where your party is centered. What kind of mood do you want? For a cocktail party, you may want to leave overhead lights off and illuminate the room with only a few table lamps that are strategically located to set off refreshment centers or pretty decorating details. Candles simply set along a mantel, for example, can add an aura of festivity or quiet elegance. The resulting shadows cast across the room, and the pretty soft golden light on the faces of your guests, will create a memorable scene.

Ventilation

In addition to appropriate lighting, for the comfort of your guests you should be sure your home is adequately ventilated, heated or cooled. You should eliminate cooking odors as much as possible. For this chore, a kitchen or stove fan works wonders.

Reduce cigarette smoke by burning candles and keeping windows open a crack to channel smoke out of a room. Scented candles are also a lovely touch to a party and help create a romantic mood in the room. If you have an everyday problem with pet odors, take some steps to alleviate them on party day by making sure that pet boxes are clean and deodorized, adding a few sprays of air freshener to the area, and brushing any animal hairs from furniture.

As for room temperature, when entertaining, keep in mind that the more guests there are, the more body heat is generated; therefore, you may want to turn your air-conditioner to a cooler setting in summer months. If you are using fans, create a gentle flow of air through rooms, but never turn fans on high, facing guests. A day or two before the party, experiment with the cooling-circulation system. Put a fan for incoming air in one window, with another fan set on exhaust in a second window. Put screens in windows to keep out unwanted insects.

In fall or winter months you have the same body-heat situation as you do in hot weather. If you have a large number of guests coming for cocktails, you will want to lower your heater. If you are also using a fireplace, you will want to keep the fire low (a romantic blaze is fine when there are just the two of you) and open windows slightly. This will keep the room from becoming too hot or stuffy. Do not group chairs too close to the fire; you may want to borrow or rent a humidifier if the air in your home is too dry in winter.

Whether you two choose to have a small party or a large one, there is always one essential you will need—a list. For a large party, you should prepare two lists or agendas: one that details chores and tasks to complete before the party; another for the day of the party, including cooking times and oven temperatures for the dishes you will be serving. It is also a good idea to prepare an overall party inventory, including all the items and accessories you will need for the special event.

In general, give yourself two to three days before a party for a thorough housecleaning. Assign one or two heavy chores for each day, such as vacuuming, scrubbing floors, cleaning windows, or doing the laundry. Do not overload your schedule by leaving these jobs until the last moment, as there is always the possibility of unexpected demands on your time as the day of the party nears. A few days in advance, begin to shop for food for your party. Do not purchase perishables such as fresh fruits, vegetables, and dairy products until the day or the morning before, as they should be as fresh as possible.

Use the following handy lists to keep your party organized so you can make it a smashing success.

All-Purpose Calendar

ONE MONTH BEFORE A LARGE PARTY
- Decide on the number of guests and prepare a list of names.
- Prepare and mail invitations.
- Start thinking about your menu, including cocktails, aperitifs, after-dinner drinks.
- For an extremely large party, you might want to consider hiring a caterer, renting tables, chairs, linens, decorations, and an outdoor tent, and hiring musicians and a bartender and waiters or waitresses.

TWO WEEKS BEFORE
• Determine your theme and plan your decor, including table settings, color schemes, linens, flowers. Survey your household and kitchen equipment and decide if you will need to borrow, rent, or buy any of the following:
• Crystal cocktail glasses
• Serving platters
• Serving utensils
• Flatware—sterling or stainless steel
• Set of dishes—bowls, plates, and cups
• Linens—tablecloth, dining and cocktail napkins
• Cooking equipment—large kettles, chafing dishes, etc.
• Coffee maker, tea service (for large gatherings)
• Ice buckets
• Extra tables, chairs
• Trays
• Punch bowl
• Vases
• Candelabra
• Fans
• Extra lamps
• Coat racks and extra hangers
• Ashtrays
• Coasters
• Plastic runners for winter boots
• Umbrella stands
• For a barbecue, grills and cooking utensils, charcoal and charcoal lighter

ONE WEEK BEFORE
• Speak to the caterer (if you plan to use one) and review all plans and menu for the party. Check all items needed, write out menu and lists.
• Purchase or order liquor.
• Prepare a food-shopping list.
• Order flowers.
• Decide on party clothes; if necessary, have them laundered or dry-cleaned.
• Purchase decorations.

THREE DAYS BEFORE
• Write out menu and/or place cards.
• Shop for food.
• Shop for bathroom supplies: extra rolls of toilet and facial tissue, extra bars of soap and air freshener.
• Prepare any foods that can be refrigerated or frozen.

TWO DAYS BEFORE
• Start or continue cooking.
• Start to clean house.
• Check off all items on inventory.
• Order extra ice, if not supplied by your caterer, to be delivered the day of the party.

ONE DAY BEFORE
- Add finishing touches to decorations.
- Defrost frozen food, have food finished or in final stages.
- Set the table or tables.
- Gather serving platters, utensils.
- Arrange coffee, tea service.
- Prepare closets for coats; arrange extra rented coat racks.
- Arrange furniture.
- Fill sugar bowls, salt and pepper shakers.
- Finish major cleaning.
- Prepare serving trays with coasters, napkins, ashtrays.
- Set out umbrella stands, runners for boots (for inclement weather).
- Clean and set up grill (if barbecueing).
- Go through a mental dress rehearsal.

THE DAY
- If using a caterer, have the staff arrive early; demonstrate duties and layout of the house and facilities.
- Light touch-up cleaning (dusting, etc.)
- Arrange flowers.
- Add final touches to recipes, including hors d'oeuvres.
- Set up serving boards or tables.
- Set out all kitchen service items: dish cloths, pot holders, etc.
- Freshen up bathroom with clean towels, fresh soap, tissue.
- Set up bar, fill ice buckets (or fill bath tub with ice).
- Chill white wines and rosés (at least 2 hours before party).
- Chill water and mixers.
- Put out dry, nibbling foods for cocktails.
- For outdoor parties, set off insect repellent.
- Ready the barbecue grill if cooking over it; assemble utensils and equipment.
- Relax, freshen up, shower, dress—take it easy!

Party Inventory List

Check to see that following items are in order and on hand:

GENERAL OVERALL PARTY NEEDS
- Invitation refusals and acceptances counted
- China
- Flatware
- Glassware
- Barware for cocktails, wine and after-dinner cordials
- Tablecloths and napkins
- Tables and chairs
- Finger bowls, if using
- Cocktail napkins and toothpicks
- Tea and coffee services, cups and saucers

FOOD PREPARATION AND PRESENTATION NEEDS

- Necessary kitchen equipment
- Grills, charcoal, cooking utensils, if required
- Bar supplies: ice, jigger, corkscrew, bottle openers, ice bucket, trays, decanters, coasters, liquor, wine, mixers, liqueurs
- Food warmers
- Necessary trays and trivets

CREATIVE COMFORTS

- Decorations and party favors, if using
- Candles and candleholders
- Flowers
- Menu and place cards
- Music, if having
- Outdoor tent, if needed
- Games and card, if using
- Coatracks and umbrella stands
- Rubber mats and plastic runners for boots (if winter)
- Ashtrays, matches and lighters
- Logs for fireplace, if required
- Supplies for bathroom, hand towels, toilet and facial tissues, and room refresher

Hiring a Capable Caterer

There will be some parties—your parents' anniversary, a reaffirmation celebration, a large formal dinner, or a baby christening—when you will want expert food preparation and service. At these extra-special times, consider hiring a caterer to do some or all of the preparation. Most professional caterers have a well-trained staff of chefs, waiters, even wine specialists, to help make your party a smash hit. There are a number of ways to scout the best caterer in your area:

- Get information from friends who have used caterers. Trusted friends can make menu recommendations and also vouch for the quality of service. Another approach is to collect names or business cards from caterers who handled good parties you have attended. Other possibilities are to ask the food editor of your local newspaper or check the listing for "Caterers" in the Yellow Pages. Before meeting with them, inquire about their menu range—do they do ethnic food, for example—as well as their equipment. Do they furnish china, glasses, linens, tables and chairs? Then get a rough estimate of their price per head for the function you are planning. It is a good idea to get estimates from three firms, as prices can differ greatly.
- When you meet with a caterer, ask to see a list of their specialties and discuss the menu extensively. Most caterers will do anything you want, from hors d'oeuvres to dessert. Review the party theme so that it coordinates with the menu. If you are uncertain about the food, ask for suggestions, keeping your budget in mind. Most often caterers supply wine and liquor, too; however, you can cut cost drastically by providing your own. Do ask to sample foods. When planning a large party, get everything in writing in a contract form. Check their credentials.

• Refer to your Party Inventory List (see Index) to determine the equipment and accessories you will need (tables, chairs, hanging lanterns, ice, etc.) and see if your caterer can provide them. Also, inquire about the caterer's cleanup service—does the base cost include dishwashing, vacuuming, clearing tables and other food-services areas?

• If you will use the caterer's service staff, decide on the waiter's outfits. Do you want black and white traditional uniforms or do you want white or pastels in summer? Do you want the bartenders to wear jackets, or is it an informal lawn party? You may want the staff dressed to match your party theme—striped T-shirts and slacks for a sailing buffet, Kelly green aprons for a St. Patrick's Day dinner, or some other dress. Make sure your plans are agreeable to the staff.

FORMAL VERSUS INFORMAL

While the terms "formal" and "informal" now tend to overlap in meaning, there are still some noteworthy traditions that distinguish one type of entertaining from another. Let us examine current etiquette for both of these occasions.

Formal Dinner

INVITATIONS

Invitations to a formal dinner should be either handwritten or engraved cards that can be filled in by the hostess. For a very special touch you can have them done in calligraphy, either by a talented friend with flawless handwriting or by a calligraphy service.

In the bottom left corner of the card you should write: "The favor of a reply is requested" or "RSVP" ("Please reply" in French). Telephone numbers can be included for all but the most formal invitations are responded to in writing.

> Mr. and Mrs. John Evans
> request the pleasure of
> Mr. and Mrs. Christopher Walker's
> company at dinner
> on Friday the sixth of December,
> at eight o'clock.
> 127 Great Oak Lane
>
> R.S.V.P.

Address invitations to married couples as: "Mr. and Mrs." If you are inviting unmarried couples, engaged or otherwise, include both names on the invitation or send each person an invitation.

On the lower right hand corner of the invitation, indicate dress: A formal dinner party is either "White Tie" or "Black Tie." If the party has a special theme, such as "masked ball" or "black and white," specify this on the invitation. If you want to relax the formality a slight bit, you can specify "Dark Suits," and men will wear suits and women evening dress or appropriate attire.

Invitations to formal dinners should be sent one month in advance.

MENU

Today, in the United States, there are usually four courses served at a formal dinner party: an appetizer or a soup, a main course, salad, and dessert. A five-course dinner features the addition of a separate fish course. The accent on food for this type of occasion is decidedly elegant and inspired, but when serving a number of courses, do not overwhelm your guests with large portions.

At least two wines are served during dinner. You might start with a white wine for the appetizer, and go on to red for the main course, if it is appropriate to the food. Sometimes champagne or a sweet after-dinner wine is served with dessert, if the meal is very festive.

TABLE SETTING

Bring out your finest china, silver, and linens for this occasion. Incorporate all the wonderful wedding gifts you received, as well as any gems you have inherited—crystal goblets, antique silverware, ornate candelabras, or a damask tablecloth.

At a formal dinner, elegance is the key. Decor and table settings are important to the occasion and should be beautiful and effective. Keep flowers and candles either very low or very high: a delicate bouquet of flowers in season at each place setting or tall topiaries of fresh greens and blossoms are lovely alternatives to a single center-of-the-table arrangement, which may be difficult to see over.

Include salt dishes, with their delicate spoons, individual silver pepper shakers or mills, sparkling goblets, and pastel or snowy-white napkins to adorn the table.

When setting the table, flatware and the rim of plates should be placed an inch from the edge of the table. Measure 24 inches from the center of one dinner plate to the center of the next, for the position of each setting.

A tablecloth is proper for formal dinners. However, if your table is especially beautiful and you want to expose its satiny finish and fine grain, you may use exquisitely embroidered or lace place mats. When using a tablecloth, linen, damask, and organdy are excellent choices. A lace cloth with an underliner is also attractive. The classic shades for your cloth: white, ecru, and, of course, pastel. The tablecloth should hang at least nine inches below the table's edge.

The following is a list of items used in an individual formal setting:

• *Service plate*—The service plate is usually larger and more ornate than a regular dinner plate, but you may substitute a regular dinner plate if you do not own service plates. The purpose of the service plate is to dress the table when guests are first seated, and it is therefore on the table when guests enter. The napkin may be put on the service plate before the plate for the first course appetizer or soup is served. The service plate is removed after the first course; if dinner plates are being used, exchange them with another set for the main course.
• *Dinner plate*—This plate is used for the main course, or can double as a service plate.
• *Soup plate and cream soup cup*—The flat rimmed soup plate is used for most soups. The two-handled cup with saucer is used for cream soups and bouillon. It is permissible to hold a cream soup cup by the handles to drink soup broth, but any noodles or vegetables should be eaten with a spoon.
• *Bread-and-butter plate*—At formal American dinner parties bread or rolls are often not served. If you elect to do so, you can follow the French formal rule according to which dinner rolls are tucked into the folded napkin on the service plate; or today you have the option to use the bread-and-butter plate. Place it at the left side of each place setting, just above the forks. The butter knife is placed across the plate, with the

handle on the right, and the edge toward the table edge. Butter balls or curls are usually put on the dish before guests are seated; the plate is removed before dessert.

• *Salad plate*—This plate is smaller than the dinner plate and can be used for appetizers and dessert as well as salad.

• *Dessert plate*—Dessert plates are sometimes larger than salad plates, but the two can be used interchangeably.

• *Flatware*—The simple rule to keep in mind is that you "eat toward the plate." Thus, all flatware is placed from the outside in. All forks are placed to the left of the dinner plate. The exception is the oyster fork, which is placed on the right side of the dinner plate.

The dinner knife is always put on the right of the dinner plate, with its blade facing the plate, and a soup spoon, if required during the meal, to its right. A seafood or oyster fork, when needed, is put at the right of the soup spoon. If a second knife is used to cut cheese with the salad, it should be put between the soup spoon and dinner knife. At a formal dinner, the dessert fork and spoon are brought in with the dessert plate, not before. They are placed left and right, respectively, on the plate. Coffee spoons or teaspoons are never put on the table.

• *Salt and pepper*—At a formal occasion, individual salt and pepper sets are used and set above each service plate. If you do not have enough individual sets, put one between each table setting for two people to share. Salt and pepper are removed before dessert is served.

• *Glassware*—Glasses should be placed as follows: The goblet or larger water glass is filled with ice water and put above the knife; glasses for wines are put at the right of the goblet, either on a diagonal line or in a triangle. The wine to be drunk first is the glass farthest on the right. Wineglasses are filled as each course is served.

TABLE SERVICE

At a formal seated dinner there are several options for serving guests. You can enlist the service of a maid or butler to serve from a platter, in which case the maid or butler would serve the hostess first so that she can see if the food is correctly arranged, or the two of you can serve your guests yourselves. One way to do this is to put serving dishes and platters in front of the hostess, or on a small cart placed near the dining table. From either of these places the hostess can serve each guest's individual plate. This is the way most formal meals are served in Europe. Plates can also be prepared—in what is known as American style—in the kitchen and placed before seated guests at the dining table.

In these cases, the female guest of honor is always served first, followed by the other female guests; the male guest of honor is served next, and then the remaining male guests. The host and hostess are served last.

FINGER BOWLS

Finger bowls are a charming custom that date back as far as the ancient Romans and Egyptians, whose primary eating utensils were their fingers. The finger bowl is a small (usually glass) dish that is three quarters filled with tepid water. Often a thin slice of lemon floats on the surface. At a formal dinner the finger bowl is offered before dessert and is presented along with a fresh napkin on a small plate covered with a doily. One hand at a time, fingertips are lightly dipped into the water and then dried, with the napkin held near your lap. A gracious hostess will use her finger bowl immediately so that guests who are unfamiliar with its use can learn by example.

COFFEE

Once dessert is finished, coffee may be served at the table. If the hostess thinks it may be more comfortable for her guests, it is conventional practice at a formal dinner to invite everyone to retire to the living room or a study so that guests can relax and enjoy their after-dinner coffee and liquors. The hostess should arrange the necessary coffeepots, one for regular and one for decaffeinated, and cups and saucers on a low table in front of her. She should individually pour coffee for each guest. Another tray should hold assorted liqueurs and brandies, cordial glasses and brandy snifters.

MISCELLANY

Ashtrays should be kept off the table in order to discourage smoking during dinner, as it affects the taste of food and is discourteous to nonsmokers. After dinner, you may make individual ashtrays available.

PLACE CARDS

Place cards, bearing each individual's name, are necessary for identifying the seating position of each guest at the table. Names are generally handwritten or in calligraphy on a flat card or a card that is folded in half, with the name centered on the lower half. The folded card is put on the tablecloth, centered above each place setting; a thoughtful hostess writes on both sides of the place card so the guest opposite may also see the name. A flat place card may be put on the dinner napkin, if it is resting on the service plate.

MENU CARDS

Menu cards are a lovely touch at a formal party, as they are at a more informal meal or buffet. The purpose of these cards is to allow guests to see what fare lies ahead so that they can both savor the anticipation and pace themselves. They may be placed directly on the table if you have enough for each guest to read or keep as a souvenir. For a buffet you might prepare a card to stand upright or placed on a small stand. Generally, they can be written in English, but if your menu is international, try to use the native language of each dish, which will usually be indicated in the recipe, and give the English translation alongside it.

SEATING ETIQUETTE

Americans are rarely concerned with stiff formalities in a seating plan, unless it involves an official occasion. There are a few simple rules of proper etiquette for formal party seating that most people adhere to:

1. The host and hostess usually sit at opposite heads of the table, with the female guest of honor seated to the host's right and the male guest of honor at the hostess's right. If there is a secondary set of honored guests, they are seated at the host and hostess's left. Positions of honor are given to official or distinguished guests, visitors from another country, guests for whom the occasion has been planned, older people, and those who are visiting your home for the first time.
2. Husbands and wives are never seated together, although engaged couples may be.
3. Men and women are seated alternately, unless they are uneven in number.
4. In general, try to match guests who seem most compatible with each other; separate friends who see each other frequently, in order to give them a chance to meet new acquaintances.

Formal Luncheon

INVITATIONS

Invitations to a formal luncheon may be telephoned, but they should be followed by a written note or engraved cards filled in by the hostess. The request for a reply can also include the telephone number. When you issue invitations by telephone, you should mention to your guests the dress code for men, which is usually "jacket and tie." Send your written reminders at least one week before the lunch. Also include directions, if necessary, on how to get to your house.

MENU

The luncheon menu is always simpler than that of the formal dinner, although the accent is still on distinctive cuisine. There is a maximum of four courses served, but usually three: a first course, including an appetizer or a soup; a main course; and a dessert. Quite often, dishes served as the first course for dinner may be used as the main course at the luncheon, such as a soufflé, egg dish, soup, hot or cold mousse, aspic, or, of course, salad.

Two wines may be served, although there is usually only one. In warm weather, iced tea or coffee may be served as an alternative to wine.

TABLE SETTING

At a luncheon, it is optional to use an elegant tablecloth; often a simple cloth or pretty place mats will do. Here, the setting can be more festive, with decorative touches of fruit or candles in bowls, and bouquets of fresh flowers.

Napkins are usually smaller at this party than at dinner; however, your finest china and silverware should be used. Candles are never used at a luncheon, because it is held in daylight hours. It is proper to use both menu and place cards for a formal lunch.

SERVICE AND SEATING PLAN

The rules of etiquette concerning service and seating remain the same for a formal luncheon as for a dinner. Because of the shorter menu, service may be less complicated. Also, it will not be necessary to use service plates or finger bowls, and unlike a formal dinner coffee and tea may be served at the table.

Informal Dinner

INVITATIONS

Invitations to an informal dinner are usually extended over the telephone or in the course of conversation, with a written reminder sent one week before the party. Dress is casual day or evening wear, depending on the hosts' discretion. The best plan is to give guests an idea of what you yourselves plan to wear for the evening.

MENU

The menu for an informal party consists of two to three courses: an appetizer or soup, a main course, and dessert. In a very casual situation, the first course can be omitted, with only the main course and vegetables, salad, and/or dessert served at the table; hors d'oeuvres are offered during cocktails or a first course may be served informally before guests are seated at the table. Food for informal entertaining tends to be more robust and less pretentious a hearty jambalaya or Alsatian choucroute might be a suitable choice. You also have more options in beverages: beer, ale, sangría, and/or fruit juice are delightful thirst-quenchers at an informal dinner. Wine bottles or decanters can be left on the table throughout the meal. If you are planning a three-course dinner, you may serve more than one wine.

TABLE SETTING

Whether your meal is formal or informal, you should always make the effort to set an attractive table. If you use your everyday dinnerware, add special accessories and playful touches like miniature flags to suit an ethnic menu. A simple trick—such as a clever napkin fold, a basket filled with flowers, or a pretty runner to accent the place mats—can make your table exciting. (For more ideas, see "Creative Ideas" in the Index.)

Because there are fewer courses in a casual meal, you will need fewer dishes and eating utensils. The first course may be set on the table before guests are seated. You also have the option of putting the dessert fork and spoon on the table. Put them above the dinner plate, with the fork pointing to the right and the spoon above it, pointing to the left. No service plates need be used. Separate salad plates and forks are optional, as salad can be eaten from the dinner plates.

SEATING PLAN

In order to avoid "musical chairs" confusion, it is important to let your guests know where to sit. Use place cards, centering them above where the dinner plate goes, or make a mental note of your seating plan.

TABLE SERVICE

The main distinction between a formal and informal dinner party is service: The hosts may serve their guests, especially if platters are very heavy; guests may serve themselves, family style; or it may be a combination of both methods. The husband and wife, of course, can share the duties of service; the host may serve cocktails and carve the meat, while the hostess serves the food.

The main dish can be placed in front of the hostess. She will then serve it on individual, heated plates and pass them to guests along the table. Side dishes of vegetables can be put on the table so guests may help themselves. The hosts can also serve individual filled plates from the kitchen or a serving table.

As with formal dinners, wine should be poured as the food is served, but at informal meals the host can serve the first glass to guests, after which they may serve themselves. Be sure the bottle or bottles are within their reach.

Informal Luncheon

INVITATIONS

You can extend informal invitations person-to-person or by telephone. Invitations can also be written on personal notepaper.

MENU

A light appetizer, a main course, and a dessert are substantial fare for an informal luncheon. But you may omit serving the first course or the dessert. Rarely is more than one wine, if any, served. It is, however, acceptable to serve an aperitif, such as a spritzer (white wine and sparkling water), before lunch. For the weekend luncheon or brunch, a pleasant addition to the menu is a Bloody Mary. In warm weather, iced tea or coffee is a refreshing beverage. Unless it is held on a Sunday, when a longer menu may be featured, the informal luncheon is generally simple.

TABLE SETTING AND SERVICE

Setting and service are informal, so use your imagination to come up with gala table settings for this kind of meal. You might use colorful plates on bright straw mats or have a centerpiece of bright and cheerful flowers on a red and white checked table-cloth. Please the eye as well as the plate. For another centerpiece idea, you might fill a rustic wooden bowl with luscious fruit or vegetables.

The flatware and service are the same as for an informal dinner, with the option of putting a cup and saucer for tea or coffee on the table.

Buffet

By its very nature, the buffet is an informal way to entertain. Guests and hosts serve themselves from a table or tables on which the food courses are displayed. A buffet is a perfect solution to entertaining in a home that does not have sufficient dining-table facilities to accommodate a large number of guests. Such occasions as a brunch, bridal or baby shower, housewarming, and informal dinner party are perfectly suited to the use of a buffet.

INVITATIONS

Guests may receive written or verbal invitations when invited to attend a buffet party (see Index for "Informal Invitations").

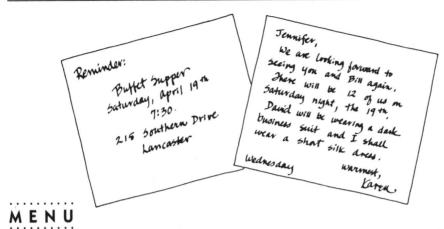

Reminder:
Buffet Supper
Saturday, April 19th
7:30.
215 Southern Drive
Lancaster

Jennifer,
We are looking forward to
seeing you and Bill again.
There will be 12 of us on
Saturday night, the 19th.
David will be wearing a dark
business suit and I shall
wear a short silk dress.
Wednesday   warmest,
                              Karen.

MENU

A buffet menu usually offers more than one main course, with additional selections of vegetables, sauces, salads, breads, and desserts. A large buffet might include both hot and cold food, with hot casseroles, sliced cold meat or poultry, salads, a stew, stuffed crêpes, and rice or pasta dishes. To avoid congestion at a buffet, you should place the table in the center of a room, so that guests can serve themselves from all sides. The buffet table or tables should be set up in a logical way so that guests approaching the buffet find dinner plates first, then the main dishes, side dishes, salads, rolls or bread, butter, napkins, and flatware. Beverages may be put at the end of a long buffet table, or on a separate smaller table. Dishes should be set out for dessert with cups and saucers and the necessary flatware for dessert and coffee.

Because guests must serve themselves from the buffet table, food should be manageable and easily transportable to the plate. Avoid serving foods that are difficult to handle, such as soups or long-stranded spaghetti. Buffet food should also be easy to eat—at the most requiring a fork unless all guests will be able to have a place at the table.

Because of the casual attitude when dining from a buffet, guests will be helping themselves to the food at different times. If it is to stay warm, food must be kept on a heating tray or over an alcohol burner.

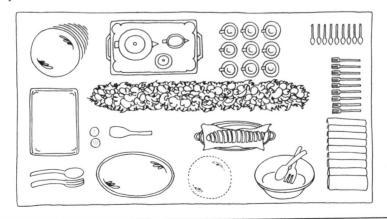

You can be as imaginative as you please with the decor of a buffet. Just be sure the serving pieces have a common theme and coordinated style to ensure that your table looks graceful and attractive. Because of the potential for messy spots, your best tablecloth is not the best choice for a buffet table. Instead, you might use a multi-colored cloth that can camouflage any food stains. Extra tips on setting up the buffet:

1. Put serving utensils next to each serving dish. After the first guest has served himself, utensils will be in the bowl or dish.
2. Leave dishes of food open, without their covers. After all the guests have served themselves, cover them to keep food warm.
3. Leave ample room between serving platters so that guests can set their plates down on the table. This is particularly important when filling a plate with any food that requires holding two serving utensils.

SEATING

Basically there are four options for seating your guests when serving buffet style:

1. Arrange individual tables where space permits to seat small groups of people. Folding card tables are perfect for this, round folding tables are available and square ones can be enlarged to accommodate more than four people by covering them with round boards disguised with pretty tablecloths. These round tops can be found at hardware stores, or have your own cut at a lumberyard. (See p. 313 for more details.)
2. Provide an individual snack table for each guest. You might even preset these with all the needed table-setting accessories, other than the dinner plate.
3. When you do not have enough tables, guests must use their laps to hold their dishes. Provide extra-large lap mats in addition to napkins (see Index). These lap mats will prevent food from soiling clothes and furniture. Wherever possible, attempt to have tables convenient for resting glasses and beverages.
4. It is also possible to serve an informal buffet meal from a sideboard or extra serving table—guests help themselves and then are seated together at the dining-room table. This idea can also be used in conjunction with seating ideas 1 and 2.

Cocktail Party

Fun-filled and high-spirited, the cocktail party mingles old and new friends from varying backgrounds in an informal, get-acquainted atmosphere. For the host and hostess, a cocktail party is the easiest way to entertain a large number of people.

INVITATIONS

Invitations to this party are usually written and sent out two to three weeks in advance. You can request a response or simply "Regrets Only" with your telephone number. The usual hours for cocktails are between 5 or 6 and 8 P.M. Guests may come and go as they please.

DRINKS

At larger parties the general rule of thumb is to serve one or two different kinds of mixed drinks (Bloody Marys and sangría, for example) and a standard assortment of hard liquors with mixers: vodka and tonic or whiskey and soda. Because of the

Cocktail Buffet

Saturday, June 8th   6:30 o'clock

10 Hobart Rd.

Regrets only 550-1212

popularity of wine in this country, you should also serve quality red and white wines, as well as bottled beer. Also include nonalcoholic drinks, such as vegetable and fruit juices, and soda.

FOOD

Because people often stand or mill about at cocktail parties, make sure that the food you serve is easy to eat with fingers. Cocktail foods can be hot, cold, or both. You can serve dried snacks or nuts; cheese platters with a variety of crackers or small breads; crudités or raw vegetables cut into small pieces and accompanying dips; and, of course, the quintessential cocktail food, canapés, and hors d'oeuvres. These take on many flavors and shapes. Just to name a few: stuffed eggs or mushrooms; snow peas filled with bleu cheese; small hamburgers; dainty sandwiches made with turkey, ham, lobster, crab meat, or cucumber fillings; and international favorites such as rumaki (water chestnuts and chicken livers wrapped and broiled in strips of bacon).

SETTING AND SERVICE

It is a good idea to clear furniture to create enough space for people to stand or walk about. Also remove your valued possessions, or they may get broken in the crush.

Hors d'oeuvre trays can be passed around to guests, or set up in several convenient areas of the room. Make sure a stack of napkins is placed on each tray, with toothpicks in foods that require them. Smaller bowls of nibbling foods, such as pretzels and nuts, can be scattered throughout the house.

THE BAR

If you plan on entertaining a large number of guests, you would be advised to hire a professional bartender or a student who is schooled in making drinks. Often the professional will bring extra glasses and ice, but you must request them in advance. Discuss the drinks and hors d'oeuvres with the bartender ahead of time. Be sure to supply him with the necessary equipment—bottle openers, corkscrews, bar knife, swizzle sticks, and lined garbage pails or buckets for storing ice. The bartender can individually prepare drinks for guests at a mixing station set up in the living room.

If you entertain without assistance, there are a number of ways to make the job easy for yourself.

1. Consider the space available. If you have a large house or apartment, you can set up mini-bars in different rooms: one in the living room, one in the dining room, and one in the den. Then guests can prepare their own drinks.
2. If you do not have the space, you can premix the drinks and pass them around on

trays with cocktail napkins.
3. The host can also set up a bar station in one room, with large pitchers of premixed drinks so guests can help themselves.

Impromptu Entertaining

Impromptu parties can be enormous fun. Consider this the next time you decide to invite guests over on the spur of the moment. Remember, under such casual circumstances people do not expect to be entertained lavishly; they are looking for gaiety! As hosts, you should not feel obligated to produce an elaborate meal. Keep it simple, but delicious.

The way to make these impromptu situations easy to handle is by stocking your pantry and freezer with some emergency foods. It is wise to keep foods at hand for your own use, anyway, when you are caught working very late evenings. Reserve a corner in one cupboard for these last-minute entertaining staples: canned corned beef, pâté, smoked oysters, tuna fish and salmon; cookies, crackers, and processed cheeses; pasta and rice; dried or canned soups; and cocktail napkins and toothpicks. Keep your freezer stocked with precooked casseroles, quiches, pastry shells, and meats. Do not forget to take advantage of yesterday's leftovers in the refrigerator. It is amazing how odds and ends of vegetables, dairy products, and other foods can turn into delicious salads, side dishes, or dips.

Tea

While formal teas are often held in stately mansions to host government officials or visiting celebrities, an informal version of this time-honored tradition adds a refreshing change to today's fast-paced everyday world. A tea signifies the ultimate in relaxation, and a stimulant for gentle conversation. It is also an excellent format for having a business meeting at home or gathering members together from a club or organization.

INVITATIONS

Invitations to tea can be exchanged in person or telephoned if the occasion is totally informal, such as a charity event meeting. If the event is formal, such as the occasion of a tea for your aunt's eightieth birthday, invitations should be handwritten on personal stationery. The traditional tea hour is from 4 to 6 P.M., before the cocktail hour and dinner. Dress is daytime or office wear—rarely is more formal dress required.

MENU

Because a tea is followed by dinner, there should never be a lavish amount of food served. There can be dainty sandwiches or suitable sweets, such as small cookies or tarts. If you are serving plain, buttered, or cinammon toast, the crusts may be left on. Other hot delectables are croissants, gingerbread, biscuits, and scones. They can be served on a covered platter, or wrapped in a napkin on a tray. Cake should be cut into thin, delicate slices and served on dessert plates with dessert forks.

TABLE SETTING AND SERVICE

The tea ceremony should be held in the dining room or living room, wherever there is adequate space for people to sit, stand, or mill about with their teacups, finger foods, or plates.

Traditionally at a tea party, the hostess pours the tea and hands the cups directly to her guests. Guests do not serve themselves, because it is the ritual more than the beverage that counts. At a large tea a hostess may appoint friends or relatives to help serve the tea. Tea bags should never be used—only looseleaf tea. Select a high-quality tea with which you can serve milk, lemon, or honey.

You will need the following equipment for a tea party:

- Large tray (preferably silver) with no cloth
- Teapot large enough for the number of guests you are serving; one that retains heat
- Strainer and basin for discarded leaves
- Pitcher of milk (preheated, if you prefer)
- Bowl of sugar lumps with tongs, or a sugar bowl with a teaspoon
- Small plate with thin lemon slices and a small fork
- Necessary number of teacups, saucers, and spoons. For larger parties, teacups can be stacked by twos, as well as saucers. But never pile on several, or your tea service will resemble a counter at a diner.
- Decanter of sherry and appropriate small glasses
- If the tray is not large enough for the tea service and food, you can put the food on a second tray on the table. Add plates and forks, if required.
- Napkins—there are tea napkins, but luncheon-size ones will do. They should be white, ecru, or pastel.

SPIRITS AND WINE

It makes it so easy to casually invite friends to come by for a leisurely drink if you keep a well-stocked bar. It is also a pleasure to simply reach into your wine selection for a good bottle at a moment's notice or to reap the benefits of purchasing a new and young wine at minimal cost by storing it at home until it becomes a well-aged treasure. Here are details and suggestions to start you on your way to storing and serving spirits and wine.

Setting Up the Bar

The following spirits and equipment are the basics for a well-stocked bar, and what you will need to make most drinks. The ingredients can be kept at the bar or in the kitchen. Naturally, you will want to add your own favorites to this list, especially those from the vast selection of fascinating liqueurs.

SPIRITS AND WINE
Bourbon
Vodka
Whiskey
Gin
Rum
Scotch
Tequila
Red Wine
White Wine
Beer
Dry Vermouth
Sweet Vermouth
Brandy
Assorted Liqueurs

EQUIPMENT
Bar knife
1½-ounce jigger
Can opener
Corkscrew
Glass rod or long spoon for stirring
Shaker, blender, or hand mixer to froth up the drinks
Ice strainer for the shaker

Water pitcher
Ice bucket and tongs to serve cubes
Ice crusher for tall drinks sipped through straws
Juicer for squeezing limes, lemons, and oranges
Cocktail napkins and coasters
Drink recipe book
Towels

INGREDIENTS
Mixers: Tonic, club soda, cola, collins mix, ginger ale, lemon/lime soda
Fresh lemons and limes
Lemon and lime peels
Angostura bitters
Tabasco sauce
Maraschino cherries
Cocktail olives
Cocktail onions
Tomato juice
Pineapple juice
Orange juice
Other fruit juices
Powdered, superfine sugar

Grenadine
Fruit and vegetable garnishes
Sugar
Salt

Pepper
Cream
Cream of coconut

Certainly cocktails are easier to prepare than the rest of the menu, but guests deserve no less of your hosting perfection in their drinks than they do in their main course. Use a recipe when first mixing a drink, and refer to the following tips for always successful refreshments.

• *Chilling and Frosting Glasses*—Keep cocktails cold without ice by pouring them into chilled glasses. Chill cocktail glasses by storing them in the refrigerator for at least half an hour, or in the freezer for 10 minutes (be cautious if putting very delicate crystal in the freezer). If you do not have time to prechill glasses, fill them with cracked ice, let stand for 2 minutes, empty ice, and pour in chilled drink. If you want to frost a glass, dip it in water and freeze for 30 minutes.

• *Egg White*—Use egg whites in some blender or shaker cocktails to help create and hold a foamy head on the drink. Use approximately ¼ to ½ egg white for each drink.

• *Garnishes*—Add eye appeal to drinks with fruit garnishes. Cut orange and lemon slices slightly thick so they do not curl or wilt. When using a lime, lemon, or orange peel for a garnish, first remove the bitter white pith; then twist the peel over the glass to free the fruit's oils before dropping it into the drink.

• *Ice*—Keep ice made ahead of when you will use it. Use crushed or shaved ice to chill glasses or for frozen frappés; cubes for anything on the rocks. Ice should go in the glass first, then liquor, followed by the mixer. For fresh drinks, do not rinse ice or reuse it. Throw out melting cubes at the bottom of the blender. Always remove ice from the drink remaining in the shaker or blender, to avoid diluting it.

• *Lemon and Limes*—Three ways to render the maximum amount of juice from lemons and limes: Roll them with your palm on a hard surface; soak them in warm water for 5 minutes before squeezing; heat them in a warm oven for 2 to 3 minutes. It is best to only use fresh lemon and lime juice. Do not substitute lemon for lime juice; it will not be tangy enough.

• *Quantity*—Count on 20 drinks from a 750-ml bottle; this is based on 1½ ounces per drink. Estimate that guests will usually consume two drinks the first hour, and one every hour after that.

• *Stirring Sparkling Mixers*—Gently stir drinks with sparkling mixers, just enough to cool and mix, being careful to preserve the sparkle in the soda.

• *Sugar and Salt Rims*—Moisten the edges of chilled glasses with lemon or lime slices; then dip the rims in powdered sugar, for daiquiris or sours; dip in salt for margaritas.

Wine

A good bottle of wine is the ideal complement to a well-prepared meal. As you taste various wines you will find those you enjoy most and will learn which ones are best suited to certain foods. Never concern yourself with thinking it necessary to serve expensive, pretentious wines to guests. In fact, a real wine connoisseur is a person who can find and serve the most enjoyable wines at the least cost. Anyone can simply buy a famous and expensive wine; but certainly with all the choices on the market, from both local vineyards and imported wines, it is easy and far more satisfying to find your own special, little-known jewel that does not cost a fortune.

Whenever you drink a wine that you like at a restaurant or someone's home, make a note of its name, vintage, producer, and any foods that seem compatible with it. An even more memorable way to record wines you have enjoyed is to request or save the labels. You might keep these in an album, or even use a collection to decorate a wine rack, bar counter, or wine closet. Of course, the most important part of the wine bottle is what's inside.

What follows is a brief introduction to wine-tasting terms, descriptions of various wines, recommendations for use with appropriate foods, as well as serving and storing.

WINE-TASTING TERMS

acidity: A necessary element to give wine balance—with too much, wine can be harsh; with too little, dull.

balance: The ideal combination of acid, sugar, fruit, and tannin.

body: Texture or feel of the wine in your mouth, which adds to the flavor intensity.

bouquet: The smell or aroma, which adds greatly to the experience of taste.

complexity: Quality of being many-faceted in flavor, body, balance, and bouquet.

dry: The absence of residual sugar; not sweet.

finesse: Harmony, balance, and refinement.

finish: The aftertaste or lingering flavor in the mouth.

flowery: The ability of the bouquet to suggest flowers such as honeysuckle, jasmine, or violets.

fruity: The flavor in the wine that suggests the impression and comparison of fruit in the flavor, such as raspberries, cherries, peaches, or apricots.

generic: Wine having the name of a specific region, such as Chablis, Burgundy, or Rhine.

robust: Full-bodied and intensely flavored wine.

soft: Not robust, but pleasant and gentle—might also imply that wine has poor balance.

spicy: A sense of pleasing, peppery complexity.

tannic: A necessary aspect of red wines—if drunk young, wine with a high tannic level can be harsh, but it aids graceful maturing.

varietal: Wine having the name of the grape that produced it, such as Chardonnay, Chenin Blanc, Cabernet Sauvignon, Zinfandel, and Pinot Noir.

WHITE WINES

White wines should be served chilled (1 hour in the refrigerator or 30 minutes in an ice bucket).

WINE	DESCRIPTION	APPROPRIATE FOOD
Chablis	Pale straw yellow color, extremely dry, with austere, flinty quality, crisp and refreshing.	Oysters, poultry, and light meat.
Chardonnay	Varies in style with production, but generally best are dry, full-bodied, with crisp acidic balance. Those aged in oak barrels have a rich buttery finesse; others have a crisp, varietal flavor.	Poultry, light meat, and fish.
Chenin Blanc	Taste ranges from lightly dry to slightly sweet, best full-bodied with good acid, drunk young.	Poultry, light meat, and excellent with salmon.
Gewürztraminer	Highly perfumed and floral bouquet with unique, spicy, peppery flavor.	Chinese food, grilled meat, and poultry.
Muscadet	A fragrant bouquet with a light, crisp, bone-dry taste.	Shellfish and poultry.
Pinot Grigio	A light-bodied, dry, refreshing wine best drunk young.	Poultry, light meat, and fish.
Riesling	A true floral bouquet, taste ranges from slightly dry to increasing sweetness.	Dryer ones with poultry and pork: sweeter ones with dessert and fruit.
Sancerre	Very fragrant and fresh with a crisp dry finish, best drunk young.	Poultry, light meat, and fish.
Sauternes	Highly perfumed and lusciously rich, sweet wines.	Pâté de foie gras, desserts, fruit, and blue-veined cheese.

Sauvignon Blanc (also labeled Fumé Blanc)	An aromatic bouquet, medium body, and dry. Some have a pleasantly smoky scent.	Poultry, light meat, and fish.
Soave	Subtle bouquet, light body, very dry, crisp, and fresh.	Poultry, light meat, fish, and pasta.
Vinho Verde	These Portuguese wines are dry, with crisp acid, usually low in alcohol and have a faint sparkle. Best drunk young.	Poultry, light meat, and seafood.

RED WINES

Red wines should be served at 65 to 68 degrees.

WINE	DESCRIPTION	APPROPRIATE FOOD
Beaujolais	Medium body with berryish fruit. Drink young and, contrary to the rules, moderately chilled.	Compatible with almost all foods.
Bordeaux (also known as Claret)	This basic wine type is best full-bodied and complex. High tannin levels require bottle aging to attain full flavor potential.	Red meat, game, and cheese.
Burgundy	Best French ones are deep red, full-bodied, fruity, and with a unique bouquet, often compared to cherries.	Red meat, game, and cheese.
Cabernet Sauvignon	Robust and astringent when young, with a substantial level of tannin. Requires bottle aging to mellow and for development of characteristic grape flavor.	Red meat, game, and cheese.

Chianti	Full-bodied, robust, and tart when young—will soften and mature with bottle aging.	Richly seasoned foods, pastas, and red meat.
Côtes du Rhône	Light-bodied, uncomplicated, best drunk when young.	Compatible with almost all foods.
Dão	Portuguese full-bodied robust wine. Certain vintage years may require bottle aging.	Red meat, game, and cheese.
Merlot	Often blended into Bordeaux and Cabernet Sauvignon to tone down astringency, this fragrant, fruity, mellow wine is generally ready to drink without much bottle aging.	Red meat, game, and cheese.
Pinot Noir (French)	A varietal wine, Pinot Noirs are dry, full-bodied, with a gentle finesse. (This grape, one of the most noble in French wine making, is used in Burgundies, champagne, and rosés.)	Red meat, game, and cheese.
Rosé	Generally fragrant, slightly sweet, without complexity.	Compatible with almost all foods.
Saint-Emilion	A deeply colored, full-bodied wine. Generally matures within a short time after bottling.	Red meat, game, and cheese.
Valpolicella	Ruby color, subtle bouquet, full rich flavor finishing with a pleasant bite.	Spicy foods, red meat, game, and cheese.
Zinfandel	A rich berrylike bouquet and flavor with the unique addition of a touch of spice.	Red meat, game, and cheese.

GLASSWARE

Glasses for the proper enjoyment of red or white wine should be clear, graceful and generous in size. The glass should be large enough to hold at least four ounces of wine with sufficient room left to swirl the wine in the glass in order to release the full extent of its bouquet.

STORAGE

After you have purchased the wine, store it in a cool, dark place. The ideal storing temperature is 55 to 57 degrees Fahrenheit, but this exact control is not always possible. The most important condition is that the wine simply stay at a relatively constant temperature year round, approximately 68 to 72 degrees. If you live in a warmer climate, wine will tend to age faster.

The next important requirement is to keep wine bottles resting on their sides, labels facing up. This position keeps the corks from drying out and becoming loose. With the labels facing up, you can identify the wine quickly and easily without having to disturb any sediment that may have settled out of the wine during aging. Keep the wine away from vibrations, such as those from a refrigerator or other appliance. Sparkling wines with plastic tops and bottles with screw caps can be stored standing up, because they have no cork.

OPENING AND SERVING WINE

Remove the capsule (foil or plastic covering over the cork) by running a knife blade under the bulge on the bottle's neck. Wipe clean any mold or leakage around the cork's seals. Put the point of the corkscrew slightly off center and it will spiral down into the center of the cork. When uncorking, use a slow steady motion so as not to break the cork. Special tools are sold to retrieve corks that break and fall into the bottle, but first try removing them by using a piece of cord with a large knot at one end. Use this to direct the cork back into the neck of the bottle; then, with the knot under the cork, pull it up through the neck. If a cork shreds in the bottle, it will be necessary to strain the wine into a clean decanter. When pouring, finish with a little twist of the bottle mouth over the glass so the wine will not drip down the bottle. To decant red wines that have collected sediment, first gently turn them from a horizontal to a vertical position and let them stand for several hours until all the sediment settles on the bottom. Uncork and slowly pour the contents of the bottle into a decanter. Put a candle or light behind the neck of the bottle as you pour so you can watch for the approaching sediment.

Red wines are usually drunk at room temperature. If you are planning to serve white, sparkling, or rosé wines, chill them in the refrigerator for at least two hours. If you have not refrigerated the wine ahead of time, put the bottle in a bucket with water and ice and twirl the bottle occasionally; it should chill in 20 to 30 minutes.

Examine the wine's appearance, taste, and aftertaste. Hold the wineglass up to the light or against a white cloth and note the wine's clarity, brilliance, and color. Swirl the wine in your glass to let it mix with the air and enhance its aroma. A large part of your sense of taste is based on your sense of smell. To taste wine fully, you must first experience its bouquet.

Discuss the wine's qualities with your friends. Is the aroma flowery—like violets, perhaps? Often, the more complex the bouquet, the better the wine. Is it tart, dry, sweet? Does it have body, a nice balance, a lingering finish? Only part of the joy of wine is the warm and glowing feeling it gives; the rest of its pleasures lie on the tongue, in the eyes, and in the nose.

LEFTOVER WINE

Save bottle corks to stop up leftover wine. Better still, pour the remaining wine into a smaller bottle, to keep out as much air as possible. Exposed to air for a few hours, wine oxidizes and loses its vitality. Leftover reds can be stored at room temperature; whites in your refrigerator. Both should last a few days and can be used in cooking.

Champagne

Special celebrations, such as a job promotion, a wedding engagement, or an anniversary, call for opening a bottle of champagne. But champagne has a unique way of adding excitement and sparkle to any occasion. The two of you should open a bottle on impulse one night, for no reason at all; the enjoyment you have together, sipping, sharing, laughing, and loving, is a celebration all in itself.

GLASSWARE

The best way to experience the effervescence, character, and delightful taste of champagne is to serve it in tall flute- or tulip-shaped glasses. These shapes keep the bubbles and bouquet steadily rising to the top. Glasses such as bowls or saucers tend to dissipate the bubbles too quickly and can spoil the wine and the fun.

CHILLING

Champagne should be chilled, but never ice-cold. Put the bottle in a bucket filled with water and ice for 30 minutes, or place the bottle in the refrigerator for two or more hours before serving. Do not put the wine in the freezer, as you can make it too cold to really taste, and if you forget it in the freezer you can damage the wine.

OPENING AND SERVING

To open the bottle, find the wire loop beneath the foil-wrapped bottle neck; untwist it and loosen the wire cage. Remove the cage and outer foil. Immediately put your thumb over the cork to prevent the risk of popping the cork.

Covering the cork with a napkin, tilt the bottle away from you at a 45-degree angle, but not pointing at anyone else. Twist the bottle (not the cork) and gently pry out the cork with your thumbs, allowing the internal pressure to slowly be reduced. Contrary to some opinions, the "big bang" is not the most desirable effect; not only will you lose much of the champagne, you will release some of the gas that makes it bubble. When the cork is free, keep the bottle at an angle for a few seconds so it will not overflow when turned upright.

Wipe the bottle rim clean and pour the champagne into a glass. Froth will gush to the top when you first pour. Wait until it subsides, then fill each glass one third to one half full, and be sure to make a champagne toast!

CREATIVE IDEAS FOR PARTY PLANNING & TABLE SETTING

The two of you will dedicate great care and thought to the planning and preparation of a delicious and tantalizing menu for yourselves or your guests. Be sure to do your culinary efforts justice with a beautifully prepared table.

You need not be artists or spend a small fortune on decorations and accessories to make a table look exciting. By taking advantage of the treasures you have at hand, plus of time and imagination, you can create a stunning centerpiece or table setting with eye-catching appeal.

When you invite family and friends to dinner it is especially nice to incorporate their wedding gifts in your decorating scheme. This thoughtful gesture will make them beam with pride.

Following are a number of ideas for party planning and creative table settings that are all inexpensive and easy.

Holiday Table Decorations

CHRISTMAS

• Create an ornamental tree with a stripped bare tree branch. Leave it natural or spray-paint it gold, white, or silver. Secure the branch in a basket or vase with florist's clay; cover the base with moss and holly. Hang ornaments from the branches, such as Christmas-tree bulbs, red velvet bows, or Christmas cards.

• Make a luscious red-and-white-striped candy cane vase. Line the outside of a clear, tall vase with real candy canes, facing outward; secure in place with a red ribbon tied tightly. Fill with candies or flowers.

CANDY CANE VASE

302

EDIBLE HOLIDAY CENTERPIECE

• For a decoration on any table surface, lay a bed of fresh pine sprigs and holly. Add a toy sleigh filled with tiny packages, teddy bears, or other whimsical figurines.

• In the center of the dinner table, lay a bed of ferns, pine branches, and holly. Place tall candles securely nestled among the greens. Generously scatter on the branches bright red bows, rosy kumquats, miniature red-and-white candy canes, pinecones, colorful fruits, and nuts. When it is time for dessert, you will have a partly edible centerpiece for all to share. Christmas dinner will never be more festive.

THANKSGIVING

• On your dinner table arrange a straw or wicker cornucopia horn overflowing with an abundance of fall leaves, small colorful gourds, Indian corn, nuts, apples, and the like. This is a perfect seasonal decoration to represent the bounty and beauty of the earth.

• For a centerpiece, arrange a basket filled with autumn flowers and pinecones.

• At each place setting, put a tiny basket with miniature pinecones, acorns, or flowers tied with pretty ribbons. Put a place card in or near each small basket, which can later be given as party favors.

• On a table top securely place large column candles on wooden discs or holders and set in a bed of colorful autumn leaves.

• For your door or over your fireplace, make a wreath of vine branches and ferns; fasten with thin copper wire. Add miniature shellacked gourds, dried flowers, kumquats, berries, and nuts.

EASTER

• For your dining table use a pretty straw basket as a vase, fill it with florist's moss and tall fresh spring flowers, such as daffodils; tuck in painted Easter eggs so that they peek out of the moss.

• To make a unique clustered centerpiece on the table, use a collection of lovely old colored glass bottles—or individual bud vases—and fill each with dainty flowers.

• To create a maypole effect for your table, from a centerpiece vase tie pastel ribbons to individual bud vases or nosegays, one per place setting. The nosegays can be worn by female guests after the meal.

• For an ornamental spring tree, take a tree branch and spray paint it white and hang lovely hand-painted wooden Easter eggs.

• Create floral wreaths to decorate the top rim of each place setting's service plate. Take crescent-shaped young twigs or bend florist's wire into an arc to fit the outer rim of the service plate. With additional wire, attach an assortment of fresh spring flowers to create a half wreath and place on each plate. This is especially effective when used to decorate service plates under the dessert course.

INDIVIDUAL SERVICE PLATE WITH FLORAL DECORATION

VALENTINE'S DAY

• On your dining table, put tall, tapered candles in the center, in candleholders. At their base, cluster a cascading pile of store-bought chocolate hearts wrapped in red foil. The light will bounce off the foil and create a lovely pink glow.
• For whimsical valentine place mats, cut out large hearts from red paper and glue crinkled white kraft paper around the border of each heart.

NEW YEAR'S EVE

• For the table, tie together a bouquet of brightly colored helium-filled balloons and fasten to a basket in the center. Fill the basket with party favors. You can also tie a balloon to the back of each chair and put a party favor at each plate.
• For a dramatic and glittering centerpiece, gather branches with leaves and spray-paint them silver. Arrange in a large vase with white helium-filled balloons.

FOURTH OF JULY

• For your table, use a red, white, and blue decorating scheme. Crisscross plaid red, white, and blue ribbons on a white tablecloth so the colors stand out. Put miniature store-bought paper American flags at each place setting, and alternate red and blue napkins around the table.

Table Decorations for Miscellaneous Moods

• For a musical-theme centerpiece, buy a number of miniature toy horns, violins, guitars, and banjos at a toy store. If you like, spray paint them in gold, silver, or another color. Arrange instruments in the center of the table, surrounded by rolled sheet music. You can also put a toy instrument at each place setting.

• For a bridesmaids' luncheon, festively wrap small packages and tie each with pastel ribbon or cord. (They might even contain small gifts.) Stack packages attractively in a cluster in the center of the table. For a baby shower, clip a big diaper pin to each napkin.

• To add a Continental touch to a casual place setting, serve wine as the country folk do in Europe, using short stemless glasses. Another European custom is to turn the flatware facedown on the table. This is especially attractive if the decorative hallmarks appear on the back of the flatware, as they do on European silver.

• For an athletic theme—particularly if there is a jogger in the family who has just finished a race—stencil or hand-write "FINISH LINE" on a wide length of ribbon and attach it to two lightweight poles or flags, which can be mounted in pots with florist's clay. This makes a knockout centerpiece, and it will be the center of attention for a dinner celebration.

• For a dramatic summer buffet centerpiece, tilt a small hand-painted Chinese umbrella on its side. Fill with florist's moss and greens, and nestle in the bottom half of the umbrella bunches of grapes, peaches, cherries, melons, and other seasonal fruits and flowers.

CHINESE UMBRELLA BUFFET CENTERPIECE

TABLECLOTHS AND TABLE TRIMMINGS

• For a quaint tablecloth with a country feeling, use your grandmother's handmade patchwork quilt.

• For another old-fashioned mood, cover a white or pastel tablecloth with an antique lace or woven shawl.

• For a seafood buffet, drape a fishnet on a solid-colored cloth. Add shells you have collected at the beach.

• For an artistic, playful party, cover the table with a long roll of white kraft paper. At each setting, write in the guest's name and leave a cup of crayons for doodling. You will be surprised at the number of artists you have!

• For a housewarming party, use architectural graph paper for a tablecloth, add large clipboards for place mats and fasten napkins under the clips.

• Tulle—the multicolored fine netting made of rayon or nylon—is a great craft item for decorating. Tie accent pieces of it around the stems of toasting glasses or wrap a loose collar of tulle at the top of a vase of flowers for an especially pretty and delicate effect. You can also gather it to make pompoms or "cloud puffs"; then pin a silk flower or bow in the center of each puff and fasten the puffs onto added swags to decorate a full-length cloth draped over a table.

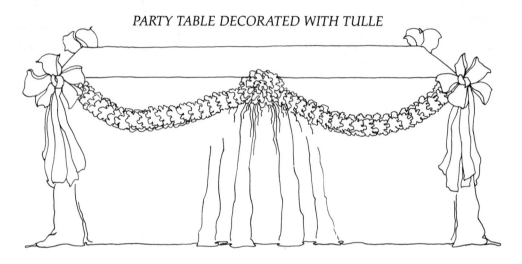

PARTY TABLE DECORATED WITH TULLE

PLACE SETTINGS

• Use hand-painted Chinese or Japanese paper fans for place mats.
• Use any large plant or tree leaf, such as rhododendron, for summery place mats.
• Gather all your favorite collectibles—little bells, figurines, toy cars, perfume bottles—and playfully accent each place setting with a different object.

HATS

You will be surprised at how many ways you can utilize hats at a party. Here are just a few suggestions:

• For special party fun, gather all the hats that the two of you own to represent the personalities of your guests and make it a humorous occasion. For example, use a cowboy hat or a construction worker's hard hat for the rough-and-ready personality; select a pretty straw hat for a dreamy-eyed nature lover; a beret for an artist; a baseball hat for a sports buff; an aviator's hat for the adventurer; a nurse's cap for the nurturer; an Indian headdress for the historian; a sailor's hat for the traveler; or a black velvet hat with veil for the sultry romantic. Tie each hat to the back of the chair, and let each guest guess where he or she sits.

• For a summery buffet, line a large broad-brimmed straw hat with a bright napkin and fill it with an array of fruits or crudités.

• If you have an old-fashioned top hat, line it with a glass or plastic cylinder and use as a champagne cooler.

VASES

There are many creative ideas for making flower holders and dressing up old ones.
• Antique porcelain pitchers, delicate teapots, or any handled pourers make delightful country-style vases.
• Brandy snifters for individual bouquets of flowers serve as dramatic holders at individual place settings.
• Low crystal bowls make elegant vases for floating flower petals and blossoms.
• Chemists' beakers of different sizes add a contemporary touch and are excellent flower holders.
• A chipped or cracked vase—or even a coffee can—can be called into service as a container. Hide the holder: Take a pretty square scarf, lay it flat on a table, and set the container in the center of the scarf. Gather the fabric around the vase-to-be tightly and tie two opposing corners together over the open rim of the container. Repeat with the other two corners. If necessary, secure with ribbon.

*FABRIC-WRAPPED
FLOWER VASE*

INCREDIBLE EDIBLES

Fruits and vegetables come in so many beautiful shapes, they can be nature's own serving pieces.
• For pumpkin soup bowls, use the pumpkins themselves. Slice off just enough of the bottom to make each pumpkin sit flat and balanced on a plate. Cut off the top quarter with stem, and scoop out the pumpkin flesh (be sure not to make the walls too thin, or to pierce the walls of the pumpkin). Use this pulp to prepare the soup (see Index). When the soup is ready to be served, pour into each pumpkin half. Top with the lid to keep it hot. This idea also works well with acorn squash.
• For a punch or fruit salad bowl, use a large scooped-out watermelon.
• For crudité dip cups, use a cut and hollowed green pepper, squash, or gourd. You can also core out heads of cabbage, put the dip in the center, and pull back the leaves to look like roses.

• For serving finger foods, shrimps or other seafood appetizers, use thoroughly washed scallop, oyster, or clam shells.
• For holding finger foods at tropical theme parties—such as a luau—use cleaned medium to large sturdy plant leaves.
• As a container for a cheese spread, select a large round loaf of bread. Scoop out the center and fill with the spread.
• Loaves of brioche make wonderful individual servers for such food as chicken or shrimp salad. Slice off the crown, remove dough inside, add chicken or shrimp and replace the lid.
• For a natural bud vase, slice the stem tip off a pear. Using an apple corer or small sharp knife, tunnel a hole from the top to the center of the pear. Insert the flowers in the hole.

PEAR BUD VASE

GARNISHES

Garnishes add excitement, color, and finesse to the foods they accent. Used on each individual dish, or on serving platters, these embellishments not only enhance the food's presentation, but they also represent your thoughtfulness in adding to your guest's dining pleasure.

Following are a few simple-to-create garnishes, using basic fruits and vegetables, each of which can be used in a variety of ways.

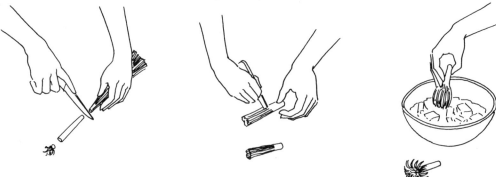

SCALLION BRUSH

1. Remove root tip of scallion and cut 3-inch length of white part.
2. With a small, sharp knife make as many thin vertical slices as possible through ¾ of the length.
3. Immerse the sliced scallion in ice water; in a short time it will curl. This garnish goes especially well with cold foods and Oriental dishes.

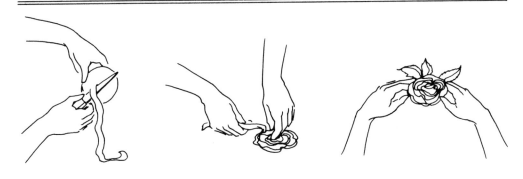

TOMATO ROSE

1. Starting at the top of the tomato, peel it with a small, sharp knife in one continuous strip about ½ inch wide.
2. To shape the rose, wrap the peel around itself in a spiral.
3. You can further embellish the tomato rose with small green leaves or pieces of lettuce and use it to garnish platters or individual dishes.

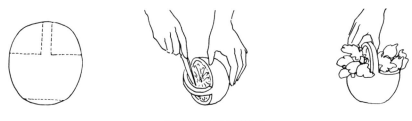

CITRUS BASKET

1. Cut two right-angled sections out of the top third of the lemon or orange, leaving a strip down the middle. Then slice a thin piece off the bottom of the fruit to keep it level.
2. With a small, sharp knife trim away the pulp around the center strip to form a handle, and core out the pulp in the cavity to form a basket.
3. The basket can be filled with watercress or parsley and used for a garnish, or filled with sorbet made with the fruit pulp.

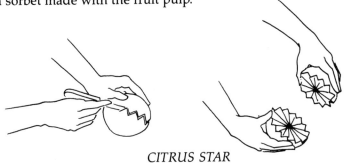

CITRUS STAR

1. With a small, sharp knife make a series of sawtooth cuts all the way around the fruit, each time penetrating the knife into the center.
2. After all the cuts have been made, the fruit will separate into two pieces. This

cut can also be used on tomatoes, which can then be hollowed out with a spoon and used as decorative cups to hold other food.

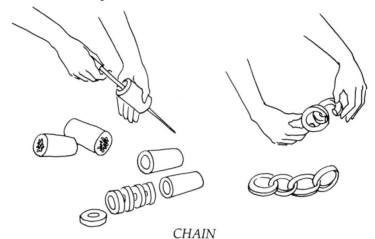

CHAIN

1. Peel cucumber, trim ends, and cut in half crosswise. With a thin knife remove the core of the cucumber. Slice into ⅜-inch rings and slit every other ring.
2. Alternating slit and solid rings, link them together to form a chain. Use two or three to garnish an individual dish or a longer length for a platter. Zucchini can also be used.

CREATIVE INVITATIONS

• For a homespun invitation, write on strips of birch bark.
• With a New Year's Eve invitation, put a pinch of confetti in the envelope.
• For a birthday party, get a number of multicolored balloons; blow them up and, using permanent felt-tip markers, write the party details on the balloons—the time, place, and dress. Deflate and send balloons in an envelope. People who receive these invitations will get a bang—if not a pop—out of them!
• For a Halloween party, write invitations on the back of face masks and send, wrapped in tissue paper, in large envelopes.
• For a housewarming, if you are artistically inclined, draw a humorous sketch of your house on paper; in the doorway, write your address and the day and time of your party. Have it printed, or Xerox it, and send to guests.
• For a Valentine's Day party, write your invitations in the center of a doily, fold, and mail in an envelope.
• For a beach party, write your invitations with a permanent felt-tip marker on the smooth surface of a clamshell. Wrap in tissue paper before putting in a mailing envelope.

PARTY FAVORS

• For New Year's Eve party favors, buy a few inexpensive paperback astrology books. Tear out the appropriate pages for guests' signs, roll in scrolls, and tie with cord. Put at their table settings.
• For a spring or summer luncheon, place a small potted starter plant of a flower or

herb—or a decorative seed packet—at each setting.
• Line small gift or pastry boxes with waxed paper or pretty cellophane. Put a slice of cake or pie in each and gift-wrap in colorful paper bags as take-home treats. Tag the box with your recipe.
• For holiday favors, fill small preserve jars with your favorite homemade jams and jellies. Tie with a festive bow and tag with your recipe.
• For Christmas, sew colorful little cloth bags with drawstring ribbons. Fill each with inexpensive, personalized gifts for each guest: a headband for the jogger or runner; an oven thermometer for the chef *extraordinaire*; a Japanese paintbrush for the artist; a miniature toy car for the auto buff; a special pen or small notebook for the writer.
• For Oriental dinner party favors, write fortunes or old Chinese proverbs on scrolls of paper. Roll and tie with a cord, write the name of guest on the outside, and set at the appropriate place.
• For a bon voyage party, prepare a traveler's kit for the departing guests of honor. Fill a cigar or gift box with the following items: a collection of miniature liquor bottles, a small foreign phrase book, a container of aspirin, a small first-aid kit with Band-Aids, tiny cologne-sample vials, a miniature sewing kit, and pre-addressed postcards, as a hint to the voyagers. Add whatever else suits your fancy.

DECORATIVE ICE

Ice decorations add a particularly festive note to any occasion. Here are a few ideas:
• Insert a bottle of vodka in a tall metal or plastic cylinder—or you can use a paper half-gallon milk container. Fill container with water and stuff leaves and flowers, such as roses, carnations, into the water along the sides of the container (but not in the vodka bottle). Freeze the container with bottle and flowers upright in the freezer overnight, or until water forms a solid block of ice. Just before using, heat the metal or plastic container under hot tap water for a few seconds, and gently loosen the ice block with the vodka bottle from the cylinder. If using a milk container, simply peel off the paper. Set the decorated ice block in a shallow crystal bowl. To use the vodka, simply untwist the cap and pour—ice block and all!

VODKA BOTTLE
FROZEN
IN DECORATIVE
ICE BLOCK

• For decorative touches to lemonades and punches in the summer, add sliced strawberries or pitted cherries to the water in an ice cube tray. Freeze overnight. Pop individual cubes in your drinks.

To camouflage an improvised wine cooler, tie colorful scarves or fabric (see Index for vases) around metal buckets, or any useful receptacle. For holding ice or chilling numerous bottles at a party, line the inside of a large wicker basket with two extra-strength garbage bags; secure over the mouth of basket with a tight belt of ribbon.

FRAGRANCE

To disguise cooking odors or to freshen up your home before guests arrive:
• Refresh potpourri by adding a few drops of perfumed oil (such as jasmine, rose, or your favorite scent) to the flower petals.
• Tuck fragrant sachets in between cushions in the couch or chairs.
• Sprinkle a drop of perfume on well-ventilated light bulbs. The heat of the bulb will spread the scent.
• Toast a few pinches of ground cinnamon in a pan over low heat. This is especially nice in fall and winter.
• Hang citrus pomanders in your coat closets and in hallways.
• Pine needles add a naturally fresh scent indoors. Hang pine wreaths in various parts of your home, even make bouquets of pine branches.

DECORATIVE VOTIVE CANDLE HOLDERS

LIGHTING

Try these suggestions for lighting up your party:
• Wrap overlapping fresh leaves around small glass votive candle containers and hold in place with twine.
• A wonderful tradition for Christmas is to make candlelight paper-bag lanterns. Use small, lunch-size brown paper bags, filled one third of the way up with sand, and center a small votive or column candle in the sand, safely away from the sides of the bag. Light with a long fireplace match. Line your sidewalk, porch, and steps with these lanterns for a storybook effect. Small white paper bags look great for a summer patio party.
• Arrange small votive candles on mirrored mats for an evening buffet outdoors. The mirror will reflect the glow of the candles, and they will twinkle like stars.
• Turn a hand-painted Chinese umbrella into a lamp by fastening the handle at an angle to a ceiling or wall light fixture with rope or twine. Turn on the light and see the beautiful scene on the umbrella glow.

• Shape tiny wreaths of flowers and leaves, fasten with thin wire, and wrap around the mouth or base of candleholders.

ROUND TABLECLOTHS

Round tables are very popular for entertaining. It is easy to make your own round tablecloths, using yard goods or flat bed linens. For a very special party you may want to add coordinating square seat cushions for the chairs. Here are simple instructions on how to make both.

To make a round table cloth:
1. Measure the diameter of the tabletop.
2. Measure the length from the tabletop to the floor.
3. Add the diameter to twice the measurement from tabletop to floor. This number, plus 2 additional inches for seams and hem, equals your working measurement.
4. The final piece of material needed to make the cloth must be a square. Therefore, after cutting the length of the fabric to the working measurement, it may be necessary to increase its width. To do this, first determine how many inches must be added to the width to equal the length. Cut out a second piece of fabric to this additional width; then cut this new piece in half again to make two panels.
5. Sew these two narrow panels to the left and right sides of the main piece, allowing for ½-inch seams. Be sure to sew the panels so that both sets of seams are on the wrong side of the fabric.
6. After all pieces are sewn, fold the square in half and then in quarters.
7. Attach a pencil to a piece of string and cut the string to the size of half the diameter of the table.
8. Pin the free end of the string to the corner of the square where both folds meet. Using the string and pencil like a compass, draw an arc connecting opposite points on the square.
9. Following the penciled arced line, cut through the four layers of fabric. Pin fabric so that it does not shift as you cut.
10. Unfold, and hem or add trim to finish the bottom of the cloth.

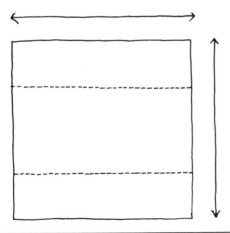 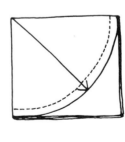

To make a square seat cushion:

1. Cut two squares of fabric to fit the size of the seats, plus 2 additional inches on each side.
2. With finished sides of fabric facing each other, start sewing squares together, allowing ½-inch seams. Sew together only three or three and a half sides, to leave an opening for stuffing the pillow.
3. Turn pillow right side out, and press seams if desired.
4. Stuff with batting or foam rubber cut to size.
5. Fold in unfinished edge and sew by hand.

NAPKINS AND NAPKIN FOLDING

With so many styles and textures of napkins available today, you will find that there is no end to the possibilities of mixing and matching. Experiment with some of the new materials. For example, for a contemporary look, why not contrast color and design and mix checked napkins with a striped tablecloth. Or try mixing textures. For instance, use lovely nubby linen with smooth stoneware plates. In addition, today there are also hordes of imaginative and different decorative napkin rings to accent your table. Rings are made of such materials as straw, shells, silver, and ceramics. Rings also can be of a soft material, such as lace or cord, that you can tie, with perhaps the addition of a single, seasonally fresh or silk flower. In any event, you will find that there is no end to the creative things you can do with napkins when entertaining.

Napkin folding is an art that, happily, can be quickly and easily mastered. Napkin folds always look elegant and special. For formal dinners it goes without saying that you must use a simple napkin fold. But for casual parties, be as creative as you want. Use one fold for the women and a different one for the men. You can make napkins into flowers, into fan shapes, or put napkins in glasses or baskets. See facing page for instructions on various napkin folds.

LAP NAPKINS

You can also create your own special buffet lap mats, which are handy at parties when there are not enough tables for guests. These are made by sewing a small pocket of coordinating fabric onto the left side of a soft or quilted place mat—or any large piece of fabric. Attach two pieces of coordinating cord or ribbon to the mat's left edge. Roll the mat so that the pocket is on top. Stuff the pocket with a pretty napkin and the flatware; secure the roll by tying with the cord. Guests can use the lap mats to protect their clothes or other surfaces on which they rest their plates. Large pretty tea towels can also be offered at buffets for lap coverings in addition to napkins.

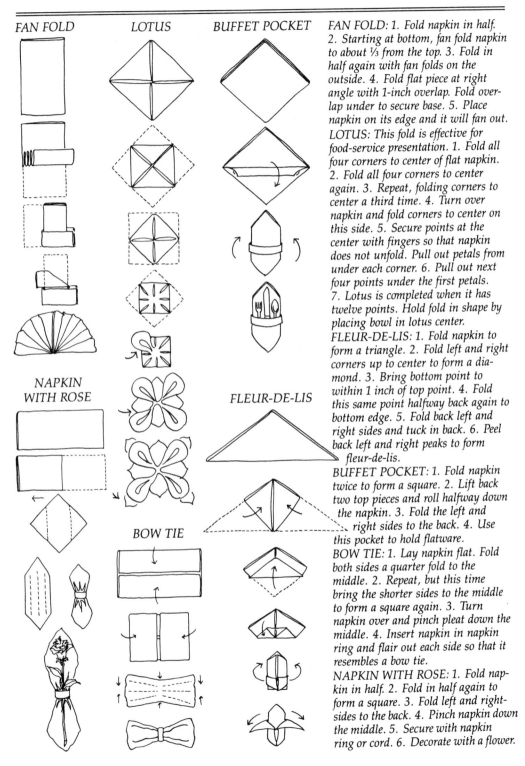

FAN FOLD   LOTUS   BUFFET POCKET

NAPKIN
WITH ROSE

FLEUR-DE-LIS

BOW TIE

FAN FOLD: 1. Fold napkin in half. 2. Starting at bottom, fan fold napkin to about ⅓ from the top. 3. Fold in half again with fan folds on the outside. 4. Fold flat piece at right angle with 1-inch overlap. Fold overlap under to secure base. 5. Place napkin on its edge and it will fan out.

LOTUS: This fold is effective for food-service presentation. 1. Fold all four corners to center of flat napkin. 2. Fold all four corners to center again. 3. Repeat, folding corners to center a third time. 4. Turn over napkin and fold corners to center on this side. 5. Secure points at the center with fingers so that napkin does not unfold. Pull out petals from under each corner. 6. Pull out next four points under the first petals. 7. Lotus is completed when it has twelve points. Hold fold in shape by placing bowl in lotus center.

FLEUR-DE-LIS: 1. Fold napkin to form a triangle. 2. Fold left and right corners up to center to form a diamond. 3. Bring bottom point to within 1 inch of top point. 4. Fold this same point halfway back again to bottom edge. 5. Fold back left and right sides and tuck in back. 6. Peel back left and right peaks to form fleur-de-lis.

BUFFET POCKET: 1. Fold napkin twice to form a square. 2. Lift back two top pieces and roll halfway down the napkin. 3. Fold the left and right sides to the back. 4. Use this pocket to hold flatware.

BOW TIE: 1. Lay napkin flat. Fold both sides a quarter fold to the middle. 2. Repeat, but this time bring the shorter sides to the middle to form a square again. 3. Turn napkin over and pinch pleat down the middle. 4. Insert napkin in napkin ring and flair out each side so that it resembles a bow tie.

NAPKIN WITH ROSE: 1. Fold napkin in half. 2. Fold in half again to form a square. 3. Fold left and right-sides to the back. 4. Pinch napkin down the middle. 5. Secure with napkin ring or cord. 6. Decorate with a flower.

315

HELPFUL HOSTING HINTS

Party time can be hassle-free. The next time you entertain, try a few of these handy tips and shortcuts:

TO KEEP FLOWERS FRESH

• When you bring flowers home from the store, cut the stems at an angle; this helps stems absorb water instead of sitting flat on the bottom of the vase. Use room-temperature water. Wash vase and change water every day or every other day to eliminate bacteria buildup. Trim stems every other day.

• Keep flowers away from direct light and heat. If you buy flowers in advance of a party, store them in a cool dark place.

REMOVING STAINS

• Always check the manufacturer's care instructions before attempting to remove stains. Some fabrics cannot be soaked or dabbed with water and must always be dry-cleaned.

• To remove stains from milk and eggs, soak as soon as possible with cold water, then wash in warm suds; or soak material in cold water with an enzyme-based presoak product.

• Remove bloodstains as soon as possible with cold water; or soak material in cold water with an enzyme-based presoak product.

• For fruit juice stains, first rinse with cold water as soon as possible. Then stretch fabric over a bowl and pour boiling water over the stain from a height of two to three feet.

• For grease stains, use dry-cleaning fluid or sudsy detergent. You can also sprinkle the grease mark with cornstarch, cover with a paper towel, and heat with a warm iron. The cornstarch should absorb the stain.

• Rinse coffee stains immediately with cold water or club soda.

• Rub a wine stain with salt, then rinse with cold water or club soda.

REMOVING CANDLE WAX

• To remove wax from fabric, quickly lift off as much wax as you can. Then put the wax spot between double layers of paper towel or brown paper bag and go over it with a warm iron.

• Never use a sharp knife to scrape off candle wax from precious materials—use a plastic credit card or an extremely dull knife.

• To remove wax from candlesticks, put them in the refrigerator until cold, then flick off the wax with your fingers. The remaining wax film can be washed off with hot, soapy water.

SILVER POLISHING AND STORAGE

• Do not store silver in contact with rubber or newspaper, which promote tarnishing.

• Do not serve egg- or vinegar-based foods in sterling silver, as prolonged contact can cause discoloration of the metal.

• Silver pieces are best stored wrapped in soft, tarnish-proof bags or fabrics. These bags often contain silver particles, which interact with the oxygen and prevent tarnish from collecting on the silverware.

• Using your sterling flatware regularly is the best protection against tarnish, and the silver will never wear out. If you must store it for a long time, you can store it wrapped in a paper napkin and seal individually or grouped by place setting or by utensil in a plastic bag.

• As you use your silver, it will develop a warm, attractive patina (tiny surface scratches). To develop an even finish on all pieces, rotate flatware in its storage box. Every month, take the top fork and put it on the bottom of the stack. As you continue this cycle, all pieces will develop an even amount of patina. Do the same with knives and spoons.

• Tiny scratches from repeated use give your sterling silver a lovely old-fashioned finish, but washing your silver pieces in a crowded dishwasher flatware basket may only cause deep knicks and scratches.

• Never use tarnish dips. They will remove the dark antiquing that may have purposely been added to provide contrast in the design.

CRYSTAL

• To remove a tiny chip in a crystal goblet, use a super-fine emery board or fine diamond sanding tool. Gently file the chip down, using a rotary motion; then run a little water over it. A jeweler may also be able to do this for you.

• When storing crystal goblets or other dishes, keep them dust-free by covering with plastic bags.

• Never crowd crystal on a shelf. If necessary, you can store every other glass upside down to make the most use of your storage area. Line shelves beforehand with shelf liner or fabric.

• It is best to hand-wash crystal, because the heat and motion of dishwashers can damage crystal and dull its brilliance. Line the sink or washbasin with a thick terry cloth towel and put a rubber aerator on the end of your faucet, to avoid cracking the crystal. And take off your rings, which can cause chips.

• Add shine and sparkle to crystal with a little ammonia and water. Rinse thoroughly.

CHINA

• Keep stored china dust-free and ready to use by wrapping each piece in a plastic bag.

• Protect plates by separating them with sheets of felt or foam; or store in individual felt cases. You can also use paper or fabric napkins or paper plates between them.

• Always hand-wash any hand-painted china. Strong dishwasher detergents can fade and damage the design.

• Occasionally polish the gold and platinum bands on china or crystal with a little bit of metal polish, to enhance their gleam.

• Never stack more than two china cups or crystal glasses—they could get stuck together and then break. If they do get stuck, dip the outer cup or glass in warm water and fill the inner one with cold water. The warmer glass will expand and the colder one contract, making it easier to separate them.

KEEPING FOODS AND PLATES HOT

To warm plates:
• Place in the oven at a low temperature.
• Put them on an electric hot plate.
• Wrap them in store-bought felt bags equipped with electric heating wires.
• Put in the dishwasher and turn on to heat-drying cycle.
• Rinse cups, mugs, and glasses in hot water. Dry quickly.

To keep food warm:
• Sprinkle a little water on the tops of casseroles or side dishes, cover with aluminum foil, and put in a warm oven.
• Warm sauces and gravies in the top of a double boiler set over simmering water. For buffets, put food in a chafing dish that has a double container and fill bottom with boiling water.

TO CHILL FOODS AND DISHES

• Chill tempered glasses or mugs in the freezer for a refreshingly cool cocktail or glass of beer: Rinse in water and freeze for 10–15 minutes.
• Chill bowls and plates in the refrigerator.
• To keep foods cool, put packed ice or ice cubes in a large bowl; garnish ice with greens and flowers. Set food directly in ice, or in a smaller serving dish nestled in the ice. To keep a punch or other beverage chilled, nestle the smaller bowl, filled with punch, in a larger one filled with ice. To avoid diluting punch by adding ice cubes, prefreeze some of the punch in plastic storage containers, then remove from containers and use frozen punch instead of ice cubes.

IMPROVISING

• To extend a table, have your local lumberyard or hardware store cut a large round or rectangular plywood top. Use this to cover a card table or other small table, with a thin foam pad underneath to keep the top from sliding. Disguise the whole construction with a tablecloth.
• For a makeshift table, balance a plywood board firmly on top of two sawhorses and cover with a cloth. When the party is over, disassemble the pieces and store in your basement or garage.
• For extra umbrella stands in bad weather, use large clay garden pots or old-fashioned milk buckets.
• For snowy-day parties, line a corner of your hall or an out-of-the-way spot with several thicknesses of kraft paper for a boot mat, or invest in a yard of plastic carpet runner.

Index

INDEX

321

Your Own Recipes and Notes